Avant-garde Performance

Other titles by the author:

Avant-garde Performance

Live Events and Electronic Technologies

Günter Berghaus

First published 2005 by
PALGRAVE MACMILLAN

Palgrave Macmillan in the UK is an imprint of Macmillan Publishers Limited,
registered in England, company number 785998, of Houndmills, Basingstoke,
Hampshire RG21 6XS.

Palgrave Macmillan in the US is a division of St Martin's Press LLC,
175 Fifth Avenue, New York, NY 10010.

Palgrave Macmillan is the global academic imprint of the above companies
and has companies and representatives throughout the world.

Palgrave® and Macmillan® are registered trademarks in the United States,
the United Kingdom, Europe and other countries.

ISBN 13: 978 1-4039-4644-7   hardback
ISBN 10: 1-4039-4644-2   hardback
ISBN 13: 975 1-4039-4645-5   paperback
ISBN 10: 1-4039-4645-0   paperback

This book is printed on paper suitable for recycling and made from fully
managed and sustained forest sources. Logging, pulping and manufacturing
processes are expected to conform to the environmental regulations of the
country of origin.

A catalogue record for this book is available from the British Library.

Library of Congress Cataloging-in-Publication Data

Berghaus, Günter, 1953–
  Avant-garde performance : live events and electronic technologies /
    Günter Berghaus.
      p. cm.
  Includes bibliographical references and index.
  ISBN-10: 1-4039-4644-2 (cloth)
  ISBN-13: 978-1-4039-4644-7 (cloth)
  ISBN-10: 1-4039-4645-0 (pbk.)
  ISBN-13: 978-1-4039-4645-4 (pbk.)
  1. Experimental theater. 2. Performance art. 3. Digital media. I. Title.

PN2193.E86B47 2005
792.02'23—dc22

2004065797

Printed and bound in Great Britain by
CPI Antony Rowe, Chippenham and Eastbourne

Comme l'amour, la scène est toujours réciproque
(Roland Barthes, *Fragments d'un discours amoureux*, 1977, p. 246)

For Kate, Tristan and Andreas

Contents

List of Illustrations

8   Epilogue: the Future of the Avant-garde   **259**

List of Tables

List of Boxes

List of Chronologies

Acknowledgements

This volume would have been unthinkable without the debates that were an integral part of my lectures, seminars and performance projects at Bristol University. The critical responses of hundreds of students made me reflect on my views on the avant-garde, rethink my attitude towards certain artists, and develop a deeper and keener appreciation of the performances discussed in this study.

Two grants from the British Academy and the Arts and Humanities Research Board of Great Britain enabled me to collect documents, to visit artists, to interview eyewitnesses of performances, and to travel to various countries in order to visit stage shows and exhibitions.

The writing of this manuscript has been made possible through a research leave granted by the University of Bristol, and a generously low teaching load during my year as guest professor at Brown University.

Ian Watson and Jean-Marie Pradier offered valuable support in the preparation phase of this project, and I received constructive comments on my draft manuscript from Ted Braun, George Brandt, Hubert van den Berg, Vera Hoffmann, Thomas Hoffmann, John Emigh, Dietrich Scheunemann and, as usual, from my wife Kate Berghaus.

Many of the artists discussed in this volume helped me at one point or another by granting me access to their private collections, by answering my queries, by sending me photographs, videos, etc. Without this active collaboration my attempts at conveying the quality and significance of their work to a twenty-first-century reader would have been doomed to failure.

I also need to mention some book dealers and private collectors, such as Barbara Moore, Steve Clay and Jan van der Donk in New York, who allowed my to copy material from their priceless possessions. In public institutions, I found some extremely supportive librarians and archivists, who often provided an excellent service far beyond their call of duty. For this valuable support I am particularly grateful to David Smith at the New York Public Library; Jennifer Tobias at the Museum of Modern Art Library; Jennifer Krivickas of the Widener Library of Harvard University; Mary Clare Altenhofen at the Fine Arts Library of Harvard University; Annette Fern at the Theatre Collection of Harvard University; Jean

Rainwater at the John Hay Library, Nancy Jakubowski at the Music Library, and Steven Thompson at the Rockefeller Library of Brown University; Vincent Giroud at Yale University Library; Ruth Dar at the Slade/Duveen Art Library of University College London; Danièle Roussell and Amalia Rausch at the Archiv des Wiener Aktionismus in Zurndorf; Angelika Ander at the Nationalbibliothek Wien; Barbara Wilk-Mincu at the Staatsbibliothek Berlin; Anita Kühnel at the Kunstbibliothek Berlin; Regine Herrmann and Renate Rätz at the Akademie der Künste in Berlin; Hedwig Müller at the Theatermuseum Köln; Everhard Kleinertz at the Historisches Archiv der Stadt Köln; Elke Tausgraf at the Deutsche Bibliothek Frankfurt; Kazuko Yamamoto at the Fukuoka Art Museum.

A number of people supplied illustrative material and granted permission to reproduce it in this volume. For this I should like to thank Vito Acconci, Valie Export, Kenji Ishiguro, Sean Kelly, Anne Marchand, Makiko Mirakami, Hermann Nitsch, Kiyoji Ohtsuji, Ulrike Rosenbach, Carolee Schneemann, Yacov Sharir, Amanda Steggell, Stelarc, the Stadt- und Universitätsbibliothek Frankfurt am Main, Theatermuseum Köln, and Historisches Archiv der Stadt Köln.

Preface

This study is largely the result of a lecture cycle that I delivered at the University of Bristol in alternating years between 1989 and 1999. The recurrence of the series afforded me the opportunity to undertake further research and to teach related topics in the form of seminars and performance projects. The response I received from my students stimulated further investigations and, as a result, the form and content of my lectures changed significantly over the years. A first draft of this manuscript was completed in 2000 and served as a basis for a further set of lectures and seminars given at Brown University in Providence, Rhode Island, in 2001/2, which then developed into the form presented in this volume.

When in 1999 I drafted a first table of contents for this study, it contained over fifty names, mostly of artists who are now widely recognized as leading innovators in the performing arts. However, it soon became obvious to me that it was impossible to cover in a comprehensive fashion the myriad of avant-garde performances mounted in the course of the past fifty years. Faced with the choice of writing an encyclopedic 'who's who in avant-garde performance' or focusing on some two dozen key figures placed in a historical, social and aesthetic context, I opted for the latter. I wanted to give individual artists and their creations sufficiently detailed coverage, and at the same time present some of the general characteristics of postwar avant-garde performance. Thus, I hoped to devise a map that identifies paths and trajectories through a landscape which, to the uninitiated, often appears like a jungle. In a complex terrain that is notoriously difficult to survey, I have chosen trends and events that were symptomatic of a given genre or movement, which stimulated discussions amongst contemporaries and exercised considerable influence on later generations, thereby fostering the growth of new aesthetics in the performing arts and leaving a lasting mark on late twentieth-century culture.

Although I myself have been an interested observer of many avant-garde performances in the last third of the twentieth century, I would not necessarily consider myself a reliable and objective witness of these events. The vagaries of personal taste and predilection, of temporary fads and fashions, as well as the limitations of accessibility, travel budgets, time schedules, etc. determined what I could or would see. This, inevitably, meant that I missed out on some great opportunities; but even shows that I did manage to see began to fade in my memory after ten, fifteen years. For this reason, all performances discussed in this volume had to be revisited by examining written or visual accounts recovered from archives, libraries, museums and private collections. These included, in the first instance, papers left behind by artists, such as texts, scores, scenarios, designs, essays, interviews, etc. Some artists still alive were willing to answer questions, provide oral or written information and show me photographs, films and videos.

Needless to say, records of this kind require careful evaluation, as they tend to be highly selective and determined by the interests of the person who produces (or preserves) them, as well as by the characteristics and restrictions of the medium in which they were recorded. I have therefore complemented these documents with descriptions and interpretations published by people who witnessed the performances (as audience members or critics) in the form of memoirs, letters and reviews. However, as avant-garde performances aim to provoke personal responses rather than linear or uniform 'readings', every viewer experiences a performance differently. Audiences bring with them their partial tastes and inclinations and react to the stage events according to their idiosyncratic predispositions. Furthermore, many of the works dealt with in this study were extremely challenging and could go far beyond the level of acceptance which spectators were able or willing to muster. This, of course, is the inherent obligation of the avant-garde. But it also means that eyewitness accounts can be as unreliable as artists' descriptions of their work. An artistic intention does not necessarily become realized on stage, and an audience member's interpretation of the event can be even further removed from what is conveyed in a script or scenario. Therefore, for a scholarly assessment of whether, how, and to what degree an artistic mission has been fulfilled and how it has been perceived by an audience, *all* of these factors need to be taken into consideration, weighed up against each other, evaluated and subjected to a comparative analysis.

But, this is not where the conundrum stops. Also the scholar's research is influenced by a number of variables that need to be fed into the equation. Academics select their objects of analysis according to personal interests and examine them in line with their socialization, ideological viewpoints, professional training, the established narratives of their discipline, etc. Even if I were to attempt an objective evaluation of a performance, I could not eliminate the subjective factors of appreciation. In fact, both have their role to play if we want to arrive at a meaningful analysis of a performance. Before a theatre historian is able to describe and analyse a live event, it has to come alive on his or her interior screen as a re-lived performance. This subjective experience will then have to be combined with objective analytical methods of evaluation, and together they will form the basis of an evocative and inspiring study.

This, of course, means that in this volume I can only offer *one* of many possible readings of the avant-garde in performance. Researching and writing this publication made me re-live some of my early encounters with the avant-garde and rediscover how performances impacted on my views on art, and on theatre in particular. The avant-garde is by its very nature a contested and controversial terrain and does not lend itself as a topic for polite conversation. Responses to works seen, heard or read tend to be extreme, either on the enthusiastic or at the dismissive end of the scale. Even in academic discourses such as this one, one cannot escape the controversial nature of the subject. Many of the artists I write about gave me great inspiration, or irritation, at the time I first became acquainted with their work, and I don't feel a need to apologize if this still shines through in subsequent chapters. In some cases, over the years, enthusiasm turned into indifference, and vexation into appreciation. This was due, in part, to my own personal development, but also to the changing artistic and cultural environment in which I was operating. Composing this volume became for me a self-reflective exercise and a meditation on how artistic climates have changed over the past decades. In the end, this knowledge could be used productively to reflect on the performances from a more objective viewpoint.

Retrospectively, I feel I was fortunate to grow up in the Rhineland, as it possessed at the time one of the liveliest art scenes to be found anywhere in Europe and afforded me the opportunity to catch a glimpse of the last signs of avant-garde vitality before it went into (terminal?) decline. Beuys, Vostell, Stockhausen, Paik, etc. provided me with some of my formative experiences as far as the performing arts were concerned. Later, as a student in Berlin, I was rarely able to repeat such encounters. Instead, I was brought into contact with the theory of the avant-garde, itself a controversial topic at the time.[1] I disagree here with the many critics who maintain that access to avant-garde practices is impossible without being intimately familiar with the theory behind them. My early contacts with the avant-garde were visceral rather than intellectual. I was taken in by the energy, exuberance, wit and intensity of what I was watching. I admired the artists' irreverent attitude to established institutions and traditions, their challenge to political, cultural, aesthetic and sexual orthodoxies. This pretty much reflected my own attitudes towards the conservative institutions that formed part of my own upbringing.

Only at a later stage did I begin to *study* the deeper meaning, the historical context, the traditions out of which the avant-garde emerged. Although I remember going to some of Peter Bürger's lectures, I don't believe that his post-1968 necrology of the failed utopias of the avant-garde had any particular impact on my outlook on the subject. I was probably more affected by the controversial discussions we had in the NGBK (New Society for Fine Arts, a predominantly Marxist organization attached to politically motivated Realist models of art), where the avant-garde was portrayed as being essentially a bourgeois, frivolous, faddish affair. Given my past experiences, I could not subscribe to such an assessment of the avant-garde as being an apolitical phenomenon effectively supporting the political status quo. To me, the avant-garde combined two types of subversion: one directed at mainstream art, the other at bourgeois politics.

Several years later, as a university lecturer in Britain and an occasional visitor at avant-garde performances in the USA, I found that the older generation of avant-garde artists had largely lost their revolutionary impetus and that their works had turned into commodities with a firm place on the art market and performance circuit. Heated debates had given way to diagnoses of the death of the avant-garde, and numerous academic studies, handbooks, even encyclopedias had been compiled to assign it a firm place in the history of twentieth-century culture. Yet, within my own institution I found that some of the most inspiring forms of expression I had encountered in the past decade were still considered illegitimate art forms that did not deserve to be given representation in a Theatre Studies curriculum. Therefore, I found myself embroiled again in discussions that repeated my earlier experiences with the conservatives of the Left and Right.

Thus, avant-garde culture never developed for me into a purely academic, safe and uncontroversial topic. There were still artists around who clung to their 'anti-bourgeois' attitudes; in fact, in the performing arts their number was steadily growing. The theatre industry may have treated them 'like house pets. A little soil on the national carpet',[2] but most of the novel and interesting developments that could be observed in the performing arts of the past decades were largely due to these performers, who took more of an interest in expanding their medium of expression than in adding to their bank account. Time and again I could experience how avant-garde performance, in contrast to conventional mainstream theatre or the hackneyed fare of the entertainment industry, could still be a source of conflict, resistance and controversy. In my pedagogical role as a university teacher I saw it as an important aspect of my work to introduce students to the history of the avant-garde and to the current state of affairs in the experimental sector of the theatre profession.[3] Response to my lectures, seminars and performance projects indicated that the oppositional stance of the avant-garde could still inspire students to create works that went against the grain of expectation, foster in them an attitude of personal engagement and risk-taking, and spawn a creative energy that was often lacking in other, though technically more accomplished, works.

Personal experiences like the ones described above may explain some of the features of the volume presented here. It has never been my intention to offer with this study an original contribution to a theory of the avant-garde in performance; in fact, if anything it sidelines theory and gives much wider representation to artistic praxis in the performance medium. The reason for this is not to be found in my resistance to theoretical inquiry (see below), but in a desire to redress an imbalance between theory and practice in the scholarly literature on the avant-garde.

In my university courses I often introduced a topic with an outline of some key theories of the avant-garde and gave students essay questions that encouraged them to discuss the œuvre of artist A or B in the light of the theories of critic C or D. However, I soon realized that this encouraged an attitude of 'provide me with a theory and I'll explain to you what an artist is up to', which subjected both theorists and artists to undue generalizations and simplifications. A more productive engagement with the dialectics of theory and praxis resulted from discussing the role of theory in the development of avant-garde performance as a whole. Irrespective of some artists' testimony to the contrary, art is never the sole product of a direct and unmediated impulse coming straight from the heart. In as much as an artist is cognizant of aesthetic practices of past and present – conveyed by academic training, informal discussions between artists, reading of art journals etc. – s/he is enmeshed in a matrix of critical discourses. Avant-garde works of art are not autonomous creations destined for aesthetic contemplation, but controversial statements thrown into the public arena. They are, as Paul Mann emphasizes, 'not only supported by discourse but [themselves] a fully discursive phenomenon'.[4] The art of the avant-garde is the result of an active engagement with aesthetic, social and political forces. Avant-garde artists take a stand, usually an oppositional one. To defend their position, they need to possess a reflective consciousness and be aware of the conceptual framework within which they are operating. In most cases, such an undertaking is echoed in their theoretical statements (manifestos, essays, interviews, etc.).

This is not to say that works of art cannot be created without explicit theoretical verbalization, or that the works are only illustrations of a theory. But it is in the nature of the avant-garde that it challenges received notions of art, questions its established categories and fundamental premises, and contests its production and reception mechanisms. Such a thorough and wide-ranging re-evaluation of art as product and process requires from the artists a highly developed awareness of the philosophical, political and aesthetic implications of their operations. Theory was an essential and integral component of the creative process and functioned as a corrective and inspirational tool. Without it, the forceful engagement with the material and the (usually hostile) public would have been unthinkable.

Audiences are usually capable of appreciating a performance even when they do not 'understand' what they see. The multifaceted, sensual experiences provided by theatre make it possible that 'meaning' or intellectual content often take second place to an engagement with its material qualities (space, bodies, light, sound etc.). Even highly conceptual performances, in as much as they require a body to act in space, tend to have a sensual or spiritual dimension that appeals to the audience's emotion, fantasy and imagination rather than intellect.[5] Therefore, the rise of a theory of the avant-garde (or rather, of a body of theories that accompanied, explained and conditioned artistic discourses) affected artists and audiences in different measures.

As the century progressed, artistic production became increasingly dependent on theory to justify its *raison d'être*. Anecdotes of children playing football with Warhol's Brillo Boxes, a janitor scraping Beuys' *Fettecke* off a wall, or a passer-by joining a Happening thinking that it is a real-life event, attest to the fact that without knowledge of theory, uninitiated audiences may be unable to distinguish between artistic and non-artistic objects or processes. It was the avowed aim of the historical avant-garde to sublate art into life. But when it became more important for artists to attend philosophy courses than drawing classes, art sublated itself into theory and sounded its own death knell. However, the widely acknowledged 'theory death of the avant-garde' was also due to other factors. Much has been written about the neo-avant-garde's inability to establish viable alternatives to the institutionalization of the historical avant-garde. The arguments, largely inspired by Peter Bürger, do not need to be repeated here. What seems more relevant in the context of this Preface is the fact that by the 1970s a meta-theoretical discourse on the avant-garde had been established which affected not only artists and critics, but also scholars like myself. My reflections on the avant-garde contribute to the formation of academic discourses, of 'canonical' histories of the avant-garde, of 'authoritative' interpretations of groundbreaking 'masterworks', and so on. These cultural practices form part of the institutional embrace of the avant-garde as much as the exhibition of Duchamp's urinal in the Museum of Modern Art, the performance of a

Schwitters play in the Hanover municipal theatre, or the inclusion of a Fluxus poem in a literary anthology.

It is unavoidable that each chapter of my publication here assigns status to a given artist or performance. And for each artist excised from my account (and there are many), the omission implies a judgement of 'worthiness' that cannot be separated from dominant ideologies of art, politics, etc. As Paul Mann has pointed out, the construction of a history of the avant-garde belongs as much to the ideological regime as does the absorption of avant-garde works into the mainstream of galleries and museums. However, it seems symptomatic that Mann excludes from his discussion performances of an avant-garde nature. Assigning status to works of fine art appears to be a comparatively easy task, given the available information on the impact of certain works of art on contemporary and subsequent generations. Boccioni's sculpture *Forme uniche della continuità nello spazio* has been viewed by hundreds of thousands of museum visitors. But whoever saw the first (and usually only) performance of an avant-garde 'classic' in the theatre? In fact, many avant-garde performances assumed notoriety and 'classical' status exactly because hardly anybody (in relative terms) witnessed their unique form unfolding in time and space. Edward Braun in his insightful analysis of some groundbreaking performances of the Modernist period rightly remarked that many of these productions were shambolic and incoherent, yet this did not prejudice their later fame as crucial turning points in the history of theatre.[6] Subsequent embroidering often enhanced the mythical status and reception of avant-garde performances and made it much more difficult to pronounce incontrovertible judgements than in the fine arts. Even in the (unlikely) event of a sudden string of revivals of such works – e.g. Allan Kaprow's *18 Happenings in 6 Parts*, Nam June Paik's *Opera sextronique*, Carolee Schneemann's *Interior Scroll* or Joseph Beuys' *I Like America and America Likes Me* – we would not be talking about re-experiencing the impact these works made in their original setting.

For the reasons noted above it is a difficult, if not impossible task to construct an 'authoritative' account of the avant-garde in performance. I have therefore set myself a much more modest objective and have assembled here some selective readings in the history of avant-garde performance, predominantly for a target audience of students pursuing a degree in Theatre and Performance Studies, Fine Arts and Media Studies. Each chapter is introduced by a general outline of the historical and cultural framework within which artists operated. As many of the artists came from a Fine Arts background and approached performance as a 'time-based', rather than dramatic, art, I have given less consideration to theatre history than to art historical concepts and aesthetics. My primary focus on alternative modes of production and my relatively narrow definition of avant-garde performance compelled me to exclude from this investigation a large number of theatre practitioners who would have otherwise been relevant to my analyses. I am fully aware that I differ here from certain colleagues, whose books on 'avant-garde theatre' hardly mention the works discussed in my study and instead dedicate much space to artists who fall outside my roster of exemplars.

Avant-garde artists were not only ahead of their time, but also assumed an attitude of opposition to their cultural surroundings. Such a stance is, of course, difficult to maintain if the means of production are collectively rather than individually owned. Whereas in the earlier part of the twentieth century, many avant-garde performers still adhered to theatrical forms of presentation, the postwar avant-garde largely operated without the paraphernalia of institutionalized theatre. The avant-garde painters and sculptors who in the 1970s turned to the performance medium did so in order to overcome the object character of art and to ward off the commodification of their creative impulses. This resulted in unique, unrepeatable and unsaleable art events, labelled at the time as 'Performance Art'. This new medium was given official recognition at the *documenta 6*;[7] but some ten years later the performance curator of the *documenta 8*, Elisabeth Jappe, still found that the genre 'remained first and foremost a medium of the fine arts'.[8] Even so, artists from a variety of disciplines contributed to the development of alternative, experimental performance practices. Other terms much in vogue then for distinctly untheatrical and non-dramatic performances were 'Happening', 'Action' or 'Event'. In the 1980s, these expressions were largely replaced by the generic term 'Live Art'.

Given this plethora of genre designations, I have favoured in this study the neutral term 'performance' as it covers a wide range of cultural manifestations. I use the word 'theatre' to designate (a) a cultural institution charged with the exhibition of plays, operas and ballets, or (b) an artistic medium, usually operating with a narrative structure and involving fictional characters represented by professionally trained actors. Although avant-garde performers succeeded in demolishing the restrictive modus of operation that characterizes theatre, they rarely achieved a total separation from it. Many art performances retained a certain 'theatrical' quality ('theatricality' here meaning an attachment to role play, stylized body language, the accoutrements of costumes, sets, lighting etc.) and even brought some of their novel forms of expression back to the theatre (see, for example, the productions by Robert Wilson, Robert Lepage, Achim Freyer, Giorgio Barberio Corsetti, etc., or of companies such as the Wooster Group, Forced Entertainment, Gaia Scienza, La Fura dels Baus).

With the unfolding of the Information Age, theatre tended to become displaced, if not superseded, by television and electronic media. As a counter-reaction to this, an emphatic re-auratization of the singular, non-repeatable live performance could be observed across the Western world.[9] None the less, the exploitative embrace of the market (galleries, museums, festivals, etc.), which put an end to Performance Art in the 1980s, also caught up with Live Artists. Museums attempted to 'preserve' art performances by exhibiting their relics and documenting them in catalogues.[10] Consequently, many performers returned to easel and chisel, or moved into the new domain of Media Art. Here, they developed new concepts of performativity, allotted new, interactive, roles to the audience, and transformed performance from object or product into an open-ended process.

In this publication I place particular emphasis on the new forms of performance made possible by electronic and digital media. The massive expansion of information technologies since the 1960s has transformed both the external realities of the world and the way we perceive them. But they also fostered new trends in the performing arts such as Ritual and Body Art, which gave special recognition to embodied existence and the liveness of a performance event. At the end of the twentieth century, this resulted in performances in which both live and mediated elements entered into a fruitful coexistence. In my view it is yet to be seen whether these recent trends can be regarded as the swan song of the avant-garde, or whether the new media technologies ushered in a second modernity and a new era of avant-garde experimentation.

Given that electronic and digital technologies are truly global phenomena, I intended this volume to cover a broad geographic horizon and not to be confined to Europe. I therefore begin my discussion of the postwar avant-garde in Chapter 3 with an examination of the last flourishing of a Modernist culture in the United States of America. Although initially linked to European avant-garde culture, Late-Modernism in the USA developed some highly original features, which eventually also influenced Europe and other parts of the world. But I regret that in the end I have not been able to include a chapter on developments in Latin America, Africa and Asia. This is not intended to suggest that the experience of modernity by-passed these continents. In fact, many publications have shown how Modernist and postmodernist movements had immediate and long-term repercussions outside Europe and the USA. However, repeated visits to Africa and Latin America convinced me that the 'classic' definition of the avant-garde, as explicated in the introductory first chapter of this volume, cannot simply be applied to non-Western cultures. The complex interactions between centre and periphery have triggered a process of rejection and assimilation both of artistic discourses and of the value systems that underpin them. In some economically advanced countries of the Eastern or Southern hemispheres a lively performance practice with strong avant-garde qualities has been in existence throughout the twentieth century (as a representative example I discuss Japan in Chapter 4. But also here, a complex transculturation process led to conceptions of the avant-garde that were emphatically different from those in Western countries. Therefore, my original intention to dedicate a final chapter to these developments was foiled by the sheer complexity of the task, which requires specialist knowledge outside my area of competence. In my view, the non-Western avant-garde deserves separate study, or rather, several studies to be carried out by specialists intimately familiar with the cultural traditions in those countries or continents.

1
The Genesis of Modernity and of the Avant-garde

The Evolution of Modernity

Conventional periodization of Western history dissects the past 2500–3000 years into a tripartite Antiquity – Middle Ages – Modern Period. The Renaissance rang in the Early Modern Era (1500–1789) and prepared the ground for the modern age through the opening up of geographical horizons, the expansion of trade and commerce beyond the European world, the growth of towns, the foundation of an industrial economy, the scientific revolution, technological progress, and so on. The 'long nineteenth century', stretching from the French Revolution to the First World War, consolidated the maturation process of a bourgeois society and transformed the feudal economy into a capitalist system of production – a process that was accompanied by great upheavals in the political world and tumultuous changes in the social and economic fields.

Until the nineteenth century, the vast majority of the population lived and worked in the countryside. During the Industrial Revolution, factories gravitated towards the cities or prompted the growth of new towns near coalfields and iron deposits. They attracted impoverished peasants and farm labourers in search of work and created a great concentration of people in compact urban agglomerations.[1] These vast demographic changes in the nineteenth century produced a new phenomenon: the Big City.

The old forms of habitation and traditional urban structures were unable to accommodate the massive influx of new citizens. Consequently, during the 1820s and 1830s, European cities experienced a reconstruction on a massive scale. Congested roadways were opened up and lined with large apartment blocks, shops, restaurants, cafés and theatres. Typical features of modern life such as leisure and entertainment industries, mass media,

1

Table 1.1   **Population growth in some major European cities, 1800–1900 (in thousands)**

	London	Paris	St Petersburg	Vienna	Moscow	Berlin
1800	1,117	581	336	247	250	172
1900	6,586	2,714	1,267	1,675	989	1,889

consumer palaces, and so on all made their first appearance. The metropolis as a colourful arena of pleasure and diversion came into existence, providing its inhabitants with new comforts and amenities such as running water, sewers, mains gas supplies, etc.

Statistics show that the net increase of population in major European cities (see Table 1.1[2]) was not due to new births but to immigration, and that the majority of the newcomers were single men and women. Many adults never married, and of those who did, many remained childless, and experienced divorce rates ten times higher than in the countryside. Consequently, the traditional family network and the comfort of the domestic hearth were unknown to large sections of the urban citizenship, and the resulting isolation, autonomization and alienation of the individual developed into typical features of life in the metropolis.

Migration from countryside to city was complemented by an analogous mobility *intra muros*. However, the latter term could not be taken literally any longer, as nearly everywhere the old city walls, ramparts and bastions were demolished and former suburbs were integrated into the city. This geographic growth of cities necessitated an improved transportation system. The growth of railways, shown in Table 1.2,[3] ushered in 'an age of movement – an age of hurry and precipitation', as a contemporary observer called it.[4]

Whereas, in the past, suburban populations worked and lived in the same district and rarely passed the city gates, after 1830 they commuted from periphery to centre on a regular basis. In Paris, for example, St Lazare became the main railway station for traffic to and from the suburbs. In 1869, 13,254,000 passengers passed through its gates, of which some 11 million, or 83 per cent, represented suburban traffic. This revolution in urban transport was complemented by a newly instituted omnibus system. In 1828, horse-drawn buses appeared for the first time in Paris; in the 1850s they were replaced by tramcars, and in 1873 there existed some thirty-two routes, transporting 111 million passengers.[5]

Mobility and the new experience of time and space found an extension

Table 1.2 **Growth of railway networks in selected European countries, 1840–1900**

	England	Germany	France	Italy
1840	2,390 km	469 km	410 km	20 km
1850	9,797 km	5,856 km	2,915 km	620 km
1875	23,365 km	27,970 km	19,357 km	8,018 km
1900	30,079 km	51,678 km	38,109 km	16,479 km

in a culture of peripatetic existence. An American visitor to Paris in 1867 was struck by the restless lifestyle of the typical city tenant, who

> dwelled in a kind of metropolitan encampment, requiring no domicile except a bedroom for seven hours in the twenty-four, and passing the remainder of each day and night as nomadic cosmopolites: going to the café to breakfast, a restaurant to dine, an estaminet to smoke, a national library to study, a cabinet de lecture to read the gazettes, a public bath for ablution etc.[6]

Another typical feature of the period – much described and reflected upon – was the *flâneur*, an uninvolved observer of modern life, usually a well-heeled middle-class man who could afford the time for a leisurely stroll down the avenues, to sit in the cafés and bars and soak in the atmosphere of his surroundings.[7] The boulevard,[8] as his preferred haunt, was a fashionable meeting place of all classes of society: 'The boulevards are now par excellence the social centre of Paris. Here the aristocrat comes to lounge, and the stranger to gaze,' found Edward King in 1867.[9] But also the poorer classes, who could hardly afford this 'extensive theatre for lounging',[10] still observed the spectacle from a nearby bench. Another contemporary observer regarded *flânerie* as 'the finest expression of modern civilization . . . where thousands of actors of different temperament, habit and character compete for the major parts'.[11]

Linked to the ritual of gazing, and partly overlapping with it, was the ritual of shopping. With the installation of gas lights, the spectacle of the street became an all-night affair and extended to the new consumer palaces: the shopping malls (or arcades, as they were called in the nineteenth century – see Illustration 1[12]) and the department stores (*magasins de nouveautés*, or *grands magasins*[13]). Based on cross-shaped church architecture, arcades were true temples of consumption, with boutique-like shops fitting into niches like chapels along the aisles, and opulent displays in glass vitrines resembling magical icons (or fetishes) in a shrine.

1 A Parisian arcade: the Passage des Princes, c. 1860

Similarly, the new department stores were, as Zola wrote, 'cathedrals of modern commerce'.[14] Visiting these places became an equivalent to a stroll on the boulevards. Shopping turned from a utilitarian act into a pastime that transcended needs. The luxuries put on view were there to be gazed at, and many people did just that. Without having the intention (or means) to buy, they entered into the mythical dream world of commodity capitalism and forgot about the imperfections of everyday life:

> It was not enough for the arcades to deliver the passer-by from the perils of the streets; they had to hold him, to enslave him, body and soul. And as soon as he entered the corrupting arcades he felt so bewitched that he forgot everything: wife, children, office, and dinner.[15]

People unable to participate in these 'consuming spectacles' still had a vicarious access to the brave new world of commodity capitalism through advertising. Major department stores spent between 500,000 and 1,000,000 francs a year on publicity. Edward King judged it to be 'a science in the gay city' and came across it at every turn, on shop fronts, on blank walls of houses, even on 'little dogs run loose in the streets with their sides painted with some dealer's name'.[16] In the past, advertising had been a word-centred method of informing potential customers about new goods; now it became a visual art designed to seduce and to engage curiosity. The new technologies of the printing press, which turned newspapers into illustrated magazines, allowed publicity to reach out into every sector of society. New mass-circulation papers such as *London Illustrated News*, *La Vie parisienne*, *Le Boulevard*, *La Vie moderne*, and *Leipziger Illustrierte Zeitung* propagated fashionable lifestyles throughout the population. A multifaceted concoction of make-believe and commodity description insinuated that pleasures and satisfactions could be obtained through the consumption of *signs* of happiness. Thus, social dissatisfaction could be deflected by projecting the desire for fulfilment and completeness onto the sphere of consumption.

The ubiquitous parade of a profusion of commodities had a lasting effect on the consciousness of all strata of society. Walter Benjamin compared the spectacle-like element of commerce ('schaustückhafte Element des Handels') to the Roman *ludi circenses*,[17] and Lefebvre called the exhibitions 'rhetorical happenings without clear boundaries between imaginary consumption, the consumption of make-believe, and real consumption'.[18] The modern concept of window shopping has its roots in the nineteenth century, where department stores employed gas light to enhance the *mise-en-scène* of their displays and give them an appearance of 'grand and magical splendour'.[19] Stores such as the Magasin du Louvre indicated in their name how much they were influenced by spectatorial practices in museums.[20] Crowds of people assembled in front of brightly lit shop windows and participated in a 'spectacle of consumption' which in real life they often had to forgo (see Illustration 2).

Much of this new visual culture was directed towards women, whose lives had previously been restricted to the domestic sphere, and who now entered the domain of public life – as consumers.[21] The times when public spaces were dominated by men, and respectable women avoided being seen on the streets, had come to an end. Camille Debans described the boulevard as 'a meeting place of the whole world . . . with women playing an elevated role here' (see Illustration 3).[22] As if to warn visitors from less advanced countries, one of the Paris guides commented: 'One thing that will strike the stranger is the immense proportion of women in the streets as compared with men.'[23] Many of these undoubtedly engaged in purposeful activities, but others were *flâneuses*,[24] attracted by the spectacle of modern life and the nascent leisure industry.[25]

2   Window shopping in Paris: the spectacular displays of the Grand Magasin du Louvre (engraving by Jules-Descartes Férat)

The nineteenth century saw the rise of new forms of popular entertainments as well as a thorough remodelling of old ones. The panorama and diorama counted amongst the most fashionable 'phantasmagoria into which people entered to be distracted',[26] and prepared the way for the ultimate experience of virtual travel in time and space: the cinema.[27] However, before the advent of this 'ninth art', the theatre, which derived its name from the act of watching (*theaesthai* in Greek), continued to provide the most significant form of artistic recreation. In the mid-nineteenth century, Paris had 41 theatres giving daily performances, and 67 others who only performed once or twice a week.[28] Together, they showed some 200 to 300 plays a year, generated an income of 16 million francs, and provided work for some 2,000 actors and singers.[29] It has been calculated that on an average night in 1867, Paris theatres had 30,000 visitors, while cafés-concerts, circuses and similar venues tallied a further 24,000.[30]

The pleasures and diversions of Paris were emulated in other European capitals and gave rise to a thoroughly commercialized theatre business, whose function was more centred on *delectare* than *protesse*. It has been suggested by Foucault and others that the cult of diversion and the democratization of leisure activities, complemented by commodity consumption, functioned as a regulatory device and a means of stifling political unrest. This was certainly the view of several contemporary observers, such as Catherine Gore, who in 1841 wrote that public recreations were offered to the lower classes as part of a *panem et circenses* policy of the State.[31] J. J. Jarves, drawing on official statistics, wrote in 1852 that the French government paid theatres a yearly subsidy of 648,420 francs, 65,790 francs for concerts and 8,593 francs for exhibitions.[32] This funding caused the socialist Jules Vallès to remark caustically: 'The people lack bread, but they are given spectacles.'[33]

'Modern' as an Aesthetic Term and Period Designation

By the 1880s, there was agreement amongst intellectuals and the common population that European society had undergone a profound transformation and that a truly modern civilization had come into existence. Artists and writers belonging to the Naturalist and Symbolist schools declared themselves champions of modernity and ushered in an extensive debate, documented in many publications, on what was to be classified as 'modern'. The term, of course, was not a recent invention. As the philologist and cultural historian E. R. Curtius informs us, it was originally coined in the early Middle Ages, as an adjective to *modo* (recently, now), analogous to *hodier-*

3 Boulevard Montmartre (engraving by Jules Pelcoq, 1869)

nus/hodie (of today), and as an antonym to *antiquus, vetus,* or *priscus*
(old). It replaced the term *neotericus,* which Cicero had introduced when
a need arose to characterize the writers of his day as distinct from those
of ancient Greece.[34] Thus, a creation was considered 'modern' when it
contained a number of innovative features that set it apart from other
products of the past. In the early modern period, the veneration of classical art and literature usually meant that the term 'modern', when
contrasted with 'ancient', had a pejorative undertone. A positive valorization of contemporaneous works of art came to be introduced with the
Querelle des Anciens et Modernes, when people such as Théophile de
Viau berated the idolatry of the past and insisted: 'One has to write in a
modern manner' ('Il faut écrire à la moderne').[35] In the course of the
seventeenth century, the term 'modern' was firmly established as a category of aesthetic criticism, sometimes with a ring of 'iconoclasm'
attached to it. The 'Moderns' questioned the view that the present was
only a figuration of the eternal and demanded that art and literature be
firmly linked to contemporary society. Furthermore, the concept of
progress was transferred from the domain of science to the arts, thus
opening up a perspective of universal and continuous perfection for
humankind through cultural evolution.

With the Romantics, the term 'modern' came to refer to something
more far-reaching than just a recent innovation, or a new aesthetic trend.
Friedrich Schlegel was amongst the first to understand modernity as an
epochal change, or the birth of a new era. Entries in his notebooks of
1797–1803 describe 'the absolute difference between antiquity and
modernity', especially the amorphous, chaotic and frightening character
of modernity, and the key features of a 'modern aesthetics'.[36] From then
on, consensus emerged that modernity was an expression of a new civilization, linked to the development of an industrial society and its
concomitant features of urbanization, secularization, deracination of the
individual, democratization of society, etc.

In the wake of the Industrial Revolution, a number of artistic movements arose which directed their focus on the new contemporary realities.
Romanticism, Realism, Naturalism and Symbolism attempted to capture
the essence of modernity in both its fascinating and frightening aspects.
They played a significant role in preparing the ground for Modernism and
contained features that we shall find again in the historical avant-gardes
of the twentieth century (see Box 1.1).

By the turn of the century, the terms 'modern' and 'modernity' had
become so pervasive that many felt that they had outlived their usefulness. They could function as a period designation (the present time as an

BOX 1.1   SOME MODERNIST FEATURES IN NINETEENTH-CENTURY ART

- Focus on contemporary subject matter.
- Search for new methods of transposing objective reality into visual or literary media.
- Break with the aesthetics of preceding generations.
- Autonomy of artists and writers from traditional patrons and dependency on an anonymous market.
- Oppositional attitudes towards the new dominant middle classes, ranging from the bohemian desire to *épater le bourgeois*, via socialist engagement, to anarchist intransigence.
- Expansion of mediating agencies and the development of modern forms of mass communication.
- Increased focus on the processes and means of artistic production.
- Scepticism towards the traditional forms of representation, and emancipation from the dictats of mimeticism and narrativity.
- Abandonment of the claim of reflecting reality as an organic whole; instead fragmentation of the object of artistic observation.
- Foregrounding of aesthetic means and techniques, self-conscious use of form, and presentation of art as artifice.
- Exploration of the subjective element in apprehending reality and transposing it into art.
- A loss of faith in the ability of language to signify meaning.

age that is substantially different from the previous epoch), a factual term (describing new features not known before), and a value judgement (characterizing, for example, the vagaries of fashion as opposed to the time-honoured values of tradition; the great achievements, or deplorable degenerations, of the present time that stand in contrast to the attainments of the past).

In 1902 Michael Georg Conrad wrote a first 'history of modernity'[37] and in 1904 Samuel Lublinski found it opportune to draw up a 'balance sheet of modernity'.[38] In another volume he announced 'the exit of modernity'[39] and summarized a feeling widely shared amongst intellectuals: modernity had reached a crisis point and had turned into a condition that was more frightening than exhilarating.

The Crisis of Modernity and the Advent of Modernism

At the end of the nineteenth century, a large number of new technologies and inventions, such as synthetic fibres and dyes, electric light, wireless telegraphy, motorcars, cinema etc., made a profound impact on the everyday life of most citizens in the industrialized world. An increased speed of urbanization transformed people's living environment and had far-reaching repercussions on their social existence. The revolutionized means of transportation and the new modes of communication shook up people's conception of a linear time–space continuum and altered their cognitive mapping of the world. In the course of just one generation, the face of Europe came to be transformed, mentally and physically, beyond recognition. Whereas previously renewal had been experienced as something happening gradually and over a long period of time, towards the end of the nineteenth century a feeling of cataclysmic commotion with profound and far-reaching consequences gained ground.

The changing conditions of contemporary life imposed new forms of expression on the artistic production of the period. From *c.* 1890 onwards, Europe was rife with new schools and movements that rallied behind Rimbaud's call, 'One has to be absolutely modern.'[40] The 'Moderns' sought to create works that were qualitatively different from those of the past. They wanted to reflect the changing conditions of contemporary life, the hustle and bustle of the metropolis, the myriad of sense impressions that incessantly showered the city-dweller's mind. But in doing so, they wanted to transcend the traditional 'mirror' concepts of Realism. Their emphasis on experimentation with new means of expression was not, as Lukács et al. intimated, pure aestheticism and formalism, but an attempt to capture the realities of the 'modern' world with new forms of representation. These innovative and often highly experimental works of art presented reality as it was processed by human consciousness. If in the artist's mind a shattered, incoherent and absurd world conjured up images of chaos, energy, noisiness, etc., then the forms employed to express this experience had to be similarly dissonant, disjointed and fragmentary.

The effort of finding new artistic languages for capturing the modern experience caused the Moderns to be highly self-conscious in the use of their media of expression. This problematization of language is rightly considered to be a fundamental and constitutive aspect of modern art. But rather than being just a formal device, it also expressed a wide-reaching epistemological crisis. Whereas nineteenth-century art was based on a positivist–materialist understanding of the world, the Moderns had to grapple with a vanishing concept of reality. New scientific discoveries destroyed the classical understanding of the physical universe, provoked new philosophical explanations of an unstable and indeterminate state of existence and offered a different perspective on individual and society. A world that seemed to be an impenetrable labyrinth could no longer be represented in a traditional manner. Karl Pinthus expressed this clearly in the introduction to his anthology *The Twilight of Humanity*:

> The poetry of this generation reveals the chaotic character of the modern age, the disintegration of traditional social forms, despair and yearning, but also the fanatical craving for new potentials of human life, and it does so with just the same noisiness and wildness as one can encounter in reality.[41]

Rationalism as an imbedded social practice of the modern age gave way to an irrational dynamics. The artist, caught in the maelstrom of modernity, focused on the illogical, unconscious, primitive aspects of life and was forced to depart from measured, rational, realistic depictions of human existence.

Whereas in the nineteenth century, artists belonging to the 'Modern' school tended to adopt a positive attitude towards the new realities, mixed in, maybe, with a healthy dose of scepticism, many artists of the early twentieth century developed an awareness of the flipside of modernity. Their works described the destructive forces of industrialization, the standardized, rationalized, secularized existence of the big-city dweller and the threatening void of a disintegrating society. Such dystopic visions of an urban wasteland offered a fundamental critique of the 'grand narratives' of progress, emancipation, perfectability of the world, which since the Enlightenment had dominated European thinking.

The subject of modernity became the focus of an ever-increasing corpus of theoretical reflections. Of course, there was no lack of theoretical statements issued by nineteenth-century artists and writers, but these were, on the whole, by-products of a creative practice. In the early twentieth century, something substantially different came into existence. Between 1890 and 1930, a plethora of groups, schools and movements propagated their artistic doctrines in journals, newspapers, magazines, or as broadsheets, flyers and pamphlets. This 'manifesto mania' resulted from a desire not only to be new, modern and innovative, but also to establish clear boundaries and distinctions from what had gone on before and what coexisted on the contemporary scene.

The emergence of organized schools and movements presenting a wide range of new artistic concepts in a formal, theoretical manner makes it useful to have an omnibus term to denote the underlying similarities between these groups. The generic term 'Modernism,' as opposed to 'modern,' characterizes an artistic consciousness that focused on the modern features of society and represented these with the new and innovative means of expression (although contemporary language continued to give preference to the term 'modern' and reserved 'Modern*ism*' to the meaning of 'to be modern at all cost'). However, I would not go as far as some critics, who use the term 'Modernism' to cover nearly all post-Romantic developments. When 'Modernism' is understood as the noun of 'modern', it becomes a very wide-ranging portmanteau term and eliminates the fundamental differences between nineteenth-century descriptions of industrial society and the highly experimental, non-Realist representations of a technological civilization in the early twentieth-century.

BOX 1.2 MODERNITY, MODERNISM AND THE AVANT-GARDE

Modernity
A historical and social condition that reached a peak with the Industrial Revolution and the establishment of capitalism as the determining force in society. The formation of modernity brought about radical changes, which affected all spheres of social life: mass-migration, urban growth, new means of transport and communication, the break-up of social ties, secularization, commodification, etc. The rapid transformation of society and everyday life in nineteenth-century Europe produced an historical consciousness of a new epoch and gave rise to a cultural attitude that valorized present over past. It rejected traditions and customary conventions as anachronistic remnants of the past, and took a positive stance towards the narratives of technological progress, prosperity, individualism and universal liberation.

Modernism
An artistic response to the advent of the modern age which consciously broke away from classical methods of representation and instead explored forms of expression better suited to the altered experience of time and space. Rather than adhering to conventional themes and academic repertoires of styles, artists focused on the present and made use of the changed forms of communication in advanced industrial societies. As a generic term, 'Modernism' encompasses a multitude of distinct,

→

→

yet closely related schools and movements such as Expressionism, Cubism, Futurism, Dadaism, Surrealism, whose adherents sought to express the spirit of modernity and the novel experiences in the contemporary world. Although these groups shared certain attitudes and formal features, they could vary substantially in the way they emphasized the exhilarating aspects of modernity or the disquieting aspects of mass society and technological civilization.

Avant-garde
Originally a military term, it came to be applied to political and aesthetic domains, where it denoted a practice of assaulting traditional authorities and cultural institutions. The avant-garde in the arts propagated a radical break with preceding formulae of artistic production and promoted creativity as part of a wider cultural–political revolution. The artists opposed conventional concepts, values and standards, and instead aimed at absolute originality in their creations. The avant-garde shared with the Modernists an interest in experimentation and new techniques of representation, but took a far more transgressive and subversive stance towards the institutional framework of the production, distribution and reception of cultural artefacts. Avant-garde artists shunned museums, theatres, and mainstream publishing houses and reached their audiences through alternative outlets. They operated in uncharted terrain with genuinely novel means of expression, creating works of art that were substantially and significantly different from the average production of their time, and were initially only appreciated by a small number of connoisseurs.

Avant-garde, Modernism and the Mainstream

Related to the concept of Modernism, yet different in emphasis and intention, was that of the avant-garde, which emerged in the nineteenth century more or less in parallel with the development of modernity (for a summary of these terms, see Box 1.2). The term itself dates back to the Middle Ages, where it was used in military language to designate the advance troops of an army. The concept of an artistic avant-garde was first introduced in the Renaissance. Étienne Pasquier was possibly the first author to characterize a number of writers as 'the avant-garde; or, if you prefer, the forerunners of other poets'.[42] Around the time of the French Revolution, the concept of a political avant-garde emerged and the word was applied to Jacobin politics and Utopian, future-oriented philosophies. The metaphor appealed to radical intellectuals who regarded themselves as an advance guard leading the rest of mankind into a liberated future. Henri de Saint-Simon, for example, held that artists should play a leading role in society and should even be put in charge of the State.[43] And his pupil Olinde Rodrigues propagated the idea of the artist as a leader, priest and Messiah, who would 'serve as the avant-garde' of a new society.[44] The concept of the vanguard artist as the herald of a better world exercised considerable influence in the years to come. Gabriel-Désiré Laverdan, another pupil of Saint-Simon, attached the ideas of progress and social justice to art and arrived at the conclusion that if 'art as an expression of society expresses in its most elevated forms the most advanced social tendencies and is a forerunner and discoverer . . . then art is worthy of its role of initiator and the artist of belonging to the avant-garde'.[45]

In the nineteenth century, the older, military understanding of the term was successively supplanted by a socio-political meaning, and then complemented by a concept of an artistic–cultural vanguard.[46] However, the military subtext never disappeared altogether. Avant-garde artists regarded themselves as militant revolutionaries in the 'culture wars' of their period. For example, the Futurists ascribed to themselves the role of scouting the enemy territory, attacking the barriers erected by the forces of tradition, forcing a breach and then moving into the uncharted terrain of the future. The 'advance guard' would then be followed by the regular 'army' of Modernist artists, who shared with the élite corps an oppositional, progressive stance, but were less reckless in their actions and did not expose themselves to the same risks.[47] The Dadaists also advocated militancy, radical dissent from the established canons of art and opposition to the guardians of tradition and social propriety: 'We were in no doubt that the world had to be overturned. We wanted to prepare an attack that went beyond anything the war-waging nations had ever seen.'[48] Their all-out assault on the institutions of bourgeois society was continued by the Surrealists, who allied themselves with the Communist Party, and the Constructivists, who played a significant role in the Russian Revolution.

Such a combination of engaged art and political radicalism was usually missing from Modernist art and literature. The Modernists may have held a critical mirror to society, but did not necessarily intervene in the political battles or promote through their art a liberated world order. In contrast, avant-garde artists attacked the dominant ideology of bourgeois society, analysed the reconciliatory functions of the category of 'art' in capitalist culture, criticized the prevailing aesthetic conventions, and subverted the institutions of artistic production and distribution. They revealed art to be an ideological construct sanctioned by custom and tradition, divested it of aesthetic forms that could offer refuge from the ugly realities of capitalism, and destroyed any illusions of organic perfection, self-contained wholeness, inner harmony and beauty. The avant-garde advocated rupture, revolution and destruction as vehicles of liberation; it employed transgression and shock as means of bringing about innovation; it even advocated the transitory death of art as a necessary therapeutic measure.

Such an attitude was markedly different from that of nineteenth-century innovators, who sought to effect a gradual evolution of artistic forms and social constellations. Artists belonging to the Modernist schools placed themselves somewhere between these two positions. They were more forceful in their criticism and reformist zeal than nineteenth-century reformers, yet never displayed the same attitude of radical opposition as avant-garde artists did in their manifestos, political actions and works of art. The Modernists struggled against entrenched rules and conventions, yet never challenged the guardians of established cultural institutions. This, in turn, has caused a widespread interpretation of Modernism as an invigorating social influence and of the avant-garde as a nihilistic and destructive force. However, avant-garde art was not only characterized by opposition, protest, negativity; it also experimented with new forms of expression and anticipated in its creations a liberated art practice. The bleak description of the modern 'wasteland' revealed, implicitly or explicitly, a desire to transcend the current state of alienation, either through social action (hence the artists' affiliation with radical parties and organizations) or through artistic creativity (hence the status of the work of art as a counter-image to social reality and rising above an alienated life praxis).

Given this intimate bond of art and anti-art, destructive impulses and forward-looking visions, the relationship between artist and society can be described as falling into three categories:

(a) The conventional artist, who produces for the mass market and has an uncritical, affirmative attitude towards society.

(b) The Modernist artist, who seeks to capture those aspects of the contemporary world that are transforming traditional culture and society. As such, the Modernist artist is at odds with the conservative forces, who try to preserve the civilization of a by-gone era.

(c) The avant-garde artist, who has an intuitive perception of impending changes, expresses a vision of how these will affect society, and seeks to open up a terrain for these innovations to take place. As such, the avant-garde artist attempts to provoke radical change before others see a need for it. Here, art takes on a visionary role and acts as an instrument of social change.

The twentieth-century avant-garde was never a homogeneous phenomenon, but encompassed a wide range of artists who were opposed to the aesthetic and social conventions of their day. They formed an integral element of Modernist culture, but differed from its mainstream spectrum on account of their radicalism and political outlook. Avant-garde art was produced by small, close-knit groups of nonconformist individualists, whereas Modernism was a 'broad church' that included many hangers-on and undistinguished associates. The avant-garde formulated the most advanced and forward-looking concepts, and then left it to its followers to translate these visions into concrete reality. The Modernists were like the rank and file who follow the shock-troopers after they have occupied a new territory. To take the military metaphor a stage further: after the Modernists have explored the 'virgin soils', the mainstream artists move in, exploit the land and use it to cultivate staple products for mass consumption.

The avant-garde was the 'cutting edge' of Modernism and produced genuinely novel and original works of art. Modernist artists assumed the task of translating the innovative achievements of the avant-garde into 'a movement-idiolect or a period-idiolect',[49] which would then become a characteristic feature of a given period and produce new norms accepted by society. The Modernists emphasized the need to go with the times, but they did not ignore the roots of the modern culture in older traditions. George Steiner has gone as far as claiming that Modernism was a deliberate attempt at salvaging a cultural past that was in danger of complete dissolution, and could therefore amount to 'a strategy of conservation'.[50] Other critics see Modernism as the 'new tradition' of the modern era; it superseded the older, Realist tradition, but remained liable to academic institutionalization.

Modernist artists operated in close cooperation with the mediating agencies of museums, theatres, newspapers, etc., whereas avant-garde artists refused to fulfil any subservient functions in bourgeois society. They established a critical distance from the reified and alienating life praxis in middle-class society and confronted the bourgeoisie with a distorted, fragmented, decentred image of reality. In order to perform its critical, anticipatory functions, avant-garde art relied on its autonomous status, yet at the same time tried to escape this position by turning artistic creativity into an emancipatory social praxis. The possibility of the work of art fulfilling its progressive, transformational and liberating function was thus predicated on the autonomy it tried to overcome.

As artistic autonomy was such an important issue in the aesthetic debates of the late nineteenth and early twentieth centuries, the dividing line between different types of autonomy needs to be clearly established:

(a) The *l'art pour l'art* concept of aestheticism: detachment of art from the functionalist, utilitarian life praxis in bourgeois society provided a sacred realm in which humanity could recover its lost wholeness. These sanctuaries of art isolated from the social sphere offered an escape from everyday routines and allowed an experience of a life in harmony with itself. It masked the contradictions of an alienated existence and promised to resolve them in an aesthetic refuge, pretending that real needs could be satisfied in an unreal world.

(b) The Modernist insistence on autonomy: artists could protect the independence of works of art from non-aesthetic functionality, concern themselves with the medium itself and focus on its inherent aesthetic qualities. This led to formalist concerns with innovation and technical perfection. Content and social purpose were seen to be of minor significance. This self-reflexive (and often self-absorbed and self-sufficient) art stood for an aesthetic revolution without consequences in the social world.

(c) The avant-garde concept of autonomy: artists aimed at establishing a critical distance from social determinism and from the affirmative role of art in capitalist society. They offered a critique of the ideology of art in bourgeois society and demonstrated an awareness of the institutionalized conditions of artistic production. The avant-garde artist was a Utopian seer or prophet of a society in which the instrumental rationality of the capitalist system would be eradicated. Art served as a model for a liberated future and anticipated a non-alienated existence, to be accomplished through a creative art/life praxis.

As bourgeois society was not monolithic in terms of ideology and social practices, artists found a variety of modes of relating to the cultural bodies of their epoch. Yet, rejecting bourgeois society while at the same time operating within its artistic institutions caught the artist in a paradoxical situation that knew no easy solution. Although the avant-garde opposed the reactionary or traditionalist aspects of bourgeois art, this opposition also strengthened a structural feature of capitalist society: its constant drive to renew and advance itself. Market economies rely on internal competition in order to sustain growth. Both avant-garde and Modernist artists were caught up in this dilemma; the difference in their response to this problem was only a matter of degree, and was effectively annulled by their joint operational platform within the bourgeois art establishment. Both counter-cultures succumbed to the institutional embrace and ended up being yoked to the very system they had tried to overcome. The concepts of alterity they promoted came to be incorporated into the machinery of progress and were neutralized in just the same manner as the attempts to break up the institutionalized distance of art from life.

Once the concepts of the avant-garde had become absorbed by the wider community of artists and popularized amongst the modern public, they ceased to be in the forefront of aesthetic innovation and had to be replaced with new ideas. The avant-garde always conceived of itself as a highly ephemeral phenomenon, and not as an institution. Marinetti, for example, described Futurism as a short-lived affair, soon to be overtaken by 'younger and stronger men, who will probably throw us into the waste paper bin like useless manuscripts – we want it to happen!'[51] The same attitude pertained to avant-garde creations. At the *Manifestation Dada* at the Grand Palais (5 February 1920), Picabia challenged his spectators with the statement: 'Dada works must not exist for any longer than six hours.'[52] However, despite this intention of being a transitory phenomenon, the avant-garde built up its own tradition, and eventually became part of the establishment. As early as 1917, a visitor to the Cabaret Voltaire could declare: 'It is nearly like an academy. They are building their own tradition.'[53] In 1920, Huelsenbeck foresaw the danger of Dada becoming commodified by the culture industry: 'The mediocrities and the gentry in search of "something mad" are beginning to conquer Dada.'[54]

For this reason, avant-garde artists liked to employ the most ephemeral of all media, performance, to express their artistic concerns. A single, unrepeatable and therefore unique stage event counted for much more than a poem printed in a magazine or a painting exhibited in a gallery. Also, performance as a live event involved a direct confrontation with the audience, whose reactions could be responded to in an improvised manner. If avant-garde practices were a means of combat, this battle could be fought most effectively within the framework of a performance. The following chapter will give us a few examples of the forms such militant engagement with the bourgeoisie could take.

BOX 1.3   SOME KEY FEATURES OF AVANT-GARDE ART

- Being against the autonomous status of art in bourgeois society: art should not be a sanctuary separate from the everyday business of politics and economics and should not offer any illusion of wholesomeness, ideal beauty, redemption, contemplation and edification.
- Favouring a merging of art and life: instead of being restricted to operating within the established cultural institutions, art should engage with a new life praxis and organize everyday existence according to creative principles.
- Negotiating a position between the paradoxes of art and anti-art, autonomy and intervention. There exists a double bind between revolt against art and a creative engagement with it, between establishing a critical distance from society and overcoming the artist's detachment from society.
- Changing the established cultural and political order by means of shock, provocation, disturbance, intervention etc., calling into question the habitual communication structures and discourses, and rejecting aesthetic canons, conventions and precepts.
- A crisis of language: questioning the referential and communicative functions of art and revealing verbal and visual language to be a construction or artifice determined by social context and artistic intention. Form reflects on itself, its codes, referential status and signifying power.
- A crisis of representation: artists opposing the concept of art as a mirror held up to nature and the organic and closed concept of art. 'An object has not one absolute form – it has many; it has as many as there are planes in the region of perception.'[55] New techniques of fragmentation, collage and montage; multi-focal perspective, simultaneity, discontinuity; juxtaposition of material; disjointed discourses rather than linear renderings.
- Self-reflexivity: the work of art is not a mimetic copy of an objective reality but an expression of the artist's consciousness of that reality. These mental filters are foregrounded in the portrayal and enhance the audience's awareness of the artificiality of the construction.
- A crisis of individuality: disintegration of the organic, coherent, integrated subject (Rimbaud's 'Je est un autre'[56]). Not only reality has lost its coherent structure, but also the observ-

→

→ ing subject. Perception is a stream of experiences and sensations. There is an emphasis on subjectivity in the production and reception process, placing the spectators at the centre of the work and forcing them to take an active role in the aesthetic experience.

- The audience as co-producer: instead of existing in splendid isolation from the work of art and taking an objective, distanced stance towards its presentation, the spectator has to re-synthesize the fragmented reality exhibited in the artwork through an active engagement with its form and content.
- New Utopianism. A futurist refashioning of the world on a changed basis. Constructivist ideas of a human and industrial future. A positive attitude towards the liberating potential of technology. The machine as a metaphor of creativity and progress.

2

Towards an Avant-garde Performance Practice, 1896–1919

In the nineteenth century, theatre was predominantly a sector of the entertainment industry and catered for bourgeois audiences with a taste for escapist, melodramatic, and sentimental drama. The art theatre of the period only occupied a small, albeit influential position in the cultural landscape. Its authors and directors made a conscious effort to address the pressing issues of the time and produced a steady stream of works categorized by their authors, audiences and critics as 'modern'. This designation could refer either to a subject matter taken from contemporary life, or to the use of stylistic devices that defied the classic Aristotelian model. Büchner, Chekhov, Tolstoy, Ibsen, Strindberg, Hauptmann, and Granville-Barker were the best known representatives of this trend, and were supported in their undertaking by directors such as Laube, Brahm, Antoine, Stanislavsky, Reinhardt, among others.

Towards the end of the nineteenth century, one can observe a distinct counter-trend, in both dramatic writing and theatrical production. Several of the founding fathers of the modern stage sought to demolish the narrow confines of Realist aesthetics. Wedekind, Strindberg, Maeterlinck and many other playwrights directed their attention to the subjective experience or spiritual dimension of reality. Craig, Appia, Fuchs, Fort, Lugné-Poë, and others stripped down the Naturalistic paraphernalia that cluttered the stage and instead worked with a stylized, symbolic or abstract décor. Dramatists and directors discovered the scenic spectacle and the physical craft of the actor as artforms in their own right, and the work undertaken by these reformers prepared the stage for the acceptance of Modernism in the theatre.

The years 1890–1914 were a transitional period, which saw the historical avant-garde emerging out of a cultural climate of renewal and experimentation that had been prepared by the Post-Impressionists, Symbolists, Art Nouveau artists, etc. Critics regularly refer to this generation as 'the first avant-garde' or 'the first wave of Modernism'. I have no principal objection to this, but I would still classify these artists as innovative reformers rather than exemplary figures of Modernism or representatives of the avant-garde. The founding fathers of the modern stage pursued an artistic programme that was certainly modern, in some ways even ahead of their time, but they still treated theatre as a handmaiden of dramatic literature. They retained the concept of theatre as a fixed and repeatable spectacle and never questioned the unspoken assumptions about the indispensable components of a theatrical production. It fell to the historical avant-garde to challenge the criteria of what constitutes a scenic work of art and to create performances that were not just interpretations of dramatic texts, but autonomous, transient events that attained power and impact from their temporal and physical immediacy. Of course, every performance is a unique and unrepeatable event; but the avant-garde in its most radical manifestations abolished the product-oriented working method of institutionalized theatre. Instead of mounting a well-rehearsed and tightly controlled production, fixed for cyclical reproduction, they created unpredictable fields of action that attained their unique quality through improvisation and the active participation of the audience.[1] As an illustration of this new principle I should like to discuss a few representative examples taken from the early avant-garde movements.

Alfred Jarry, *Ubu Roi*

Alfred Jarry was a person who, more than anybody else in this transitional period, presented himself and his artistic œuvre as a model of avant-garde creativity. In 1894, he met the influential theatre director Lugné-Poë and decided to refashion a juvenile puppet play, *Les Polonais*, which he had occasionally performed to friends in his private marionette theatre and also recited, mimed and acted out in various literary soirées and salons. On 8 January 1896, he proposed to Lugné-Poë a production of the play at the Théâtre de l'Œuvre and in April/May he had it published in Paul Fort's review *Livre d'art*. On 11 June, a first book edition, issued by the *Mercure de France*, appeared and gained him an appointment as secretary and dramaturg at the Théâtre de l'Œuvre. As the critical response to the playtext was predominantly negative,[2] Jarry felt his artistic sensibility had been badly hurt and began to adopt in his private life a behaviour that was extreme even by the standards of the Parisian bohème.

When, on 9 and 10 December 1896, *Ubu Roi* was given the only two performances during the author's lifetime, it caused one of the greatest scandals in French theatre history and became a benchmark against which future avant-garde events were to be measured. Jarry and his small circle of supporters at the Théâtre de l'Œuvre used the theatre as a means of setting themselves apart from the bourgeois patrons of the arts in France. The controversies surrounding *Ubu Roi* established a clear demarcation between the avant-garde and the mainstream. The publication of the text was preparatory work for this undertaking; but its full oppositional force could only be experienced in a public theatre performance. For this reason, the two nights of scandal that shook the Théâtre de l'Œuvre in 1896 were principally different in intention and effect from the publication of a book, however provocative the text may have been.

The outrage caused by the première of *Ubu Roi* should not make us forget that Jarry possessed a serious, albeit radical, conception of the theatre.[3] He felt that European theatre since the introduction of the Italianate system of scenery and stage architecture had exhausted itself in a meaningless duplication of life. In order to find a way out of the cul-de-sac created by the Realist/Naturalist tradition and its 'slice-of-life' aesthetics, the stage needed to be re-theatricalized. Jarry sought to shatter the illusion of reality by extreme simplification. He argued for a theatre of artifice and demanded that the stage sets and properties be iconic, suggestive and evocative. Schematic and highly stylized scenery with a deliberate crudeness and naivety was to offer a visual manifestation of the substance of a play. Rather than being tied to narrative, psychology and contemporary issues, Jarry's theatre was to present universal topics in a distinctly timeless and abstract manner, and convey its underlying themes by means of archetypal images. Jarry wanted to use theatre as a catalyst that stimulated the imagination and allowed the audience to conceive of new worlds rather than cling to the banalities of everyday existence. He sought to eliminate all that impedes the creative act in the mind of the audience. Thereby, the spectator would become an active participant and co-producer of the spectacle, rather than a passive consumer of a theatrical entertainment.

At a time when leading actors and actresses were fashionable high-society figures who used the stage for satisfying their egomania rather than furthering the dramatic arts, Jarry wanted to submit the actor to the control of the playwright and theatre director.[4] He demanded a de-individualized, mechanical type of acting, with a monotonous delivery style, expressive gestures and movements, a heightened physicality and an emphasis on non-verbal forms of communication, primarily derived from the marionette theatre, the Elizabethan Dumb-Show and medieval Mystery plays.

However, in the 1890s there was little opportunity for bringing such ideas to fruition. The two dominant types of theatre – the Boulevard stage with its unashamed commercialism, and the Realist/Naturalist tradition – were still unassailable institutions. Parisian theatre, and in effect, most European theatre at the time, was a commercial institution concerned with trivial histrionic displays, bound by moribund conventions, and exploited by financial speculators. Jarry felt that if one wished to re-institute theatre as a serious art, one had to destroy first of all the prevailing artistic and social conventions of this bastion of tradition. The Symbolist reformers, with Paul Fort and Lugné-Poë at the forefront, took a serious interest in Jarry's absurdist conceptions, but were unwilling to lend full support to his radical visions. Conversely, Jarry entertained a certain sympathy with the idealist bias of Symbolist theatre, but also felt that its archetypal universality was rather vague in conception and would benefit from a more radical approach. Jarry was serious about his innovative ideas and pursued them with great zeal. At the same time, he held the bourgeoisie in absolute contempt, as they possessed no understanding of and no interest in the artistic side of theatre. Therefore, *Ubu Roi* was designed to function as a dynamite thrown at an audience who visited playhouses only to parade their dresses and jewels and to seek superficial diversion in the merry company of stars and starlets.

Jarry's anarchist convictions, combined with his antagonistic and erratic personality, produced a rather explosive constellation that erupted in the first performances of *Ubu Roi*. His correspondence from the time of setting up the production indicates that he was consciously striving 'to react against established traditions' and to introduce elements that would 'incite the old ladies and make certain people shout "Scandal!"' [5] He wanted the stage 'to act like a mirror' that would make the audience 'dumbfounded at the sight of its ignoble double'.[6] And as he was effectively in charge of the show (Lugné-Poë was little more than nominal director), he was able to put his ideas into practice. The accounts of the première certainly show that his provocations and shock tactics bore fruit.[7]

As was the custom at the Théâtre de l'Œuvre, Jarry delivered a lecture before the performance, in a clownish outfit, with dishevelled hair and in an exaggerated enunciation. When the curtain went up, the stage set did not bear any resemblance to Poland or any of the locations Ubu visited on his perambulations. In accordance with Jarry's writings, the décor looked like a naive children's painting that mixed indoor with outdoor elements and resembled simultaneous scenography in the medieval manner. It cobbled together the arctic and temperate zones, showed an apple tree in bloom, a palm tree with snow falling from the blue sky, and a bare tree growing at the foot of a bed. On one side of the backdrop a skeleton dangled from the gallows, on the other side was painted a bed, complete with chamber pot, and a fireplace that served for the characters' entrances and exits. Scene changes were indicated by placards brought on by a black-suited 'Father Time' figure. Nobles, financiers and magistrates consigned to the 'mince grinder' in Act III were 'acted' by marionettes, and the Horse of Phynance was a pantomime dummy. Many of the costumes were incongruous to the characters (e.g. Bordure attired like a Hungarian Gypsy musician; Bougrelas in a baby dress with bonnet; Ubu wearing a black suit with one trouser leg rolled up to his thigh). The actors wore masks, spoke with strange accents and imitated the stiff and jerky gait of marionettes. The Gargantuan farce was accompanied by fairground music played on two pianos and various percussive instruments.

The public dress rehearsal on 9 December 1896 was attended mainly by an invited audience, who only began to voice their displeasure in Act III, scene 5. The official première on 10 December 1896 found a more turbulent reception from the very beginning of the show. In order to pacify the rioting spectators, actors improvised a range of scenic actions not foreseen in the playtext. These were mainly routines taken from the popular stage, and in an odd manner fitted the style of a play; however, the resulting chaos made it impossible for the audience to understand the plot of this savage and unsavoury charade of a play. The actors' attempts at placating the audience were countermanded by several friends of the dramatist, who fanned the unrest by booing when the spectators clapped, and *vice versa*.[8] In the end, the exasperated actors observed from the stage an unscheduled performance unfolding in the auditorium.[9] The traditionalists and curiosity seekers, who objected to the play's scatological and obscene humour, reacted with indignation and finally paroxysms of rage. But as the press reviews made abundantly clear, the cultured élites of Paris also felt insulted by the play and its presentation. The critics described the drama as a vulgar hoax devoid of artistic value, and interpreted the production as an anarchist insurrection equivalent to the bombs that had recently shaken Paris (the *Figaro* called it a 'literary form of terror' by 'anarchists of art'[10]). Others surmised that Jarry had directed a political satire at the bourgeoisie and the present government. It is not astonishing therefore that Lugné-Poë drew the necessary conclusions, cancelled subsequent performances, and severed his contact with the scandalous author.

Jarry's *Ubu Roi* was widely discussed in artistic circles, and not only by those who had actually seen the performance at the Œuvre. Reviews in literary journals were also read outside France and copies of the play found their way into the hands of writers across Europe. In Italy, Jarry found an ardent admirer in F. T. Marinetti, who established an epistolary contact with the infamous writer and came to Paris to make his acquaintance.[11] A few years later, he published a play, *Le Roi Bombance*, that was closely modelled on *Ubu Roi*, and had it put on by the Théâtre de l'Œuvre.[12] In the following years, he developed a new approach to theatre which pursued the provocation of scandal, uproar and outrage in a systematic and highly accomplished manner. Before discussing this practice in the section on 'The Futurist *Serate*', I should like to present an event that pre-dates the Futurist soirées by a few years and relates to another Modernist school that developed more or less in parallel with Futurism.

Oskar Kokoschka, *Murderer Hope of Women*

Oskar Kokoschka was an important forerunner of Expressionism, and in the 1910s one of its most important representatives. Although trained as painter, he was equally interested in the theatre, wrote a number of plays and also designed the works of other dramatists. His production of *Murderer Hope of Women* had the hallmark of an avant-garde event of the first order and established him as a major source of irritation on the Viennese cultural scene.

This Austrian artist was born in 1886 and made his theatrical debut on 28 October 1907 with a shadow play, *The Speckled Egg*. A year later, he presented some of his paintings in a major collective exhibition, the Wiener Kunstschau. Gustav Klimt liked his works very much and called him 'the greatest talent of the younger generation', but the general public reacted to his works with consternation and incomprehension. In response to this, Kokoschka began to adopt a new public persona. His appearances in public gave a vivid demonstration of an avant-garde artist living in opposition to society and the artistic establishment. He distanced himself more and more from the Art Nouveau style, which at that time dominated Vienna, he joined the bohemian circle of Peter Altenberg, shaved his head and presented himself in Viennese cafés as a wild 'punk' (or to use his own words, as a 'bull in a china shop'[13]).

On 29 March 1909, his play *Sphinx and Strawman* was performed at the Cabaret Fledermaus, and Kokoschka discussed with his cast the production of an as yet unfinished play, *Murderer Hope of Women*. Aware of the attention he had received at the first Kunstschau, he planned a *succès de scandale* for the next edition of the show, approached the organizers of the exhibition, and received their permission to have both plays staged in the garden of the building.

Murderer Hope of Women was written, as Kokoschka stated in his auto-biography, as a means 'to express my attitude to the world' and as 'an anti-dote to the torpor that, for the most part, one experiences in the theatre today'.[14] Kokoschka approached theatre with the attitude of a painter rather than poet or dramatist. Instead of using conventional dramatic language he composed theatrical images that gave visual expression to his concepts and ideas. The 1907 draft of *Murderer Hope of Women* operated only with stage pictures, and in the later versions of the play the stage directions take up more space than the dialogues. The text did not adhere to any rules of grammar or syntax. Just as a painter would arrange shapes and colours on a canvas, Kokoschka placed words next to each other. He was interested in their aural qualities and semantic associations rather than literal meaning. He made rhythmic speech patterns clash with melodious flows of soft vowels and consonants, and set clusters of harsh sounds against ariose sentences. The characters' intense states of mind were meant to be given physical realization by means of body language and vocal production, and not through conventional acting techniques. None of this had ever been explored in the theatre before but in the following years, many of these characteristics became hallmarks of Expressionist theatre. A later perfor-mance of Kokoschka's play, directed by the leading Expressionist actor Heinrich George, is shown in Illustration 4.

On 10 June 1909, an advertisement for 'A Kokoschka Evening' appeared in the Viennese press, announcing 'a drama followed by a comedy, directed by Ernst Reinhold'.[15] Kokoschka fuelled public curios-ity by distributing all over Vienna a garish poster with a repulsive treat-ment of the *pietà* theme, which 'sent the Viennese into paroxysms of rage'[16] and confirmed to the wider public what the newspapers had writ-ten about him: that he was a 'wild savage' (*Oberwildling*) intent on shocking the bourgeoisie. As it happened, the performance had to be post-poned and an actress from the court theatre was no longer able to partic-ipate. Some last-minute alterations in the cast were required, with little time left for rehearsals. This is probably why Kokoschka wrote in his autobiography:

> I had simply improvised with my friends the play at a night-time rehearsal in the garden. I gave the principals and other players an outline of the action and wrote down each of their parts in short key phrases on slips of paper, after first acting out the essentials of the play for them, complete with all the variations of pitch, rhythm and expression.[17]

4 *Murderer Hope of Women*, directed by Heinrich George at the Neues Theater in Frankfurt (1920)

However, the reports in the local press do not confirm Kokoschka's claim that the whole production was 'simply improvised'. Rather, they suggest that Kokoschka's planning went slightly awry, but there was still enough time to engage a musician, Paul Zinner, to write a score with lots of brass and percussion for the play. A surviving photograph of Kokoschka, Reinhold and another friend gives the clear impression of a group of young, self-consciously rebellious artists taking on the artistic establishment and delighting in their ability to *épater le bourgeois*. The performance on 4 July 1909 certainly established their reputation and served as a useful public relations exercise for promoting their artistic ideas.

The Viennese newspapers inform us that 'the exotic poster, which in recent days had been beckoning from every street corner'[18] attracted 'a very distinguished audience, which awaited the Kokoschka evening with great anticipation'. Apparently, they interjected some sarcastic comments, but otherwise reacted with 'well-meaning hilarity' to 'the manneristically constructed word excesses, the incomprehensible, ecstatic screaming, the staggering movements of human clusters on stage'. The leading actress, Marianne Heller, interpreted her role with 'Salome ardour' and 'was able to grab the audience's attention with verve and style'. The chorus of men and women shouted the text to the sound of drums and cymbals, ran around with torches in their hands, and made little attempt to link words to actions. At the end there was applause, mingled with a few boos, and when the audience demanded to see the author, a stagehand informed them that 'Mr. Kokoschka had retired to avoid accepting the ovations'.

The reviews confirm that 'performers, most of them drama students, hurled themselves into their parts, as if acting for dear life'.[19] Although the critics did not describe the costumes, they are invoked in Kokoschka's statement: 'As there was no money, I dressed [the actors] in makeshift costumes of rags and scraps of cloth and painted their faces and bodies . . . with nerve lines, muscles and tendons, just as they can be seen in my old drawings.'[20] These 'old drawings' are presumably the woodcuts that accompanied the text in its first published version in *Der Sturm*, and are likely to reflect the style of the 1909 production. Kokoschka described the performance as having caused a riot in the audience, the intervention of a regiment of Bosnian soldiers, and his near arrest by the police. As nothing of the kind is reported in the Viennese press, we should handle this statement with a certain degree of scepticism. But there is no doubt that for weeks the event prompted major debates in coffee houses and at dinner tables on the role of art and theatre in modern society.

The Futurist *Serate*

The year 1909 also saw the establishment of another artistic movement, Futurism, directed by the already mentioned F. T. Marinetti. Futurism was arguably the first organized avant-garde movement with a clearly formulated artistic and political aim. As Marinetti was a theatre critic, a dramatist and an experienced and controversial performer himself, he took a strong interest in the theatre and sought to employ it as a means of 'cultural combat'. Marinetti believed that the theatre could 'introduce the fist into the artistic battle'[21] and cause 'the brutal entry of life into art'.[22] He hoped that it would force the artists out of their ivory tower and give them a chance 'to participate, like the workers or soldiers, in the battle for world progress'.[23] The Futurist performer became the advance guard of the Futurist revolution, employing fighting methods that were derived from the anarchists' *beaux gestes destructifs*.[24] Theatre, when imbued with such a bellicose spirit, would have the necessary strength, Marinetti believed, 'to snatch the soul of the audience away from base everyday reality'[25] and have a liberating effect on society at large. Futurism as an artistic and political practice was designed to obliterate the contemplative, intellectual concept of culture and bring about a total and permanent revolution in all spheres of human existence. What was later called 'Futurist Reconstruction of the Universe' was aimed at a transformation of humankind through a remodelling of the social, political, physiological and psychological conditions prevailing in the modern metropolis.

Marinetti gave a first demonstration of his revolutionary concept of theatre in the productions of his plays *Poupées électriques* (performed in Turin on 15 January 1909) and *Le Roi Bombance* (organized by the Théâtre de l'Œuvre and performed from 3 to 5 April 1909 at the Théâtre Marigny in Paris). However, both plays were written long before Futurism had come into existence. The real innovation brought to the theatrical medium by the group of artists belonging to Marinetti's circle was the transformation of literary soirées (*serate*) into vehicles of public scandal and outrage. As of 1910, the term 'Futurist *serata*' meant: presenting the key ideas of the Futurist movement in a large theatre and offering the audience examples of how these principles could be translated into performative language. The first *serate* always contained a combination of (a) the reading of manifestos, and (b) the presentation of artistic creations that had arisen from these theories. This allowed Marinetti to introduce the Italian public, successively, to Futurist poetry, painting and music.

5 Filiberto Mateldi: Marinetti at a Futurist *serata* (1921)

For more than ten years, Marinetti had gathered experience as a reciter of Symbolist and anarchist poetry in various French and Italian theatres, often causing altercations and agitated audience reactions. He used this experience to launch a new, Futurist, type of recitation, characterized by visual and gestural presentation of poetic and theoretical texts (see Illustration 5).[26] However, from the first *serata* in Trieste onwards, another key element formed an integral part of the programme: Futurist politics. The *serate* had the function not only of familiarizing the art world with the aesthetic principles of Futurism, but also of propagating their ideology of anti-traditionalism, patriotism, dynamism, etc. Marinetti called events such as the Milan *serata* of 15 February 1910 a *comizio artistico*, that is, a political meeting with an artistic format.[27] In an essay of 1914 he tried to establish six key criteria that differentiate a Futurist *serata* from other events of a similarly noisy type, and included amongst them, besides several artistic principles, the systematic demolition of traditional art and politics.[28]

In this respect, the declamation of a manifesto or of selected examples of Futurist poetry no longer aimed at interpreting a literary text with artistic finesse, as had been the case in the poetry recitations during Symbolist soirées. The Futurist declaimer now served as an object the audience could react *against*. The reading set in motion a mechanism that went far beyond the appreciation of an artistic creation. The text functioned as a score, the reciter as a conductor, and the audience as the orchestra. The main task of the declaimer was to challenge the spectators and to provoke them into reactions of an unpremeditated kind.

The *serate* were a weapon in the political and artistic fight for a total renewal of Italian public life. They were an all-round attack on the cult of the past and the social forces that sustained it. Not only did they serve to glorify war and revolution, they *were* an act of insurrection, 'like the throwing of a well-primed hand-grenade over the heads of our contemporaries'.[29] But they also contained performances of an artistic nature, and it was in this combination of art and politics that the anarchist tradition of 'generative violence' found its concrete application. The Futurist *serata* was a medium in which art and life could be joined together in a compact union. Marinetti's *arte-azione* (Art-in-Action) was an artistic-political battle directed *against* an audience he regarded as reactionary, passive, lazy, complacent, etc. In order to shake these spectators out of their stupor, the *serate* had to be provocative. Depending on where the performances took place, a different composition of the programme ensured that nobody in the auditorium could remain unaffected by what was presented on stage.

As the Futurists gained experience with this loose format of the *serate*, they mastered the art of provocation and learned how to retaliate to the audience's counter-attacks. This aggressive stance turned every performance into a veritable battlefield (see Illustration 6). Initially, the Futurists had difficulty in handling the audience reactions and controlling the progress of the performance. But after a while they developed a certain virtuosity in the 'martial art' of theatre. They learned how to handle aggression (verbal or physical) and to channel audience reactions as they saw fit.

The riots and scandals that surrounded the *serate* served as an excellent public-relations exercise for the Futurists and brought the movement to the attention of the wider public. They made Marinetti a household name all over Europe – more so than any of his previous activities had done. The *serate* gave the Futurists a bad name in some circles (which the artists did not mind, since they regarded these people as passéists and beyond redemption anyway), but others felt admiration for this small group of artists, who within the span of a few years had captured the public imagination and exercised a growing influence on the cultural climate of the country.

A number of critics acknowledged that the *serate* served as a catalyst and remedial tonic that revitalized the ailing Italian theatre system. The genre was also an innovatory force because it gave encouragement to other artists and motivated them to pursue similar (or diverse, but nevertheless innovatory) artistic ideas. And, finally, it altered audiences' expectations and changed their idea of what constitutes a theatrical work of art.

One example may suffice here to give an impression of the atmosphere that reigned at a Futurist *serata*, of the performance strategies employed by Marinetti and his collaborators, and of the audience reactions they provoked.[30]

On 30 November 1913, an important exhibition of Futurist paintings organized by the journal *Lacerba* opened at the Libreria Gonnelli in Florence. To coincide with this major show, the local Futurist circle planned to hold a *serata*, and the publisher Vallecchi hired the Teatro Verdi for 12 December. The performance went down in the chronicles of Futurist theatre as the 'Battle of Florence'. Hours before the performance, the playhouse was surrounded by a clambering crowd. Estimates of how many people managed to squeeze into the auditorium vary between 5,000 (*Lacerba*) and 7,000 (*Corriere della sera*). The spectators opened the proceedings by whistling on keys, operating sirens and honking car horns. As one of the Futurists remarked, they 'had not arrived in the theatre with the intention to listen, but only to raise hell and make a racket'.[31] The general spirit of excitement and expectation created a tense atmosphere that needed only a tiny spark to set off an explosion. When, finally, the performers appeared on stage,

> an inferno broke out. Before any of us could open his mouth, the hall was boiling over, resounding with savage voices in the fever of excitement. There was an atmosphere like that of an execution field before the capital punishment is about to be carried out.[32]

6   Giovanni Manca: Futurist *serata* at the Politeama Chiarella in Turin (1910)

And Cangiullo remembered:

> When the curtain went up, a howling tribe of cannibals raised their thousands of arms and greeted our apparition with a volley of objects from the animal, vegetable and mineral world. . . . No one thought of taking the first word. We were totally overwhelmed by this reception. We looked at our audience and began to read the banners that were displayed from the dress circle: 'Perverts! Pederasts! Pimps! Charlatans! Buffoons!'[33]

After about five minutes, the audience began to calm down. Marinetti approached the footlights and exclaimed: 'I have the impression I am down below the Turkish Fortresses in the Dardanelles. I can see your munitions running out and they still have not hit us.' And immediately he was given proof that his assumption was wrong. The spectators had still masses of missiles left, causing Viviani to ask himself why neither the management of the theatre nor the many policemen had forbidden people to carry sackloads of projectiles into the auditorium. But it was not only the ammunition that caused disturbances. People had also arrived with car horns, cow-bells, whistles, pipes, rattles etc. Those who could not command any such instrument, at least made use of their door keys. After a while, Marinetti managed to interject another couple of sentences:

> It seems to me that this game has been going on too long. We shall wait until there is at least an intermittent silence. We ask those who support us to get the upper hand over the crowd, if necessary with force. Listen to us first, and when you've heard our new ideas, then you may whistle. Your asphyxiating and stinking missiles only demonstrate that traditionalism seeks to defend itself as best it can.[34]

As was to be expected, the audience retaliated with an ear-splitting clamour. Marinetti was exhorted: 'Get off and hide in a lunatic asylum!' To which he replied: 'I prefer our loony bin to your Pantheon!' And immediately the fracas started again. Marinetti advised his fellow-players: 'We have to attack at all cost.'

Amidst a barrage of vegetables which covered their heads in a shroud of pulp, the performers tried their best to get through the programme they had announced on the posters and in the newspapers: Soffici talking on Futurist painting, Carrà slating the art critics and explaining his theory of paintings of odours, Boccioni speaking on plastic dynamism, Marinetti and Cangiullo declaiming poems, and as the 'clou' of the evening, Papini giving a lecture against passéist Florence. Since hardly any of the words reached the ears of the spectators, the speeches were printed in the next issue of *Lacerba*. The paper *L'unità cattolica* wrote with amazement: 'Not only the working-class audience perched on the balcony were throwing potatoes. No, the upper classes and the petty bourgeoisie too gave a nice demonstration of the civil education they had received in their colleges and grammar schools.' There were a few dozen friends of the artists who made some attempt at cooling down the spectators. However, brandishing a club that had been broken out of the banister only produced the opposite effect. Brawls erupted between supporters and opponents of Futurism. Ottone Rosai describes how he and a few friends sought to pacify their opponents:

> Holding their arms we prevented them from throwing their projectiles down onto the heads of the calmer part of the audience. We did not always succeed in grabbing them on time. One of them hit Marinetti's eye with a light bulb, and other actors were struck by further missiles. Up in the gods, Zanini and I took a fanatic by his legs and let him dangle for a few minutes from the parapet. When we pulled him up again, he was the calmest and humblest person in this tide of frenetic beings.[35]

Police intervened to prevent worse incidents from happening, but the turmoil continued. Cangiullo and Papini watched the audience from the stage and smoked a cigarette. Marinetti took out some binoculars and had a closer look at the scenes unfolding on the balcony. After a while, the hail of vegetables turned the stage into a cesspit. 'Throw an idea, not a potato, you idiot!' Carrà hissed at a spectator, whose neighbour answered by blowing a children's trumpet. Marinetti commented, to everybody's amusement: 'That's the signal for the departure of his intelligence!' And Boccioni shouted: 'The projectiles you are throwing with such profusion are the fruit of your cowardice multiplied by your ignorance.' A spectator came up to the stage and offered Marinetti a pistol. 'Go on, commit suicide,' he suggested, to which Marinetti replied: 'If I deserve a bullet of lead, you deserve a bullet of shit!' But it was not only the actors who had to suffer from the transgressive behaviour of their enemies. Soffici remembered:

> Not everything that was destined to hit us actually reached its target. A cauliflower, an egg, a slice of maize cake, a chestnut pudding thrown from the upper balcony hit the bald heads and shoulders of gentlemen in dinner jackets, the elegant hats of the ladies down in the stalls, where they provoked violent protests and screams. . . . We could observe from the stage how here and there in the auditorium altercations of words developed into altercations of fists. Infuriated people in the dress circle leaned forward and disputed with those bending down from above. They may have been members of high society, but their vocabulary was that of hawkers and fishwives. Given the impossibility of developing an orderly argument, the whole thing degenerated into an exchange of heated phrases and a skirmish of invective and repartees between stage and auditorium.[36]

Towards the end of the performance, Marinetti tried to explain the *Futurist Political Programme*, which had been published three months earlier in *Lacerba*. His attacks on 'the cowardly pacifists and eunuchs' and 'the miserable mire of Socialists and Republicans' finally brought the house down. The police came on stage and declared the performance to be over.

The *serate* were the Futurists' first attempt at revolutionizing the established forms of theatrical communication. And indeed, the *serate* represented a clear break with the conventions and traditions of theatrical culture. They were not 'scandals' in the normal sense of the word, i.e. spontaneous eruptions of public ire, like those after the first performance of *Hernani* or *Ubu Roi*. Marinetti had *planned* and *organized* the events in a systematic and logical manner in order to *provoke* such reactions. He had initiated the *serate* with a clear political aim in mind: to storm the citadels of bourgeois culture and turn them into a battleground of a new socio-political praxis. Or as Carrà put it: 'Having issued our appeal to youth with a manifesto, we realized that this was still too indirect a way to rouse public opinion. We felt the need to enter into a more immediate contact with the people: thus were born the famous Futurist *serate*.'[37]

Although the programme of each *serata* contained items of an artistic nature, these were often only an excuse for political agitation or for propaganda for the Futurist movement. The Futurist artists slipped into the role of performers, but they eschewed all characteristics associated with the acting profession. They did not transform themselves into fictitious characters. They wore neutral evening clothes (only Balla sported his colourful waistcoats or cravats), and instead of realistic settings the stage was equipped with a few functional pieces of furniture (usually a table and a couple of chairs). At this early phase of the Futurist movement, Marinetti did not choose the theatre because of the artistic possibilities it offered, but rather because it was the most effective medium for polemics and propaganda in an evolving mass society. ('As only 10% of Italians read books and magazines but 90% go to the theatre, the only way to inculcate a warlike spirit in Italians is through the medium of theatre.'[38]) Papini underlined this fact when he wrote that through the *serate* the Futurists could divulge their ideas to a large number of people,

who otherwise would not have taken notice of them, had they simply and quietly been issued in printed form. In many ways, the theatre has taken the place of the old church. Modern man, who wants to put himself into contact with the masses, can put this modern temple to good use.[39]

The Dada Soirées in Zurich

Reports on the Futurist *serate* filled the pages of newspapers not only in Italy, but also abroad. In Germany, they inspired a number of artists emerging from the Expressionist school to stage some similar events. Hugo Ball, a student from Max Reinhardt's acting school in Berlin and dramaturg at the Kammerspiele in Munich, came into contact with Futurist art in November 1913, when he saw the Futurist exhibition that had started a European tour in Paris in 1912. It inspired him to plan an exhibition of Cubist, Futurist, and Expressionist paintings and to organize a Futurist soirée, however, because of the outbreak of the First World War, this never came to fruition.

If Ball's artistic development took a new turn following his contacts with Futurism, his position became even more radical when he witnessed the mass killings on the western front. He wrote to his sister on 7 August 1914: 'Art? That's had its day and has become a laughing matter. It's cast to the winds and has no longer any meaning.'[40] A few months later he noted in his diary: 'The whole machinery and the devil himself have broken loose now. Ideals are only labels that have been stuck on. Everything has been shaken to its very foundation.'[41] In October 1914, Ball moved to Berlin, where intensive studies of Kropotkin, Bakunin and other anarchist writers prepared him for 'a new, anarcho-revolutionary, life'.[42] He frequented the political circles of Gustav Landauer, a prominent anarchist later to become a leader in the Munich Soviet. Else Hadwiger, the translator of Marinetti's *Futuristische Dichtungen* (1912), informed him about the theatre evenings that had caused such scandals in Milan, Florence and Rome and inspired him to organize three similar soirées in Berlin. Ball was supported in this undertaking by his friend Richard Huelsenbeck, and together they wrote a manifesto, which expressed a pre-Dadaist position based on 'Expressionism, colourfulness, adventurousness, Futurism, action'.[43] The leaflet was distributed during a soirée held on 12 February 1915 at the Berlin Architektenhaus. The second soirée, on 26 March at the Café Austria, had a more sober, political orientation; but the next event, at the Harmoniumsaal on 12 May 1915, included self-composed 'Negro poems' by Huelsenbeck and contributions by Emmy Hennings, a cabaret singer who had become Ball's lover.[44] The atmosphere was such that the critic of the *Vossische Zeitung* could describe it as 'a protest against Germany, in favour of Marinetti'.[45]

Soon afterwards, Ball and Hennings emigrated to Switzerland, where they made the acquaintance of Fritz Brupbacher, a Swiss anarcho-syndicalist and editor of the journal *Der Revoluzzer*. Together, they attended political meetings and participated in activities of revolutionary groups. The couple's financial situation was desperate. Hennings tried to earn some money as singer with the Marcelli concert agent and to supplement her meagre income with occasional prostitution. In October 1915, they accepted an engagement with the Variety ensemble 'Maxim'. After a while, they tired of their perambulatory existence and sought to set up their own company, called 'Arabella'. Their ultimate aim was to find a venue where they could arrange artistic events on a regular basis and under their own aegis.

The opportunity offered itself in December 1915, when they met Jan Ephraim, owner of the Meierei, a run-down bar in the disreputable Niederdorfviertel of Zurich. The publican hoped to increase his clientele by offering some cabaret entertainment, and Ball and Hennings had just the right background to provide that. The Cabaret Voltaire was set up in January 1916, as a 'centre for artistic entertainment . . . with daily meetings where visiting artists will perform their music and poetry. The younger artists of Zurich are invited to bring along their ideas and contributions.'[46] The venue was located in a small room next to the bar and had some 15 to 20 tables, giving it a capacity of not more than 50 per night. Although the walls had been decorated with what nowadays would be priceless paintings and collages, the stage was without décor and offered only a tattered screen for costume changes. Performances were given daily except Fridays, and instead of an entrance fee a slightly raised cloakroom fee was charged. Judging by Huelsenbeck's memoirs, the audience consisted mainly of young people, often students, who had spent a raunchy night in the amusement venues of Niederdorf and dropped for a late-night drink and to look for easy girls. Other memoirs mention a petty-bourgeois clientele who had come to the Meierei because of its restaurant service and who stayed on for the cabaret just out of curiosity. These were the sections of the audience who voiced the strongest objections to the high-brow offerings on stage and had to be reprimanded: 'The Cabaret Voltaire is not a common music-hall. We have not gathered here to offer you *frou-frous* and naked thighs and cheap ditties. The Cabaret Voltaire is a cultural institution!'[47] Then there was the motley crew of emigrés living in or near Zurich – artists, writers, dancers and musicians – who felt attracted to the cabaret because of its international ambience and who were curious about the growing fame, or rather notoriety, of the enterprise.[48] Occasionally also, members of high society strayed in, whom Guggenheim described as 'visitors in evening dress who seem to have descended to the lower depths after a classy dinner'.[49] A painting of the Cabaret by Marcel Janco is shown in Illustration 7, and described by Hans Arp. On the stage we see, from left to

7 Marcel Janco: *Cabaret Voltaire*, lost painting of 1916

right: Ball at the piano, Tzara wringing his hands, Arp; Huelsenbeck behind them with the big drum, Janco behind him; Hennings and Glauser dancing to the right. Hans Arp described the painting in the following manner:

> On a platform in an overcrowded room, splotched with color, are seated several fantastic characters who are supposed to represent Tzara, Janco, Ball, Huelsenbeck, Madame Hennings, and your humble servant. We are putting on one of our big Sabbaths. The people around us are shouting, laughing, gesticulating. We reply with sighs of love, salvos of hiccups, poems, and the bow-wows and meows of mediaeval bruitists. Tzara makes his bottom jump like the belly of an oriental dancer. Janco plays an invisible violin and bows down to the ground. Madame Hennings with a face like a madonna attempts a split. Huelsenbeck keeps pounding on a big drum, while Ball, pale as a plaster dummy, accompanies him on the piano.[50]

The first evenings in February 1916 offered a mixture of light entertainment and poetry readings. This relaxed and loose format of an artists' cabaret may have been to Mr Ephraim's satisfaction as it increased the turnover of his bar, but it did not live up to Ball's expectation. The venue had been set up as 'a gathering place for all artistic trends, not just modern ones',[51] and the local community of literati offered more contributions than could possibly be accommodated. But Ball did not wish the cabaret to become a platform for mediocre artists performing regurgitated wares. He wanted to institute a more avant-garde programme, something akin to what he had performed in Berlin. As it happened, a former acquaintance, the Italian journalist Alberto Spaini, relocated to Zurich and advised him how the Cabaret could be turned into a more exciting venue. Spaini was a friend of the Florentine Futurists and a great admirer of Marinetti. In 1914 he had recited several poems by Marinetti at a Sturm Gallery soirée, and as he had experienced a number of Futurist *serate* in Italy, he could give Ball some first-hand accounts of Marinetti's performance art.

Consequently, the Meierei was furnished with a new décor, including Futurist paintings and graphic poems on the walls. On 23 March 1916, the group advertised in two Zurich newspapers that they were going to perform 'a Futurist comedy and some Futurist programme-music'. Previously, on 12 February 1916, they had announced in *Das Volksrecht* that Hugo Ball was going to recite poems by Marinetti, Buzzi, and Palazzeschi. On 12 May 1917, Spaini introduced a Futurist style of recitation when he performed Meriano's *Gemma* and, on 14 April 1917, Marinetti's *Bombardment of Adrianopoli*.

The first soirée that truly deserved to be called 'Dadaist' took place on

30 March 1916, and had Huelsenbeck reciting 'Negro' poetry with trembling nostrils and raised eyebrows, a cane in his hand, to the accompaniment of a bass drum.[52] He then recited, together with Tzara and Janco, the simultaneous poem *L'Amiral cherche une maison à louer*, in three different languages to the accompaniment of a whistle, rattle and bass drum. Afterwards, they dressed up in black cowls and sang/danced/recited *Chant nègre I* and *II*.

The Dada circus, which according to Ball was 'both a buffoonery and a requiem mass',[53] had begun. Although most of the audience enjoyed the unique and highly experimental presentations, others, who had come for some light entertainment, took objection to the high-brow poetry recitations and incomprehensible 'negro songs'. They shouted, booed, demanded their money back, but usually calmed down again when Emmy Hennings appeared on stage to deliver her chansons. As Hugo Ball said: 'The people get terribly agitated, as they expect the Cabaret Voltaire to be a normal night club. One first has to teach these students what a political cabaret is.'[54] However, it was not only the students who objected to the presentations; also the local press and the conservative bourgeoisie began to regard Dada 'as a dissolute monster, a revolutionary villain, a barbarous Asiatic'.[55] This attitude was not astonishing, as Janco explained: 'At the Cabaret Voltaire we began by shocking the bourgeois, demolishing his idea of art, attacking common sense, public opinion, education, institutions, museums, good taste, in short, the whole prevailing order.'[56]

The new direction of the Cabaret Voltaire gave Ball a fresh lease of life. His diary for these months is full of ideas and reflections about the new art they were in the process of developing:

> Our cabaret is a gesture. Every word that is spoken or sung here proves at least that this humiliating age has not succeeded in winning our respect. What could be respectable and impressive about it? Its cannons? Our big drum is louder. Its idealism? That became a laughing stock a long time ago, in its popular as well as in its academic form. The grandiose butchery and cannibalistic exploits? Our deliberate foolishness and enthusiasm for illusion will annihilate it.[57]

During the following months, the group extended their activities into holding exhibitions of Dadaist, Cubist and Futurist paintings, publishing an anthology (*Cabaret Voltaire*) and a magazine (*Dada*). Soon, Hugo Ball was on the brink of exhaustion, and in July 1916 the Cabaret Voltaire closed its doors. A second series of performances started after the opening of the Galerie Dada (29 March 1917), featuring poetry recitations, Expressionist dances, noise music, simultaneous poems, and even short plays. The last major Dada event in Zurich was a soirée at the Saal zur Kaufleuten (9 April 1919), a public venue with an audience that resembled a normal cross-section of society and attracted over 1,000 people.

Hans Richter said that 'Tzara had organised the whole thing with the magnificent precision of a ringmaster.'[58] This in no way contradicted the improvised nature of the stage events themselves. Apart from allowing the performers room for creative self-expression, the soirées had the equally important function of provoking the largely bourgeois audience,[59] and this could only succeed if the whole programme was well organized. However, as the audience would arrive at the hall with the expectation that they would experience a provocative event, Tzara arranged a programme that defied all expectations and delivered exactly the opposite of what people had come for. Viking Eggeling introduced the evening with serious lecture on abstract and constructivist art. After this prosaic beginning, which provoked simply by being so unprovocative, there followed a piano recital of music by Schönberg, Satie and Cyril Scott, given by Suzanne Perrottet. Käthe Wulff recited poems by Huelsenbeck, Arp and Kandinsky, which prepared the ground for Tzara's simultaneous poem for twenty performers, *The Fever of the Male*. This 'hellish spectacle enraged the other half of the audience and unleashed the "signal of blood". Revolt of the past and of education.'[60] The spectators were now in a state of agitation; but before they could bring the evening to a close, an intermission was called.

In the second half, the same method of defying popular expectation was used again and brought the audience to new heights of indignation. There was a talk by Richter on Dadaism, which 'cursed the audience with moderation', atonal music by Hans Heusser, a recitation by Arp from his *Cloud Pump*, and Perrottet's *Black Cockatoo Dances*, performed by five dancers in sombre, oversized outfits. When Tzara read out his *Proclamation Dada*, he was showered with coins, oranges and similar objects. Amongst the booing and whistling he hardly succeeded in making his manifesto heard. But things got even worse when the climax of the evening arrived: the entrance of Walter Serner, a tall, elegant figure dressed in an immaculate black coat and striped trousers, with a grey cravat. When he read out the provocative statements of his Dada manifesto, *Final Dissolution*, he received such a tumultuous reception that he had to withdraw into the wings. When finally he returned to the stage, people expected him to proceed with the next item on the programme, a recitation of his own poems. But instead, he carried on stage a headless tailor's dummy, gave it a bunch of roses to smell, and placed the flowers at the mannequin's feet. He then brought a chair and sat astride it, but with his back to the audience. Hans Richter described the spectators' reaction to this act of defiance:

The tension in the hall became unbearable. At first it was so quiet that you could have heard a pin drop. Then the catcalls began, scornful at first, then furious. 'Rat, bastard, you've got a nerve!' until the noise almost entirely drowned Serner's voice, which could be heard, during a momentary lull, saying the words 'Napoleon was a big strong oaf, after all'. That really did it. What Napoleon had to do with it, I don't know. He wasn't Swiss. But the young men, most of whom were in the gallery, leaped on to the stage, brandishing pieces of the balustrade (which had survived intact for several hundred years), chased Serner into the wings and out of the building, smashed the tailor's dummy and the chair, and stamped on the bouquet. The whole place was in an uproar.[61]

So finally the provocation had worked. But this was only due to the fact that Tzara had masterminded the show with a clear vision of how the various sections of the programme would affect the audience, who after three years of Dada activities were no longer naive in their expectations, but arrived in order to be shocked and affronted. Once the spectators began to enjoy the spectacle on stage, and the conventional roles of performers and onlookers were reinstated, Dada performance had failed in one of its major functions: to provoke its bourgeois audience to the extent that they reversed the direction of theatrical communication and 'performed the script in the hall'.[62]

The Influence of the Historical Avant-garde on Mainstream Theatre

At the beginning of the chapter, I described the years 1896–1914 as a transitional period between the late nineteenth-century culture of renewal and the postwar consolidation of the avant-garde impetus. Some of the most radical facets of avant-garde aesthetics were to be found in this early era. In the theatre, performances derive their revolutionary drive from the artists' defiance of conventional theatre practices and their militant opposition to the bourgeois patrons of the arts, which in turn provoked scandals and pitched battles between progressive and conservative members of the audience. These unmistakable features of the historical avant-garde began to change after the First World War. The reconstruction of western European economies demanded a positive response to the pressing tasks of the time and led to what is variously described as a *rappel à l'ordre* or an *esprit nouveau*. One of its most conspicuous signs was the transformation of Dada into Surrealism, and its partial sublation in the Constructivist movement.

News about the Dada activities circulated in Paris without, initially, causing much of a reaction. This changed in early 1919, when *Dada 3* passed around Apollinaire's circle of friends and Picabia, freshly arrived from Zurich, planned a Paris edition of his magazine *391*. Marcel Janco, too, visited Paris and reported in great detail to Breton and Soupault what exactly had happened at the Cabaret Voltaire. On 4 January 1920, Breton visited Picabia for the first time, and their meeting became the 'true début of the Dada movement in Paris'.[63] Now everybody was waiting for the arrival of Tristan Tzara, the new Messiah of modern literature. The event took place on 17 January 1920, and in the following eighteen months a string of Dada events were organized, including a number of performances along the lines already explored in Zurich. However, in Spring 1921, Breton and Picabia fell out with Tzara and began to surround themselves with a new circle of friends. This became the core of the Surrealist group, which issued its first manifesto in October 1924.

Although the Surrealists often scandalized bourgeois society, they never advocated the same rupture with past traditions as could be observed amongst the Dadaists. In political terms, the group's sympathy with the Communist Party indicated that the old dream of a union between revolutionaries in the artistic and political arenas was still virulent. However, the coalition was extremely fragile and did not lead to many concrete results.

Around 1922, several of the Dadaists began to sympathize with the aims of Constructivism. At a congress of the International Union of Progressive Artists in Düsseldorf (29–31 May 1922), an 'International Faction of Constructivists' undertook a critical review of Dada and Expressionism and signed a manifesto in which they protested 'against the predominance of subjectivity in art and against the arbitrariness of lyrical values'. Instead they demanded that 'the new principle of creation must be based on the systematic organization of the means of expression and produce an art that is universally comprehensible'.[64] From now on, the dialectic relationship between anti-art and art was tilting more and more towards the latter.[65] Although some Dada members continued their activities until 1923, it became apparent that as a pure protest the movement had outlived its usefulness and had become an anachronism. In 1924, van Doesburg declared categorically: 'The epoch of destruction has come to an end. A new epoch has begun: the great epoch of construction.'[66]

In Italy, the Constructivist manifesto found a positive response from Enrico Prampolini and Ruggero Vasari, who were major representatives of Futurist mechanical art, a trend that dominated the movement until the early 1930s. The *Futurist Manifesto of Mechanical Art*[67] was widely distributed in Europe and found a positive reception amongst De Stijl artists. Reyner Banham has shown how the Dutch theorists 'transmogrified' the Futurists' romantic enthusiasm for the machine and thus became the 'true founders of that enlightened Machine Aesthetic that inspired the best work of the Twenties'.[68] Enrico Crispolti ascribed a similar role to the

L'Esprit nouveau group in Paris,[69] where Léger's work was linked so often with the Futurists that he had declared publicly: 'I like the forms necessitated by modern industry and I use them [. . . but] I am not a Futurist.'[70] Consequently, there was a great deal of overlap between different artistic schools and movements. Although they tended to claim absolute originality and independence from competing trends of the time, mutual influences were in fact as important as the novel features of their creativity. For this reason, one should avoid the neat compartmentalizations that are commonly employed in art-historical textbooks. Such simplifications do not do justice to the wide range of aspirations pursued by different branches of the avant-garde and do not reflect the complex traffic of ideas that existed between them.

After Europe had recovered from the devastations of the First World War, artists undertook a serious and genuine attempt to re-balance the relationship between art and anti-art and to pursue a positive, constructive line of research and experimentation. It is therefore not astonishing that mainstream playhouses took note of these performances and became receptive to some of the ideas expressed in them. Just as there existed an osmosis between the different avant-garde movements, their methods and artistic concepts also filtered through into the mainstream. Already before the First World War, theatre directors increasingly felt that the Realist/Naturalist mode of production had reached a cul-de-sac and that the repertoire of scenic means of expression ought to be expanded. The work of the great reformers of the early twentieth century was finally taking effect and led to the acceptance of a more radical refashioning of theatre aesthetics at the hand of directors such as Meyerhold, Tairov, Brecht, Piscator, Jessner, Copeau, Pitoëff, Dullin and so on.

An extensive critical literature on these major representatives of the modern stage has clearly established the lines of influence that connected them to the avant-garde movements mentioned above. A much smaller range of studies has investigated the work undertaken by avant-garde artists in conventional playhouses. The very fact that by the late 1920s every major European capital possessed a number of playhouses dedicated to theatre as an artistic rather than purely commercial activity makes it abundantly clear that the forces of tradition and retrospection had lost a major battle. Many of the productions mounted in these houses were indebted to ideas and techniques first promulgated by the avant-garde, which had then been taken up by various Modernist schools and circles, and had finally filtered through into the mainstream. There can be little doubt that the great scenic revolutions of the early twentieth century would have been unthinkable without the influence of the historical avant-gardes.

3

From Late-Modernism to Postmodernism

As I outlined in the previous chapter, Modernism and the concept of an avant-garde were closely linked to the changes that took place in the wake of European industrialization, c. 1830 to 1940. The emergence of a post-industrial information society is considered by many to have been a momentous event with consequences as far-reaching as those of the Industrial Revolution in the nineteenth century. This chapter maps out some of the fundamental transformations that unfolded during the second half of the twentieth century and outlines some of the ways in which these developments affected social and intellectual life in the Western world. In Chapters 4 to 8 of this volume I shall then discuss how these eventful changes impacted on a range of avant-garde performance artists and how they responded, in their creations, to the challenges of a post-industrial, postmodern information society.

The Emergence of a Post-industrial Information Society

One of the main tasks that politicians and planners had to confront in the postwar period was the reconstruction of European economies and the expansion of the new industries that had matured in the interwar years, such as car manufacturing, ship building, iron and steel, petrochemicals, electronics, transport and communication. The USA was the only major country to emerge from the devastation of the Second World War in a strengthened economic position. For the next decade, North America benefited from the lack of industrial competitors and an increased demand for goods in a Europe recovering from the war. Fear that a further deterioration of the living conditions would make these countries an easy prey of Communism led to the installation of a European Recovery Programme in April 1948.[1] American

48

aid provided under the Marshall Plan did much to promote Fordism[2] as a dominant system of industrial production, designed to produce stable growth rates, a disciplined workforce, and expanding markets through mass consumerism. Western economists regarded Fordism as an engine for a dynamic capitalist system, but it also came to be seen as a symbol of the American Way of Life and of rising living standards across social strata.

In most people's mind, the Industrial Revolution was symbolized by smoke-stacked factories, steam engines and opulent villas belonging to capitalist entrepreneurs as the organizing force behind the production process. In the postwar period, these images were replaced by those of computer-studded offices and smart-looking employees representing the clean technologies of the information age. The centrality of theoretical knowledge in the production process dislodged industrial labour from its position of pre-eminence and assigned a pivotal role to the professional and technical classes of scientists, engineers, economists and managers. The post-Fordist economic system did not entirely displace traditional industries, but most goods-producing sectors became increasingly dependent on theoretical work ('Research and Development') prior to production. Daniel Bell described these developments in his influential book *The Coming of Post-industrial Society* (1973), and outlined how the transition from a commodity to a service economy created a technocratic society determined by information technology.

The economic boom of the 1950s brought about a massive expansion of world trade, international finance, and global markets. Rising competition amongst the industrialized nations forced these into reducing costs and increasing productivity. In order to achieve these aims, multinational companies took advantage of cheap labour in Third World countries and 'outsourced' entire production facilities across the world whilst keeping managerial control centralized in Western capitals. Although large sections of industrial production, manufacturing business and mid-stream technology were shifted from the industrialized countries to low-wage, surplus-population zones of the world, the 'core countries' (United States, Japan, Germany etc.) developed their highly skilled workforce and technologically advanced production lines. The functional integration of such internationally dispersed activities, combined with the globalization of financial markets, produced a radical transformation of the world economic order and led to fundamental changes in the occupational structures in Western countries. In the new social composition of society, the technical intelligentsia became the largest and most prominent sector and served as the 'new proletariat' (or 'cognitariat', as Charles Jencks called it[3]) in the technocratic mode of production (see Table 3.1[4]).

Table 3.1   **Statistics for US experienced civilian labour force, 1800–1980 (sector's percentage of total labour force)**

Year	Agricultural	Industrial	Service	Information
1800	87.2	1.4	11.3	0.2
1850	49.5	33.8	12.5	4.2
1900	35.3	26.8	25.1	12.8
1930	20.4	35.3	19.8	24.5
1950	11.9	38.3	19.0	30.8
1960	6.0	34.8	17.2	42.0
1970	3.1	28.6	21.9	46.4
1980	2.1	22.5	28.8	46.6

Cross-national production networks and the complex international division of labour required the collection, storing, retrieving, processing and transmission of enormous quantities of data. The development of a new generation of computers and their integration into electronic communication networks was an important precondition of this development. However, the resulting Information Revolution was as much the product of military planning as it was of industrial necessities. The Cold War between the USSR and USA had led to an arms race (1949: the Russians exploded their first atomic device) and a competition in space programmes (1957: Sputnik I; 1958: Explorer I). In the 1950s and 1960s, the largest part of funding of electronic research came from government defence budgets. The improvement of rocket, radar and satellite systems necessitated more reliable electronic components, better and faster computers, and digital processing equipment to convert data into telecommunicatable form.[5] This was provided by the integrated circuits of silicone chips[6] and image processing techniques (computer vision and automation of sight[7]), which also found a profitable application on the consumer market. This, in turn, led to the micro-chip revolution of the 1970s, with electronic goods representing some 20 per cent of the US gross domestic product.[8] The growth in US transistor production is shown in Table 3.2,[9] and the uses of those transistors in the three main market sectors in 1963 is shown in Table 3.3.[10]

From Mechanical to Electronic Culture

Just as the Industrial Revolution took off when the invention of mechanical devices such as the steam engine was complemented by new transportation

Table 3.2   **US transistor production, 1957–65**

	1957	1960	1963	1965
Germanium				
Units (million)	27	119	249	333
Cost ($)	1.85	1.70	0.69	0.50
Silicon				
Units (million)	1	9	51	275
Cost ($)	17.81	11.27	2.65	0.86

and distribution networks, information technology (IT) revolutionized society by the introduction of new communication systems (fibre-glass optics, satellites, etc.) and the creation of a digitalized 'nervous system' for world distribution of information. In the 1980s it became possible for multinational companies to link computers via electronic networks and to make vast amounts of information stored on data banks available to terminals anywhere in the world.

In the advanced information society, an increasing number of human activities were replaced, supplemented or mediated by cybernetic machines in three key applications: perceptual (telecommunications, audio-visual technology), conceptual (computers, calculators, Artificial Intelligent machines), and motoric (robots). This resulted in a fundamental transformation of the economic, social and cultural domains in all Western societies. Initially, the Information Revolution affected people's lives only at the workplace and had little tangible effect on the domestic sphere. Mainframe computers of the 1960s and 1970s were accessible only to highly specialized professions, and computer-controlled, automated production lines were the exclusive domain of large-scale industrial plants. But in the 1980s and 1990s, the advent of the personal computer and the IT

Table 3.3   **US users of transistors in 1963 (value in $ million)**

Military		Industrial		Consumer	
Space	33	Computers	47	Car radios	20.6
Aircraft	23	Communications	16	Portable radios	12.6
Missiles	20	Tests and measuring	12	Organs and hearing aids	7.3
Communications	17	Controls	12	Television	0.3
Others	26	Others	5		
Total	**119**	**Total**	**92**	**Total**	**41**

revolution in offices[11] changed the social patterns of the work environment. People spent more time in front of a computer screen, had less face-to-face contacts with other humans and increasingly felt as if they were becoming part of a machine. This elimination, or reduction, of the human factor in the work environment began to have an effect on people's private life as well, as it altered their communicative behaviour and interpersonal relationships. Furthermore, management tended to introduce new technology in order to rationalize and control work operations more effectively. This led to changing work patterns, flexible work hours, teleworking, contract work, temporary employment, and so on.

Although working hours have been nominally reduced in Western countries, much of the 'freed' time has been used for 'informal' work at home. Continuing education became compulsory for keeping abreast of changes in one's profession; consumption of the new technology (hard and software) evolved into a means of acquiring social and professional 'competence', credibility and status. Consequently, work and leisure time overlapped to a considerable degree and became largely dependent on each other. Soon, IT came to be seen as an unavoidable framework for all levels of human activity. The individual had no choice but to adapt to the changes and to operate within the new structures. Widespread fear of IT in the 1970s – largely caused by the threat of unemployment – changed to ambivalence in the 1980s (favourable assessment of leisure and work-saving aspects versus scepticism about employment prospects), and to pragmatism in the 1990s (resigned acceptance combined with appreciation of the positive features of IT).

Back in the 1980s, 80 per cent of IT business was to be found in the public sector and only 20 per cent with private customers, with 70 per cent of the latter dedicated to entertainment.[12] In the late twentieth century, information technology became an integral element of people's domestic life. Satellite or cable TV, video recorders, computer games, credit and switch cards, mobile phones, fax and email radically changed life in urban societies. The convergence and integration of computer technology and telecommunications brought about a globalized culture in the industrialized world and established worldwide trends in leisure and popular entertainment. For a summary of the history of computing, see Chronology 3.1.

A ceaseless flow of migrant workers turned urban centres into multicultural 'world spaces'. Multinational corporations dispersed more or less identical goods to every corner of the globe, where they were sold in virtually identical shopping malls and department stores. Credit cards became a currency without national barriers, and every city of the Western world participated in the same revelry of consumption following identical trends

CHRONOLOGY 3.1: HISTORY OF COMPUTING

17th c. Mechanical calculation machines.

1830s First automatic computer conceived by Charles Babbage.

1880s Introduction of punched cards in data processing.

Early 20th c. Gödel develops a formal logic, which provides the basis for Turing's concept of a computing machine, published in 1936. These simple analogue computers are about 50 times faster than a skilled mathematician.

1944 Harvard Mark I, an automatic sequence controlled calculator.

1945 ENIAC (Electronic Numerical Integrator and Calculator), the first computer where all mechanical components were replaced by electronic ones. The development is funded by the US Department of Defense, who need a machine to calculate the trajectories of shells and bombs. ENIAC can do so 500 times faster than the early analogue computers, but weighs 30 tons, occupies 144 square metres of floor space and is about 3 metres high.

1945–7 John von Neumann lays the basis for a modern digital computer.

1948 Bell Laboratories invent the transistor, which replaces the vacuum valves.

1949 EDSAC (Electronic Delay Storage Automatic Calculator), the first stored-programme computer, built in Cambridge, UK.

1950s FORTRAN and COBOL programming languages.

1954 Texas Instruments produces the first silicon transistor.

1958 Defense Advanced Research Projects Agency established in the USA. Its funding policies determine much of the computer research over the next decades.

→

→

1960	Second-generation computers use transistors and magnetic core memory, allowing 100,000 instructions per second.
1960s	Some 6,000 computers are in operation in the USA.
1969	US Department of Defense Advanced Research Projects Agency introduces ARPAnet, the first distributed, non-hierarchical computer network.
1970s	Microprocessor revolution increases memory on same-size chips from 64 bits in 1968 to 262kb in 1985, at the same time reducing cost from 2 cents to 0.01 cents.
Mid-1970s	Integrated circuits (IC) of micro-chips and large-scale integration (LSI) of thousands of transistors place the entire workings of a computer on a single integrated circuit. First minicomputers small enough to fit onto a desk or table. Average cost per 100,000 calculations reduced from $1.25 (1952) to $0.005 (1977). At the same time, the cost of a machine falls from $3 mill. to $3,000 and the number of computers installed in the USA rises from 50 to 200,000.
1975	Bill Gates and Paul Allen form Micro-Soft, which together with Apple, Tandy and Commodore launch the personal-computer revolution, initially in the business sector.
1980	Microsoft develops MS-DOS, which becomes the operating system for most personal computers. Over the next three years, software sales rise from $149 million to $1.6 billion.
1980s	Very large-scale integration (VLSI) vastly increases circuit density and leads to microcomputers for home use.
1981	IBM launches its first personal computer and makes it the industry standard. More than 6 million PCs are sold over the next three years.
1985	Microsoft launches its WINDOWS operating system, selling more than 2 million copies over the next four years.

→

→

1985	NASA presents its first head-mounted virtual reality (VR) system.
1989	The Intel i860 Central Processor Unit surpasses the one-million-transistor mark (500 times more powerful than the first microprocessors, with each transistor occupying a thousand times less space than those of the early 1970s).
1991	First VR systems become commercially available as leisure industry items.
1992	World-wide-web launched, which ten years later has over 100 million users.
1996	US factory sales of computers reach $50 billion (with a 70 per cent market segment of personal computers), surpassed only by Japan ($55 billion)

and fashions. Modern mass media became international in content, style, technology and ownership. A homogenized, global consumer society shaped the intercultural tastes of citizens around the world, thereby contributing markedly to the disintegration or transformation of local cultures.

However, the globalization of economies and financial markets does not necessarily equate with global connectivity. Given the concentration of economic and political power in Western nations, the postindustrial information society has largely reinforced the imbalance between First World and developing countries and has disqualified the majority of the world's population from citizenship in the 'global village'. At the end of the twentieth century, the World-Wide Web – symbol of globalization and 'universal' connectivity – had 97 per cent of its users concentrated in Western countries, while less than 1 per cent of Third World populations possessed as much as a telephone connection.[13] Therefore, the cultural developments described below hardly affected the average citizen in Africa and Asia, although the economic repercussions of globalization had a bearing on the way of life well beyond the educated (and economically potent) élites.

The Formation of a Postmodern Identity

In traditional societies, people were born into a fixed framework of existence, where identity was relatively stable once the process of social validation and mutual recognition had been completed and status had been achieved. The modern age made people socially and geographically mobile and subjected the individual to a process of deracination and alienation; yet, even in the modern metropolis, human beings shared many collective experiences in the family, at the workplace, in political associations, religious communities, and so on, and could therefore still believe in a pre-existent, essential and unchanging self.

In the postmodern age, the transformation of society accelerated to such a degree that identity became a highly problematic concept. The economic forces of a globalized information society affected the very core of human existence as it prevented the individual from finding any long-term mooring in social or institutional settings. Even temporary stability was undermined by the culture of the electronic age. This left a lasting mark on the identity formation of those members of society who, as children and young adults, had spent more time communicating with IT equipment than with other human beings. But also in the older generation, people's conception of the world, their social identity and self-image were fundamentally transformed, first by mechanical, then by electronic means of representation.

The urban centres of the postindustrial age produced ephemeral and amorphous societies in which individuals found it hard to participate in collective experiences. To compensate for this lack, the dislocated postmodern subject searching for human encounter joined virtual communities 'online', and cyberspace developed into an 'agora' of postmodern life. The resulting 'global villages' and computer-mediated 'neighbourhoods' re-created a sense of 'family' and recovered communal values that had gone missing in the real world.[14] Instead of entertaining physical contact with an organic community, the 'nomadic' subject increasingly identified with abstract and distant symbols of 'conviviality' offered by electronic culture. But as face-to-face communication came to be complemented or replaced by electronic means of communication, social practices shifted even further from public to privatized, home-centred activities. The spread of television, which played a major role in this process, is shown in Chronology 3.2.

Immersed in a networked, virtual mediascape, the individual found him/herself free-floating in a sea of cultural signifiers. But when identity is no longer experienced as an innate, inalienable and essential part of the self, then latent insecurity and anxiety are an unavoidable outcome. The culture industry has responded to the individual's desperate search for new objects of identification by offering a plethora of new sites of consumption and entertainment. Pop stars and TV celebrities demonstrate how gender, class, race, etc. could be morphed or reconfigured according to the taste of the individual concerned. The impression thus created is that identity is a matter of free choice, or at least a negotiable item.

Needless to say, personality features modelled on mass-media images are just as unstable as communities based on lifestyle choices, leisure activities and communication in cyberspace. The person who believes that the purchase of status-enhancing commodities on the consumer market and participation in the virtual communities of the 'global village' would indeed offer a reconstitution or redemption of the Ego, falls prey to a key marketing pitch of a multi-billion dollar electronic industry:

> Techno-reality is where identity crisis can be denied or disavowed, and coherence sustained through the fiction of protean imagination; or it is where the stressful and distressing consequences of fragmentation can be neutralized, and the condition experienced in terms of perverse pleasure and play.[15]

The traditional assumption of a coherent and unified subject, of a unity of mind and body, could no longer be brought into agreement with the postmodern realities of the Information Age. Increasingly, the postmodern subject experienced him/herself as a fractured, decentred individual; yet the engineers and purveyors of electronic mass media promised to their customers a reintegration of the self by means of adopting alternative identities in a commercialized digital environment. Robert Dunn summed up the process as follows:

> the source of identity has historically shifted from the internalization and integration of social roles to the appropriation of disposable commodities, images, and techniques, selected and discarded at will from the extensive repertoire of consumer culture. Communication and information technologies supplant older forms of association, roles and identities lose their interactional quality, becoming an extension of the instrumental and performative functions of various cultural media.[16]

But, of course, identity is not just a question of taste, desire and spending power. The media may provide an unlimited choice of identification, but the postmodern subject is both acting and being acted upon. As Terry Eagleton has argued in *The Illusions of Postmodernity*, the subject's position is highly contradictory: autonomous and free in some respects, yet conditioned and over-determined in others. An essentially ephemeral and fragmented, self-determined identity is externally framed by the choices offered by the culture industry. Although no longer imposed once and for all by the fate of origin (sex, class, race etc.), the degree of personal freedom is still circumscribed by the conditions of consumption (and large proportions of the population are excluded by dint of their insufficient spending power). Therefore, relinquishing a fixed identity can only be partially liberating. In the end, the postmodern subject finds him/herself as much determined by exterior agencies as the city dweller of the modernist age, enriched, maybe, only by a few more illusions.

CHRONOLOGY 3.2:   HISTORY OF TELEVISION

1884   Paul Nipkow applies for a German patent for an 'Electric Telescope'.

1902   Otto von Bronk applies for a German patent for a colour television.

1907   Boris Rozing applies for a Russian patent for a television system using a cathode ray tube as a receiver.

1909   Three different television systems are built and demonstrated by Max Dieckmann, Ernst Ruhmer and Georges Rignoux.

1911   First demonstration of a televison system by Boris Rozing in St Petersburg.

1922   Charles Francis Jenkins applies for a patent for transmitting pictures by wireless, and a year later demonstrates his first television apparatus.

1923   John Logie Baird applies for a television patent.

1923   August Karolus demonstrates a 48-line television.

1925   Bell Telephone Laboratories set up a television research programme.

1925   John Logie Baird gives a three-week public demonstration of television at Selfridges in London.

1926   Édouard Belin gives a demonstration of his television system in Paris

1927   AT&T give their first public demonstration of television, generally considered to be of excellent quality.

1928   General Electric broadcast first live picture.
Westinghouse Electric gives a demonstration of 'radio movies'.

→

→

1929   Baird Television Ltd operates a first TV service for BBC. German Reichs Postal Central Office in Berlin tests first TV broadcasts in Germany.

1930   First TV broadcasts by National Broadcasting Company (NBC) in New York. BBC transmits a theatrical show synchronizing sight and sound from the Coliseum Theatre in London's West End.

1935   German Post Office starts regular public TV broadcasts from Berlin.

1936   Berlin Olympics shown on German television. Walter Bruch and Otto von Bronk start first trials with colour television at Telefunken. London Television Service starts regular broadcasts. There are about 2,000 television sets in use around the world.

1939   Some 20,000 TV sets in use in the London area. First public US television service.

1940   National Television Systems Committee (NTSC) sets a universal standard for TV signals.

1941   Commercial television starts in USA, with 15 stations operational by 1946.

1946   BBC London re-introduces regular TV broadcasts.

1949   First daily news programme (*Journal Télévisé*) on French TV.

1950   CBS initiates a regular one-hour commercial colour TV programme. There are more than 100 TV stations operating in 38 US states; 8 million American homes have television sets.

1951   Ampex Electric Corporation demonstrates first video signals recorded on magnetic tape.

1952   15 million TV sets sold in USA, 1.2 million in UK.

1954   Colour television broadcasting begins in USA using the NTSC standard.

1955   36 million TV sets sold in USA, 4.5 million in UK, 0.3 million in the rest of Europe.

→

→

1956	First broadcast of a programme produced with video technology.
1958	US television advertising revenues exceed $1 billion.
1961	90 per cent of American homes now own television sets. Number of TV sets in operation worldwide exceeds 100 million Launch of Telstar, first communication satellite.
1968	200 million TV sets in operation worldwide: 78 million in the USA, 25 million in the USSR, 20 million in Japan, 19 million in the UK, 13.5 million in W. Germany and 10 million in France.
1972	First TV cable network (Home Box Office).
1976	A study indicates that the average American child will have spent 10,800 hours in school by the time he or she is 18, but will have watched an average 20,000 hours of television.
1994	Start of digital satellite TV in Europe: EUTELSAT Hot Bird.

Postwar Art in Europe and the USA

The outline given above of some of the fundamental changes that affected Western societies in the postwar era had a profound impact on the arts of the time. In the following pages I shall discuss some general features of this cultural production, which may then serve as a framework for our discussion of the performance artists active in the same period.

The first quarter of the twentieth century had been an extraordinary period of cultural innovation, with a whole phalanx of writers, artists and musicians producing works soon to be considered cornerstones of modern culture. But by the mid-1920s, the avant-garde had lost its radical drive, and with the economic crisis of the late 1920s it finally come to a halt. Even middle-of-the-road Modernism, whose innovative energies had become widely acceptable during the 'Jazz Age', was curbed by the establishment of fascist and para-fascist regimes in several European countries. For a while, the École de Paris acted as a centre of gravitation for modern artists of all denominations, but none of the circles and associations founded there in the 1930s arrived at any genuinely new departures from what had been achieved in the previous decade. Although Paris continued to be a lively, cosmopolitan centre playing host to a large number of creative geniuses, the Modernist impulse had reached a point of exhaustion and was finally brought to a halt by the Nazi invasion of France in 1940. Only limited aspects of Modernism survived during the 1930s and 1940s, usually in narrowly defined domains and always heavily controlled.

While for the next five years Europe was embroiled in the most destructive war ever waged, the hub of artistic creativity shifted to the USA, where New York took on the role of international centre of artistic research. Until then, the United States had been relatively unaffected by Modernism. In the early 1900s, the Ashcan school had emancipated American art from the stronghold of Academism and had directed artists' attention towards modern urban realities. The so-called 'American Scene' that developed from it pursued a similarly anti-academic stance and, not unlike nineteenth-century Realism, pitched truth against beauty, naturalism against artificiality, social significance against refined aestheticism. Both in its Regionalist and Socialist Realist variants, the school consciously rejected all Modernist styles as élitist and incompatible with the American sensibility. Instead, artists sought to immerse themselves in their 'native land' and detached themselves from all foreign influences, thus manoeuvring US-American art into a provincial and isolationist position. Consequently, the only two showcases of real significance – the 1913 International Exhibition of Modern Art in New York (better known as the Armory Show[17]) and the 1915 Panama-Pacific International Exposition in San Francisco – came more of a shock than a revelation to the American public. Many visitors regarded what was presented there as a foreign aberration, and most established artists took an equally negative stance towards the works displayed. However, in the younger generation it fostered a serious interest in international Modernism, and led to a brief flowering of Synchromism, Precisionism and New York Dada. New galleries emerged to exhibit European works, and once it became safe to travel to Europe, artists immersed themselves fully in the advanced language of Modernist experimentation. Upon their return, they found few opportunities to show their works in the USA. When Duchamp, Picabia, Gleizes and Crotti visited New York, they were bitterly disappointed that the modernity of native US urban life did not extend to the arts. Although Stieglitz's Gallery 291, the Folsom Galleries, the salon of Walter and Louise Arensberg and Katherine Dreier's Société Anonyme provided meeting places for people interested in the avant-garde, for the time being this had little influence on public taste.

Similarly in the area of theatre, Modernism remained a foreign import with next to no impact on the profession. The European Art Theatre movement, which was so crucial for the rise of Modernism in the performing arts, was never replicated in the USA and caused Sheldon Cheney in 1927 to deplore 'the lack of one permanent art theater acting company in these United States'.[18] The first attempt to introduce a European-style Art Theatre – the New Theatre in New York (1909–11) – failed miserably. The Little Theatre movement in the 1910s provided some potential for broadening the palette of theatrical expression, but it was largely an amateur affair and highly eclectic. The Theatre Guild, founded in 1919, produced plays that did not find a home in the commercial theatre, but in its performance style it never emulated the experimental 'director's theatre' approach of the Russians, French or Germans. Similarly, the Group Theatre (from 1931) brought little stylistic innovation. Hence, the adaptation of selected stylistic features of Expressionism or Futurism in the plays of Eugene O'Neill, Thornton Wilder or Elmer Rice remained isolated examples and did not bring about a move towards avant-garde experimentation that could compare in scale or vigour with the developments in Europe.

In 1944, Royal Cortissoz could unambiguously state in the last sentence of his updated edition of Samuel Isham's *History of American Painting*: 'The bulk of American painting is untouched by modernism.' This, however, was not to remain so for long, and the situation had already begun to change in New York. Artists and critics returning to the USA after several years of military service found that Social Realism and American Scene painting had been replaced by Surrealist and abstract art as the dominant trend in New York galleries. For example, Milton W. Brown noted in 1946: 'I have returned to find with some surprise that in the interim the dark horse of abstraction has swept into the lead. . . . All along the streets are evidences that the vogue today is for abstraction. Three years ago this tendency was evident; today it is swarming all over the stage.'[19] Clement Greenberg even feared that 'we are in danger of having a new kind of official art foisted on us – official 'modern' art'.[20]

The single most important factor bringing this about was the exodus of thousands of artists from totalitarian regimes and war-torn Europe to America. Many key figures of the prewar avant-garde settled in the USA or remained there for as long as it was unsafe to return to their homelands. Suddenly the second-hand and third-hand knowledge of Modernism that had produced so many misunderstandings in the 1910s and 1920s gave way to informed, authentic voices, who through their exhibitions, writings and teaching introduced the American public to the great artistic achievements of the early twentieth century. The Museum of Modern Art, which after its foundation in 1929 had focused nearly exclusively on Impressionism and post-Impressionism, suddenly began to exhibit major artists from the Modernist schools of Europe. The Solomon R. Guggenheim Museum, opened in 1939, followed suit, and several private galleries (some of them founded by émigrés) held exhibitions of significant figures of the European avant-garde. The catalogues published on these occasions often contained for the first time translations of key texts and manifestos, which were complemented by essays and reproductions in the 'Little Magazines' of the period. Several art historians and critics amongst the émigrés found teaching positions at American universities, and leading artists of the avant-garde conveyed their rich knowledge and experience to the younger generation at art colleges or through private teaching. The New Bauhaus in Chicago provided a whole phalanx of artists with a formative training in modern art, and the émigrés at the Black Mountain College gave artists from a variety of disciplines a fundamental introduction to avant-garde concepts of experimentation, which prepared them for the major roles they were later going to play in dance, theatre and music.

These displaced Europeans transported across the Atlantic not only skill and knowledge, but also a different role model for what it meant to be an artist. For a while it seemed as if the bohemian community of Montmartre had found a new home in Greenwich Village. A closely knit artist community came into existence – often referred to as the New York School – where, after an initial stage of absorbing the rich inheritance of European Modernism, an originally American brand of vanguard art came into existence. Abstract Expressionism, Action Painting and Colour-Field Painting were the first US-American contributions to Late-Modernism. The works created in the 1940s and 1950s were very distinct from their predecessors of the 1910s and 1920s, yet at the same time unthinkable without their European pedigree (in fact many members of the new schools had studied in Europe, or with European émigrés, or were of European extraction).

Also in Europe, the avant-garde went through a series of permutations and transformations. After years of pseudo-Realism and 'heroic' idealism imposed by fascist regimes, the return of Modernism seemed like an act of liberation. Europeans were looking across the Atlantic and found inspiration from the artists of the New York School. Their popularity was no doubt strengthened by a general admiration for the American way of life, which because of the low standard of living in the ruins of postwar Europe appeared like a progressive culture worth striving for. But behind the façade of a brave new transatlantic world a whole range of political agendas lay hidden. Just like the Marshall Plan, which was a calculated move to root out any sympathies for Communism, the State-funded promotion of Abstract Expressionism and geometrical abstraction served to depoliticize

Modernist art and make artists relinquish their adherence to left-wing ideologies. Following the fascists' instrumentalization of art for political purposes the depoliticization of art appeared like a necessary step, but in actual fact the revived ideology of 'art for art's sake' was a politically motivated move primarily directed against the Socialist-Realist modes of expression prevalent in the Eastern bloc.

The banning of Modernist and US-American culture during the fascist era had awakened a natural curiosity in the works of, say, Aaron Copland, George Gershwin, Gian Carlo Menotti, Thornton Wilder, Eugene O'Neill, Tennessee Williams, John Steinbeck, William Faulkner, Ernest Hemingway, and others. The USA responded to this interest in their cultural foreign policy and organized a number of high-profile festivals and touring programmes, thus giving representatives of recent American art prominent showcases in Berlin, Paris, Milan, Madrid, etc.[21] This, in itself, was a positive development, which only took on a new dimension when, in 1947, the CIA as a peace-time intelligence organization took on the role of a *kulturkampf* apparatus to complement the economic aid granted under the Marshall Plan.

The Truman Doctrine and National Security Act of 1947 sanctioned aggressive political intervention by the USA abroad in order to counteract Soviet influence in Europe and other parts of the world. A Manichean world view, promoted by often religiously motivated apostles of a messianic anti-Communism, portrayed the Soviet Union as an evil monster and Communism as an ideology masterminded by Satan. These self-righteous and intransigent Cold War strategists saw in the USA 'the protector of western civilization'[22] and displayed an attitude of 'we've won the war, now we're going to reorganize Europe our way'.[23] Seized by an acute superiority complex, they reckoned that a country with unrivalled industrial and military might should also possess a matching cultural power that could be imposed on the rest of the world. Consequently, the US government created a new cultural *imperium* that could at times become as undemocratic, manipulative and totalitarian as the one it was supposed to be fighting against.

From 1947 onwards, the United States championed a rigorously anti-Communist foreign policy and sought to counteract Soviet influence with a twin approach of political containment and covert psychological warfare. Ironically, the US government, while campaigning for civil liberties behind the Iron Curtain, established a garrison mentality within its own borders. McCarthy's Committee of Un-American Activities fomented a national paranoia about Communist subversion and instigated a cancerous system of investigation.[24] Spy fever gripped the administration, who in the course of six years investigated the political loyalty of 4,756,705 citizens[25] and dispelled tens of thousands of them from their jobs because they held, or had held, or were believed to hold, left-wing views (deemed to be 'treason' rather than political opinion).

The US foreign-policy machinery was provided with instruments of cultural propaganda designed to promote a *pax americana* and the American way of life in the rest of the world. Protected by the tightest secrecy, the CIA developed an expansive conception of the USA's security requirements, which included sophisticated propaganda measures 'so planned and executed that any U.S. government responsibility for them is not evident to unauthorized persons, and that if discovered the U.S. government can plausibly disclaim any responsibility for them'.[26] Altogether, the secret war chest of the CIA disbursed some $200 million per annum, of which $125 million were spent on psychological warfare and 'constructive measures' designed to thwart Soviet propaganda. The Office of Policy Coordination became the fastest-growing department of the CIA, commanding in 1952 a personnel of 2,812 stationed in the USA and 3,142 abroad, and a budget of $82 million.[27] The Central Intelligence Agency, supported by the United States Information Agency,[28] directed their propaganda at both a general populace and a cultured élite, at apolitical individuals and non-communist leftists. The main charge was to correct the Soviet portrayal of the US as a materialist, trigger-happy, uncultured nation and to promote the benefits of art and culture under capitalism.

In the years 1947–60, the US government discovered culture to be a useful political tool in its attempt to fight a battle for people's minds and to inoculate the Western world against the contagion of Communism. The arsenal of weapons in this cultural call-to-arms comprised high-profile touring exhibitions of modern American art and consumer products,[29] performances of American theatre, ballet and opera companies, international conferences, prizes for artists and writers, etc. Several bills were presented to the US Congress 'to establish a program of cultural interchange with foreign countries to meet the challenge of competitive coexistence of Communism'.[30] Consequently, vast sums of money were spent to build American cultural bases in Europe and to provide them with the wherewithal to act as spearheads of political propaganda. With millions of dollars being pumped into the Congress for Cultural Freedom, the National Committee for a Free Europe, the Truth Campaign, the Moral Rearmament Movement, the Crusade for Freedom, the Voice of America, etc., 'the CIA was in effect acting as America's Ministry of Culture'.[31]

However, in the immediate postwar period, there was little consensus as to what aspect of American culture ought to be promoted abroad. Many politicians in the USA were extremely conservative in their cultural tastes and considered Modernism to be part of a worldwide conspiracy designed to weaken American spiritual health. Congressman George A. Dondero was no exception when he demanded that government-sponsored art ought to 'glorify our beautiful country, our cheerful and smiling people, and our material progress . . . in plain, simple terms that everyone can understand'.[32] President Truman's judgement that the 'so-called modern art . . . is merely the vaporings of half-baked lazy people'[33] found a resonant echo in Dondero's congressional speech of 16 August 1949, in which he deplored modern art as being 'hog-scrapple' and 'trash' and accused Modernist artists to be 'depraved', 'decadent', 'degenerate', 'a horde of foreign art manglers', a 'polyglot rabble of subversives', 'neurotic left-wingers', 'instruments of destruction' and 'active weapons of the Kremlin'. He asked:

> What have we, the plain American people, done to deserve this sore affliction that has been visited upon us so direly; who has brought down this curse upon us; who has let into our homeland this horde of germ-carrying art vermin? . . . How did we ever let this horde of art distortionists, these international art thugs descend upon us? . . . Communist art, aided and abetted by misguided Americans, is stabbing our glorious American art in the back with murderous intent.[34]

Dondero's repeated attacks on modern art did not go unheeded in intelligence quarters, as recent examinations of FBI dossiers on 'suspect' artists believed to wield their art as a 'communist cultural weapon' show.[35] Richard Nixon, later to become President of the USA, took up the cue and charged a committee of Congress with a thorough investigation of art in government buildings, 'with a view to obtaining removal of all that is found to be inconsistent with American ideals and principles'.[36] Consequently, the philistines led by the Hearst press forced the withdrawal of a travel exhibition, 'Advancing American Art', arguing that it featured 'the work of left-wing painters who are members of the Red fascist organizations', that it was 'incomprehensible junk . . . with roots in the alien cultures, ideas, philosophy and sickness of Europe', and that it represented attitudes that were not 'indigenous to our soil'.[37]

Although the political establishment favoured Realist art, none of its American variants could be imposed on a world that had been primed by half a century of Modernist experimentation. There was certainly no chance of exporting a home-spun Realism of the Regionalist or American Scene variety. The more enlightened and liberal politicians therefore saw it as more opportune to exploit the fact that abstract art and most schools of the historical avant-garde had been banned in Stalin's Russia.[38] Although large sections of the political and social establishment had no personal predilection for abstract or Expressionist painting, they saw it as politically expedient to promote Modernism as an antithesis of Socialist Realism and a symbol of free expression. Thus instrumentalized as a weapon against Communism, abstract art came to be elevated to the position of *art officiel* of the Democratic West.

Circumventing the reservations of conservative congressmen, the CIA promoted an image of American society that was so tolerant and ideologically unencumbered that it allowed and even supported the most perplexing forms of Modernism. A number of authors have examined the promotion of Abstract Expressionism and Action Painting as a political measure during the Cold War[39] and have shown how these schools became integrated into a matrix of American apolitical liberalism *versus* Soviet instrumentalization of art, causing many of their representatives, who had been engaged in left-wing politics, to detach themselves from all Leftist organizations and embrace the ideology of art-standing-above-politics.[40] Abstract Expressionism was given a massive boost by the Museum of Modern Art (MoMA), which put together a series of exhibitions destined for foreign consumption (by 1956 they amounted to 33 altogether). The selection of works was specifically designed to give Abstract Expressionism canonical recognition and to show that the artistic vanguard, along with industrial and political leadership, had traversed from Europe to the USA. MoMA's International Council designed a programme of 'benevolent propaganda for foreign intelligentsia', in which they could convey the message that 'American art is the sole trustee of the avant-garde.'[41] Russell Lynes characterized these developments at MoMA:

> The Museum now had, and was delighted to have, the whole world (or at least the world outside the Iron Curtain) in which to proselytize – though this time the exportable religion was home-grown rather than what had been in the past its primary message, the importable faith from Europe.[42]

One of the results of this gigantic enterprise of cultural manipulation was that none of the figural forms of representation, which had been an important facet of early twentieth-century art, experienced a revival after the Second World War. In the fine arts, Tachism and Art Informel[43] as the European equivalent to Abstract Expressionism and Action Painting received an official sign of approval. In the performing arts, it was the Theatre of the Absurd that found the strongest backing from fund-holders.

Many European adherents of the new styles merged the American impulse with the older Modernist traditions while at the same time eliminating their Utopian political content.

By the 1950s, the New York School was considered to be on an equal footing with prewar Modernism centred on Paris, Berlin, Rome, etc. The international success of modern US-American culture suggested that the most innovative developments in the arts were now to be found in the USA rather than Europe. But whereas the founding fathers of American Modernism had been motivated by deeply personal and often existential reasons, the second generation was much more propelled by commercial motivations. This laid the ground for what Harold Rosenberg in 1959 could refer to as 'the tradition of the new'.[44] The changed conditions of a highly commercialized art market imposed on the avant-garde, which for many intellectuals had functioned as an *ersatz* religion, a process of secularization. A large number of artists were roped into a political game and – knowingly or not – became players in the Cold War theatre of the 1950s. To some of them it was an occasional ride on the gravy-train – to be given an exhibition in Paris, to receive a handsome advance on a novel, to have a play produced in a major theatre – whilst others were systematically built up to stardom by being provided with a colour-spread in *Time Life* magazine, a *Vogue* special feature, a prime-time television exposé, etc. Of course, when reproductions of their works graced the coffee-tables of the chattering classes around Fifth Avenue or Cape Cod, the price of their paintings soared sky-high. Therefore, it is no wonder that amongst the artists and intellectuals orbiting in the CIA galaxy one could observe an inevitable amnesia of formerly leftish views and bohemian attitudes and a sudden taste for Mediterranean cruises, ski holidays in Gstaad and *villeggiatura* on Martha's Vineyard.

But also other Late-Modernists, who had achieved bourgeois respectability and were now fêted by bankers, industrialists and conservative politicians, relinquished their commitment to political causes and social change. 'The modern artist is apolitical. . . . Political expertise belongs to the politician. As with art, only the full-time career can yield results', was the advice Allan Kaprow gave to his fellow artists.[45] The old commandment 'Thou shouldst not contaminate art with gain' was overturned; bohemian artists turned into businessmen, and creativity came to be judged by the criteria of commercial success. During the first ten years of the Cold War, hardly any artist driven by a genuine quest for the betterment of society could maintain a position on the west European art market. The often messianic visions of Expressionists and Constructivists, who in their majority had belonged to the Left-wing, and often Communist, community of artists, gave way to a rather inane Utopian optimism and to works of austere minimalism that bore no relation to any kind of experienceable reality. Late-Modernism as a watered-down version of 'classic' Modernist art was predominantly supported and bought by pretentious connoisseurs of middle-class origin. There was certainly nothing disturbing or scandalous about the 'corporate modernism' of the 1950s, which graced the walls of banks, boardrooms and bourgeois villas. The former avant-garde, which had defined itself through its opposition to society and its artistic institutions, had moved from the margins of society into the mainstream. It became an object of 'smart investment',[46] was absorbed by academic institutions, and ended up as an integral element of the culture industry. The last permutations of Modernism produced a never-ending supply of '-isms', a scrambling for novelty and an unrelenting quest for the New, which could be exploited by the art market and commended to the bourgeoisie as the latest fashion fad and lifestyle accessory. An acceptable form of Modernism, where form dominated over content, had become a 'modern tradition' functioning as the 'official' art in advanced capitalist countries.

In the mid-1950s, the pendulum swung back in the other direction, and a return to Realist means of representation could be observed both in Europe and in the United States. Slowly but steadily, the trickle of figurative paintings inspired by the new urban culture of the postwar period swelled in size. What initially had been a faint counter-trend to High-Modernist abstraction became a rising tide, for which Lawrence Alloway in 1958 coined the term 'Pop-Art'.[47] In France, the new trend was called 'Nouveau Réalisme'. Artists as far afield as London, Paris, Düsseldorf and Milan turned towards this new form of Realism without ever developing much of a group mentality or common programme. Each artist possessed a recognizable, individual stance, yet at the same time shared many of his fellow artists' concerns, which Henry Geldzahler defined thus:

> The new art draws on everyday objects and images. They are isolated from their ordinary context, and typified and intensified. What we are left with is a heightened awareness of the object and image, *and* of the context from which they have been ripped, that is, our environment.[48]

Pop Art was a reflection of postwar consumer society and the lifestyles it had given rise to. The flood of new consumer products, the rising tide of images produced by a proliferating media industry, the bewildering barrage of sensations and visual stimuli assaulting people's nerves: all this was a new experience, which abstract art could not give adequate expression to. The media-dominated urban culture offered artists new themes and techniques, and consequently they turned to recycling the motifs of advertisements, billboards, magazines, newspapers, comics, photographs, television, cinema, etc. However, merely reproducing the new urban reality in painterly form was a rather meaningless undertaking. 'I think a picture is more like the real world when it's made out of the real world,' Robert Rauschenberg discovered.[49] Like many others, he began to work with available materials and to include fragments of ordinary reality in his pictures. Collage became a popular stylistic device, which in a neo-Dadaist gesture was linked to the Nihilist and Existentialist philosophy of the post-war period.[50] The resulting works looked as chaotic and meaningless as the reality they depicted. Artists embraced the profusion of fragmented and multi-layered imagery promulgated by the media and transformed the visual diarrhoea of popular magazines, television programmes and pulp movies into works where the traditional opposition of high and low art lost all significance.

The first signs of Pop Art could be observed in England, where the post-war economic depression followed by a prolonged period of austerity contrasted markedly with the consumer boom in the United States. Hence, a new generation of artists looked across the Atlantic for inspiration, as, in the past, they had travelled to Paris. The American 'Society of Abundance' was regarded as a cultural alternative to a declining post-Imperial Britain. American magazines, music, films and novels were avidly received by intellectuals and artists, who soon turned their attention to pre-packed convenience food, brand-name consumer products, streamlined technology, etc. Following the first meetings of the Independent Group at the ICA in 1952 and the thematic exhibitions 'Parallel of Art and Life' (1953) and 'Man, Machine and Motion' (1955), the depiction of contemporary popular culture included a sophisticated analysis of the conventions and implicit messages of modern mass-media.

Pop Art, as it was practised in the United States, by and large evaded political commentary and displayed an affirmative attitude towards social realities, or at most, humorous detachment. American Pop Art was certainly not didactic. European Pop artists, on the other hand, expressed a far more critical attitude to the brave new world of modern technology and electronic culture. Their transformation of popular imagery involved devices that were similar to Brecht's Alienation Effect. Without forcing one singular viewpoint on the recipient, they addressed a range of questions with an open-minded, yet critical stance, inviting the viewer to participate in the reflective process and to develop an independent position towards the subject matter presented. Rather than offering a pure 'spectacle' of popular culture, they raised questions on the persuasion techniques of advertising and television. Images were not taken at face value. Illusionary reality was revealed as being fabricated. In fact, it became a major concern of European Pop artists to create an awareness of the dangers inherent in a culture where the 'real' world is transformed into an image of reality that seems more perfect and desirable than the 'real' thing it draws on. This act of transformation was a process that could of course be best captured in time-based performance art, which in its various forms and configurations will be the subject of the following chapters.

Postmodernism and the End of the Avant-garde

It was in this situation, towards the late 1960s or early 1970s, that post-modernism became a major, and then the dominant, trend in Western art. The complex network of economic, social, and intellectual forces that in the postwar period had allowed a last flourishing of Modernist art, had undergone a profound transformation. The changed realities of the emerging post-industrial information society could no longer be captured in Late-Modernist art, and a new generation of artists felt that Modernism had run out of steam. They regarded the 'establishment', who still subscribed to its tenets, as being out of touch with contemporary realities. Bored with the pretensions of abstract art and the introspective character of Art Informel, they found in Pop Art and New Realism alternative models to draw on, and developed from this a new aesthetics, usually referred to as 'post-modernism' (see Box 3.1). Both as a theory and as an artistic practice, this new movement was concerned with power structures and domination strategies in the social world and investigated how these give rise to cultural discourses. The aim was to expose the politics of representation in the new media of communication and to show how orthodox cultural practices functioned as tools in the hand of hegemonic social groups.

The postmodern condition of Western societies in the 1960s and 1970s was closely linked to the new electronic culture, which had demolished the concept of the individual, fixed in time and space, or moving in a linear fashion from A to B. Hegemonic systems of vision and representation had become fragmented; singularity of viewpoint had been broken up. The individual's consciousness and relationship with the outside world (Nature, society) were no longer determined by face-to-face communication, but mediated through multiple, artificial, ephemeral images, which could be scanned and processed, but no longer viewed and critiqued with the classic apparatus of perception (which includes judgement, appreciation, values). The subject had to navigate through a world of signifiers and absorb a

BOX 3.1:   SOME KEY CHARACTERISTICS OF POSTMODERN ART

- self-consciousness
- ambiguity of meaning
- statements in inverted commas
- irony
- parodic appropriation of non-systemic material
- quoting of elements from different cultures and periods
- mixing of high art and mass culture
- incongruity of composition
- use of pastiche and collage
- crossing of genre boundaries
- mixing of media

dynamic, multi-focal experience that conveyed messages without constructing manifest meanings. The result was a semiotic crisis that affected the very core of the epistemic system.

The infinite possibilities of transformation and combination of computer-generated texts and electronically produced images dissolve the supposedly fixed relationship between the signifier and the signified. In a digital environment, the referent for a text or image is no longer an objective reality, but concepts of reality. One sign relates to another sign, which forms part of a chain of signifiers. The liberated nexus of signification makes a unified representation of the world impossible because all that can be apprehended is a perpetually shifting and changing mosaic of fragments. Consequently, reality comes to be experienced as a rich phantasmagoria of artificial worlds: the fleeting images on the TV screen, the vivid sense impressions of video, the deceptive appearances of virtual-reality games, and so on. The technologies of electronic culture have replaced mechanical reflections of reality with a simulacrum, a hyper-reality, where the true and false are indistinguishable.

The cultural landscape of the 1960 and 1970s, littered with fragmented artefacts of immediate sensual appeal, gave the consumer a widened choice of 'lifestyle' artefacts and an increased ability to satisfy hedonistic desires. The resulting impression of free choice and self-determination was all the more pronounced because modern cybernetic systems and most electronic media are principally interactive. A dialogic relationship with a simulated reality opens up infinite and otherwise unrealizable possibilities of pleasurable encounters. Man interacting with Nature is a *homo faber*; man interacting with cybernetic systems is a *homo ludens*. However, as all virtual dialogues are limited by the parameters of the system, it is admissible to speak of a *simulated* intersubjectivity and, as Baudrillard said about the chimera of mass-media information, 'instead of facilitating communication, it exhausts itself in the *staging* of communication'.[51]

Human perception in the electronic age is determined by an environment in which the primacy of reality over image has been inverted. The media are no longer 'mediating' between individual and outer reality, but assume an autonomous position. They exist as a reality in their own right; they surround the individual; they may even absorb him or her to such a degree that the boundaries between self and other, between reality and simulation become suspended. The ultimate consequence of this process is the 'schizoid' condition of the postmodern subject: the stable, unified, autonomous Ego is split into differentiated selves locked in a perpetual battle with an ungraspable Other.

And how did the artists of the period respond to this novel condition of the individual 'lost forever in a fragmentary fun house of mirrors in the infinite play of superfluous, meaningless images'.[52] The politics of diversion, the promotion of a culture of consumerism, the production of needs and desires through advertising, etc. vastly expanded the profession of image producers and cultural managers. The number of visual artists in interwar Paris, Berlin, or New York could be counted in thousands; by the end of the twentieth century they amounted to hundreds of thousands, with the addition of freelance creators in the video, film and television industries, countless advertising and graphic designers, and a vast array of producers in the popular print media.

Competition between these artists and creators of cultural artefacts increased the pressure to be innovative and to set oneself apart from concurrent practices and those that preceded them. What initially had been a valid response to the rapidly changing life in the Western metropolis soon turned into a naive chasing after originality and fresh ideas. The fundamental need for an updating of forms and functions of art in industrial society gave way to an external pressure to seek novelty for novelty's sake. As a result, the shelf-life of any avant-garde movement became shorter and shorter. Artistic trends turned seasonal like fashions, until in the end the avant-garde became absorbed by the mainstream, and assumed the function of, as Paul Mann scathingly remarked, 'a research and development bureau of the capitalist factory'.[53]

By the 1980s, the concept of the avant-garde, which had given such stimulus and innovatory impulses to Western art, had reached a cul-de-sac. Already in 1974, Octavio Paz wrote: 'Modern art begins to lose its force of negation. For years now, its negations have been ritual repetitions: rebellion has turned into a blueprinted course of conduct, critique into rhetorics, transgression into ceremony. Negation has ceased to be creative.'[54] Consequently, artists jettisoned the ethical imperatives of opposition and subversion and entered into a constructive relationship with the culture industry. In the early phase of postmodernism it was still relatively easy to distinguish art from commerce. But once artists were prospering in the record industry, on the video market, in the television companies, etc., one could hardly avoid asking: are they challenging the system, or have they been co-opted by it? Or are their works possibly both, a 'complicitous critique' of post-industrial capitalism, based on the belief that there is no alternative to a liberal market economy?

Initially, postmodern art had largely been an oppositional cultural praxis, albeit with a certain ambivalence, as resistance and affirmation were often wound up in the same process. But in the 1980s, postmodernism lost its last pretensions of being an avant-garde practice and degenerated into an eclectic, largely affirmative commodity. At least, this was the case in Europe. In the United States, avant-garde and commercial art had coexisted for a long time and were not regarded as mutually exclusive. American postmodernism was an optimistic end-phase of the avant-garde, the product of an explosion of information technology and mass media, an attempt to revitalize a Modernist art which had become rather sterile and clinical.

European artists, on the other hand, were far more aware of the conservative backlash that had set in after the student rebellion of 1968, and even more so after the demise of Communism after 1989. With the establishment of liberal capitalism as the hegemonic world order, and the society of the spectacle as the dominant cultural force in every corner of the world, the concept of avant-garde art as a force of resistance and opposition became a quaint anachronism. Consequently, the 'grand narrative' of the artist as spearhead of progress and innovation transmogrified into dystopian visions of a post-industrial, or even post-human existence.

However, for the reasons outlined above, postmodernism never became a monolithic ideology or cultural practice. Critical and affirmative attitudes towards the new technologies opposed each other with the same force as could be observed in the early phase of modernity. In the art and culture of the 1980s and 1990s two dominant trends could be observed, exacerbated, no doubt, by the approaching fin-de-millennium. On the one hand there were the neo-Futurists, advocates of the electronic age, who saw in the new technologies a means of solving humanity's problems. They embraced the new developments with a Utopian optimism and propagated a euphoric scenario of increased communication by means of electronic mail, satellite telephone, the world-wide-web, etc. On the other hand, there were the neo-Primitivists, who deplored the influence of technology on our civilization and professed a technophobic, pessimistic outlook on the twenty-first century. They predicted a cultural Armageddon, an erosion of humanistic values and traditions, and the disintegration of social institutions and organic communities, all due to an increased isolation and alienation of the individual and a replacement of communal with home-centred lifestyles. Their doomladen analysis of modern and postmodern society favoured a rejection of the Moloch technology, and in a distinctly neo-Luddite manner advocated a 'politics of the ejection seat' in order to prevent humanity's 'march into Hades'.

At a time when the individual was in danger of being disembodied, sucked into cyberspace or modified by the tools of biotechnology, the rooting of the self in the physical body and an organic community became a political as well as an artistic issue (see Chapter 5). A society characterized by an abundance and overproduction of goods, images and works of culture encourages the rise of avant-garde élites to reinstate the value of singular experiences and unrepeatable acts of creativity. Vacuity of existence in a mundane world, crisis of identity, and loss of spiritual certainties foster the search for compensations in intensely personal and distinctly transcendental art 'events', which by definition are performative. Attempts at returning to a non-instrumentalized art by linking creative production to personal, social and aesthetic concerns led the artists to a mythical Ur-art, in which aesthetic and social processes were not yet separated from each other.

Technophiles were, of course, not unaware of the dangers and negative aspects of modern electronic culture, but in their view these were to be seen not as faults inherent in the media themselves but as imperfections of the way in which they were implemented, controlled and used. Mindful of the Frankfurt School's critique of the 'culture industry' (Adorno/Horkheimer) or 'consciousness-shaping industry' (Enzensberger), they criticized the frequently one-sided views of eschatological environmentalists, who disregarded the dynamic diversity of modern capitalism and the productive conflicts within post-industrial society. In their view, the electronic market showed variety as well as uniformity. Beside the multinational monopolies, there was also a plethora of small companies which provided sophisticated services and products. Even the mass media did not proffer only soporific, escapist products but also reflected social realities and contributed positively to social change. Furthermore, the latest generation of interactive technologies opened up exactly those possibilities that Enzensberger had demanded from an emancipatory media practice.[55]

Consequently, the technophiles attached great value to individual self-determination in the flourishing, small-scale 'electronic cottage industries' and trusted that isolation and alienation could be overcome through the construction of alternative social spheres, local support groups, civil rights movements, and so on. They believed that a positive valorization of difference and a freedom of choice between multiple and situationally contingent identities would by necessity lead to the dismantling of hegemonic discourses of race, sex and class and thus to an obliteration of the universalizing social practices of dominant social groups. Reducing conformism and fostering a more pluralistic society, they argued, would shift difference from the margins to the centre of society, thereby creating a flourishing system of independent, market-oriented cultural sectors that would allow for increased personal choice and greater democratic participation.

Between the two opposing ends of the scale, represented by the cyber-Futurists and neo-Primitivists, a whole spectrum of reconciliatory attitudes and often startling hybrid positions could be found. For example, there existed a strange convergence of New Age optimism and Cyber Age Utopianism. People who had had their first experiences on the 'information super-highway' expressed with starry-eyed euphoria a quasi-religious belief in the new digital world's potential to fill a spiritual void. Postmodern gurus and shamans of 'Cyberia' praised the magic and mystery of cyberspace and saw in it a post-material 'Other World' that promised happiness and fulfilment.[56] The cyberfeminists represented another sector of society who embraced information technology as a liberating force, because they saw in the Internet a Utopian space where the disembodied, androgynous user can escape gender stereotypes and the tyranny of biology. More ambivalent was the attitude of the cyberpunks, who in the case of the hacker communities acquired a phenomenal knowledge of the operational complexities of computer networks, but used this information to sabotage the smooth operations of capitalist or military organizations. A more bohemian faction embraced the cutting edge of the digital consumer industry and subverted it with a mixture of hedonism and counter-cultural 'guerrilla' tactics. Other citizens of the cyberworld were more willing to enter into a compromise with what was considered an unavoidable technological future. Embracing the positive and resisting the negative aspects of technology was seen to be a realistic way of coping and surviving the onslaught of an unstoppable force, or a possible option for controlling a development before it totally controls us (see Chapter 7).

In the following four chapters I shall look at some of the ways in which performance artists responded to the developments outlined above, how they incorporated many of the achievements of the Modernist period, and how some of these lines of experimentation changed under the conditions of an age of cybernetic systems. As in the early part of the twentieth century, avant-garde performance was a temporary site of exchange between artist and audience and, as such, markedly different from mainstream theatre geared towards commodities that could be repeated night after night *ad infinitum*. The postmodern avant-garde continued to deconstruct the unspoken conventions of 'theatre' by dislocating and fracturing the theatrical frame, valorizing process over product, encouraging the spectator to become a co-producer of the work, shifting the emphasis from looking to participating, etc.

While some performance artists immersed themselves in the new media – video, computer, interactive digital environments – others focused their attention on the body as a medium of expression, on spiritual practices and ritual encounters. With the advent of electronic theatre and post-organic performances in cyberspace, the category of the actor came to be extended from flesh body to cybernetic machine. And once humans could be fitted with interfaces that allowed them to determine the actions on stage, distinctions between performer and spectator became very fluid indeed. Fictive worlds, which formerly could only be imagined in the mind, became actual in the theatre of virtual reality. Here, the 'users' no longer watch a character's action, but slip into the 'skin' of another person. In an act of virtual schizophrenia, they can project themselves into VR space and interact with their own avatars. Clearly, the traditional concept of performance with its reliance on liveness, immediacy and presence had to be radically reconfigured in an age characterized by a symbiotic coexistence of organic and cybernetic life.

The new technologies of communication and the electronic mass media closed the gap between high and low art and had a profound effect on the techniques and conventions of painting, music, theatre and so on. Particularly towards the end of the millennium, many avant-garde artists moved from the periphery to the centre of cultural operations and entered into a symbiotic relationship with the subsidized, in some cases also the commercial, media culture. Also theatre producers learned their lessons from the avant-garde. Directors, designers and performers incorporated into their works aspects and techniques that only a decade ago had been considered avant-garde. Because in the postwar period most European countries had instituted an effective State subsidy system for the theatre, the new funding regimes allowed mainstream playhouses to operate experimental studios as a sideline to their main business, which soon exercised a profound influence on the productions in the main auditoria. This hybrid middle-ground complemented the traditional dichotomy of mainstream and avant-garde, and combined elements from both ends of the spectrum in productions which had an appeal to both modern and traditionalist audiences.

Theatre culture in the second half of the twentieth century was certainly more diverse and enterprising than before the Second World War. But none the less, it accepted and operated with the fundamental parameters of theatrical production, which avant-garde performers consciously ignored, circumvented or tried to overcome. Although it would be an interesting undertaking to study the impact of the avant-garde on late twentieth-century mainstream theatre – and some scholars have already prepared the field for this[57] – the following chapters will be reserved to artists and artistic trends who represented a last flourishing of the avant-garde.

4

Happening and Fluxus

CHRONOLOGY 4.1:   HAPPENINGS

1952

16 August(?)   *Untitled Theatre Piece* at Black Mountain College, organized by John Cage with various participants. Exact date uncertain.

1955

25 July   Opening of *Experimental Outdoor Exhibition of Modern Art to Challenge the Midsummer Burning Sun*, Ashiya, with first proto-Happenings by Gutai group.

19 October   Opening of *First Official Gutai Art Exhibition*, Tokyo, Ohara Kaikan Hall, with several Happening-like actions by Gutai group.

1956

9 April   *One-Day-Only Outdoor Exhibition*, Amagasaki, with various actions by Gutai group.

27 July   Opening of *Second Gutai Outdoor Exhibition*, Ashiya.

11 October   Opening of *Second Gutai Art Exhibition*, Tokyo, Ohara Kaikan Hall.

1957

3 April   Opening of the *Third Gutai Art Exhibition*, Kyoto, Municipal Museum of Art.

10 May   Yves Klein, *Aerostatic Sculptures*, Paris, Place Saint-Germain-de-Près.

29 May   *First Gutai On-Stage Art Show*, Osaka, Sankei Centre; repeated on 7 July at the Sankei Centre in Tokyo.

$\rightarrow$

→

1958

January	Wolf Vostell, *The Theatre Takes Place on the Street*, Paris, Passage de Tour de Vanves.
28 April	Y. Klein, *Manifestation of Emptiness*, Paris, Galerie Iris Clert.
4 April	*Second Gutai On-Stage Art Show*, Osaka, Asahi Kaikan Hall.
5 June– 19 October	*Dada: Dokumente einer Bewegung*, Düsseldorf, Kunsthalle. First major Dada exhibition after the war.
9 June	J. Tinguely, *My Stars: Concert for Seven Paintings*, Paris, Galerie Iris Clert. A second version is presented at Galerie Schmela, Düsseldorf, 30 January 1959.
14 October	John Cage, *Music Walk, for One or More Pianos*, Düsseldorf, Galerie 22.

1959

11 May, 1 June	Otto Piene, *Light Ballet*, Düsseldorf, Galerie Schmela; repeated in Wiesbaden and Heidelberg. A more complex version is performed in 1960 in Berlin, Ulm, Cologne and Düsseldorf. Various large-scale versions performed in 1961 in Vienna, Munich, Amsterdam, Stockholm etc.
August– September	W. Vostell, *TV-Dé-Coll/Age for Millions*, Cologne, Atelier Vostell.
4, 6–10 October	Allan Kaprow, *18 Happenings in 6 Parts*, New York, Reuben Gallery.
16 October– 5 November	George Brecht, *Towards Events*, New York: Reuben Gallery
13 November	Nam June Paik, *Hommage à John Cage*, Düsseldorf Galerie 22; repeated 16–18 June 1960 at Studio Bauermeister in Cologne.
18 November	Y. Klein, Sale of Immaterial Sensibility Zones, Paris, Seine Quay.
4–11 December	Red Grooms, *The Burning Building*, New York, Studio Delancy Street.

→

→

1960

12 January	Y. Klein, *Leap into the Void*, Paris, Galerie Colette Allendy (a later photographed version took place on 16 and 19 October 1960).
23 February	Y. Klein, *Anthropometries*, Paris, artist's apartment.
29 February–2 March	Various artists, *Ray Gun Spex*, New York, Judson Gallery.
9 March	Y. Klein, *Anthropometries of the Blue Epoque*, Paris, Galerie Internationale d'Art Contemporain.
14 March	Various artists, *A Concert of New Music*, New York, The Living Theatre.
17 March	Jean Tinguely, *Hommage to New York*, New York, Museum of Modern Art.
29 April–9 May	J.-J. Lebel, *Anti-Process*, Paris, Galerie des Quatre Saisons.
2 May	Al Hansen, *A Program of Happenings? Events! & Situations?*, New York, Pratt Institute.
13 May	J. Tinguely, Street parade from Impasse Ronsin to Galerie des Quatres Saisons.
11 June	Various artists, *An Evening of Sound Theatre*, New York, Reuben Gallery.
21 July	Piero Manzoni, *The Consumption of Dynamic Art by the Public Devouring Art*, Milan, Galleria Azimut.
7 October	Opening of *A Festival of Light*, Düsseldorf, Galerie Schmela, followed by three performances of the Lightballet (10, 13, 15 October) at Studio Otto Piene.
1–6 November	J. Dine, *Car Crash*, New York, Reuben Gallery.

1961

12 February	Niki de Saint Phalle, *Shooting Action*, Paris, artist's studio and Impasse Ronsin.
21–6 February	Claes Oldenburg, *Circus (Ironworks/Fotodeath)*, New York, Reuben Gallery.
22 April	P. Manzoni, *Living Sculptures*, Rome, Galleria La Tartaruga; repeated on 18 October 1961 with naked bodies at Gallerie Køpcke in Copenhagen.

→

20 June	Rauschenberg, Tinguely, Tudor, Johns, de Saint-Phalle, *The Concert*, Paris, theatre of the US Embassy.
5 July	Piene, Mack, Uecker, *Zero-Festival*, Düsseldorf, Galerie Schmela; repeated 7 December in Arnhem, Gallerie A.
13 July	*First Festival of New Realism*, Nice, Abbaye de Roseland.
15 September	W. Vostell, *Cityrama 1 for Audience*, Cologne, various street locations.

1962

Spring	Mack, Piene, Uecker, *Zero Demonstration*, Düsseldorf, Rhine Banks.
23 February–26 May	C. Oldenburg, *Ray Gun Theatre*. A series of 10 Happenings, New York, Ray Gun Mfg Co.
22–7 March	A. Kaprow, *Spring Happening*, New York, Reuben Gallery.
7 July	W. Vostell, *PC-Petite Ceinture*, Paris, PC bus route.
19 August	A. Kaprow, *Sweeping*, Woodstock, Outdoor location.
23 October–8 November	Various artists, *Festival of Misfits*, London, Gallery One.
23–5 November	A. Kaprow, *Courtyard*, New York, Mills Hotel.
27 November	J.-J. Lebel, *To Exorcise the Spirit of Catastrophe*, Paris, Galerie Cordier.

1963

8 February	*Second Festival of New Realism*, Munich, Neue Galerie im Künstlerhaus.
1–31 May	*Yam Festival*, New York, Smolin Gallery, Hardware Playhouse and various outdoor locations.
9 May	Robert Rauschenberg, *Pelican*, Washington, DC, 'America on Wheels' skating rink.
15 August	Hi Red Center, *Non-V-Day Anniversary Meal*, Tokyo, Citizen's Hall.

→

→

20 August– 4 September	*First Festival of the Avant Garde*, New York, Judson Memorial Church and Carnegie Recital Hall.
14 September	W. Vostell, *Nein-9-dé-Coll/Agen*, Wuppertal, various locations.
9–10 December	C. Oldenburg, *Autobodys*, Los Angeles, American Institute of Aeronautics.

1964

11 January	W. Vostell, *Sun in Your Head*, Amsterdam, Leidsen Plein Theater.
26–7 January	Hi Red Center, *Shelter Plan*, Tokyo, Imperial Hotel.
27 January	B. Vautier, G. Brecht, N. J. Paik, B. Patterson, 'Zen Happening', *Réalité: Le Théâtre Total*, Nice, Théâtre Artistique.
25–30 May	Various artists, *Festival of Free Expression*, Paris, American Center.
12 June	Hi Red Center, *The Great Panorama Exhibition*, Tokyo, Naiqua Gallery.
26 June	Various artists, *Bloomsday 1964: Actions, Agit-Prop, Dé-coll/age-Happenings*, Frankfurt-am-Main, Galerie Loehr.
20 July	Various artists, *Actions, Agit-Prop, Dé-coll/age-Happenings*, Aachen: Technische Hochschule.
30 August– 13 September	*Second Annual New York Avant Garde Festival*, New York, Judson Memorial Church.
13 September	R. Rauschenberg, *Elgin Tie*, Stockholm, Moderna Museet.
10 October	Hi Red Center, *Dropping Event*, Tokyo, Ikenobo building and Ochanomitsu railway station
16 October	Hi Red Center, *Movement to Promote the Cleaning-Up of the Metropolitan Area (Be Clean!)*, Tokyo, Namiki Street.
7 November	W. Vostell, *In Ulm, um Ulm und um Ulm herum*, Ulm and environs.

1965

13 March	Various artists, *Artists' Key Club*, New York, Pennsylvania station. →

→

22–3 May	C. Oldenburg, *Washes*, New York, Al Roon's Health Club.
25 May	*Second Festival of Free Expression*, Paris, American Center.
5–6 June	Various Artists, *24 Hours*, Wuppertal, Galerie Parnass.
21–2 August	A. Kaprow, *Calling*, New York and New Brunswick, NJ: various locations.
25 August–11 September	*Third Festival of the Avant Garde*, New York, Judson Church.
4 November	R. Rauschenberg, *Map Room I*, Plainfield, VT: Goddard College; revised as *Map Room II* on 1–3, 16–18 December in New York, Forty-first Street Theatre.
1–3, 16–17 December	C. Oldenburg, *Moveyhouse*, New York, Forty-first Street Theatre.
1966	
31 August–30 September	*Destruction in Art Symposium*, London and Edinburgh, Various locations.
14, 24 October	R. Rauschenberg, *Open Score*, New York, 69th Regiment Armory.

Allan Kaprow and Early Happenings in the USA

Towards the end of the 1950s, Allan Kaprow invented the term 'Happening' and presented several examples of this new performance genre. However, before the term came into general currency, other artists had already explored a variety of similar concepts and presented them in a manner that was not all that different from what later sailed under the banner of 'Happenings' (see those listed in Chronology 4.1). A prime example was the now famous *Untitled Theatre Piece #1* organized by John Cage and Merce Cunningham at Black Mountain College in the summer of 1952. Unfortunately, it has been impossible to reconstruct the details of this mixed-media event and the exact arrangement of its components (even the date of 16 August is uncertain[1]). By the time scholars recognized the significance of the performance and interviewed participants and audiences, their recollection of what had happened in the dining hall of the college was highly contradictory and often mutually exclusive. Part of this may be explained by the vagaries of memory retention, but another reason will have been the fact that everybody experienced the episode in an entirely different manner.

From the scraps of information available,[2] we can conclude that Cage organized the performance in line with his recent study of Huang Po's Doctrine of Universal Mind, a key Zen text which explained Nature as a complex of non-hierarchical events where everything has equal value. Cage developed, in conversation with David Tudor, the idea of a theatrical event that reflected these principles, and devised an evening where several things not causally related to each other would take place in a simultaneous or sequential manner. He outlined a number of time brackets – forty-five minutes altogether – and asked various artists to fill the slots with ideas that were entirely of their own invention. These could be planned or improvised and were not to be communicated to the others in advance of the performance. Framing the individual assignments was a lecture on 'Zen and Music', given by Cage himself. He organized the space in a manner that gave the performers a maximum of freedom. The audience (some 50 people altogether) sat in the middle of the hall, in triangular blocks facing each other, with enough room between blocks to create aisles for the actors to move in and out. Robert Rauschenberg suspended four of his White Paintings in a cruciform shape from the ceiling, prepared some hand-painted slides to be projected onto a wall, and he or someone else fitted several theatre lights with colourful gels. In the performance itself, Rauschenberg played scratchy Edith Piaf records at double-speed on a wind-up gramophone; Tim LaFarge and Nicholas Cernovitch projected movies and still photographs onto the ceiling and another wall of the hall; David Tudor played a radio and a 'prepared piano', while Jay Watts performed a piece on Polynesian instruments. Mary Caroline Richards, who was dragged into the hall on a hobby-horse or a little cart, interspersed Cage's lecture with a poetry reading from the top of a ladder. Charles Olson sat amongst the spectators and distributed to them fragments of his poetry, which were then read out in random fashion. All the while, Cunningham danced up and down the aisles and around the audience, periodically chased by a little dog.

The historical significance of the event was only recognized much later, when Allan Kaprow and other artists developed an interest in non-matrixed performances and a multi-focal, participatory theatre full of random actions and chance occurrences. Kaprow was a painter, who after graduation in 1952 was made aware of the European tradition of collage by the émigré Hans Hofmann. In the following years he began to extend his collages into the third dimension and to call these works 'assemblages'. Inspired by Jackson Pollock's Action Paintings he developed the technique of *action-collage*, where diverse materials were assembled, as rapidly as possible and without rational planning, into compositions that were meant to reflect unconscious states of mind. He explained the next stage: 'The action-collage then became bigger, and I introduced flashing lights and thicker hunks of matter. These parts projected farther and farther from the wall and into the room, and included more and more audible elements: sounds of ringing buzzers, bells, toys, etc.'[3] Once these assemblages had turned into environments, they were also fitted with kinetic elements. An exhibition in 1957 roused in him a desire to integrate the viewers who came to see these rooms into the composition. This is how *18 Happenings in 6 Parts* (1959) at the Reuben Gallery in New York came about.

The gallery space had been divided into three compartments, where six sequences of events occurred simultaneously. The actions had been fixed in a score and rehearsed by friends of the artist. Also the visitors of the exhibition were given precise instructions, and this enabled them to become performers carrying out actions of 'a strict nature, where the freedoms were carefully limited to certain parameters of time and space'.[4] Thereby, a four-dimensional work of art was created, which Kaprow described as 'a more tangible reality than it was possible to suggest through painting alone'.[5] However, after the event he came to realize that the actions had been too controlled. So in the following years he tended to simplify the Happenings and to relinquish rehearsals, thereby creating in the prepared rooms 'a continually active field, whose outlines are very, very uncertain so that they blend in and out of daily life'.[6] He combined planned operations with secondary, improvised actions and mixed invited guests with chance visitors, but in each case the Happenings took place in an organized framework according to a predetermined structure.

The principal aim behind these events was to provide participants with an immediate, sensual experience of reality. But what differentiates a Happening from a normal, real-life occurrence? Kaprow described his works as 'life-like but no substitute for life'. The randomness of selection procedures (he used chance elements, spur-of-the-moment ideas, indiscriminate extracts from notebooks or Yellow Pages) caused the Happenings to be as indeterminate and fragmented as real-life events. However, the structuring and the amount of attention given to them allowed the performances to develop 'a sense of magnitude, an aura of mystery' or 'a sense of spectacle'.[7]

Between 1958 and 1966 Kaprow carried out some 25 Happenings in a variety of indoor and open-air locations, which provided him with a wealth of experience summed up in his monumental documentation *Assemblage, Environment and Happenings*, of 1966. This publication also contains a useful description of what constitutes a Happening (summarized in Box 4.1).

BOX 4.1: KEY FEATURES OF HAPPENINGS, ACCORDING TO ALLAN KAPROW

- Happenings are derived from life but are not exactly like it. The dividing line between them must be kept fluid.

- They are not a representation of life but present it in a selective and focused manner.

- They must possess a strong immediacy and physical presence.

- They do not work with a traditional dramaturgy of plot, dramatic development, predetermined climaxes and endings. The artist employs chance methods in order to arrive at a score of 'root' directions, which serve as a basis for generating open-ended, life-like actions that make up the Happening.

- Their structure must be flexible and open to improvised, unpredictable interventions. Composition and arrangement must be balanced with chance and random elements.

- Usually there is a distinction between performer and spectator, but the dividing line is flexible and both are to some degree participants in a Happening. Spectators are often given tasks and are encouraged to join in the action. Also people unprepared for the event (passers-by or chance visitors) can be integrated and become authentic parts of it.

- Performers in a Happening are not acting (representing a fictional character, place and time) or expressing their inner feelings, but carry out allocated tasks without active engagement of the Ego.

- Happenings break up the continuum of time and space. They can be discontinuous events taking place simultaneously over days or weeks in a variety of locations.

- Happenings are organic events where the artist, the surroundings, the work and everybody who participates in it become one in a unique and novel experience of reality.

- Happenings escape the commodity status of art in a capitalist society. Their impermanence prevents them from being collectable works of art; their freshness and unpredictability are a countermeasure to the stale conventions of theatres, galleries and museums.

In the early 1960s, Happenings became a popular performance genre in the USA and Europe, as well as in Japan. Of course, artists did not necessarily adhere to all of the criteria laid down by Kaprow. I should therefore like to discuss in this chapter some representative examples from the wide spectrum of practices that could be observed in the early 1960s.

One of the most prominent Happening artists, with a large body of works (22 altogether created between 1960 and 1966), was Claes Oldenburg. He had moved to New York in 1956 and become part of the artist community centred on the Reuben Gallery and Judson Memorial Church. His first Happening, *Snapshots from the City*, took place in 1960 in an environment he had created at the Judson Gallery as part of the *Ray Gun Spex* exhibition-cum-performance programme. He had assembled all sorts of street debris in the gallery, which looked like a realistic representation of an urban landscape. Inhabiting the space and moving around in it completed the 'picture' of real life. Oldenburg's New Realism became even more accentuated in *The Store*, an installation that served as the scene for *Ray Gun Theatre*, a series of ten Happenings unfolding over three months in a studio he had baptized 'Ray Gun Manufacturing Company'. The fixtures and fittings of the 'store' were again taken from the Lower East Side and resembled those of any shop in that district, except that they were covered in fabric and plaster and then painted to look like 'the real thing'. Many of these sculptures became Pop Art icons shown at various exhibitions, but in their original setting in *The Store* they formed an ensemble that reflected outside reality as much as Oldenburg's inner state of mind ('The store title is in fact a play on words ... the store means for me: my consciousness'[8]). Oldenburg described his Happenings as 'a theatre of physical effects' attempting to be 'more epical than lyrical. The aim is panoramic, spatial.'[9] Oldenburg transformed Nature to fit his intention of reflecting life and its myriad features in a condensed fashion. In another statement he called it 'a theatre of real events', where

> nothing is communicated or represented except through its attachment to an object. ... It is the play of consciousness in reaction to certain objects ... a play which involves the consciousness of myself my actors and my audience. ... This differs from conventional theater in that the communication is less fixed ... more in doubt ... there is a sequence but not plot or given relation to the events and objects as they occur.[10]

Oldenburg continued to explore his concept of Happening as 'physical theatre' in other site-specific performances, such as *Autobodys*, performed in a car park of the American Institute of Aeronautics in Los Angeles;

Washes, in the swimming pool of Al Roon's Health Club; or *Moveyhouse*, in a Forty-first Street cinema. These pieces were directly inspired by the environment in which they took place, but their final form was developed in several scripting stages, which established the basic ingredients of a piece through a variety of actions. These were then tried out with the performers, whom he chose not for their acting talent but for their real-life personality. While working with them on the 'ideas score', new actions emerged out of improvisations and were incorporated into the text. The resulting 'practical script' was then tested in technical rehearsals and subsequently formed the basis of a 'performance script' that could be displayed backstage for the performers to refer to. Oldenburg believed that such detailed preparation was necessary to give his performers the security they needed in order to be able to deal with unforeseen incidents and chance features of the environment. Once a performance was under way, Oldenburg was 'able to withdraw and let the thing handle itself and find its own way'.[11] The audiences who came to these events were confronted with such a profusion of visual and audible impressions that they had to pick and choose what they wished to concentrate on. Oldenburg gave them the freedom to follow their subjective responses, focus on what seemed most interesting to them and enjoy the associations that would be triggered in their minds. This way a Happening could act as a stimulating experience and overcome the 'chronic disease of ... realism ... distance ... commercial pressures ... poor theater'.[12]

Such anti-theatrical sentiments were unknown to Robert Rauschenberg, who never severed entirely the connection between Happening and theatre. He sometimes employed the loose term 'performance' to designate his works, which could range from dance to site-specific installation pieces. Between 1954 and 1967 he created costume and stage designs for some fifty productions by Paul Taylor, Merce Cunningham and the Judson Dance Theatre. The experience gained from working with these avant-garde companies naturally affected his Happenings and Happening-like theatre pieces. And vice versa, his experience with Happenings (his own and those of other artists in which he performed) had an impact on his theatre works and, one might add, on experimental theatre in the USA as a whole.[13]

Rauschenberg's performance work in the 1950s was greatly influenced by his tutor John Cage, with whom he first collaborated in 1952 in the famous *Untitled Theatre Piece #1* at Black Mountain College. In 1953 they produced *Automobile Print*, a scroll-like 'painting' created by running the inked tyres of an automobile over a seven-metre long strip of paper in a downtown Manhattan street. In the following years, many of Rauschenberg's paintings focused on issues of time, motion and collaborative gestures. For example, on 20 June 1961 as part of a Festival of New Realism in Paris he performed, together with David Tudor, *Variations II* by John Cage. Tudor played the piano while Rauschenberg executed a painting, hidden away from the audience behind the canvas. Contact microphones were attached to the frame and easel, amplifying his brushstrokes and rubbing so that the durational aspect of the creative act could be physically demonstrated.

Pelican was the first of the eleven Happenings created between 1963 and 1967 and was performed in the *America on Wheels* skating rink in Washington, DC (9 May 1963). It had Rauschenberg and Fluxus artist Per Olof Ultvedt kneeling on a trolley and using their hands to wheel themselves into the performance space. When the dancer Carolyn Brown entered *en pointe*, they followed her on roller skates. As they swooped around her, two parachutes opened from their rucksacks and trailed behind them as they moved around the space. Occasionally they stood on the trolley and like butterflies created swirling configurations with the silken parachute fabric. The whole *pas à trois* was accompanied by taped music assembled by Rauschenberg from found noises, classical music and pop tunes. Although the actions were scored, instructions were minimal and offered only vague outlines of gestures, postures and body constellations. Most of the performance was improvised and depended in its execution on the environment, the props and the (poor) skating skills of the performers.

In *Elgin Tie* (13 September 1964) Rauschenberg performed a *pas de deux* with a cow. As the animal was led through the performance space in the Moderna Museet in Stockholm, Rauschenberg abseiled from the ceiling into a large, water-filled oil drum. It had been his intention to cover himself and the cow with white powder to make themselves look like the Elgin marbles. However, the animal did not take to the treatment and the artist had to settle for another ending, which saw him standing in a pair of large boots nailed to a cart and leaning forward at a dangerous angle while being wheeled out of the hall. Much more spectacular, yet still outside the confines of theatre, was *Map Room I and II* (1965), which had complex shadow projections, ballet dancers stuck in car tyres, contact microphones amplifying the sounds of their movements, and Rauschenberg strutting through the darkened space with dry ice in his socks and flashlights attached to his legs. In another scene he wore some insulating shoes and used his own body to pass electric currents between two neon tubes, which lit up every time he touched them. Half of the audience had large white cards attached to their backs, which served as projection screens for a movie.

Rauschenberg's interest in technical wizardry was again demonstrated in *Open Score* (14 and 24 October 1966), performed in an outdoor tennis court as part of *9 Evenings: Theatre and Technology* in New York. The rackets were wired up so that they could transmit the sounds of being hit by a ball, and triggered electrical circuits linked to flood lights, which cut out one after the other. When the whole court was thrown into darkness, five hundred volunteers entered the space and carried out actions mapped out by Rauschenberg on a score sheet. Infrared television cameras filmed the actions and projected them onto three screens hanging over the space. Finally Rauschenberg appeared, with Simone Forti hidden in a sack-cloth draped over his shoulder. Standing in a spotlight, she sang a quiet dirge and was then carried off again.

Rauschenberg was an artist who moved freely between different artistic categories, such as painting, sculpture, installation, dance and theatre. The performances that came closest to Happenings were very site-specific and made up of relatively self-contained activities, but their 'combined coexistence' nevertheless created a single image that reflected 'a world where multiple distractions are the only constant'.[14] He devised his pieces as 'vehicles for events of a particular nature that can embody and use the personalities and abilities of the performers'.[15] Rehearsals were minimal and only served to familiarize the actors with the score. The actions developed naturally out of the way the performers handled the instructions. But Rauschenberg tried to avoid improvisations as he felt that they made actors fall back on clichéd mannerisms.

Another prominent Happening artist, whose work came close to dramatic theatre, was Jim Dine. Like Rauschenberg, he met Kaprow in the late 1950s through the Reuben Gallery and participated in several of the early Happenings in New York. Like Oldenburg he was interested in installation art animated by human performers. His environment *The House* was a side piece to Oldenburg's *The Street* in the Judson Gallery and was also used as a set for a Happening entitled *The Smiling Workman* (29 February, 1 and 2 March 1960). Here, Dine was dressed like a Shaman or artist-priest and engaged in a spiritual ceremony that had him create a painting, drink a bucket of red paint (actually tomato juice), pour two buckets of paint over his head and finally destroy the painting by jumping through it. The performance played a cathartic role for Dine, as he could employ it for acting out personal traumas and so face certain aspects of his private life in public. The emphasis on violence and transformation turned up again in *Car Crash*, which he performed with three artist friends at the Reuben Gallery on 1–6 November 1960. Again, the piece had deeply personal ramifications (he and his wife had narrowly escaped death and a friend of theirs died in a car accident in 1958). In view of the technical complexity of the piece, Dine wrote a script and rehearsed the actions with his collaborators. He also designed the setting, costumes and props, which created a highly symbolic emergency-room atmosphere. The audience was placed in a central, U-shaped position around which the action unfolded, but they were not given any active participatory role in the proceedings. The car crash was impersonated by Dine, a man dressed as a woman, and a woman dressed as a man. Dramatic lighting effects were used to heighten the drama of the car chase and subsequent collision. Occasionally the house lights went up, for example when Dine used a chalkboard to relieve himself from obsessive memories of fear and pain by drawing and redrawing the crash scene. As before, the Happening served him as a kind of psycho-drama and a cathartic acting-out of horrific moments in his personal life.

Dine continued to use performative means of expression in *The Shining Bed* (16–18 December 1960, again at the Reuben Gallery), which was a highly physical monodrama on the theme of transformation, and *Natural History* (1–3 May 1965, at the RKO Theatre), another poetic and personal piece focusing on his personal life and dreams. Although these works were still called Happenings, Dine did not adhere to the conventions that had been established by other exponents of the genre, but rather adjusted them to fit his own interests and concerns. By 1965 much of the original impetus for creating Happenings had lost its driving force in the USA, and these last works were highly controlled acting pieces without any audience participation and therefore pretty much indistinguishable from theatre.

The New Realism in France, Germany and Italy

In Chapter 3 I showed how in the postwar period the subjective impulse of abstract art and Expressionism gave way to a more objective concern with the concrete features of the modern information society. The Continental-European art movement that followed on from Tachism and Art Informel is usually referred to as 'New Realism' and was centred in France around a semi-official 'school' headed by Pierre Restany.[16] Restany was, in the first instance, a critic and theoretician. He published a first Manifesto of New Realism on 16 April 1960, presented a first exhibition under the same title in May 1960 at the Galleria Apollinaire in Milan, and offically founded the group on 27 October 1960 in Yves Klein's apartment. A further manifesto was signed by Arman, Spoerri, Tinguely, Klein, Raysse and Hains, later to be joined by de Saint-Phalle, Christo and Deschamps. It was largely through Restany's organizational and publicist skills that New Realism began to be used as an umbrella term covering the whole field of artistic activities inspired by 'modern nature', i.e. the new realities of the mass media and the world of advertising and other popular imagery. Like the Pop Artists in the USA, the New Realists formed their collages or assemblages from found and processed fragments of reality and materials not commonly associated with high art. They elaborated a new methodology of perceiving and re-presenting the concrete, objective quality of contemporary urban life. The appropriation of elements of the everyday world and their *presentation* in objects that reveal the material poetics of reality followed a philosophy that was completely different from *representing* reality through the means of conventional realism.

Although Restany had organized two immensely important exhibitions of American Pop artists (July 1961, at the Galerie Rive Droite in Paris) and French New Realists (October 1962, at the Sydney Janis Gallery in New York), the beginnings of the Happening genre in the work of Allan Kaprow had remained unknown to the Parisian action artists.[17] A key figure amongst them was Yves Klein. He was an ingrained enemy of the ostentatious consumerism and materialism of postwar society and, as a kind of consequence of this, turned against the glorification of art in the form of material objects. He immersed himself in Zen Buddhism, Rosicrucianism and medieval mysticism and developed a number of projects which translated his ideas from the materially based world of painting and sculpture into the world of immaterial performance. One of them, *Aerostatic Sculptures*, was performed on 10 May 1958 on the Place Saint-Germain-des-Près, where 1001 blue balloons were released into the Parisian sky to let the immaterial sensibility permeate and impregnate the world. Unfortunately, Klein's larger projects that aimed at stimulating the 'Blue Revolution' and at leading humanity back to an authentic spiritual existence were never realized.[18]

Together with Tinguely he constructed a painting machine, and in 1958 he experimented for the first time with 'living brushes'. A first demonstration of his paint actions that employed human bodies to apply the pigments to the canvas was given in his Paris flat on 23 February 1960. His wife, Rotraut Uecker, covered a model's breasts, belly and thighs with blue paint. Then, following Klein's instructions, she pressed the woman five times against a sheet of paper that had been pinned to the wall. Pierre Restany, who was present that evening, coined the term 'Anthropometry' for this type of painting.[19]

On 9 March 1960, at the Galerie Internationale d'Art Contemporain in Paris, twenty musicians and singers performed Klein's *Monotonous Symphony*, consisting of 20 minutes of a single note and 20 minutes of silence, while Klein himself applied blue paint to the bodies of three nude models and created his first *Anthropometries of the Blue Epoque*. In the following years, more than 150 paintings of this kind were produced, using different methods for applying the pigments on the canvas. They ranged from careful impressions of individual parts of the bodies, via full imprints created through dancing and rolling on the canvas, to the large *batailles*, or battlefields, of several models fighting with each other on the canvas.

On 27 November 1960, Klein declared life to become theatre for a 24-hour period. The newspaper manifesto that announced the event all over Paris showed Klein in the action of freeing himself from all material constraints. For Klein, this 'Leap into the Void' was no Dada gag or publicity stunt, but expressed his desire to transcend the earthly realm through *pneuma*, to ascend like Christ to heaven or into nirvana. Klein saw himself as a Messiah, as the prophet of the Blue Revolution, who captured in his works the fleeting moments of the joys of life. His 'New Realism' had nothing to do with depictions of anecdotal, ephemeral 'life as observed', but was concerned with the conquest of the totality of universal Being. His celebration of life impregnated with vitality and pure sensibility could be experienced either in the spatial ambiences of the Void (stage sets for the mystery and magic of colour), or by the body turning itself into a work of art.

Because of his untimely death at the early age of 34, Klein's theatrical projects[20] were never realized. The same, unfortunately, applies to his Italian friend Piero Manzoni, whose activities covered little more than five years, 1957–63. Manzoni came to art after having studied philosophy. His desire to surmount the limitations of abstractionism first led him to Informel painting, where 'art had abandoned representation to the delirium of gesture and to the jubilation of materials'.[21] Art Informel reinforced his wish to give up painting altogether and to express ephemeral and transient gestures in pure event art. In spring 1959, he mentioned for the first time his plan to sign the bodies of friends and fellow artists and to present them as art works. (The idea was eventually carried out at the Galleria La Tartaruga in Rome on 22 April 1961, and again with naked bodies at the Gallerie Køpcke in Copenhagen on 18 October 1961.) The same year, he produced *Bodies of Air*, which consisted of wooden boxes containing a balloon and a metallic base. The balloon could be inflated by the purchaser and exhibited on the base, thereby becoming a work of art. If Manzoni himself inflated the balloon (at a price of 300 lire per litre of breath), the work was called *The Artist's Breath*. In 1959, he published the first issue of a magazine, *Azimuth*, and opened a gallery in Milan with the same name, Azimut. Both served to propagate his artistic ideas and to form international links with artists who equally sought to overcome the then dominant abstractionist trend in Western art. His main collaborators in America were Robert Rauschenberg and Jasper Johns, in Germany the Zero group, and in France Yves Klein.

On 21 July 1960, he presented at the Azimut gallery *The Consumption of Dynamic Art by the Public Devouring Art*, where he boiled a number of eggs, signed them with his thumbprint and distributed them to the invited audience. The exhibition lasted for 70 minutes and, by the end of it, all works had been consumed.[22] The performance was an ironic statement on the role of the artist and of art in consumer society. But the symbolic significance of eggs as a source of life and the references to the Last Supper also gave the act many spiritual undertones.

Manzoni's most famous and certainly most notorious action came in May 1961 when he produced and packaged ninety tins of *Artist's Shit*. The conserves were sold by weight for the equivalent of the day's price of gold. Despite the polemical nature of this action it was not just intended to ridicule the status of the artist as creative genius. Manzoni regarded the human body as a valid artwork in itself, not just as a vessel for subjective expression. He deified himself in his corporeal and material existence and stated: 'There is nothing to be said. There is only to be, there is only to live.'[23] Manzoni utilized his own body as a Ready Made and as a medium for the merging of art and life. He was an important precursor of Body Art (see below, Chapter 5) and left behind a collection of works that traces his physical existence: blood, breath, faeces, fingerprints, etc. His small œuvre is a reminder of a short life that *was* art. There were also Platonic aspects in his work, which often went unnoticed under the witticism and humour contained in his creations. His *Breath Sculptures*, for example, employed the concept of breath (*pneuma*) as an expression of the most noble and spiritual part of the artist's soul and genius, as a divine inspiration that connects the human and divine worlds.[24] Creativity based on this 'spiritual' element can only be given form in gestural actions or performances; and 'once a gesture has been made, the work becomes thereafter a documentation on the advent of an artistic fact'.[25]

Manzoni's Azimut gallery cooperated closely with the group ZERO, founded in 1957 by Otto Piene, Heinz Mack and Günther Uecker as in informal organization of young artists living and working in the Rhineland around Düsseldorf. [26] The name ZERO was chosen

> not as an expression of nihilism or a neo-dada gag but as a word indicating a zone of silence and of pure possibilities for a new beginning like at the countdown when rockets are started – zero is the incommensurable zone where the old state turns into the new.[27]

All members of the group were interested in an 'expansion of art into far-reaching projects . . . and their relation to the rhythm of life'.[28] Their first exhibitions were therefore rather unusual events, which did not last any longer than the opening night. They were called 'night exhibitions'[29] and later on 'Zero Happenings', where 'the event structure permits an exchange of experience between artist and viewer, not possessions. The event as a work of art – as process art – is largely anti-materialistic.'[30] The first events of this kind were open-air 'demonstrations' or 'festivities' (5 July 1961, repeated in December 1961 and Spring 1962) in which huge hot-air balloons and kites were carried through the streets of Düsseldorf and along the banks of the Rhine, to be finally set adrift, with searchlights following their paths up into the night sky.[31]

Different in quality were the *Light Ballets*, which Piene produced from 1959 onwards as an extension of his earlier light paintings. Instead of a brush he used hand-operated lamps and directed their beams through stencils, in order to 'enable the spectator to experience the pure sensation of his own steady dynamics'[32] and to 'transmit light as energy rather than, as in painting, to symbolize it by tonal gradients'.[33] Later versions used mechanical light projections accompanied by jazz music, and group performances where several people created colourful light spectacles, light environments and a 'light theatre' (e.g. *The Fire Flower* at the Galerie Diogenes in Berlin, 1964, and *The Proliferation of the Sun* in New York, 1966–7). Piene always emphasized that these works were designed to counteract the mono-focal direction of theatrical and cinematic presentations and to give the spectator an active, playful role in the proceedings.[34] Later, he drew many strands of his early experiments together in his spectacular *Sky Events*.[35]

Wolf Vostell and Jean-Jacques Lebel

From the many Happening artists active in Europe during the 1960s I should like to select for discussion two particularly prolific performers and organizers.[36] Wolf Vostell can be regarded as the father of the European Happening movement. He was certainly one of the most active artists in this field, building up a body of works in a continuous line of development, with 28 Happenings produced between 1961 and 1970, and a particularly active peak in 1964–6.

Vostell moved in the direction of Happening in 1954, when he came to the realization that both abstract art and Art Informel 'lacked essential categories & dimensions of our multi-material & multi-mixed technological existence . . . the totality of phenomena of our changing & pulsating life was not in the least integrated in the art of that time in any way'.[37] The result was his first 'dé-coll/age' paintings made of layers of unstuck and torn posters. Vostell commented on the next stage: 'Torn posters were my first de-coll/ages, & as i was demonstrating the de-coll/age principle in action it became an event, & out of these events grew my first de-coll/age happenings.'[38]

His intention of turning the creative process into a work of art became even more pronounced in *The Theatre Takes Place on the Street* (1958). He prepared a score[39] for the action with concrete directions that aimed at transforming passive spectators into active participants. Thereby, they were able to go beyond the level of contemplating a work of art (such as a décollage) and to reflect critically on themselves and their relationship with reality by participating in a transformation of their environment.[40] A more complex action was *Cityrama* of 1961, a 'permanent realistic demonstration at twenty-six places in Cologne, where life and reality, action and events are declared to be décollaged Total Works of Art'.[41] Here, the spectators were encouraged to go to one of the twenty-six sites (a scrapyard, bombsite, railway station, etc.) and to carry out actions such as:

> Listen to the noise of the railway and practise the art of love . . . urinate into the debris and think of your best friends . . . observe the children play, then take a fish in your mouth and go for a walk . . . enter a laundry and ask which year we are living in . . . examine uninterruptedly for one hour the display of a butcher's shop.

The first action Vostell called a Happening was *PC-Petite Ceinture*, performed on 7 July 1962 in Paris. The audience was asked to board a bus of the 'PC' Circle Line, drive around Paris and take note of the acoustic and visual impressions gained during the journey. In the following years, these open-air Happenings in urban landscapes became increasingly complex and large-scale. *No-Nine Dé-coll/ages* (14 September 1963) took place in nine different sites of the city of Wuppertal. The audience gathered at the Galerie Parnass and were then taken 'on a journey which equalled an indetermined, open form of composition'.[42] They were driven in a bus to a cinema, where they could watch *Sun in Your Head*, a décollaged television programme by Vostell, and a number of live actions: Vostell brushing his teeth, pouring water into a glass, leafing through a book, vacuuming the floor, etc. Then they drove to a marshalling yard surrounded by allotments. While one of the actors performed an everyday scene (selling sausages), people working in their vegetable patch could witness the spectacular destruction of a Mercedes 170 by two locomotives. Stage three of the journey was a garden centre. Three large household mixers were used to grind a tabloid paper to pulp and to mix it with eau de cologne, pepper and plant-seeds. The resulting paste was poured over the flowerbeds. Then they drove on to a quarry where Vostell had set up a TV set. The audience settled down to watch a popular quiz show, which Vostell, from the upper part of the quarry constantly jammed or 'décollaged'. Finally, he blew up the television. The spectators were taken back to the city and driven down into a dark underground garage. They had to remain seated on the bus and watch through the windows how Vostell décollaged a number of objects. Next came a short interlude on the street, where they had to wrap passers-by in plastic foil. Site seven was a cellar in a factory, formerly used as an air-raid shelter, and number eight a room that looked like a prison. Here twelve simultaneous actions unfolded amongst the audience, including slide projections and the transformation, with the aid of barbed wire, of a TV set into a sculpture. The ninth and last venue was the same as the starting point, the Galerie Parnass, where Vostell melted a number of plastic toys on an electric stove and sculpted them into a 'décollage à la verticale'.

Vostell's interest in the fetishes of modern civilization and mass communication also found an expression in his video art and intermedia installations, where he sought to demonstrate the inner contradictions of the modern media of communication and the conflict between their positive potential and actual destructiveness. The first event of this kind was *TV Décollage Events and Actions for Millions*.[43] The idea was to produce a TV broadcast with décollaged images, which encouraged the viewer to respond to the broadcast and to carry out actions suggested during the programme: kiss the person on the TV screen; sit in front of the TV and brush your teeth; press your belly against the monitor; drink a can of Coca-Cola, but think of the adverts for Pepsi-Cola; feed the TV set with TV food, etc. In the introduction to the script, Vostell commented:

> The viewer who submits to the events or acts against them experiences the absurdity and the dubious quality of mass manipulation through the means of communication. The broadcast aims at revealing that TV has already reached our subconscious and has acted out all these actions or has stored and spread them everywhere. The absurd and critical game ought to produce consciousness of these facts.[44]

Vostell tried to encourage the spectator to see television as a *tableau vivant* designed to reproduce life in a fatally flawed manner: it is more real than real and therefore false. His TV décollages used electronic images as a basis for the generation of new images, which reveal the medium's potential to be manipulated. 'Décollage' meant stripping off the layers of falsity in the electronically produced simulacrum of reality. Destroying the images through obstructing them, or physically by shooting at the TV set (as in the *No-Nine* Happening in Wuppertal) or burying it (as at the *Yam* Festival in New York), was not just a destructive gesture: it showed that the human being was able to take control of the electronic media and that television could be formed, moulded, structured, sculpted etc. according to our will and desire.

These ideas were further explored in the *Technological Happening Room* of 1966.[45] Here, a room was conceived as a 'visual-acoustic laboratory in which the media can be mixed/stored/blurred/& dé-coll/aged' in order to 'generate an intense psychological and physiological period of experience by the availability of its media instruments & their informations'. A large number of electronic instruments (TV monitors, film projectors, video tapes, telephones, radios, xerox machines, record players, computers, an epidiascope and a juke box) was operated from a control desk. Only individual visitors were allowed to enter the Happening room, where they were bombarded by sounds and images from the networked media. Actions and reactions were recorded and played back to them, and in the course of the visit the relation between object and subject became blurred: 'passive' watching of images turned into 'active' producing of images, thereby dismantling the traditional nexus of representation and eliminating the gap between art and life.

Vostell developed a large number of strategies and techniques to intervene, recast, manipulate and attack the modern mass media. His décollages transformed found imagery and converted the fragments into new *gestalts*. His Happenings provided the audience with material that enabled them to engage actively and critically with their environment: 'I'm concerned with enlightening the audience through décollage. Taking everyday occurrences out of their context opens up a possibility for discussing the absurdities and demands of life, thereby shocking the audience and prompting them to reflect and react.'[46]

In contrast to Vostell's complex engagement with the politics of the information age, Jean-Jacques Lebel's aesthetics and political ideas were extremely simple to grasp and had an immediate impact on a whole generation of young Happening artists. Lebel was an extremely active publicist, who expressed his views in short statements, longer essays and even in book form. He was not a sophisticated thinker, but an able and energetic organizer who popularized the Happening genre, which he had studied first-hand in New York.[47] He linked it with the Hippy and Beat culture of the time and with Leftist actionism and shocked the bourgeois press with nudity, anarchical actions and radical political slogans.

Lebel's first major Happening was *To Conjure up the Spirit of Catastrophe*, performed in the Cordier Gallery in front of Surrealist and Neo-Dada paintings and sculptures. The gallery was used as an environment in which a large number of simultaneous actions unfolded, accompanied by the sounds of a frenetic jazz combo: Lebel, as president De Gaulle, wheeled a toy baby carriage through the audience; abstract images were projected onto a nude female body; two naked girls had newspaper headlines stuck on their bodies, then put on masks of Kennedy and Khrushchev and took a 'blood-bath' in a tub filled with chicken blood; an erotic action painting was created underneath a row of penis-shaped objects dangling from the ceiling: the painter Ferrò, dressed as a sex priest, stuck a paint brush in the form of a papier mâché phallus into paint pots which two girls clasped between their legs, and finally collapsed in a 'mystic orgasm'; Tetsumi Kudo demonstrated the 'Impotence of Philosophy' by carrying a cupboard around the gallery, opening it and revealing a womb spiked with hypodermic needles; Lebel stuck his head inside a TV monitor, signalled with his fingers the union of a penis and vagina and declared that the revolution was on the march. Finally, Lebel and some members of the audience took off their clothes, danced and produced an action painting. When the work was finished, Lebel jumped through the canvas and walked out of the gallery to shouts of 'Heil Art, Heil Sex'.[48]

A similarly Dionysian event was *Déchirex*, which *Life Magazine* called a 'Bacchanal of Nudity, Spaghetti and Poetry'.[49] On the darkened stage of the American Center in Paris two women played badminton with fluorescent rackets and were joined by two men with equally fluorescent helmets and spectacles. Like snails they slid towards the girls and began to eat their costumes made of cabbage. Suddenly, a nude woman on a motorcycle roared into the auditorium and was chased through the crowd until the house lights went off. A spotlight focused on two men demolishing an old car with axe and hammer. A woman wearing a death mask kneeled on the crushed roof and was covered with spaghetti, which she then hurled into the jeering crowd. All the while one could hear screeching fire engines, an old recording of Mayakovsky declaiming a poem, and finally a political speech by Fidel Castro. The badminton players, by now bereft of their vegetarian costume, entered the auditorium and auctioned off the demolished car. The Beat poet Lawrence Ferlinghetti read from *The Great Chinese Dragon* while a girl shaved her groin; another woman tore off the arms and legs of a doll, and a naked couple made love in a hammock.

In the last phase of his career as a Happening artist Lebel turned towards 'Political Street Theatre' linked to the political unrest in Paris in May 1968:

The May Revolution dynamited the limits of 'art' and 'culture' as it did all other social or political limits. The old avant-garde dream of turning 'life' into 'art', into a collective creative experience, finally came true. . . . The May uprising was theatrical in that it was a gigantic fiesta, a revelatory and sensuous explosion outside the 'normal' pattern of politics. [50]

The merging of art and life in a revolutionary situation led him to the conclusion: 'I have ceased to be an artist. I'm still creative as much and as often as I can, especially producing collective, spontaneous, dangerous, consciousness-busting, empirical events (sometimes one can call them Happenings, sometimes, more often, they are simply life).'[51] However, this 'permanent revolutionary process', as he called it in the letter, came to an abrupt halt in 1969, and soon afterwards Lebel withdrew from the performance scene and went into self-imposed 'exile'.

Lebel, probably more than any other artist of the 1960s, popularized the genre of Happening and brought it to the attention of a mass audience. This was not only because of the reports in the daily press on the events he organized, but also due to his copious writings, from which some key elements of a performance theory, as listed in Box 4.2, can be deduced.

Action Art in Japan: the Gutai Group, Neo-Dada Organizers and Hi Red Center

Japan's defeat in the Second World War was a watershed event, that left a lasting mark on the social and cultural development of the country. The collapse of the Meiji constitution and the imposition of a democratic order deeply affected traditional élites and forced the common people into accepting a new value system. Many taboos began to crumble and a hitherto unknown freedom of expression emerged from under the encrusted surface of the old order. To a certain degree, Japan had been prepared for the event by the Meiji Revolution of 1868, which had released the country from its self-imposed isolation and introduced a rigorous modernization programme in line with Western models. However, acknowledging the superiority of Western technology and scientific learning did not extend to the wider cultural or artistic fields; in fact many leaders believed that art was one of the areas where Japan could stand up to the West or be superior to it.

In the early twentieth century, Japan's rapidly changing identity brought about a re-evaluation of the country's artistic traditions in a wider, global perspective. The opening up of channels to Western art movements such as

BOX 4.2:   KEY FEATURES OF HAPPENINGS, ACCORDING TO
JEAN-JACQUES LEBEL

- Happenings are an open and fluid art form with no beginning, middle or end. The scenic actions are not mapped out in any detail and therefore allow plenty of room for improvisation. They only happen once and cannot be repeated.

- Happenings are participatory events and stir spectators out of the habitual passivity to which literary theatre and the mass media have conditioned them. Happenings do not offer space for contemplation, but rather bring the participants into contact with life as it unfolds in time, and foster active intervention, exchange and collaboration. It is a central aim of Happenings to convert mono-directional communication into dialogue and the circulation of ideas.

- Happenings are a means of breaking down the barriers between art and life. However, they do not accept life as it is, but are 'cosmogony in action'. They intervene in our everyday existence, transform human beings, and make them change their old ways of seeing, feeling, and being.

- Happenings express people's innermost feelings in an intense and playful manner. They re-establish contact with our instincts, fight alienation and erotic sublimation, and turn dreams into actions.

- Happenings protest against the power of the State, the politics of the bourgeoisie, the impositions of the law and the control exercised by the censors. Happenings evade the art market and cultural industry and give the artist a free and creative role in society. Happenings are a combative art form, an expression of a political and sexual revolution.

Cubism, Futurism, Dada, Surrealism, and Abstract Art caused some artists, dissatisfied with the government-sponsored, official system, to embrace the foreign ideals, travel to the West and seek recognition amongst the international avant-garde. However, the influence of these artists on Japanese art as a whole remained strictly limited. This was partly because the Modernist tenets of individualism, freedom of expression, and opposition to cultural orthodoxy sat uncomfortably within the conformist structures that regulated Japanese society, and partly because the majority of Japanese artists and intellectuals did not wish to equate modernization with Westernization. Rather, they promoted a revival of the country's nativist spirit and disapproved of uncritical imports and shallow imitations of Western avant-garde practices. Even radical avant-garde artists such as Murayama proclaimed: 'Throw away your albums. Stand up by yourselves. I beg you to stop acting like monkeys. . . . It makes you want to puke. Oh mates, how far will you be slaves?'[52]

The possibilities for exhibiting Western-style art were very limited at a time when Japan possessed hardly any commercial galleries and very few collectors with an interest in modern art. Consequently, artists professing avant-gardist ideas and leading a bohemian lifestyle found it virtually impossible to make a living. As Ichiro Hariu pointed out, they 'had an average life expectancy of about thirty years, and many died even younger, either as a result of poverty, dissipation or illness'.[53] During the years of fascism and war, when the country was put under rigid military control and Western ideas of Modernist art were considered a threat to the cultural establishment, there was the added danger of being imprisoned. Japanese Surrealists were suspected of being Communist sympathizers, and the police treated all avant-garde activities as potentially subversive. Consequently, many artists were attacked, placed under surveillance, or detained.

The situation only began to change after the Second World War, when the defeat of Japanese imperialism brought about a general loss of belief in the age-old national cultural values. The occupation of Japan (1945–52) and the continued US presence during the Cold War led to a sudden influx of American modern art, and traditional Japanese-style painting came to be equated with the reactionary forces responsible for the war disaster. The US–Japan Security Treaty (ANPO, 1951) turned Japan into a military base for operations against China and Korea. For the next ten years, a rapidly advancing global information society led to many cross-cultural appropriations and a lively cultural exchange with Western countries. Independent galleries and free artists' associations sprang up; it became common practice to hold democratically run exhibitions, and several large-scale showcases of recent Western art found an enthusiastic response. But still, modernity and Modernism assumed different meanings in Japan from those in the West and led to a fusion of imported and indigenous concepts, of traditional and modern forms. The Left criticized the mass media for propagating an American lifestyle and instead attempted to revive the native spirit of Japanese art and culture. Other artists shunned such a blanket anti-Western attitude and sought to assert a typically Japanese form of modernity and Modernism. Alexandra Munroe, in an essay on postwar Japanese art, commented on this:

The Japanese avant-garde has struggled with how to preserve, transform, or universalize cultural legacy, and beneath the veneer of appropriation, has deeply resisted the blind assimilation of Western culture. . . . The Japanese avant-garde too found itself 'on strike' (*en grève*) against society. But if the object of European antipathy was the capitalist bourgeoisie, the Japanese confronted the entrenched system of nationalism at home and the hegemony of Euro-American modernism worldwide.[54]

The Japanese avant-garde strove to create works that were modern in a Japanese way, incorporating and opposing at the same time local and Western influences. Not unlike Baudelaire a hundred years earlier, Japanese artists and writers believed in a timeless essence of tradition, which interacted with the ever-changing constellations of the modern. So even when accepting certain aspects of Western Modernism, the artists avoided wholesale acceptance, second-hand adaptation or uncritical emulation of Western models. By incorporating autochthonous elements they added an Eastern perspective on the global practice of Modernism and avant-garde art.

The first Japanese avant-garde association to appear on the scene after the great upheavals of the postwar era was the Gutai group, founded in 1954 by Jiro Yoshihara, initially as a loose group of young painters who would discuss each others' works and seek the advice and guidance of their master. Yoshihara encouraged his disciples to be absolutely true to their own creative impulses and to develop an artistic language that was entirely different from anything else they might have encountered. In 1955 they published a journal, *Gutai* (Concrete), of which twelve issues appeared over the next ten years, spreading the ideas and concepts of the group in Japan as well as abroad.

The group's operational headquarters was in Ashiya near Osaka, where from 25 July to 6 August 1955 they held an *Experimental Outdoor Exhibition of Modern Art to Challenge the Midsummer Burning Sun*. The artists used a pine grove for a site-specific installation that required an active role from the visitors in order to achieve its artistic aims. The artists altered their exhibits during their period of presentation, thereby staging the very act of creation, and conferring art status to the process rather than to the object of their creativity. On the closing day of the exhibition they burned the works, as if to emphasize with this Neo-Dada gesture the primacy of play and action over static objectification and commodification. The first official Gutai art exhibition was held from 19 to 28 October 1955 at the Ohara Centre in Tokyo. Amongst its most innovative pieces were a 'sound painting' by Atsuko Tanaka (a set of bells linked by an electric cable, which could be set off by the visitors as they moved around the hall) and *Electric Dress* by the same artist, made of hundreds of electric bulbs and tubes and serving both as a theatrical costume and as a piece of sculpture. From among the programme of events and actions one must mention Kazuo Shiraga's *Challenging Mud*, in which the half-naked artist dived into a large pile of clay and wrestled with it until a sculpture emerged from this violent material action. Saburo Murakami hurled himself through a set of large-scale frames covered with wrapping paper, thus creating *At One Moment Opening Six Holes* (see Illustration 8). He repeated the action on subsequent occasions and commented on this early form of Body Art: 'When one rejects the existing sense for beauty which yearns for certainties, and grasps evasive qualities and boldly chooses danger, will not possibilities open up for the discovery of a new facet of beauty?'[55]

The Gutai members used their body as a medium of expression and created works where the live act of creation was far more important than the resulting object. For this reason the performances were carried out in front of an audience and documented on photo and film.[56] For the next event, an exhibition held in an old shipyard on the Hanshin River near Amagasaki for one day only (9 April 1956), they invited *Life Magazine* to cover the performances, which were intimately aligned to the surrounding environment. Similarly, the *Second Gutai Outdoor Exhibition* of 27 July–5 August 1956 was meticulously documented, showing, for example, Shozo Shimamoto creating a painting by shooting paint at a canvas with a handmade cannon, or Shiraga erecting ten logs covered with red paint in the form of a cone and then scarring their surface with the aid of an axe. The *Second Gutai Art Exhibition*, in Tokyo (11–17 October 1956), had Shimamoto throwing paint-filled bottles at a rock and creating a drip painting on a canvas stretched underneath, and Shiraga executed a painting with his feet while hanging on a rope and swinging over a canvas that was nailed to the floor. At the *Third Gutai Art Exhibition,* in Kyoto (3–10 April 1957), Akira Kanayama demonstrated a mechanical way of creating a painting: he placed lacerated containers filled with paint on remote-controlled toy cars and let the paint drip onto the canvas as they moved across the floor.

From these gallery and open-air actions it was only a natural progression to arrive at *Gutai On-Stage Art Shows*. The first of these took place on 29 May 1957 in the Sankei Centre in Osaka, repeated on 7 July 1957 in the Sankei Centre in Tokyo, and the second was on 4 April 1958 in the Asahi Centre in Osaka. They involved music, film projections and lighting effects and therefore had to be carefully planned, though not rehearsed in a conventional theatrical manner. Some of the two dozen pieces performed

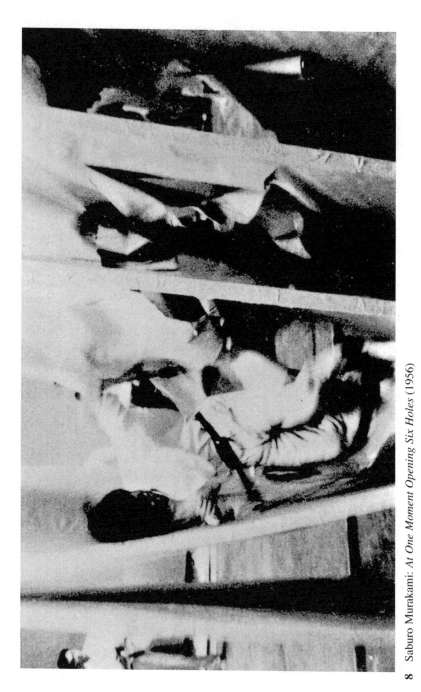

8 Saburo Murakami: *At One Moment Opening Six Holes* (1956)

on these occasions had been presented in similar form before. Featuring amongst the new items was Shiraga's dance-pantomime *Sambaso Ultra-modern*; Yoshihara's *Two Spaces* used a dark stage with occasional flashing lights and undefineable sounds, which demonstrated the Zen concept of *mu*, an empty space pregnant with potentialities; Toshio Yoshida's *Ceremony by Cloth* was a wedding ritual in which the couple was wrapped in long strips of fabric until eventually they were entirely covered like a cocoon; Sadamasa Motonaga used a smoke machine to create large smoke rings, which were given a luminous appearance as they wafted into the auditorium; Koichi Nakahashi and Yasuo Sumi, to the accompaniment of a specially composed soundtrack, created an Action Painting by throwing paint-soaked balls at a white back wall; and Tanaka stripped off layers and layers of a paper dress until in the end she stood on stage in a leotard decorated with blinking lights.

With these performances in Tokyo and Osaka the Gutai group came close to producing theatre. But none of the pieces presented were based on literary drama, nor were they any longer actions that resulted in the production of art objects. None the less, several of the works used symbolic or even representational elements and resembled dramatic actions born from a chance encounter of theatrical space, sound, light and human bodies.[57] Yoshihara acknowledged this fact in an essay published after the 1957 stage shows, but emphasized that the performances did not subordinate fine art to the scenic arts. Rather, it had been the group's intention 'to leave the traditional notions of fine arts behind and to confront from an independent position the problems that are peculiar to scenic space, to grapple with the theatre's specific *modus operandi*, and to address the functions of sound, light and time'.[58] In the following years, economic necessities forced the group to relinquish their focus on action art and again to execute sculptures and paintings that could be sold in galleries. Instead of the Dionysian, visceral, body-centred 'Happenings' they concentrated on running a *Gutai Pinacotheca*, mounting exhibitions abroad and arranging shows of foreign artists in Japan. Occasional forays into the performance medium, as with a kite event during the Osaka International Sky Festival (19–24 April 1960), or *Don't Worry! The Moon Won't Fall!*, a collaboration with the Morita Modern Dance Company (Sankei Centre, Osaka, 6 November 1962), no longer had the startling, innovative character of the early actions, which had left audiences speechless and critics perplexed and confused.

The 1960s ushered in a new development in Japanese avant-garde performance, which went a few stages beyond the Gutai experimentation and produced works that were akin to Fluxus and Punk art. Despite their emphasis on the creative process rather than the object character of art, the

Gutai Happenings often resulted in works which nowadays grace the walls of museums and are considered masterpieces of contemporary Japanese art. This was rarely the case with the action art of subsequent generations of avant-garde artists, who shunned museums, were often considered too outrageous to be granted exhibition space in galleries, and presented their violent struggle with materials in the entirely ephemeral medium of performance art.

In the 1960s, the early Japanese avant-garde inspired by Futurism and Dada experienced a revival. Concepts and ideas which in the 1920s and 1930s had been unacceptable in Japan, were reintroduced by artists who for political reasons had turned their back on Japanese society. In 1960, the US–Japan Security Treaty came to an end and large sections of the population considered the time opportune for re-establishing Japan's independence. Therefore, the announcement by the pro-American government that the treaty would be renewed without substantial revisions led to the so-called ANPO crisis, characterized by mass rallies, strikes and demonstrations. Many avant-garde artists participated in these events and formed a radical opposition to the political and cultural establishment. From this culture of controversy and discord emerged two groups, Neo-Dada Organizers and Hi Red Center, who produced some of the most radical forms of avant-garde performance in Japanese postwar history. They severed the last links to Action Painting, Art Informel, Tachism etc. and instead promoted anti-art as a non-élitist activity merging with the political struggle and the social processes of urban societies. Their work was first seen at the Yomiuri Andepandan-ten, a jury-free showcase organized between 1949 and 1963 by the *Yomiuri* newspaper at the Tokyo Metropolitan Museum of Art. This annual event was the only exhibition opportunity for young and radical artists who wished to go beyond Gutai aesthetics and felt inspired by the 1920s Japanese avant-garde, who had in vain sought to promote the role of the artist as an iconoclast, of art as an expression of individualism, self-identity and primitive inner urges, to lead art back to life and merge it with the world of everyday life. It was characteristic for these Yomiuri Andepandan groups to create works from found objects and the debris of urban life. Like the New Realists, they were primarily interested in the act of assembling objects in a performance. To underline this disregard for permanence they often destroyed the works immediately after their creation.

In April 1960, the Neo-Dada Organizers held their first exhibition, which was much more like a series of actions than a display of artworks. The artists filled the gallery with junk and found objects; Sho Kazekura stuck his head in a bucket of water and started shouting 'The War, the War, the Third World War!' Others destroyed some chairs with well-aimed karate chops and smashed a dozen beer bottles, while Genpei Akasegawa read out a manifesto that declared: 'We enter the ring on an Earth gone mad in this 20.6th century – the century which has stamped out serious works of art. The only way we will be spared the massacre is to become slaughterers ourselves.'[59] In a destructive spree, they destroyed the whole content of the gallery and ended their performance with the singing of a traditional Japanese folk-song, 'The only thing that is left to do is crying'. For the next months, the group met regularly at Masunobu Yoshimura's studio, where they held two exhibitions. On 15 June 1960, they staged an *Anpo Episode Event*, where in an 'excrescence of destructive energy' (Akasegawa) the half-naked, half-drunk artists destroyed most of the studio's inventory. On 1 July 1960 they opened another exhibition with a 'happening' (Yoshino) that included Yoshimura pouring vitriol onto a steel-plate; over it hung a mobile of human figures, which performed an eerie dance in the acid fumes. Akasegawa poured liquid rubber over the floor and stuck radio tubes into it; Shinohara gave a wooden sculpture an 'irokese' hairdo by hammering six-inch nails into it, and Takkai Yoshino occasionally cast the room into glaring light by setting fire to magnesium powder. Their third exhibition, in August 1960, was held in the open air on Zaimoku-za Beach in Kamakura. For a show at the Hibiya Metropolitan Gallery they paraded through the Ginza district, covered in bandages and light bulbs, and when they reached Hibiya Park, they stripped half-naked, performed a body-paint event and smashed a number of steel sculptures in a savagely violent action (see Illustration 9). Another action designed to shock and provoke was carried out by Sho Kazekura at the 1962 Yomiuri Indépendent show of 1962: he exhibited himself, stark-naked, in the gallery, and when he was asked what he was doing there and where his work was, he replied: 'It's me right here. It's called *The Real Thing*.'[60]

As a result of such actions and various other riotous tendencies the newspaper *Yomiuri Shimbun* eventually withdrew its sponsorship and the annual exhibition came to a close in 1963. In the run-up to the 1964 Tokyo Olympic Games, the government tried to curb anarchical and violent manifestations. Nevertheless, publicly staged performances by avant-garde groups continued even without sponsorship, and in the forefront of this was Hi Red Center, formed in May 1963 by Genpei Akasegawa, Natsuyuki Nakanishi and Jiro Takamatsu (the name was an acronym of the first syllables of the members' surnames, Taka = High, Aka = Red, Naka = Centre).[61] These artists had come together because of their common interest in converging art and life in public performances, as for example in 1962 when they carried out various actions in the Tokyo Underground and in railway stations. Their first joint Happening was *Miniature Restaurant*,

9 Ushio Shinohara of Neo-Dada Organizers in an untitled action in Hibiya Park, Tokyo (1960)

a food event at the last Yomiuri Andepandan-ten. On 7 May 1963 they had a show called *Mixer Plan* at the Shinjiku Daiichi Gallery in Tokyo, which brought together various works they had previously shown at the Yomiuri Indépendent. These were presented to the audience in a strangely formal ceremony designed to satirize the conventional behaviour at art auctions. On 15 August 1963, a *Non-V-Day Anniversary Meal* was held at Tokyo's Citizen's Hall in protest against the Japanese hypocrisy over their defeat in the Second World War. The group sold very expensive tickets to an unsuspecting audience, and when the guests arrived for what they believed would be a splendid dinner, they discovered that they were only entitled to watch Hi Red Center devouring the meal, which ended at midnight with Kazekura branding his chest with a red-hot iron. On 26–7 January 1964 they held an event called *Shelter Plan*, in which they booked a suite at Tokyo's Imperial Hotel under the pretence of selling 'custom-made' bomb-shelter boxes. For this purpose they measured and photographed various body parts of guests they brought up from the lobby, and of invited friends such as Nam June Paik and Yoko Ono. In June 1964 they presented *The Great Panorama Exhibition*, where they closed the gallery on the opening day, and opened it again when the show was finished. *Movement to Promote the Cleaning-Up of the Metropolitan Area (Be Clean!)* saw them scubbing the pavements of the Ginza district during the Summer Olympics of 1964. *Dropping Event*, on 10 October 1964, consisted of throwing various objects from the rooftop of a building to the street below, collecting the items in a suitcase and placing it in a locker at a railway station. They then sent the locker key to a person randomly picked out of a telephone directory.

In the following years, Hi Red Center became integrated into the Fluxus movement and took on a predominantly artistic rather than political character. The outrageous and sometimes dangerous actions that had been a feature of Japanese avant-garde art abated and a more sophisticated interaction with the forces of globalization and technological progress set in.

CHRONOLOGY 4.2: FLUXUS

1962

9 June	George Maciunas et al., *Little Summer Fête: Après John Cage*, Wuppertal, Galerie Parnass.
16 June	Nam June Paik et al., *Neo-Dada in Music*, Düsseldorf, Kammerspiele.

→

→

1–23 September	*Fluxus: International Festival of Newest Music,* 14 concerts, Wiesbaden, Städtisches Museum.
5 October	Various artists, *Festival of New Music,* Amsterdam, Galerie Monet.
23–8 November	Various artists, *Fluxus: Music and Anti-Music. Acoustic Theatre,* Copenhagen, Nikolajkirke and Allé Scenen.
3–8 December	Various artists, *Festum Fluxorum,* Paris, American Centre.
1963	
2–3 February	*Festum Fluxorum Fluxus,* Düsseldorf, Staatliche Kunstakademie.
1 March	*Fluxus, Happenings, Danger Music,* Stockholm, Alleteatern.
10–20 March	Nam June Paik, *Exposition of Music – Electronic Television,* Wuppertal, Galerie Parnass.
28 March	*Fluxus Concert,* Oslo, Studentekroa.
23 and 28 June	*Fluxus Festival,* Amsterdam, Hypocriterion Theatre, and The Hague, Bleijenburg.
25 July– 3 August	*Fluxus Festival,* Nice, Nouveau Casino and various street locations.
27–30 September	*Two International Concerts of Newest Acoustic Theatre and Anti-Art,* Copenhagen, Nikolajkirke.
18 December	*International Programme of Newest Music, Theatre, Literature,* Amsterdam, Kleine Komedie.
1964	
11 April– 23 May	*Fully Guaranteed 12 Fluxus Concerts,* New York, Fluxhall, 359 Canal St.
27 June	*Fluxus Concert (Fluxus Symphony Orchestra),* New York, Carnegie Hall.
6 July	*Fluxus: A Little Festival of New Music,* London, Goldsmiths' College.
18 September– 3 November	*Perpetual Fluxfest,* New York, Washington Square Gallery.
16 November	*Recitals d'avanguardia,* Milan, Galleria Blue.
23 November– December	*Flux Festival,* Rotterdam: De Lantaren, Amsterdam, Galerie Amstel.

→

1965	
14 June	*Fluxus Concert*, Berlin, Galerie René Block.
5 September– 19 December	*Perpetual Fluxfest*, New York, New Cinematheque.

George Maciunas and the Birth of Fluxus

Maciunas's father was a Lithuanian engineer who had studied architecture in Berlin and was employed during the Second World War by Siemens to construct and maintain electric power stations in his home country. When, in 1944, Russia occupied Lithuania, he was considered a collaborator and his family had to flee with the retreating troops to Germany, where young Yurgis grew up as Jürgen Matschunas in the spa town of Bad Nauheim. The desolate economic situation forced the family in 1948 to emigrate to the USA, where Maciunas senior became a professor at the City College of New York, and Yurgis, now called George Maciunas, studied architecture at the Carnegie Institute of Technology in Pittsburgh. Disappointment with the profession made him take up postgraduate studies in art history at New York University, where in 1960 he met a fellow Lithuanian, Almus Salcius, who ran a small gallery in Great Neck, Long Island. They decided to found a Lithuanian Cultural Club and in December 1960 rented premises at 925 Madison Avenue. They called the venue by the acronym of their first names, AG Gallery, and decided to found a magazine to support their artistic venture. Being immigrants, they considered calling it *Influx*, but then settled on the name *Fluxus*.[62] Maciunas designed the gallery space and rebuilt it to fit his tastes and requirements. He intended the venue to become a meeting place of the avant-garde in fine arts, music and theatre and therefore organized twelve events to complement the exhibitions. Each lecture, concert or reading was followed by a discussion and 'a repast of hors d'oeuvre and wine. Entry contribution of $3 will help to publish FLUXUS magazine.'[63] Henry Flynt, who met Maciunas in June 1961, described the gallerist as a young man professing a 'reasonable, academic modernism'[64] and planning mainly exhibitions of abstract art, Action Paintings and Tachist works. In order to graduate to a more adventurous form of avant-garde aesthetics he was in need of inspiration from other, more advanced quarters.

Around that time there were several experimental groups of artists operating in Manhattan. Apart from the Happening circle discussed at the beginning of this chapter, there was John Cage's class at the New School for Social Research, whose members performed their pieces in a variety of New York venues. Maciunas never studied with Cage, but regularly went to Richard Maxwell's classes in electronic music, where he met several of his future collaborators. Another circle congregated at Yoko Ono's loft in Chambers Street and held performance festivals under the organizational guidance of La Monte Young. These included a number of Japanese artists who would later play a major role in Fluxus. Maciunas established contacts with many of these avant-garde artists, cooperated with them for his performance programme at the AG Gallery and had them contribute to an anthology of contemporary experimental writing that he was in the process of putting together with La Monte Young and Jackson MacLow.

Maciunas's exhibitions were badly attended, and his poetry evenings fared no better. As to the presentation of 'Musica antiqua et nova' (ancient music played on original instruments), and 'Concerts of New Sounds and Noises' (modern electronic compositions by Richard Maxfield, John Cage, and others), they were even less of a commercial proposition in the early 1960s. The Lithuanian exile community boycotted the gallery because of Maciunas's communist leanings, and it was only his income as a graphic designer that kept the gallery going for nearly a year. He later recalled: 'To La Monte's concert for instance only 5 came. Imagine 8 performers and 5 audience!! We will run into same difficulty if we don't promote Fluxus. And we must promote without expenditures – that's the trick, since I won't have a job in N.Y. & will have no $$$.'[65] The accumulated debts from the gallery and the cost of printing *An Anthology* brought Maciunas into conflict with his creditors and forced him, in autumn 1961, to leave the USA.

He returned to Germany and took a job as architect–designer for the American Air Force in Wiesbaden. Before escaping from New York, he had collected names and addresses of European people of influence who were interested in avant-garde art, music and theatre. Once he had settled in the Taunus mountains, he wrote to them or visited them, soliciting their support for his Fluxus venture and using their connections to rent a gallery, concert hall or theatre.[66] As the term 'Fluxus' had no artistic connotations in Germany, he initially sought to promote the events under the heading 'Neo-Dada'. Raoul Hausmann discouraged him and said that his programme was 'bruitist-futurist and not dadaist'.[67] In some ways Maciunas admired the Russian Kom-futs (Communist Futurists) and LEF (Left Front of the Arts) for their vision of a socially productive artist, but he still thought that a Dada-like deconstruction of the dominant ideology of art was called for. He therefore planned to sell his *Fluxus* magazine in a 'nice box of a disposable enema unit' and to distribute the Fluxus prospectus in a small tube 'so people can stick it up their ass and squeeze gently ... until strong urge is felt'.[68]

Of the various groups and individuals Maciunas entered into contact with, five stand out as being of particular influence on his later life: Jean-Pierre Wilhelm and Alfred Schmela, who ran two galleries in Düsseldorf,[69] Mary Bauermeister, who had instituted a very active performance programme in her studio in Cologne,[70] the artists of the Galerie Parnass in Wuppertal,[71] and the Darmstadt group of Brock, Bremer, Spoerri and Mon, who produced some of the most experimental theatre productions in the German-speaking countries.[72] Within half a year of his return to Germany, Maciunas was in contact with a large number of individuals from various countries who shared his artistic tastes and sensibilities and were willing to join him in a series of 'concerts', fifteen in all, to be given in Wiesbaden, Cologne, Berlin, London and Paris (a second series was planned for Czechoslovakia, Poland, Lithuania and the USSR). Although he was an immensely able organizer who, like a general, marshalled his forces in a meticulously planned and tightly packed schedule, several of these events never came off the ground and others were switched at short notice to different locations. As in New York, he put all his financial resources (USAF salary plus income from commercial design jobs) into the Fluxus venture, which he ran from his home in Ehlhalten near Wiesbaden.

In spring 1962 Maciunas was ready to hold his first event and wrote to Mary Bauermeister: 'Dear Mary . . . Could we hold festival in your studio June or July? It would be a good beginning for fluxus series.'[73] Despite their shared interests in experimental music and time-based art, Bauermeister could not help out and the event did not take place. But a few weeks later, on 9 June, he gathered several artists from her circle at the Galerie Parnass for a Neo-Dada event held on the opening of the exhibition *Après John Cage*. It included performances of new musical works by Higgins, Maciunas, Patterson, Riley,[74] and a lecture on *Neo-Dada in Music, Theatre, Poetry and Art*. In the text, which is often considered the first Fluxus manifesto, Maciunas presented to the German public the latest developments in art, namely 'concretism', which engages with 'the world of concrete reality rather than the artificial abstraction of illusionism'.[75] When applied to the theatre, it meant the replacement of artificial plots and predetermined acts on stage with 'unrehearsed and undetermined events resulting from spontaneous and improvised actions of a group of people who have been given by the author only specific tasks or a general outline of actions'.[76] In another section he spoke of 'chance procedures as a compositional method', where the artist only delivers the concept or method of production and allows the work of art to unfold undisturbed by the originator's artistic ego. Maciunas did not use the terms 'Happening' or 'New Realism' in the lecture, but these were clearly the reference points in his first, introductory part dedicated to the Cage school of New York artists. However, in the following sections he went a stage further and spoke of anti-art and art-nihilism as the determining factors of his aesthetics. It was designed to abolish art as a professional pursuit, to overcome the artificial separation between creator/spectator or performer/audience, and to create 'works of life' that are formless, meaningless and without purpose ('anti-art is life, Nature, true reality'[77]). As Maciunas was a shy man with no oratory skills, the text was read out by Carlheinz Caspari and was illustrated with graphs and charts mounted on boards that were held up by Maciunas and Nam June Paik behind the speaker.

A week later, on 16 June, the same group met again in Düsseldorf, where Jean-Pierre Wilhelm had organized for Nam June Paik a late-night event at the Kammerspiele, entitled *Neo-Dada in Music* (see Chronology 4.2). It contained five compositions by Paik, one of them performed in parallel with other pieces by Sylvano Bussotti, Dieter Schnebel, Wolf Vostell, Dick Higgins, Jackson MacLow, Ben Patterson, Toshi Ishiyanagi, La Monte Young, Jed Curtis and Maciunas. Through the good services of Jean-Pierre Wilhelm, the municipal museum in Wiesbaden allowed Maciunas to use its lecture hall for a series of concerts, designed to promote material to be published in a Fluxus magazine. Under the banner of 'Fluxus – International Festival of Newest Music' fourteen concerts were announced, as well as the imminent appearance of *Fluxus – An International Journal of Newest Art, Anti-Art, Music, Anti-Music, Poetry, Anti-Poetry etc.* Maciunas invited artists not only resident in the Rhineland and various other parts of Germany, but also from neighbouring countries and the USA. Dick Higgins, for example, arrived with a suitcase full of material that was used in the second weekend of the Wiesbaden concerts. Other participants included artists whom he had met at the Galerie Parnass and at the Neo-Dada evening in Düsseldorf. They performed more than 100 pieces over four weekends, some of them works written over the previous ten years, and other compositions and scenarios of a truly avant-garde nature moving into entirely new directions.[78] Dick Higgins recalled some of them in *Postface*:

> We did Emmett Williams's german opera, 'ja, es war noch da' in English: it was the longest three-quarters of an hour I have ever spent, since it is mostly tapping on a pan in regular rhythms a prescribed number of times. We did a one-hour version of La Monte Young's B–F sharp held, unvarying, sung and accompanied

by Benjamin Patterson's bass viol. We invented a piece by a mythical Japanese and improvised it for an hour. . . . We did Danger Music No. 3 by shaving my head and heaving political pamphlets into the audience and Danger Music No. 16 by 'working with butter and eggs for a while' so as to make an inedible waste instead of an omelette. I felt that was what Wiesbaden needed. For a while eggs were flying through the air every couple of minutes. . . . We did Corner's 'Piano Activities' by taking apart a grand piano and auctioning off the parts. Most of my 'Requiem for Wagner the Criminal Mayor' was done, to the delight of the house super, who left in the middle and came back with his whole family, they liked the goings-on so much.[79]

The local newspapers provide a great deal more information on the opening concert, given by the Norwegian pianist Karl-Erik Welin. The first, more serious part, contained *Variation 1 and 2* by Boguslaw Schaeffer, *Piano Piece A and B* by Jerry Jennings, and *Folio* by Earle Brown. In the interval there were various clownesque and acrobatic offerings, which tied over into the second part. It included a piece called *Sitting*, in which Werle sat in the auditorium and played three minutes of 'pause'; *566* consisted of 566 repetitive, dissonant sounds, and was followed by several works of a similarly cacophonous nature, such as *Piano Piece no. 3* by Sylvano Bussotti, *Piece for Barbecue and Piano* by Lars Johan Werle, *Piece 3, 4 and 7* by La Monte Young, and *Incidental Music* by George Brecht. On the execution of the programme we are informed:

Amongst others, we could hear the sounds of a matchbox and a beer bottle being scraped over the piano strings, a carnivalesque piece for toy trumpet and clothes' pegs, the noise of a piano lid being slammed (although this may have been unintentional) and fists banging on the piano. The artist attired himself most solemnly in a blue toga, lit a Christmas candle and heated a piano string until it turned red hot. He then jumped up and down on the instrument. Following this, the artist brought a push-chair with a teddy bear on stage. He carefully combed the bear and gave him some beaten egg to drink. He then very quietly piled up some children's building blocks inside the piano and let them fall onto the strings, creating some weird and wonderful sounds and a long pause. What was the purpose of it all? Was it meant to be a provocation? If so, then those to be provoked had not shown up. The audience's unequivocal signs of hilarity left the artist unperturbed and showed no trace of aggravation.[80]

The high point of the concert was undoubtedly the destruction of a piano in Phil Corner's *Piano Activities*. The *Wiesbadener Kurier* felt that this piece for 'crowbar, drill, stones, planks and pliers . . . showed most clearly the mental state of these international disciples of the muses'.[81] It certainly gave the Wiesbaden festival notoriety and caused the event to be covered even on German television. Reporters turned the name Fluxus into a label for any kind of weird stage event that was not performance art wrapped up in the attire of 'theatre', but unpretentious activities of a banal, everyday nature.

For the next three years, Fluxus became the organizational network of far-flung artists from the worlds of music, poetry and the fine arts. There was a 'hard core' of about a dozen people, who grounded their art in a concrete, quotidian reality and shared an interest in artistic creation that shifted attention away from object to process (see Box 4.3 for the main aims of the Fluxus movement). They met regularly at various *festa fluxorum* and formed an intimate circle held together by Maciunas as impresario and chief-ideologue. They were more or less united behind a common programme, which Maciunas defined in the following terms:

> Fluxus opposed serious art or culture and its institutions, as well as Europeanism. It is also opposed to artistic professionalism and art as a commercial object or means to a personal income, it is opposed to any form of art that promotes the artist's ego. Fluxus rejects opera and theater (Kaprow, Stockhausen etc.), which represent the institutionalizing of serious art, and instead of opera and theater is for vaudeville or the circus, which represent a more popular art form or totally nonartistic amusement (which have been considered false by 'cultivated' intellectuals). Hence Fluxus concerts tend to be vaudevillian or many times satires of serious concerts. They are certainly not 'great operas', which once in a while, for unexplained reasons, are called 'happenings'.[82]

This circle widened considerably when Maciunas returned to the USA, following his dismissal from the Air Force on health grounds. From September 1963 until his death in 1978 he incorporated dozens of American artists into the Fluxus fold. Occasional attempts at excommunicating members and imposing a strict line on who was allowed to represent Fluxus to the wider world did not have any lasting effect, and nobody ever appears to have shared his political beliefs ('We laughed about them, gave our opinion, and then put them aside', one member of the group commented[83]). After a while, Maciunas resigned himself to his roles of chairman, publicity manager and organizer of events, and after 1965 he concentrated on the production of Flux boxes and on turning Fluxus into a positive social force by buying 27 buildings in SoHo, redeveloping them and turning them into cooperatively run Flux houses for artists.

Although this latter project earned him the admiration of some Fluxus members, the underlying idea of phasing out art and culture and turning the artist into a useful, productive member of society (preferably a socialist one) never won general support. Fluxus artists shared with each other a concern for their social environment and a commitment to creative interaction with the world at large, but rejected any attempt to define this attitude in narrow political terms. They often referred to themselves as a 'Flux Circus' and were only willing to operate under the Fluxus umbrella as long as Maciunas kept an 'open church' approach and allowed them to pursue their own individual interests. Occasionally, this necessitated members uniting against their chairman, as for example when Maciunas organized a protest action against Stockhausen's *Originale* in New York (29 April, 30 August, 8 September 1964). Debunking the aura of High Art was one thing; aggressive attacks on a member of the artists' community were an entirely different task. Similarly, they opposed some of his suggestions for the merging of art and life in street actions ('it's free, we don't have to advertise & we get audiences'[84]), as they would have a negative effect on society at large:

> Prearranged 'breakdowns' of a fleet of Fluxus autos and trucks bearing posters, exhibits etc. in the middle of the busiest traffic intersections, such as Times Square, 5th Avenue, 57th and 42nd Streets, tunnel and bridge entries. . . . and selling on street corners 'revised' & 'prepared' editions of the *New York Times*, *Daily News* etc. with Fluxus announcements. . . . Posting and mailing announcements (to libraries, newspapers etc.) with totally revised dates of various concerts, plays, movies, exhibits etc.[85]

In its final phase, Fluxus transformed performance into a quasi-ritual domain centred on Flux banquets, Flux weddings, Flux holidays, Flux Masses, Flux olympics, etc., which served as 'cultural performances' that reinforced group cohesion and the social identity of an otherwise fragmented and geographically dispersed community. [86] They were akin to Erving Goffman's concept of the performance of self in everyday life, and although conceptually related to the Fluxus aim of joining art and life in a compact union, they no longer had any impact on the art world at large.

Nam June Paik and Charlotte Moorman

Nam June Paik was born in Seoul (Korea), studied musicology, art history and philosophy in Tokyo, and in 1956 moved to Germany to pursue postgraduate studies in music and composition. Over the next five years he made the acquaintance of some of the leading experimental composers of his age (Cage, Stockhausen, Nono, Kagel, Cardew, Tudor, Young, etc.). Between 1958 and 1963 he lived in Cologne, worked with Kagel and

BOX 4.3:   SOME KEY CHARACTERISTICS OF FLUXUS

- Fluxus is opposed to the illusionistic character of conventional art, the metaphysical underpinnings of abstract art, the subjectivity of Expressionism.

- Fluxus locates art in the concrete, lived world and fosters an active, creative engagement with everyday existence. It aspires to an utmost realism (anti-art or non-art), and because of its simplicity and minimalism stands in contrast to the time-consuming and material-intensive Happenings.

- It opens up the mind to an appreciation of reality through its enactment, participates in the flux of life without following predetermined goals, and explores the nature of existence by treating all experiences as having essentially the same value.

- Fluxus art is produced without emotional involvement and the intervention of the conscious mind, and demands from the performer an attitude of uninvolved detachment.

- The Fluxus artist embraces reality with an open, unprejudiced mind and experiences it as situationally determined. Improvisation is a key trait of creativity.

- Fluxus seeks to destroy the élitism and exclusiveness of High Art and aims at a democratization of the production and consumption of art. It opposes the concept of the artist as a separate category from the rest of the population. Everybody is an artist.

- Fluxus dismantles the ego of the artist and the ideology of the artist as genius. The use of chance methods reduces the author's influence on form and content and allows the work of art to make itself (automorphism).

- Fluxus pieces are simple, natural, unpretentious and easy to produce. They do not require training, skills or theatrical experience. The scores are short and describe straightforward tasks, which just about anyone, especially non-artists and ordinary people, can perform. They debunk the occidental mania of perfection. Personal variations are idiosyncratic accidentals that do not interfere with the substantive intentions of a script.

- Fluxus pieces are ephemeral and can only be experienced in the here and now. They are not made for posterity; there is no

→

→

commercial intention behind them and they play no role on the official art market and in the theatre industry.

- Fluxus art is humorous and playful, uses gags, jokes, irony and elements of satire. It ridicules academic art and cultural traditions and allows the performer to have a pleasurable time while standing on stage.

- Fluxus art can take a provocative stance designed to shock and outrage. Anarchical destructiveness (e.g. smashing a violin or sawing a piano to pieces) is a tactical strategy to undermine expectations, but also to suggest alternatives to the pompous, all-hallowed status quo of art.

- As there is no distinction between art and life, the conventional boundaries between different arts are untenable.

- Fluxus performances compel spectators and performers to confront their attitude towards reality, redirect their attention to the multifaceted aspects of quotidian life, and revise their modes of perception. This is to produce new patterns of behaviour and alternative social practices.

- On a practical level, Fluxus performances do not rely on a complex technical apparatus. Props are minimal and can be carried from one performance to the next, or can be acquired at minimal cost at the venue. The only exceptions are musical compositions that require specific instruments.

- The cost of organizing a Fluxus performance is minimal. Concerts can be given in any hall that is available at no cost or at a minimal rent. Participants do not receive any remuneration and usually have to pay for their own incidental expenses such as transport and accommodation.

Stockhausen at the WDR Studio for Electronic Music, and became involved with Mary Bauermeister's Studio. Like many of the artists of this circle, Paik was deeply impressed by the first major Dada exhibition held after the war (5 September to 19 October 1958, Düsseldorf Kunsthalle) and started to give performances in a similar vein.[87] In 1961, he met George Maciunas and became a key member of the European Fluxus group. In the following years his main interest shifted towards electronic media and he would have given up performing altogether had he not met Charlotte

Moorman, with whom he collaborated from 1964 to 1991 on a series of projects performed at more than a hundred venues all over the world. Like Vostell, Beuys and several other early Fluxus members, Paik pursued a wide range of interests and artistic concepts that did not fit into Maciunas's definition of Fluxus. Although Paik remained associated with the movement, personal relations with Maciunas deteriorated, and Moorman became something of a bête noire for the Fluxus chief. For this reason it seems appropriate to discuss their performance work in a separate section of this chapter.

Paik's career as a composer fell into three phases: conventionally notated serial music (1947–57); experimental, electronic and action music influenced by Cage, Kagel, Stockhausen and Fluxus (1957–63); the collaborations with Charlotte Moorman (1964–91).[88] His first major performance was *Hommage à John Cage: Music for Tape and Piano* (Gallery 22, Düsseldorf, 13 November 1959; Studio Bauermeister, Cologne, 16–18 June 1960),[89] a piece of 'pure theatre' in the Dada tradition,[90] which combined 'action music' with his interests in electronic production of sounds and images. It consisted of three movements: the first mixed a live radio news broadcast with a pre-recorded tape of primitive vocal sounds, and had the artist running around the hall with a musical clock and a metronome, sitting down at the piano to play a few bars of music and then hammering on it with various implements. The second movement was, according to Paik, 'as boring as Proust', and issued 'a warning against the German economic miracle with its combination of thriftiness and stupidity'.[91] It made use of a prepared piano, a rattling toy car, a tuning whistle and a plastic locomotive. The third act demonstrated his idea of how to 'escape from suffocating musical theatre'[92] and contained taped quotations from Artaud and Rimbaud, toppling over a piano, releasing a live chicken, smashing glass on the floor, throwing an egg against the wall, setting off Chinese crackers, switching off the light and projecting slides of gruesome and aggressive images.

Although the event had been scored and carefully planned, most of the action was in the end improvised. Paik explained this turn of events to the composer Gottfried Michael König: 'When it is impossible to distinguish between art and Nature, then it is unnecessary to write a composition. One only needs a certain expertise to elevate Nature to the status of art.'[93] This attitude became even more apparent in *Étude for Piano Forte* (Studio Bauermeister, Cologne, 6 October 1960). One of the planned actions – cutting John Cage's tail-coat as a protest against his formal appearance at concerts – did not take place as the composer turned up in normal, everyday clothes. Similarly, the piano that Paik had nearly demolished at the previous concert did not behave as expected, so he jumped on it and played it with his feet. However, the electronic support functioned smoothly so that the audience could hear the noises of audience whisper and orchestra tuning before a concert, and Stravinsky's *Petroushka* played at enhanced speed. Other actions included shampooing Cage's and Tudor's heads with shaving cream, and Paik running out of the hall and phoning in from a telephone box in the street, announcing that the piece was over.[94]

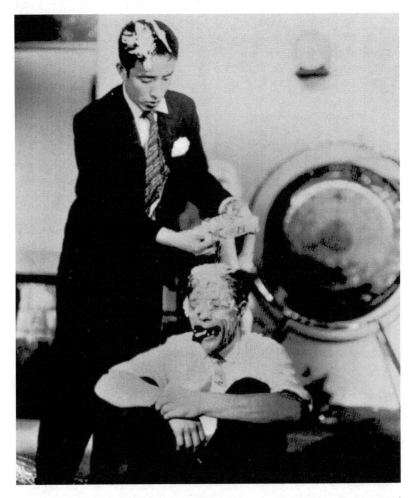

10 Nam June Paik and Carlheinz Caspari in *Simple*, performed as part of Stockhausen's *Originale* in Cologne, Theater am Dom, 26 October to 6 November 1961

On 26 October 1961 Paik participated in a performance of Stockhausen's *Originale* with a rather idiosyncratic scene of his own making (see Illustration 10): two tape recorders with collages of electronic and natural sounds were played together with a gramophone recording of Haydn's string quartet, which formed the basis of the *Deutschlandlied*. All the while, Paik was dashing back and forth on stage, throwing beans into the auditorium, unrolling a long scroll of paper, smearing a tube of shaving cream on his face, emptying a bag of flour over his head, diving into a bath tub, sitting down at a piano with his soaking-wet black suit, playing a sentimental tune with a baby dummy in his mouth, and then hammering on the keys with his head.

Paik gave another demonstration of his concept of 'visual music' in an installation at the Düsseldorf Kunsthalle, entitled *Memories of the Twentieth Century: Marilyn Monroe* (1962), which introduced a feature that has formed part of his career until the present day: the archaeology of acoustic and electronic instruments, here exhibited in the form of an ancient gramophone cabinet containing piles of newspapers reporting the death of the actress on 4 August 1962. A year later he was given an opportunity to show on a much larger scale what he understood to be 'exposition of music' and 'music-graphic': these 'new genres of art' not only translated sounds into images, but gave the audience the freedom to create their own music.[95] Paik's intermedia interests were the driving force behind his attempts at relating electronic sounds to optical signals, and to create a 'meta-medium', where the differences between these media were sublated and a new artistic discipline was created.

> I am tired of renewing the form of music. . . . I must renew the ontological form of music. . . . In the *Symphony for 20 Rooms* the sounds etc. move and the audience moves also. In my *Omnibus Music no. 1* (1961) the sounds sit down, the audience visits them. In the *Music Exposition*, the sounds sit, the audience plays or attacks them.[96]

Paik's experience with electronic music fostered his interest in other electronic media, in particular television and video, which became his main focus of attention and which will be discussed below in Chapter 6. However, in this second stage of his career he was still interested in performance practices derived from concerts and theatre shows, which he combined with electronic instruments and redesigned to activate his audiences. In 1961 he started collecting old TV monitors and altered their inside components in order to create an electronic equivalent to Cage's 'prepared piano'. To Paik, television was a musical and visual instrument, which required the input of a skilled artist and competent composer in order to fulfil its true potential as a creative medium. The result of this thinking was his 'prepared television', which transformed and manipulated broadcast images by means of magnets, and a series of action concerts with Charlotte Moorman, which aimed at integrating electronics, music and the human body.

Paik had only reluctantly continued his career as a performer under the Fluxus umbrella. According to his own testimonial, he had lost interest in stage appearances as early as 1961, and it was only due to Charlotte Moorman that he developed a new enthusiasm for the stage.[97] Paik met the classical cellist and organizer of the New York Avant Garde Festival in 1964. They struck up an immediate friendship, and after reading his manifesto 'Music History Needs His D. H. Lawrence,' she agreed to perform his 'Sex-Music', for which, until then, he had not found an interpreter.[98] Their first joint concert was *Variations on a Theme by Saint-Saëns* (1964), in which Moorman wore a transparent garment and played, with Paik at the piano, what initially sounded like a classical interpretation of 'Le Cygne'. In the middle of the piece she suddenly stopped, climbed up a stepladder and jumped into a barrel of water. She then returned, dripping wet, and completed the composition. In *Robot Opera* (1964), Moorman sat on a 'human chair' and played her cello while Robot K456, built and operated by Paik, strutted on stage, defecated beans and blasted out unusual sounds from his twenty radio and ten tape channels. John Cage's *26'1.1499''* (1965) was an action piece with Moorman blowing a whistle, smashing a bottle with a hammer, bursting a balloon, playing with a cymbal and a buzzer, frying an egg on a hotplate, etc. and occasionally slapping Paik's face and using him, semi-nude kneeling in front of her, as a human cello. *Sonata no. 1 for Adults Only* (1965) had Moorman taking off her garments behind a screen on which a film by Robert Breer was projected, and intermittently playing sections of Bach's third cello suite. *Opera sextronique* (1967) was performed by Moorman in a formal gown skirt and an 'electric bikini top' made of triangles and flashing six-volt light bulbs. The first part consisted of Paik's *Variations on Massenet's Élégie*, played together with Paik at the piano. The second part (Paik's *Variations on Brahm's Lullaby*) showed Moorman topless with a gas mask and a battery-driven propeller attached to her nipples. In the last part, which was not played at the première in New York owing to police intervention, she intended to produce an unusual barrage of sounds and noises by sawing an amplified bomb shell to pieces. *TV Bra for Living Sculpture* (1969) was a pun on the clichéd 'Boob-Tube' and a reference to television functioning as a parent substitute and nutrient akin to mother's milk. As Moorman was playing the cello, the sounds of her instrument triggered a variety of images on tiny monitors covering her breasts. *Peace Sonata* (originally *Sonata opus 69*, 1966; then renamed *Military Piece* and *New Piece for Charlotte*, 1970) had Moorman in combat gear crawling onto the stage with a cello strapped to her back. Originally, the work had been written to be performed in public squares next to a war memorial, but in the late 1960s she turned it into a protest piece against the Vietnam War. In *Concerto for TV – Cello and Video Tape* (1971), the entrails of a TV monitor were extracted from the casing and put into a plexiglass cello. The sounds of the instrument were transformed into electronic signals that interacted with images on the cello. *TV Bed* (1972) was created for a performance at The Kitchen in New York and consisted of ten monitors fitted into a bed frame, playing pre-recorded and live television broadcasts. It allowed Moorman, who was recovering from an operation, to play her cello in a reclining position.

The artistic collaboration between these two highly skilled classical musicians in a series of actions (the above list is far from complete[99]) performed at dozens of festivals and on tours around the world, was a sustained effort to examine the role of the human body in musical performance. It was a rare attempt at integrating sex and music and focusing the audience's mind on the erotics of musical performance. As Paik wrote in the programme to *Opera sextronique*:

> After three emancipations in 20th century music (serial-indeterministic, actional) ...
> I have found that there is still one more chain to lose ... that is ... pre-Freudian hypocrisy.
> Why is sex a predominant theme in art and literature prohibited ONLY in music?

Charlotte Moorman was a leading figure of the New York avant-garde scene and organizer of fifteen editions of the New York Avant Garde Festival between 1963 and 1980. As a musician she also collaborated with other composers (Jim McWilliams, Takehisa Kosugi, Mieko Shiomi, Yoko Ono), but with Paik she created a body of works that became emblematic of the mixing of avant-garde music and performance art. 'Moorman, the topless cellist' became an iconic image of the experimental art scene of the 1960s and was no doubt an important factor in popularizing Nam June Paik's work. Moorman was not only a star interpreter of Paik's compositions, but also an active collaborator and trusted medium who conveyed their joint message to the world. Their performances – which cost Moorman her position as cellist with Stokowski's American Symphony Orchestra – offered a mixture of straight-faced seriousness, cheeky humour and parody of the ossified codes of conduct in concerts of classical music. The sensationalism of some of their performances was intentional, as was their entertainment value. Paik and Moorman undermined the High Art traditions not only in music but also in the fine arts, and made Fluxus and Happening as well as experimental music accessible to people with only a casual interest in these art forms. Although feminist critics objected to Paik's use of nudity because this subjected a woman's body to a voyeuristic gaze, others interpreted it as subverting bourgeois morality and serving as a means of undermining US obscenity laws (in fact, they were subsequently rebuked, at least partially because of a court case brought against Moorman). To Moorman, the abolition of concert rituals was an issue for which she risked her career and reputation as a classical musician, and to Paik the eroticism in the works was successful 'because Charlotte did it. If any other lady cellist did it, it would have been just a gimmick.'[100]

Conceptual Performances by Robert Filliou and Ben Vautier

Robert Filliou was one of the most elusive Fluxus artists, in both a literal and a figurative sense. Although he participated in many Flux festivals, he never fully subscribed to any artistic dogma:

> I have never joined any group. I dislike -isms. In art, in life I reject theories. Manifestos bore me. The spirit in which things are done interests me. So, in so far as what I read in Fluxus did exist in Fluxus, Fluxus is the sort of non-group I've felt closest to, while keeping my own counsel and independence.[101]

Filliou shunned both traditional and modern performance genres and pushed Fluxus into the direction of purely conceptual art. Faced with a marketing system that judged art and the artist by their commodity value, Filliou refused his collaboration and treated everyone as a genius who only has to discover his or her creative potential: 'To be a man or a woman is to be a genius, but most people forget it (they're too busy exploiting their talents).'[102] Filliou regarded himself as an 'arteur' and sought to provide people with a key to unlock[103] their hidden genius and to provide them with the secret of the 'Permanent Creation'. His 'art' was in the first instance a source of energy and provocation. His activities consisted of small and unusual gestures, which encouraged spectators to establish connections between seemingly unrelated elements of reality and to react to them according to their own desires. Performances were carried out with utmost simplicity, and instead of imposing any fixed ideas or structures on the audience they only pointed out the direction of *possibilities*.

Playfulness (*ludisme*) as a lifestyle forced Filliou to become a 'man of the theatre outside the theatre'. One of his key principles was: 'I hate work which is not play'. His *République Géniale* became the imaginary territory of his research aimed at 'liberating the child in us'.[104] Although his performances were informed by a sophisticated theory, they were never didactic or simply illustrations of his aesthetic concepts. The element of chance and improvisation prevented them from becoming mere realizations of preconceived scenarios. He relished the visual and sense-bound side of theatre and wrote several plays for it.[105]

From January 1962 onwards, Filliou roamed the streets with his *Galerie légitime*, an art gallery contained in a cap, later on in a bowler hat. He offered passers-by small artworks for a few francs or a drink. Some of the works on sale consisted of simple questions, such as: 'What do you do if you have meat but no teeth?' 'What do you do if you are afraid of death but have also no fun in life?' 'What do you do if you are happy with the colour of your skin, but still preferred it were different?'

On 8 February 1965 at the Café A Go Go in New York, Filliou and Alison Knowles performed *The Ideal Filliou*. While Knowles recited from *Yes*, a text by Filliou, he sat on a chair, cross-legged, emotionless and silent. Then he stood up, read out another of his compositions and returned to his former position. At the same time, Philip Corner improvised an almost silent piece of music. This continued until the audience had left the hall.[106] At the Festival of Misfits at Gallery One in London (23 October to 8 November 1962) he performed a 'roulette poem'. He attached a bicycle wheel to a board on which the words of the poem were written. He then moved the wheel as one would a roulette wheel, and read out the poem as determined by a pointer on the wheel. As a variation, the audience was placed in charge of moving the wheel and had to carry out instructions given to them by the poem.

The principle of chance and audience participation ran through much of Filliou's œuvre and was complemented by another type of work, which he called 'No-Art'. For example, his *No-Play* of 1964 begins: 'This is a play nobody must come and see. That is, the not-coming of anyone makes the play.' He explained the concept behind this in an interview with Klaus Liebig[107]: from the point of view of Permanent Creation it is of equal value whether something is well made, badly made, or not made (*bien fait, mal fait, pas fait*). The essential task of an artist is to make the tools of creativity, spontaneity and inventiveness available to others. Art is 'a form of organization of leisure'[108] and an expression of a practical attitude to the world, where art becomes part of the texture of life. Art has value in itself. According to his 'Principle of Equivalence', it does not matter whether it is well made (like industrial production or art created for a market) or badly made (like Filliou's works). From the concept of the badly made he then progressed to the concept of the not-made, consciously avoiding this being mistaken for anti-art: 'The absolute secret of permanent creation is not wanting, not deciding, not choosing, aware of self, wide awake, sitting quietly, doing nothing.'[109] (It is worthwhile mentioning that Filliou was a Zen Buddhist and ended his life in a monastery.)

Filliou's performances shared many characteristics with the works of Ben Vautier, which had a similar conceptual basis and were also badly documented (excepting his activities at Fluxus festivals). Unable to offer any detailed analysis of Vautier's performances, I shall at least outline his art theory and comment on some of the scripts and scenarios published in the 1960s.

Vautier concerned himself with the creation of a post-Dadaist and, in particular, a post-Duchampian art. Finding new forms of expression that went beyond Dada aesthetics and ideology forced Vautier into re-examining the formula Art = Life and finding new proofs that met the conditions of a postmodern culture. Vautier applied himself to the history of artistic development, since Duchamp's Bottle Rack admitted that he had not found a solution for post-Dadaist art. When all forms of activity can be called art, no further development can be expected on a formal level. He therefore saw his task as 'investigating the status of the artist and, more exactly, the mechanism of the creative act'.[110] Vautier's work was primarily concerned with a fundamental questioning of the art market, the role of the artist, the revalorization of simple and common activities as art. His work relied on thoughts and words, as for example in a show at the Galerie Daniel Templon in Paris (1970), where he exhibited a large wooden chest on which was written: 'The reason I am in this box and that I am not eating is that everybody is eating and nobody is in a box – but when I think it over twice I think the whole thing is nonsense so I shall go to sleep. Ben.' He communicated his 'work in progress' not through objects (sculpture, painting etc.), but through linguistic and physical gestures. He placed himself at the centre of his works. This was not an attempt to put himself into the limelight but to express doubt. 'To change art – destroy ego' was the key phrase in his œuvre. Other, related ones, were:

Ben doute de tout. [Ben doubts everything.]

Prise de possession du tout. [Taking possession of everything.]

Art = Ben. Art Total. [Art = Ben. Total Art.]

Ben = Rien. Ben = Tout. [Ben = Nothing. Ben = Everything.]

Théâtre d'Art Total: Regardez moi. Cela suffit. [Total Art Theatre: Look at me. That's enough.]

L'Art Total est d'abandonner l'Art. [Total Art means abandoning Art.]

J'ai honte d'être artiste. [I feel ashamed being an artist.]

By exhibiting his ego and making it the centre of his 'exhibitions' he raised questions about the category of the 'artist' and the demarcation line between the two assumed classes of human beings: artists and non-artists, hence the banality of much of his work. To exhibit a banderole in the street saying 'yesterday, 12.30, i ate a hard-boiled egg' has nothing to do with aesthetics, but concerns the ideology of art and the criteria that determine the social role of an artist. By exhibiting himself, his doubts, his convictions, his problems with his position as an artist/non-artist, Vautier provoked more questions than he could possibly answer.

Ben Vautier declared himself to be influenced by the performance works of Dadaists and Surrealists, John Cage, the Gutai group and the Theatre of the Absurd.[111] But his dematerialization of the most immaterial art form, performance, went a stage further than that attempted by his predecessors. In his 'Zen Happening "Réalité" ' of 27 January 1964, the totality of everyday activities carried out by himself and a group of Fluxus friends (Brecht, Paik, Patterson) on the stage of the Théâtre Artistique in Nice was exhibited as a 'Total Theatre' performance. In a manifesto of April 1966, *Le Happening de Ben*,[112] Vautier distinguished between two types of Happenings: one that aims at a transformation of reality, the other at presenting reality through means taken from that reality. He saw himself operating in the latter category, where life is represented by simple and real actions that create an awareness of the fact that reality in all its aspects is a form of spectacle. This is why 'EVERYTHING IS ART and ART IS LIFE'. But this fact still needs to be communicated through the personality of the artist:

Art is not life per se, but life as communicated by X. . . . My happenings are concerned with communicating this claim. It is only possible within one frame: the acceptance of all reality. Its realization exists through my claim, which conditions and guarantees the reality which, whatever it may be, I communicate and authenticize through my signature.

In the course of the 1960s, Vautier's actions became more and more conceptual. For example, at the 1966 Venice Biennale he performed *in absentia* and explained to his audience at the French pavilion on a large poster:

> **400 miles from Venice**
> In Nice
> 32, Road Tondutti-de-l'Escarène
> From the 18th of June 1966
> During the Biennale of Venise
> BEN SHALL LIVE AS USUAL
> Everyday
> He will inscribe in a Fluxus copybook
> Unimportant and important details
> of the day
> At the end of the Biennale of Venise
> this copybook
> signed and dated
> Will represent
> EVERYDAY LIFE
> Ben's contribution to the Biennale of Venise 1966.

On 16 June 1966 he presented *Nobody*, a piece for which he sent out invitations that informed the potential audience that 'the curtain will rise precisely at 21.30 and close at precisely 22.30. Absolutely nobody will be allowed to witness the performance.' A photograph of the production shows Vautier and a group of ten friends sitting around a table on the stage. To the left of the proscenium arch on a chair stands a large placard saying *Personnne*. The rows of seats in the auditorium are empty.[113]

In its final consequence, Fluxus was the outcome of a dematerialization of art, largely inspired by the dematerialization of reality in a media-drenched information society. The ephemeral, fragmented and frenzied flow of images in postmodern mass communication forced artists to reassess the concept of realism and to direct our attention to the very foundations of our conceptual and epistemic apparatus. An artistic practice that focused on reality as a process rather than a fixed object had to confront the technical means and production mechanisms of our electronically based culture. This is where the media arts of the 1970s and 1980s, discussed in Chapters 6 and 7, came into existence as a kind of natural outgrowth of the experimental performances of 1960s Happening and Fluxus.

5

Body Art, Ritualism and Neo-Shamanic Performances

Corporeal Identities in a Postmodern Age

A comprehensive survey of Body Art would need to begin with a discussion of body-centred performance traditions in pre-modern and popular cultures (dance, mime, acrobatics, martial arts, freak shows, medical displays, striptease, etc.). In this chapter, however, I shall concern myself exclusively with recent avant-garde practices. But before doing so, we need to remind ourselves of some of the Modernist experiments which, to some degree, determined the forms of expression chosen by Body Artists in the 1970s and 1980s, and also informed the practitioners discussed in the following pages.

In the early twentieth century, artists began to take a serious interest in the performing body irrespective of its narrative or theatrical framework. Voice, gesture and movement came to be used not only as means of conveying story lines, dramatic conflicts and intellectual concepts, but also as scenic elements with a visceral quality in their own right. Modernist directors discovered the actor's physical means of expression and combined these with other scenic elements such as sound, lighting, costumes, stage sets, etc. For example, the Expressionists employed the body as a seismograph for psychic states and created extremely stylized, physically heightened renderings of mental processes that went far beyond conventional acting; the Futurists extolled 'body madness' (*fisicofollia*) and chose circus, music-hall, cabaret and Variety as models for their theatre; the Dadaists were fascinated by primitivism in its indigenous and foreign forms and made it a cornerstone of their performance aesthetic; the Constructivists analysed the anatomical laws of the human body, combined them with the abstract elements of space, colour, form, sound etc. and developed, from these basic components, a 'new ABC and grammar' of the stage.

In the postwar period, Abstract Expressionism reassessed the body in relation to the works of art created by it. In Pollock's Action Paintings, the artist physicalized an emotional energy and embodied himself in his work. Painting became the result of a drama involving mind and body and served as a highly condensed reminder of a creative act or situation where art and life were fused into one. Georges Mathieu went a stage further by staging live paint actions, and the Gutai group shifted the emphasis entirely from product to process by destroying the objects immediately after their creation (see Chapter 4). Other examples of the 1950s that pointed towards a revaluation of the artist's body in the creative process were Kazuo Shiraga's wrestling with clay in *Challenging Mud*, Yves Klein using human brushes in his *Anthropometries*, and Piero Manzoni's signing human bodies as works of art. Also, the Happening artists in the 1960s brought the performer into close physical contact with material reality, often to the point of 'ending up as dirty as a bunch of scabby dogs', as one of them said.[1] From among the Fluxus performances, where the body was placed at the centre of the creative act, one could mention Shigeko Kubota's *Vagina Painting* or Nam June Paik's *Zen for Head*.

The examples cited here indicate that in postwar avant-garde performance the body assumed a function that was clearly different from traditional theatre. However, within the wider spectrum of Modernist and postmodern art and its decidedly intellectual, formalist and purist bias, these experiments were an exception rather than a rule. Abstractionism, Conceptualism, Minimalism, Optical and Kinetic Art, etc. continued to divorce art from the primary qualities of life and thereby caused a reaction, which became generally known as Body Art. It emerged in the mid-1960s, largely transformed itself in the early 1980s into 'performance art' and 'physical theatre', but continued to be practised by a significant number of artists until the 1990s.[2]

The mid-1960s was a period of great political upheavals and social change, both in the USA and in Europe. It found its most visible manifestations in the 1968 revolt and the mass demonstrations against the Vietnam War, the Women's Liberation movement, civil rights campaigns, Black Panther activism, and so on. This political counter-culture was closely related to the 'sexual revolution', the emancipation of the individual from social repression and conformity, the liberalization of the laws on censorship etc. Re-embodying what in previous centuries had been disembodied was as much a response to the repression of the body in Christian societies as it was to the dominance of rationalist, intellectual discourses in Western culture as a whole. Exploring corporeal existence and the semantics of the body could take a variety of forms, ranging from questioning and disrupting social norms pertaining to body expression, to 'repressive desublimation' (Marcuse) of physical desire in commercial pornography.

The subject matter of Body Art was not the biological organism described in medical textbooks, but the body as a site of social inscription. 'The artists who started to "unfold" their bodies in public . . . aimed at peeling off the sedimented layers of signification with which the body, their body, was historically and culturally coated.'[3] Performances focused on racial difference and placed the discriminated, non-normative body in a historical context of colonialism, Orientalism, racialist ethnography, and so on. This gave rise to the innovative and radical work of artists such as Coco Fusco, Guillermo Gómez-Peña, and Adrian Piper. Others directed their attention to the topic of sexual identity and demonstrated the political nature of their most private life sphere. As in most political theatre of the period, these performers tended to emphasize the content of their message rather than the means of presentation, and consequently fell into the category of 'radical theatre' rather than Body Art. Of course, there were exceptions to this rule, particularly amongst women performers, who sought to problematize the whole complex of representation in Western art, theatre and mass media. Feminist performance artists and Body Artists drew attention to the female body as an object to be looked at; they stripped off the layers of cultural inscriptions and deconstructed the gendered sign 'woman' in the traditional representational framework. They sought to discover an essentialist female core under the deformations of patriarchal culture and explored ways of empowering women as creative subjects speaking with their very own voice.

Closely related to this search for a female identity was a theoretical debate about the complex question of what constitutes the female self and how it relates to the multifaceted personas created in everyday social intercourse. Feminists questioned the concept of selfhood as a biological entity expounded in the phenomenological tradition of Merleau-Ponty (the body as the last refuge of lived experience) and sided with Lévi-Strauss, who considered the body a surface for social inscription. Others regarded the self as a metaphysical construct or as a psycho-social product capable of being contested and signified in a variety of manners. Whatever the theoretical position, the body as a cultural artefact or an object of psycho-social narratives could best be demonstrated in the medium of performance. Here, the artist could 're-present' herself in a self-determined subject position and reveal both the process of inscription and ways of resisting oppressive social codes. This way, performances were expected to stimulate a healing process in actor and audience alike.

From criticizing the commodification of the female body and deconstructing its representational framework, artists proceeded to develop new artistic forms of expression. Some feminists believed that the liberation of women would need to go hand in hand with exploring the locus of difference, i.e. the female body and her sexuality. 'Writing the female body', as Cixous called it, became a prime concern of many women artists of the 1970s. Feminist Body Art challenged the conventional ways of displaying the female body in a fixed, pictorial frame or behind the proscenium arch. Placing the performer in a traditional representational nexus and then letting the displayed object take over subject functions produced a contradictory union of active and passive positions. Such ambiguity questioned the traditional apparatus of signification and representation. By foregrounding gender-specific behaviour and social expectations, feminist Body Artists unmasked the cultural construction of gender, subverted the culturally imposed mechanisms of the 'male gaze' and pointed out to what extent the sign 'woman' had become removed from the actual referent <woman> in her essentialist qualities. Eventually, these performers transformed the female body from object to subject, and developed a new imagery based on female experience rather than male desire.

By the mid-1970s, feminism had become firmly established as a liberating force in most Western countries. Women's Centres had been established in every major city, women's projects had developed new communication networks, and long-standing women's groups had fostered an atmosphere of sisterhood and intimate camaraderie. New areas of investigation emerged and new trends in feminist performance art could be observed. After a decade of being primarily concerned with power politics in a patriarchal society and the construction of gender and sexual difference, the matrix of female sexuality took a centre-stage position. The female body was reclaimed as a source of pleasure. The prudery and sexual phobias of past decades had been overcome and the female body could be re-presented to a sympathetic female audience. No longer objectified by male writers and directors, the female performer exposed, demystified, rehabilitated and reintegrated her body while inviting the spectators to see themselves mirrored in the spectacle on stage. The often explicit scenes celebrated female sexuality and the beauty of the flesh. To see and experience women's bodies from a female perspective and to discover a new, a *female*, discourse of the body, turned out to be a second liberation for many women.

It also transpired from these performances that the rather Manichaean world view of 'woman as victim – man as oppressor' no longer sufficed to explain the complexities of psycho-social and psycho-sexual behaviour. It is probably significant that by that time another age group of feminists – daughters and heirs of the first generation of 'women's libbers' – had come to the fore. They discovered that many feminist artists, after going through a phase of celebrating the body as spectacle, had ended up with a new form of idealization of the female body. Such gynocentric mythology bore little relation to the way they had experienced life – in fact it began to stand in their way when they sought to explore the multifaceted and often contradictory emotional and social condition of the female psyche. Obviously, the feminist movement had created its own taboo areas, which needed to be pulled down, too.

A new generation of radical, avant-garde performance artists began to explore the repressed, the unmentionable, the censored areas of female sexuality. Instead of celebrating the pleasurable aspects of the female body they entered into dangerous, paradoxical, bewildering realms, and they did so at great personal risk. Many performances proved to be painful and exhausting in the extreme. The fact that pain, rather than pleasure, had been a determining factor in the formation of a woman's identity explains why so many performance artists – including those discussed below – have employed this as an expressive element in their art. But when fellow feminists, shocked and disturbed by what they saw on stage, stormed out of the hall, or when the feminist press questioned the legitimacy of the performances, then the artists realized how political the personal really was.

The 1960s 'Hippie' culture had instigated a revolt of the instincts, a transgression of taboos and a liberation of repressed sexuality. This search for a more authentic existence had led many people to experiment with cathartic and therapeutic rituals and to explore those aspects of the psyche that were commonly repressed in Judaeo-Christian societies. The crisis of the subject in advanced industrial or post-industrial societies (see above, Chapter 3) and the alienation of the mind from the body was explored in these circles by means of performances that were closely related to the Body Art described above. Jorge Glusberg summed up some of these works carried out by both male and female artists: 'It is probable that one of the principal motives behind Body Art and Body Performances is a return to an organic nature, not as an idyllic atmosphere but through dramatic lacerations of the world in which we live.'[4]

The quest for an authentic and essentialist experience of the self led many performers to the study of ancient trance techniques, magic rites and healing ceremonies. Inspired by the books of Claude Lévi-Strauss and Mircea Eliade, or Castaneda's imaginative account of the teachings of a supposedly indigenous Mexican shaman, they sought to resuscitate a defunct shamanism and to rediscover the mystery cults of a by-gone era. Having grown tired of traditional religion in Western society, they sought to re-establish contact with the sacred realm by means of new rituals suited to 'the Age of Aquarius'. For many female artists this meant a reclaiming of the tradition of the female shaman, the revival of ancient goddess cults and the propagation of an ecological feminism that integrated the female body again into the natural environment. Male artists who shared their concerns, rejected the exploitative, mechanistic ('male') attitude towards the physical world and demonstrated the dependence of the biological body and of the body politic on Nature. Many of these artists, male and female, were solo performers; but there were also small groups who fled from the urban jungle into rural environments and experimented there with new forms of communality and ritual performances.[5] However, the majority of artists discussed or referred to in this chapter worked in isolation from each other, often assuming the role of a prophet in their community and propagating a 'return to the future' as the only way to save humankind.

This eco-spiritualist avant-garde offered an interesting parallel to the primitivist avant-garde at the beginning of the century, as both were using ancient rituals as countermeasures to the detrimental effects of modernity and the cerebral aspects of modern culture. Another branch of this community, whom anthropologists and social scientists refer to as 'Modern Primitives',[6] was also having an effect on Body Art. Some members of these groups used their skin as a canvas for tattoos or artificial scars; others pierced their lips, tongues, nipples, genitals etc. to carry ornaments and heighten their physical, erotic experience of the body. Much of this behaviour has been interpreted as a measure to counteract the forces of a desensitized environment; but it could also be seen as a means of inscribing corporeal subjectivity and identity. Manipulation, modification and ritual subjection of the body to physical pain was also a typical trait of Sado-Masochist activism, which during this period went increasingly public by means of mass-circulation magazines and widely advertised club events. However, presentations given at 'Slave-Balls' and 'Skin-II-Parties' tended to be private rituals enacted for the pleasure of the performers and, as such, differed in intention from performances by, say, Ron Athey, Franko B, Bob Flanagan, or Paul McCarthy, which were designed to raise consciousness and represent physical experiences for the benefit of the spiritual enrichment of the viewers.

The physical culture of the 1980s with its narcissistic and fetishistic 'Body-beautiful' ideology caused some artists to specialize in parodistic appropriations of imagery that had become ubiquitous in commercial television and in the popular press. Usually avoiding live performances, they employed photography as a means of presenting and deconstructing the glamourized body in the commercial cinema and in fashion magazines (e.g. Urs Lüthy, Yayoi Kusama and Cindy Sherman). Others, such as Orlan, enacted male-defined notions of idealized beauty; she communicated her works (e.g. her 'surgical performances') by means of video. The rise of digital media in the 1990s caused Body Artists such as Stelarc, who previously had performed spectacular body suspensions in galleries and outdoor venues, to execute their works in cyberspace. The dematerialized but not at all disembodied human being became (and still is) a major topic of debate in books and journals dedicated to the new electronic culture, which I shall discuss below in Chapter 6.

In view of the wide range of artistic trends summarized above, it is understandable that there never existed a uniform and homogeneous Body Art movement, but only a multifaceted conglomeration of artists with widely diverging aims and strategies. They never set up any organizational ties, issued any group manifestos, or appeared in public as a group (unless they were brought together by the curator of an exhibition or festival). Nevertheless, one can discern certain themes and approaches that were shared by many of them, as listed in Box 5.1.

BOX 5.1: SOME COMMON THEMES AND APPROACHES IN BODY ART

- Emphasis on the body's materiality, physicality, vitality, sensuality.

- Use of the body not as a medium to represent stories or fictitious characters, but to reveal the artist in the first person, as a physical–mental being.

- Focus on visceral experiences that are relayed to the audience in a manner that makes its members accomplices rather than distanced observers.

- Essentialist concerns with the body as a vessel of authenticity, truth, identity and selfhood.

- Deconstruction of the body as a site of social inscription.

- Feminist concerns with representations of the gendered body.

- Representation of transforming experiences of great emotional intensity and physical resonance.

- Focus on autobiographical, private, intimate, secret aspects of the self, leading to revelations of hidden desires and painful memories, or to the recovery of moments of great physical pleasure.

The role of the body in the performances discussed below could be very different depending on whether the artist was male or female: 'While male body artists from this period tended to project themselves outward, *acting on* other participants and audience members as if to prove their self-suffi-ciency as subjects, their female colleagues tended to explore their imma-nence, their contingency on others.'[7] In this chapter I have chosen artists belonging to either camp. My focus is predominantly on the 1970s and on artists working as live performers. However, as other media are also of rele-vance to our discussion here, I should like to refer the reader to some of the video artists discussed in Chapter 6, and to performances in cyberspace, analysed in Chapter 7.

Readers will notice that in this chapter I have given preference to work by female rather than male artists. This is not intended to deprecate the work of, say, Chris Burden, Dennis Oppenheim, or Paul McCarthy, but rather to highlight the fact that in this period some of the most important contribu-tions were made by women artists. As it happened, Body Art was also prac-tised by many second- and third-rate artists, whose derivative, self-indulgent and shallow creations could give the whole genre a bad name. Because Body Art, and Performance Art in general, did not demand professional skills, as required, for example, for circus acts or stand-up comedy, people could get away with a great deal of half-baked ideas and underdeveloped presenta-tions. As Marina Abramović once scathingly remarked: 'All the bad performers became the bad painters of the early '80s. It was incredible how many bad performances there were in the '70s.'[8]

When leafing through festival programmes and collective volumes of the period, one is struck by the profusion of names that have gracefully fallen into oblivion. But also, and much in contrast to the Modernist period, one cannot fail to notice the large number of women artists. Performance Art opened up a great chance to express concerns for which theatre and the fine arts had not previously offered many opportunities. Much of this work grew out of the women's movement and served many useful functions in the cultural life of the period. But like all political art that seeks to make an immediate impact, this work tended to lose its relevance very soon after its creation. The women I have chosen for discussion in this chapter clearly formed an exception. The issues they explored had more than just short-lived significance. They engaged with profound problems in a complex, serious and extremely dedicated manner. They expanded the boundaries of theatrical expression and developed truly novel ways of addressing aspects of human life with universal significance. Audiences rarely failed to be touched by their performances, and their impact still reverberates in the mythologies later embroidered around them.

Carolee Schneemann

The Happening movement of the 1960s stimulated new departures in post-war art and caused scores of painters and sculptors to introduce the dimension of time into their works. This move from the fine arts into the direction of the performing arts challenged the pictorial system of representation, but not many Happeners foregrounded their own body to any significant degree. This role fell to Carolee Schneemann, who like her male colleagues had developed 'a resistance to the conceptual deadening, the disappearance of the body' in Late-Modernist art. Experiencing 'a sensory submersion in the materiality of the process of work' had given her 'a concern for the vitality of material being taken through the self and back into space'.[9] But because of her female identity she was much more attuned to the complex issues that were at stake in the processes of visual representation of the body. In the early 1960s she became a pioneer of what was later called Body Art and Autoperformance. Since then, scores of artists have turned themselves into vehicles of their art and made their autobiographical experiences the subject of their creations. But Schneemann's historic role in this development has constantly been underestimated by male scholars and downplayed by feminist critics.[10]

Schneemann began her career as a painter in the late 1950s, working rather derivatively in an Abstract Expressionist mould. Like many artists in the early 1960s, she left easel and studio behind and moved into Happenings territory. She worked with Dick Higgins and Philip Corner on *Environment for Sound and Motion* (1962 at the Living Theatre), choreographed several pieces for the Judson dance group, became a performer in Claes Oldenburg's *Store Days* (1962), Wolf Vostell's *You* (1964) and Robert Morris's *Site* (1964), and participated in various Fluxus events in New York. Out of her involvement with the New York avant-garde scene emerged her first major installation piece, *Eye Body* (1963), where she incorporated her paint-smeared body, festooned with snakes and ropes, into a messy loft filled with broken glass, motorized umbrellas and a variety of painted panels and objects. She employed her body as material to complement the tactile sensations of her environment and undertook a series of physical transformations inspired by her study of ancient goddess cults. This private performance was communicated to the outside world by means of photographs, which showed her nude body 'as a primal, archaic force which could unify energies' and explore 'the image values of flesh as material . . . marked, written over in a text of stroke and gesture'. The title *Eye Body* indicated an intimate connection between vision and corporeal existence; the eye was for Schneemann a muscle that guides the body and directs the explorations of the mind: 'The body is in the eye; sensations received visually take hold in the total organism. Perception moves the total personality to excitation.'[11]

Schneemann's use of nudity was a political act that rejected the terms by which her body had been used in Happenings by her male colleagues. She sought to transform the object character of previous corporeal representations and determine herself how her body would be viewed, thereby subjecting the spectacle to her 'creative female will' and giving it 'personal integrity'.[12] Dan Cameron, curator of a recent exhibition of Schneemann's work, commented on her work of this period:

> Schneemann's art is probably the most consistent in terms of her focusing her performance persona in such a way that the act of being exposed to the world (and vice versa) never failed to be understood as a highly charged seizing of disputed territory. It was an outrageous act of public eroticism that not only reversed the gender-based hierarchies of representation, but actually challenged the historical dynamic of possession and control between the artist and (her) subject.[13]

Schneemann established her international reputation with *Meat Joy* (see Illustration 11) first performed in Paris in May 1964, during Lebel's Festival de la Libre Expression, and then repeated in London and New York. The work possessed an orgiastic quality that was rare to find in the performing arts of the period, and bore more of a resemblance to an erotic ritual than to a choreographed performance piece. Schneemann's 'celebration of flesh as material'[14] involved nine performers in a largely improvised encounter game rife with polymorphous eroticism, raw fish, chickens, cakes, strings of sausages, buckets of paint, and lots of paper. The one-hour action vacillated between moments of tenderness and wild abandon, between scenes of comic, joyous and repellent character. The performers painted their bodies on stage and then formed a variety of group pictures (stars, wheels, flowers, crystals). When a Maid carried in a platter of meat, the actors improvised a series of interactions with the objects until they were all covered in foodstuffs. Finally, buckets of paint, brushes and sponges were brought in and everybody engaged in an exuberant paint orgy. The soundtrack (Rock 'n' Roll and Motown music, recorded traffic noise and market cries) and lighting cues (colourful washes with shafts of directional beams) determined the sequence of scenes, but within this predetermined and rehearsed order there was a great deal of improvisation. The character of a Serving Maid functioned as a stage manager, who would ensure that props and materials were available at the right moment, and would goad the action along when necessary.

11   Carolee Schneemann, *Meat Joy,* Festival de la Libre Expression, Paris, 1964

In 1964, Schneemann turned the sexual act into a key topic of her first film, *Fuses,* which since then has become a classic in the genre of women's erotic cinema. At the time, it caused a great deal of controversy, as it usurped a male privilege (determining the rules of production and representation in erotic movies). A year later, Schneemann participated in Charlotte Moorman's New York Avant Garde Festival. Together with Nam June Paik she directed *Push and Pull* (1965), a piece by Allan Kaprow which degenerated into chaos, damaged the theatre and ended with police intervention. *Ghost Rev* (1965) was an Expanded Cinema event, in which she and the dancer Phoebe Neville acted as projection surface for a film. In 1966, she explored the human body in relation to the natural environment with *Water Light/Water Needle.* It turned the visual and sensory experience of a Venice visit into 'aerial theatre', accompanied by the music of Philip Corner, Bach and Vivaldi. Other pieces of the late 1960s focused on the Vietnam War, using images of the abused and maimed body to heighten people's awareness of the slaughter and destruction wreaked by the US army.

Up to and Including her Limits developed over a long period of time following Schneemann's return to the USA after a long sojourn in Europe.

Its first version, of 1973, was called *Tracking*, and after seven intermediate stages it became an installation at the Basle Art Fair in 1976. It evoked the gestural sweep of her early Abstract Expressionism and drew heavily on the suspension elements in *Water Light / Water Needle*, but was more private and meditative in quality, lacking form and avoiding contact with an audience. She suspended herself from the ceiling by means of a rope-and-pulley system, which allowed body movements by means of tensing and relaxation of the muscles. As she swung through the room, she created a web of automatic drawings through her markings and signs on the walls and floor. As she lived in the space throughout the day of the performance, there was no urgency to hurry through a script or scenario. Audiences wandered in and out, looked at her, or her drawings, or at a projected film starring her cat, or listened to the soundtrack. There was also a reading corner, where people could sit down and study texts she had written. Several video monitors and slide projectors showed images of Schneemann's previous performances. The artist herself lived in a kind of trance caused by the anti-gravitational state of suspension. To her as a performer it did not matter whether there was an audience or not, as she had attuned herself to an inner sensitivity that allowed her to 'simply be (and enjoy) the freedom of the body shaping an environment'.[15]

Interior Scroll (1975) took many of her previous concerns to a radical conclusion and addressed the politics of intellectual authority. The performance grew out of a *Naked Action Lecture* she had given in 1968 at the ICA in London. In a second stage she thought of elaborating on the serpent imagery she had employed in *Eye Body*; then she began to incorporate prehistoric incisions on bones and stones, which may have measured time in units of menstrual cycles. In the final stage she chose the scroll as a medium for the preservation of knowledge – including knowledge of ancient goddess cultures and matriarchal forms of living. Relating corporeal experience and self-knowledge to a natural environment and cosmic scheme led her to the symbol of the uncoiling serpent as a representation of the transition from interior thought to external signification. The knowledge received from inside the body unfolds like a scroll into the outside world, where it can empower other women. The performance took place at a women's art festival in East Hampton and was announced as a reading from her book *Cézanne, She was a Great Painter*. The text Schneemann actually recited as she extracted the scroll from her vagina was 'about the abstraction of the female body and its loss of meanings'[16] in Western civilization. It also chastized an unnamed 'happy man / a structuralist filmmaker', who had censured the 'personal clutter' and 'persistence of feelings' in her work and who had induced in her a fear that her artistic creations might be buried and lost forever.[17] The powerful visual metaphors and their underlying feminist message will have been very clear to her audience of fellow artists. However, outside this original setting the photographs of the performance caused a stir, which Schneemann had not anticipated and which made her suspend any further body works.

Schneemann challenged accepted art practices of the mainstream, of the avant-garde and in the women's movement. She soon came to realize that people responded to her images of flesh and nude bodies with their emotional rather than intellectual faculties. This also applied to feminist critics, as Schneemann deplored in an interview with Robert Sklar.[18] Her work became marginalized, because 'it ran counter to prevailing feminist politics [and] because it didn't seem to constitute a critique of patriarchy. It had a little too much pleasure, a little too much (hetero)sexuality, and an uncompromising refusal on the part of the artist to justify herself to anyone.'[19] There was no-one in NewYork except Schneemann who practised Body Art at the time, and the only encouragement she received came from Yoko Ono, from some dancer friends, and from Happening colleagues in Europe. Therefore, it took nearly two decades before her work began to be appreciated for its historical significance.

Schneemann's performances explored the body as a source of emotive power and sought to redress the tradition that made women the object rather than the subject of creative activity. Adopting a male position of authority with regard to her own body and its visual representation was a revolutionary step not acceptable to the art world of the time: 'I was permitted to be an image / but not the image maker creating her own self image.'[20] The images she created came out of her inner self. She inhabited her pictures as a real person. Her autobiography and private life were not faded out or turned into a-personal 'representations' of the self ('inanimate objects with projections of our repressed vitality'[21]). Her work had to do with 'cutting through the idealized (mostly male) mythology of the "abstracted self" or the "invented self"'[22] and with finding an organic relationship between creativity and sexuality. As a person who had grown up in the countryside in close contact with Nature ('Animals were sexual creatures and I identified that part of my nature with them'[23]), she felt shocked by the repressive attitudes she was exposed to at school and art college. What she regarded as joyful and pleasurable, others classified as pornographic and obscene. Her interest of working with the material of her own body was considered narcissistic, trivial or self-indulgent, but she did not let this critique drive a breach between her creative and erotic energies. Studying Wilhelm Reich and Simone de Beauvoir reinforced her thinking and gave her a messianic desire to confront and eroticize the sex-guilty culture that surrounded her.

Her inspiration for this endeavour came predominantly from representations of sacred sexuality in prehistoric times and the early civilization of Crete, but also from studying the books on ancient matriarchies by Johann Jakob Bachofen, Jane Harrison, Robert Graves and Erich Neumann. Schneemann's interest in mythology, archetypal dream images and the collective subconscious gave her approach to sexuality psychological ramifications as well as deeply spiritual dimensions. Much of her work had a strongly ritualistic quality: 'It becomes ritualised so that the individual elements are all addressing something that's within it but also centred beyond it.'[24] Schneemann was far from being just an 'angry girl' or transgressive taboo-breaker. However, critics and curators of the time pushed her into a 'Dionysian cul-de-sac',[25] which blocked her recognition as a 'serious' artist, and her message – which contained 'more than meat joy' – went unheard for a long time. 'I made a gift of my body to other women,' she wrote in 1974.[26] It took until the 1990s before this gift was finally being accepted.

Vito Acconci

Acconci, who is generally considered the founding father of Body Art, appeared on the New York avant-garde scene some ten years after Carolee Schneemann. He began his career as a writer concerned with concrete poetry ('language pieces'), which treated the page as 'a model space, a performance area in miniature'[27] and employed words not for their referential functions but as 'a kind of analogue to minimalist sculpture'.[28] After a while he did not want to be locked into this mental space any longer, nor to confine himself to covering the surface of the page with words. He explored the possibilities for performing his poetry on the 'Beat' scene and at Happening events, but neither were to his liking. For a while he considered fine arts as an alternative to poetry, but as he wanted to communicate his concerns directly to the public, without going through an intermediary such as painting or sculpture, he turned himself into an 'agent' and shifted from the poetry of words to the poetry of the body, from writing to performing, from printed page to architectural space. His early 'activities' (he avoided the term 'performance' as it had too many theatrical connotations for him) were a stage further from the task-like Happening and Fluxus experiments of the 1960s. They employed a gestural language that was rooted in an everyday vernacular, similar to what he had seen at the Judson Church,[29] and bore more than a passing resemblance to Allan Kaprow's later performance work, which operated with 'ready-made' behaviour and developed into 'self-performances' that used the artist's physicality and autobiography as material.[30]

In the following years, Acconci pursued several strands of experimentation: live performances (often recorded and subsequently shown as film or video), video performances (live performances combined with instantly relayed images of the stage actions), and video installations (using video tapes specially made for an exhibition). One can observe in his œuvre a gradual shift from self-reflexive to relational work, which finally led him out of the art world into social spheres where he could become a 'useful' member of society engaged in environmental issues, architecture and urbanism. Although he himself often referred to these shifts of emphasis as 'phases', they did not happen in strictly consecutive order, and none of the strands was ever abandoned altogether.[31]

At a time when Concept Art was the dominant trend in the art world, Acconci's body-centred performances were also highly conceptual in orientation and engaged primarily with the material parameters of time and space: *Drawing a Line* (1969) marked out the space between two walls; *Performance Situation Using Walking, Different Levels, a Curtain, Opening, Closing* (1969) focused on the time used to draw a curtain; in *Trademarks* (1970) he bit various parts of his body and observed the bite marks disappearing, thereby 'marking' the passage of time; in *Second Hand* (1971) he performed a circular motion on stage with his eyes fixed on a large wall clock until he felt he had become one with the clock.

Working conceptually with performance in the above manner produced in Acconci a strong sense of isolation ('I want something else to occur but I know I am back in the old realm of thinking'[32]), which he problematized in *Private Property* (1971). He lay blindfolded on a bed with his legs tied together, unable to establish physical contact with the people around him; but his hands were left free to take notes and to photograph the activities that were going on around him. Similarly, *Memory Box* (1972) dealt with his unrealized potential for establishing a relationship with the outside world. He placed a box with a cassette player inside it into the dark, enclosed space of a gallery. Visitors had to kneel or lie on a mattress to hear messages such as 'I hate myself for hesitating every time I start to touch you. . . . I am acting, groping for a way to action . . . one of these ways might lead me to you. . . . Self-hate can close me up, box me up.'

Acconci, who considered himself a political artist,[33] wanted to overcome the system of production and distribution in the institutionalized art market and release his creations from the confinement of the gallery space. This gave rise to what he called 'relational work', starting with *Following Piece* (1969): 'Choosing a person at random, in the street, any location, any day. Following him wherever he goes, however long or far he travels. (The activity ends when he enters a private house – his home, office, etc.).' This and other performances created for the exhibition 'Street Works' at the Architectural League in New York[34] led him into

> a world that was far beyond gallery walls, outside of museums. How could systems based so much on closure, based on museum as kind of fortress and on gallery as store, deal with this? This art was something that couldn't be adaptable to a store. There was nothing to buy.[35]

In a subsequent stage, after following and observing other people, Acconci wanted to 'step out of myself, view myself from above, as an observer of my behavior'.[36] Reading R. D. Laing's writings on the divided self inspired him to devise a number of performances in which he presented his body as an instrument to be 'acted' upon. This shift from a centred and unified to a decentred and fragmented subject made him an influential exponent of postmodernism.

> I started to think of art as a situation of experiencing, rather than as an object. . . . If I was thinking of these pieces as occasions where I concentrate on myself, the obvious question was how do I prove that I am concentrating on myself? One obvious way was to do something physical to myself, apply something physical to myself. So the pieces in 1970 started to involve applying some kind of stress to my own person, my body.[37]

He subjected his body to a variety of treatments, ranging from the marking pieces mentioned above and *Rubbing Piece* (1970), where he scuffed his forearm for as long as it required to produce a sore, to the attempted body modifications in *Conversions* (see below) or pieces like *Runoff* (1970), where he ran for two hours and then leaned his sweaty body against a wall, creating marks on wall and body, or *Waterways* (1971), where he filled his mouth with saliva until he could not contain it any longer and had to spit it out. He also engaged in personal rituals that allowed him to enter into a dialogue with parts of himself, as in *Trappings* (1971), where he lived in the closed space of a gallery: 'I have only myself to work with – turn in on myself – I'm dividing myself into two – turn my penis into another person.'

Acconci's early performances concentrated on the body as a source of identity and, through its dependency on other human beings, as the origin of social existence. He showed how the self fashions itself and at the same time is constructed by outside forces. By objectifying the body and making it a focus of observation, Acconci addressed this social construction of identity, especially male identity and its relation to the female 'other'. He employed a number of self-reflexive exercises to reveal how we fashion ourselves (our 'selves') by identifying with the way other people perceive us. Although these performances were presented to an audience, spectators had little opportunity to be an active partner in an exchange. Because of their solipsistic nature, these works were as much a theatre of the mind as his early literary compositions. He therefore arrived at the conclusion: 'If I am concentrating on my own person, I'm making a closed circle around myself. The viewer really has no way in. . . . So obviously something had to change. It couldn't just be I in relation to me, it had to be I in relation to you, the viewer.'[38] One line of experiments, designed to explore the boundaries between private and public space and to question the social structures that impose these categories on human beings, resulted in works such as *Room Piece* (1970), where he moved the furniture of his apartment to Gain Ground Gallery and treated the event as a performance, or *Service Area* (1970), where he had his personal mail forwarded to the Museum of Modern Art to be exhibited there in an 'Information' show.

As these performances still treated the public as an anonymous, impersonal entity, they did not successfully fulfil Acconci's intention of serving as an 'exchange point' or medium of 'transformation'.[39] Even when he approached his viewers directly, he did not achieve an active exchange, as he had experienced in *Performance Test* (1969), where he stared at members of the audience until they broke off eye contact. Edward Hall's space analyses in *The Hidden Dimension* brought him a stage further and led to *Proximity Piece*: 'Stand near a person and intrude on his personal space.' The resulting conflicts led Acconci to investigate Erving Goffman's interaction studies and Kurt Lewin's field theory, to develop a complex understanding of the dynamics of interpersonal communication, and to gain an insight into the ritualized interactions between individual and social environment. This made Acconci realize: 'I had gotten into this total isolation. So it seemed like the only move from there was that I had to become part of an interpersonal space, rather than I in this private, self-enclosed space.'[40] From now on, Acconci transgressed the boundaries that separate the 'me' from the 'other' and opened up an active exchange of energy with the outside world. A whole series of performances explored the interpersonal dynamics that exist between two human beings, or between individual and society.

His starting point was again the body as a vessel of the self and of one's autobiography. But instead of conducting his self-inquiry as a solitary monologue, he sought to project himself into social space and to create a 'stage' for the en'act'ment of the self and for exploring the construction of identity through inter'act'ion. For example, in *Untitled Piece for Pier 17*

(1971) he invited his audience to an abandoned dock in Lower Manhattan with the promise of revealing to them details of his personal life which he had never disclosed before. *Transference Zone* (1972) took place in a gallery with Acconci sitting in a small cubicle, or 'history chamber', surrounded by photographs of seven key people in his life (see Illustration 12). He talked to the images until he felt very close to the persons they represented. When visitors knocked on the door, he would let them in and react as if they were the person he had just fantasized about. He thereby released his hidden feelings and hoped to produce a response from the visitors that came close to the behaviour of the 'prime person' in the photograph. When people came to see *Reception Room* (1973) in Lucio Amelio's Modern Art Agency in Naples, they found him lying on a table surrounded

12 Vito Acconci: *Transference Zone*, Sonnabend Gallery (New York, 1972).

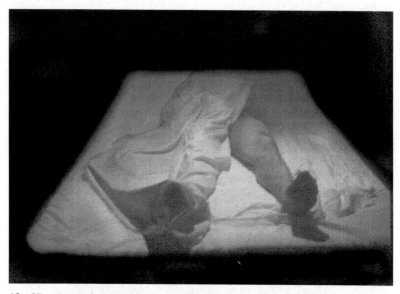

13 Vito Acconci: *Reception Room,* Modern Art Agency (Naples, 1973).

by seven stools and a spotlight above (see Illustration 13). As they entered this 'operating theatre', Acconci exposed part of his body and said: 'I am here in public, I can reveal something private. I can reveal something that I am ashamed of. I can show the pimples on my ass, . . . the size of my prick, my certainty that it is too small.'

Probably his most famous piece from this period was *Seedbed* (1970), where between 15 and 29 January 1971 he inhabited for some eight hours a day, three times a week, the space under a ramp erected in the Sonnabend Gallery. A poster made the visitors aware that they were to become an integral component of the artist's erotic fantasies. He used their presence in the space to evoke his desire, communicated to them the fantasies unfolding in his mind, and had the visitors' reactions stimulate his libido further until he would spill his seed. The austere white space of the gallery forced the visitors to concentrate on the invisible artist, whose voice was amplified through a loudspeaker. Although the ramp created a barrier between them, the boundaries of private and public space became permeable. The interior drama of a sexual fantasy, usually locked up in psychic space, was projected into public space, where it turned into a dialogue and became a shared event. The audience was no longer just an observer, but became a participant in an erotic game. The interchange between artist and visitor/accomplice was the driving force of the performance. However, in the final outcome, sexual union was denied. The unreachable other could only stimulate the artist's erotic imagination.

Revealing important and essentially private aspects of the self to other people in a structured environment bore a close resemblance to certain forms of psychotherapy ('The base of a lot of my work for the past two years is a kind of encounter group – group therapy situation.'[41]). The performances focused on issues such as the constitution of private and public spheres, anxieties and doubts about identity, the 'power field' in a partnership with its mechanisms of submission, domination, control and manipulation. However, Acconci always insisted that it was not his personal ego or hang-ups that mattered, but the general patterns that could be examined this way. Performing his 'self' in public did not lead him to any catharsis or transformation experiences. To Acconci, confessing a personal trait to his audience was less an act of self-revelation than an attempt to make them confront their own predicaments.

Many of these performances were undertaken with his partner Kathy Dillon and revealed aspects of their personal relationship, which they considered to be of general interest to other people. For example, *Pull* (1971 at the Loeb Student Center Auditorium of New York University) showed Acconci and Dillon moving around each other and keeping permanent eye contact whilst shifting direction and speed. The idea was to exert control, or 'pull', on the other, exploring who wants to control or be controlled. Whatever the outcome, top and bottom always complemented each other, and one performer was always subsumed by the other. They moved together in this closed circuit of the stage, which separated them from the viewers in the auditorium, established unity between them and made them experience performance as withdrawal.

> In some ways pieces of mine have always been some reference to some kind of power. In early pieces, that dealt with some notion of inter-personal relation. I was obviously a male. I was obviously focusing on male as dominant power wielder in this relation. I hoped that a lot of ways that I was dealing with it would be so blatant and so cartoon-like that those pieces weren't seen to glorify maleness. Hopefully, they put forward that male image as analyzable.[42]

Acconci acknowledged the influence of Bertolt Brecht's concept of alienation and used similar devices to put a frame around certain traits of human behaviour to make them stand out and look 'strange' ('it can shift into focus what is ordinarily unattended to'[43]). His performances were experiments in the Brechtian sense, employing the technique of the contradictory actor, who exhibits himself as an object of analysis and suggests a commentary on his own behaviour.[44] Acconci's staging of the self in public was designed to demonstrate the self in interaction with the other, to make visible the controlling functions of society and to show the individual as an active agent in a network of forces. Yet sometimes he felt that this was assuming too much mental sophistication from his audience. Many average viewers did not engage with his pieces in a dialectic manner, but rather identified with his actions and invitations to such a degree that it seriously compromised the intended outcome. After one such experience in Florence in 1974 he stopped live performances altogether: 'The danger is that [this] power sign is going to act as a further wielder of power rather than be analyzed as power. Just like in a lot of those earlier pieces – I think they are probably seen by a lot of people as very sexist pieces. I hoped that they would be seen as the opposite.'[45] Critics such as Amelia Jones believe that Acconci's exaggeration of male power, combined with his pathetic failure to live up to the ideals of male subjectivity, made his work 'readable', i.e. distanced enough to encourage criticism and to unhinge masculinist activities. Yet, at the same time, they could also be understood as possibly reinforcing it.[46]

Parallel to his work as a live performer, Acconci also used the medium of video to explore the power of the performer over the spectator, the boundaries of public and private, the interrelatedness of submission and domination, male and female, body and mind. He became a pioneer in this new medium and established an innovative and influential œuvre, which I shall discuss in more detail in Chapter 6.

Viennese Actionism

Various authors, including myself,[47] have discussed the 'Wiener Aktionsgruppe', which was formally constituted in July 1965, within the context of the Fluxus and Happening movement. However, members of the group had been performing their actions long before they had heard of American Happenings; and because of the unusual nature of the group's actions they were rarely invited to present their works at other Happening festivals in Europe.[48] Therefore it seems appropriate to discuss the group's basic philosophy and performance aesthetics in the light of their body-centred ritualism, which made them an important link between 1950s Action Painting and 1970s Body Art.

Otto Mühl and Hermann Nitsch, the two older members of the Aktionsgruppe, both underwent similar developments in their early artistic career. Starting off as conventional painters, they moved into more process-based works that involved them in a forceful, physical engagement with the materials they employed in their creations, not dissimilar to the artists discussed in Chapter 3. The initial impulse came from Tachism, which became known in Vienna around 1951 and was adopted by various Austrian painters from 1955 onwards. In 1959, Nitsch saw an exhibition of works by Pollock, Kline and de Kooning, and a year later he moved into the terrain of Action Painting himself.[49] From the spraying, splashing and smearing of dyes he progressed to working with blood, which he poured from a freshly slaughtered lamb onto the canvas. Before moving into Actionism proper, Nitsch had been working on the idea of a Theatre of Orgies and Mysteries and had produced the first versions of a six-day drama that mixed elements taken from the myths of Œdipus, Christ's Passion, Parsifal, the Nibelungs and other sources.[50] For Nitsch, the progression from ritual theatre to action painting to ritualistic Actionism was based on the 'dionysic-dynamic' element contained in all of these forms of expression. The use of the vital substances of blood, viscera and flesh in his paint actions of 1960–3 led him quite naturally to his 'Lamb Tearing Actions', which formed the core of his over 80 performances in the last thirty years.

Most of these actions contained a number of elements, which were combined according to a standard formula: to the sound of loud music, Nitsch acted as a High Priest and fastened a slaughtered lamb head down as if crucified. He gradually disembowelled it and let the blood and viscera fall onto a white cloth. The innards of other lambs were placed on the body of a nude human being, who was finally crucified like the lamb. The carcass of the eviscerated animal was beaten and hurled against the wall. The actors tore out lumps of flesh with their teeth and stamped on the mutilated cadavers. In between the excessive actions there were quiet moments in which the carcasses were anointed with perfumed essences and decorated with flowers. A chasuble, monstrance or similar ecclesiastical garment was laid out on the floor. The action usually ended with a totem meal that was reminiscent of the Eucharist.

The generic name Nitsch gave to these actions was *Abreaktionsspiel* (abreaction play), derived from the Freudian concept of catharsis.[51] The first of them was performed on 19 December 1962 in the flat of his friend Otto Mühl; the second was a public event at the Galerie Dvorak on 16 March 1963. Until 1970 he had performed 31 of these rituals, mainly in private apartments and studios, and some in galleries, outdoor spaces, a restaurant, and a meat market. His architectural plans for a specially constructed O.M. Theatre[52] came finally to fruition when he acquired the Prinzendorf Castle in 1971. Ever since he has been perfecting his concept of a six-day drama (see Illustrations 14 and 15).

14   Hermann Nitsch: *6tagespiel in Prinzendorf*

The origins of the abreaction plays go back to 1957, when Nitsch began to study systematically the available literature on ancient cults and rituals and the psychoanalytical writings of Freud, Rank and Jung. The most prominent myths to become a constant point of reference in his writings were those of Dionysus Zagreus, Attis, Oedipus and the *Bacchae*.[53] From these he developed his concept of a festival of orgies and mysteries with a

15   *80th Action of the OM Theatre,* 1984

sacrifice and crucifixion at its centre. In *On the Roots of Tragedy* (1963) he wrote:

> Tragedy turned from its original state into something different, something that led far away from it: playful theatre. The inner-most essence of tragedy was rooted in Nature's attempt to respond to a collective human urge to ventilate our

instincts . . . and to rebel against the censorship of our Super Ego, or at least to outwit it. When we push aside the intellectual and conscious control of our basic life-energies, we gain an insight into our subconscious, unbridled, chaotic libido. And once these vital forces have been contacted, they break free and rise to the surface, where they provide extreme satisfaction, ecstasy, joyful cruelty, sado-masochistic reactions, and excess. In Greek mythology it was Dionysus who provoked excess. He descended into animality and chaos, sacrificed himself and was torn apart. That's why tragedy is the starting point of excess. The Dionysian forces of the subconscious mind burst out into the open, gain form and, to some extent, enter our consciousness. The result is psychic cleansing (*katharsis*), which impacts on the spectators and hits their psyche. Ancient drama, like the myths on which it was based, was an expression of a collective desire for abre-action, conditioned by a restricting reality principle that has been imposed on all human beings.[54]

Nitsch established a connection between the primitive cult of Dionysus – the tearing up of animals and the eating of raw flesh in a state of ecstasy and frenzy – with the crucifixion of Christ. Totem meals were a counterpart of the Last Supper. Conquest of death, spiritual purification and redemption were as much part of the catharthic plays as the liberation of stored-up aggression and the release of libidinal forces. Nitsch's action theatre (or rather 'abreaction' theatre) was designed to have a therapeutic effect on its participants, who release their aggressive impulses in ritual acts of violence directed against a slaughtered animal, rather than in barbaric warfare against human beings. Thereby, the participants can gain insight into their aggressive instincts and turn these into art. Thus, 'erotic cruelty is over-come by aesthetic means'.[55] The performative process purified the performers and, in the end, liberated them from feelings of guilt.

If Nitsch, the Dionysian High Priest, attempted a return to the origins of tragedy, Otto Mühl, in a far more burlesque and hedonistic way, revived the tradition of the Greek satyr play. Like his friend Hermann Nitsch, Mühl arrived at Actionism through his work as a painter. His early 'Material Actions' were dominated by a very painterly aesthetics. In a way that was akin to Pop Art he employed the everyday matter of foodstuffs, de-func-tionalized them, operated with them in an Action-Painting manner to create a material assemblage, and then let them degrade again into primal matter (*Versumpfung*).

The Material Action is painting which has grown beyond the picture frame. The 'canvas' is formed by a human body, a table on which the material is layed out, or a whole room . . . In the Material Action the focus is not directed towards the body as a human, but as a material entity. . . . The Material Action is a method to expand reality, to create realities and to broaden the dimensions of life.[56]

Painting always results in a picture. Process is replaced by product. A Material Action does the opposite. Here, the picture cedes to the action. The Material Action does not aim at results. The process, the action becomes the result. . . . The Material Action is a happening, which offers a parallel medium to painting, sculpture, ballet, theatre, music, circus, yet at the same time has nothing to do with these. It renounces on artistry: no costumes, no stage sets, no illusion.[57]

In the 56 Material Actions performed between 1963 and 1969, the artist's body gained in importance over the concrete language of materials.[58] The painterly arrangements of bodies and materials (e.g. in *Still-Life of a Male, a Female and a Bovine Head* of 1964, or *Penis Still-Life* of 1964) gave way to actions, where Mühl placed his and his assistants' bodies at the centre of activity and arrived at a specific language of body gestures and improvised treatments of materials. For Mühl, the Material Action was a means of overcoming the concept of re-presentation in art and of establishing a direct, immediate contact with the visceral substance of life. He saw the essence of existence as rooted in matter and energy. The improvised Material Action was a means of liberating our vital (and especially sexual) impulses.

All avant-garde performance artists were concerned with overcoming the gap between art and life. In Vienna this took on the more specific form of breaking down the barriers between Super-Ego and Id, between social/cultural conventions and the libidinal forces. Unveiling the psychic condition of the human race was a process of socio-political critique and brought the Actionists into conflict with the representatives of State power. The extreme unpleasantness of their performances led to semi-exclusion from most 'official' Happening festivals.[59] However, the Viennese 'Aesthetics of Ugliness'[60] cannot be fully understood without recognizing its counterpoint, the emphasis on form and ritual perfection. Nitsch's reasonings on 'form as the innermost essence of art'[61] seem to reflect what another Viennese writer, Hermann Bahr, characterized as the essence of tragedy: 'extracting beauty from ugliness'.[62]

Viennese Actionism was not only an aesthetic phenomenon. The Actionists firmly believed that the therapeutic aspects of their performances had far-reaching political consequences. They linked Freud's psychological existentialism with the political psychology of the Frankfurt School and suggested that perversion was a rebellion of pleasure principle against reality principle, a protest against the functional use of sexuality in the service of procreation. Sublimating infantile partial desires for the sake of cultural and social achievement would lead, they believed, to the formation of 'authoritarian characters' (Horkheimer) and fascist social structures. Hence Mühl's declaration: 'I'm in favour of fornication, of de-mythologization of sexuality. Intercourse is not a state-supportive sacrament, but a purely bodily function.'[63]

Viennese Actionism was not only an artistic phenomenon, but also possessed a political rationale: rebellion against the remnants of Austro-Fascism and the incrustations of bourgeois society. The Austrian state responded with juridical force and drove several members of the group into exile. Nitsch remains the only member of the group still pursuing his Actionist concerns. He has found a worldwide following, who gather regularly at Prinzendorf Castle for the enactment of his Orgies-Mysteries ritual. The former 'Gedärme-Wüterich' (entrails maniac) [64] has become a 'grand-seigneur' of Austrian art, who is now allowed to represent his country at major international festivals and has been given access to the bastion of Viennese art, the State Opera House. Even the Catholic Church is nowadays taking him seriously as a modern religious artist.[65] However, such official recognition of Viennese Actionism as Austria's most important contribution to postwar art is only a very recent phenomenon. Previously, the Actionists were generally reviled by the cultural establishment and only positively acknowledged by artists such as Valie Export or Elke Krystufek. In a more indirect way they were also a factor of influence in Austrian theatre. The radical rupture with prevailing forms of art and performance served as an inspiration to people like Handke, Turrini and Bernhard – all of them virulent critics of Austrian society. The Artaudian component in their work still continues to hold a fascination for contemporary groups pursuing ritualistic concepts of theatre.

Joseph Beuys

Joseph Beuys was one of the most influential artists on the international scene and left a great legacy to the following generation of performers working in a ritual vein. His symbol-laden, shamanic actions had a magical quality and exuded a stark and mystical aura that deeply affected the spiritual life of his audiences. Beuys was extremely sceptical of the advances in modern science and felt that technology, in its present application, reduced rather than enhanced the human condition. Man mechanized by machines and conditioned by the electronic media has become a victim of his own hubris. Therefore, Beuys drew on the organic warmth of natural materials, using many metaphors of energy and transformation to indicate his desire for a return to a close and immediate contact with the forces of Nature.

Beuys' performances were heavily influenced by his 'Theory of Social Sculpture'. His use of the term *Plastik* implied the moulding of materials as well as ideas. For Beuys, any 'form-giving process' that leads from chaos to structure can be considered *Plastik*. Development of human consciousness and spiritual awareness is the most important form of *Plastik*. For art to be a useful tool in this process it has to move beyond the static and fixed boundaries of traditional painting and sculpture. Beuys sought to give symbolic expression to his idea of social sculpture through his performances, where everything was in a state of flux, change and transformation.

Beuys adopted the role of shaman following a long and painful illness, which radically transformed his life. As a pilot during the Second World War he was shot down in the Crimea. He was nearly frozen to death when some nomadic Tatars found him in the snow. They rescued him by covering his body with fat and wrapping him up in felt. He was then nursed back to life in their felt tents and fed on butter, milk and cheese. Consequently, all these materials possessed a powerful resonance for Beuys. When he returned to Germany, he gave up his plans for a career as a natural scientist and began training as a sculptor. Attempts to combine his scientific and artistic gifts pushed him into a state of crisis, which was further exacerbated by the after-effects of his war experience. Physical exhaustion and illness followed, but out of this chaos and spiritual upheaval a new direction emerged, which eventually changed his life.

Beuys likened these painful experiences to the preparatory stages and initiation rites of shamans. The crashing of his fighter plane in the Crimea in 1943 and the subsequent impasse in his professional life were like an exorcism and the start of a new life. It helped him overcome the traumas of his early life and initiated a healing process that led to a radical re-evaluation of the purpose of art and science.

In 1961, Beuys became Professor of Sculpture at the Academy of Art in Düsseldorf and took an active role on the performance scene of the Rhineland. After meeting Maciunas at the Neo-Dada concert in Düsseldorf (16 June 1962, see above p. 116, Chapter 4) he agreed to stage his *Earth Piano* piece at the Fluxus Festival in Wiesbaden (due to unforeseen circumstances he could not, in the end, participate). From 1963 to 1965, Beuys was involved in a number of Fluxus events,[66] but his actions soon moved beyond the provocative character that characterized so many of the concerts.

Beuys' transformation of Maciunas's Fluxus concepts became first obvious in *The Chief* (30 August 1963 at the Fluxus Festival in Copenhagen, and on 1 December 1964 at the René Block Gallery in Berlin). It was a nine-hour performance and emphasized the meditative and ritualistic aspect of Beuys' œuvre. The brightly lit gallery space was 'decorated' with a strip of margarine, two lumps of fat, an assembly of hair and fingernails, a felt roll wrapped around a copper staff, and two dead hares. In the centre of the room lay a large piece of felt, with Beuys rolled up inside it. At irregular intervals he transmitted messages to the outside world. These 'primary sounds', resembling the hoarse roaring of a stag, contrasted with electronic compositions played by Erik Andersen and Henning Christiansen. The meditative character of lying in the same position wrapped up in felt for nine hours was intended to have a consciousness-expanding effect on both spectators and performer. As Beuys said: 'Such an action, and indeed every action, changes me radically. In a way it's a death, a real action and not an interpretation.'[67]

In 1965, Beuys separated from the Fluxus movement and began to perform far more structured 'actions'. On 5 June 1965, at the Galerie Parnass in Wuppertal during a collaborative twenty-four-hour Happening festival, he performed . . . *and in us . . . under us . . . land beneath*. The aim was to encourage the audience to develop a new, intuitive perception of time and space. For this, he crouched on a crate that stood like an island in a large room, his feet and head resting on wedge-shaped slabs of fat. He 'listened' to the fat and reached out for objects beyond his grasp, occasionally uttering strange sounds into a microphone. His intense theatrical gestures were again a form of meditation in front of a spell-bound audience, interrupted from time to time by hammering a double-handled spade against the floor and playing fragments of music from a tape recorder. In the collective catalogue published on the occasion of the festival, Beuys printed a text that commented on his performance. It presented his concept of *Plastik* as a creative alternative to a cold, analytical rationalism of the natural sciences and as 'an expansion of time and space into the spiritual realm'.[68] If used by humans according to an 'energy plan', sculpting has the potential of transforming the earth in a positive way; if not, it leads to death and destruction:

> Life after death
>
> Over-Time
>
> Counter-Space
>
> ↑
>
> Warmth ← life on planet Earth → Coldness
>
> ↓
>
> Space
>
> Time
>
> Death[69]

In *How to Explain Pictures to a Dead Hare* at the Schmela Gallery in Düsseldorf (26 November 1965), Beuys had his head covered with honey and gold leaf and spent three hours walking through an exhibition of his works. His movements produced strange clanking noises, as his feet were stuck in shoes with an iron and a felt sole. In his arms he cradled a dead hare and made it touch the paintings with its paw. After the tour he sat down on a bench, mute, and 'explained' the images to the hare. He later described the action as dealing with the problem of language, of thought, of human consciousness and of the consciousness of animals. Just like a shaman needs a power animal, Beuys used the hare as a spirit guide in a journey of initiation. In Beuys' symbolic language, the hare was also connected to birth, and the honey to organic productivity. Covering his head with honey was meant to indicate the contrast between intuitive sensibility and abstract intellectuality. Universal communication, which includes interacting with the animal world and making contact with an existence beyond death, was presented as a spiritual and creative gift, which many humans have lost as a result of an increasingly technological and materialistic society.

On 14 and 15 October 1966 Beuys performed *Eurasia: 34th Section of the Siberian Symphony*, at the Gallery 101 in Copenhagen (repeated on 31 October 1966 at the René Block Gallery in Berlin). Again, a dead hare was his companion in the action, here symbolizing fast movement, fleetingness, transitoriness. A cross indicated the split between the West and East, and a felt-covered staff was used by the 'Wanderer' between continents in order to reconnect the circuit of energy and to create a future unity between the world of transcendentality and reason. The one and a half hour long performance consisted of pushing two crosses towards a blackboard, placing an alarm clock on each cross, writing 'Eurasia' on the blackboard, manoeuvring the dead hare along a drawn line and attaching it to some long sticks. Then the hare was taken to the board. Beuys sprinkled white powder between the legs of the animal, put a thermometer in its mouth and blew into a pipe. He took one of the crosses to the board and stamped with his iron sole on a metal plate on the floor. He then fired a bullet from a cardboard gun and recited fragments of German Romantic poetry.

His next performance was inspired by the meditations of Ignatius de Loyola. *Manresa* was presented at the Gallery Schmela in Düsseldorf on 15 December 1966 and illustrated Beuys' belief in intuition as a higher form of reason and a more profound form of perception.[70] In this action, Beuys, Henning Christiansen and Björn Nörregaard interacted between two 'elements'. Element 1 was a cross with its left part missing. The half-cross leaned against a wall, and the other part was indicated with chalk on the wall. A letter 'n' showed the zone still to be completed by human energy. It was the 'potential arithmetic or one and two integrated'.[71] Element 2 was a box filled with a number of electrical instruments and the innards of a hare. With a Geisler tube, Beuys induced electricity and made the whole environment light up. He then conducted energy through a gold-coloured hare. In front of the cross he fluttered the wings of a bird on a stick. With a bicycle pump he splattered fat against the wall. Throughout these actions, Beuys' collaborators produced a sound accompaniment. Towards the end, the word 'can', as an affirmation of human potential, dominated the score.

The ideas of energy, time, space, and language were further explored in *Mainstream* at the Franz Dahlem Gallery in Darmstadt (20 March 1967). For ten hours Beuys inhabited a bare, whitewashed space with a rust-coloured floor. The edges of the space were defined with a wall of fat. The audience was allowed to enter this space, but they kept a distance, either because of the unresponsiveness of the 'fat-dweller' or because he cleaned up any area a spectator had entered, repaired the borders that had been broken by the audience, and rebuilt the fat walls that had been damaged. There was a recurring ritual of wiping and sliding on the fat-soaked floor. He played with lumps of fat and lay down on the floor, his limbs stretching beyond the demarcation lines that surrounded him. He then got up and held an antenna to his ear, listening intently and desperately into space. Finally, as if imbued with superhuman power, he stood still with his hand placed in front of his brow. Throughout the action, Henning Christiansen operated four tape recorders that issued sounds and word fragments. Beuys himself only produced his favourite 'öö' sounds and spoke two sentences: 'This is my axe and this is the axe of my mother,' and 'It is not your fault that you said that but that they asked you.'

Celtic (Kinlock Rannoch) Scottish Symphony was first performed on 26–30 August 1970 at the Edinburgh College of Art. Again, Henning Christiansen provided a Fluxus soundtrack. Beuys went through a number of highly symbolic actions with props such as a blackboard, a spear dripping blood, an axe and a staff, and performed some very minimalist movements: standing on one leg, spending one and a half hours scraping bits of gelatine off a wall, placing them on a tray, pouring them on his head, singing 'öööö', standing still for 40 minutes. Here, as in *Celtic +* (6 April 1971 at the Civil Defence Rooms in Basle), the stage action was complemented by projections of several of his films. The Basle performance was even more ritualistic. Ambiguous conjunctions of pagan and Christian symbols, combined with the meditative pace of the piece, created some powerful moments that left a deep resonance in the consciousness of the 500 spectators.

His most famous action, which has been well documented in a book by Caroline Tisdall, was *I Like America and America Likes Me* (23–5 May 1974 at the René Block Gallery in New York). For three days, Beuys shared the gallery space with a Coyote and demonstrated the possibilities of harmonious co-habitation of man and animal. This state of natural existence was disturbed by the intrusion of capitalism, here indicated by fifty copies of the *Wall Street Journal*. Beuys covered himself with felt blankets and lived in a felt tent, always communicating with the coyote. He never took his eyes off the animal and performed a repertoire of movements that were dictated by the coyote's responses and energy levels. He commented on the performance:

> Human Universality – a total contrast to the *Wall Street Journal*, the financial newspaper which embodies most symptomatically the ultimate rigor mortis inherent in the thinking about CAPITAL (in the sense of the tyranny exerted by money and power). A symptom of our time, where CAPITAL ought to have become an ARTISTIC CONCEPT. That too is an aspect of the United States. Even more: it is a diminished and destructive interpretation of money and economics, an inorganic fixation based on unjust and unsound concepts of modern money economy, and one which can only prepare the ground for more proliferating sources of infection in all the productive areas of the body politic, in culture, in law and in society.[72]

Nearly all of Beuys' performances took place in art galleries. In 1969, he undertook a rare attempt to take his performance concepts into the theatre world. Beuys had been invited to design the sets for two theatre productions in Frankfurt, Goethe's *Iphigenia* and Shakespeare's *Titus Andronicus*.[73] He decided to perform the two plays himself, simultaneously, at the Theater am Turm during the *Experimenta 3* theatre festival. He divided the stage into a Titus corner (empty) and an Iphigenia corner (with a microphone on a stand, chalk drawings and scores written on the floor, lumps of sugar and blocks of fat). At the back of the stage, a white horse was eating hay or stomping its hoofs on a resounding iron plank. Text fragments of both plays were spoken by Claus Peymann and Wolfgang Wiens over loudspeakers. Beuys himself, initially wrapped up in white shining fur, 'played' Iphigenia. His movements echoed those of the horse as he spoke Goethe's text into the microphone. Between speeches, he walked around the stage, patted the horse, squatted down and measured his own head, made guttural noises, spat fat into the Titus corner, played the cymbals. Some of the ritual actions were repeated; others were improvised and were determined by the behaviour of the horse.

The performance was far from offering a theatrical interpretation of the two plays. The texts were used to contrast humanist idealism and brutal realism. Between these two poles there was a field of interaction between Beuys and the horse. Beuys did not aim at making exact connections between the four elements, but rather, established an intuitive field of associations between them. He sought to foster a pre-rational form of consciousness by contrasting the organic element of man and horse with the intellectual element of the play texts communicated via an electronic medium.

From about 1967 onwards, the political aspects of Beuys' actions became more and more pronounced. He not only inserted references to contemporary political realities in his works, but he himself became actively engaged in the political life of his country. Despite his aversion to parties and organizations he founded a number of groups, based on non-hierarchical and free democratic principles, and went public with his political aims. He employed many channels to promote more participatory forms of government and the creation of a different society for the future.[74] However, his idealistic concepts of democracy were often derided, and the idiosyncratic forms he chose for his propaganda meant that outside the art world few people took him seriously as a politician. In many ways, this work as an activist in the political arena was a logical extension of his attempts to bridge the gap between art and life in his Happenings and ritualized actions:

Art is now the only evolutionary-revolutionary power. Only art is capable of dismantling the repressive effects of a senile system that continues to totter along the deathline: to dismantle in order to build A SOCIAL ORGANISM AS A WORK OF ART. The most modern art discipline – Social Sculpture / Social Architecture – will only reach fruition when every living person becomes a creator, a sculptor or architect of the social organism. – Only then would the insistence on participation of the action art of FLUXUS and Happening be fulfilled.[75]

During the last years of his life, Beuys became an influential leader amongst young artists who had grown sceptical of Western society, technology and capitalism. They shared Beuys' belief that materialism and rational science has severed humankind's umbilical cord with the cosmic powers of Nature and they supported his concept of art and creativity as a powerful antidote to the crisis that had befallen planet Earth. In contrast to the techno-Futurists they advocated cultural resistance to the debilitating influence of the mass media and shared Beuys' vision of a future in which unity with the spiritual world would be re-established.

Beuys' main aim was to unlock and mobilize people's latent creativity. He employed means of communication that emphasized the role of intuition, empathy and non-intellectualized thinking. For him, every human being was an artist and able to create a social work of art. His heavily ritualized actions employed elements taken from the shamanic healing séance in order to restore a balanced cosmic order. He used power animals (hare, horse, bees, etc.) as spiritual guides to help him travel to the supernatural world. His complex iconography relied on the recurrent use of symbolic objects and substances that encapsulated organic energy and symbolized the powerful forces of Nature: the cross, batteries, bones, fat, felt, honey, etc. This encouraged or re-enforced many people's belief in the therapeutic potential of art and performance.

Gina Pane

The French-Italian artist Gina Pane began her career in the 1960s as a painter and sculptor. After an initial phase of experimentation with minimalism and land art, she increasingly focused on her own body as a means of conveying her ideas and concerns. *Displaced Stones* (Valle dell'Orco/Piedmont, July 1968), *Reading Table* (Turin, 1969), *Burying a Sunray* (Ecos/Eure, 1969), and *Continuation of a Wooden Track* (Ury, 1970) were examples of actions/installations that involved her in simple manipulations of the natural environment, documented as photography. Her intimate relationship and communication with Nature was highlighted even more in *Protected Earth 2* (Pinerolo/Piedmont, 1970), in which she covered ('protected') an earthen mound with her body stretched out in the form of a cross. Pane employed the medium of performance to transmit information received from natural environments and materials. The body acted like a sensor listening to impulses from Nature, converting them into signals and transmitting these to the viewer.

In *Second Silence Project* (Ury, 1970), it was her own body, not the earth, that was at risk and needed protection. Here, Pane was giving voice not only to the forces of Nature, but also to her inner voices, her desires and spiritual aspirations. Her intention was to climb up a steep sand cliff, only to let herself slide down a moment later. To achieve this aim, Pane had to confront the real danger of injuring her body and falling to the bottom of the cliff. Sliding down and climbing up the hill for 30 minutes was a dangerous and painful experience, but it also established an intimate dialogue between body and earth, between the physical force of gravity and the will of the artist to overcome her own fear and resistance.

Not Anaesthetized Ladder (Artist's studio in Paris, 1971) had Pane climb up and down a ladder, the rungs of which were covered with pointed protrusions. After about thirty times her bare hands and feet were bleeding and she had reached the limit of her endurance. This climb without anaesthesia was a protest against a world of indifference and insensitivity and transported her body and mind into an elevated state of consciousness through physical and moral suffering. A text distributed with photographs of the performance indicated that the protest was specifically related to the Vietnam War[76] and explained that the title of the action, *escalade* (climbing up a ladder), was a word play on the escalation of the American bombing of Vietnam. However, in an interview with Effie Stephano she also related the action to people becoming so concerned with their career path that their basic human sensibilities become totally anaesthetized.[77]

Another performance connected with socio-political issues was *Food – TV News – Fire* (private apartment, Paris, November 1971). During the first part, Pane sat at a table with a pound of raw hamburger meat in front of her. She chewed the meat, spat it out, swallowed it and vomited it out again, pounded and squashed the substance until she and her audience were filled with total disgust. In the second part she sat in front of a television with a high-wattage light bulb hanging right in front of her head. A table near the audience displayed economics journals and ecological magazines, with title pages related to agriculture and the world food crisis. Watching the news became a very painful experience and made people comment: 'It's strange, we have never consciously taken in the news before. There's actually a war going on in Vietnam, unemployment everywhere, etc.'[78] The third part was performed in an adjacent bare room, where Pane poured alcohol on a patch of sand, set light to it and proceeded to extinguish the fire with her bare hands and feet.

In this performance, the artist attacked habitual behaviour and attitudes that made people turn a blind eye to suffering and exploitation, in this instance related to the role of animals in the food chain and humans in the circulation of capital. By presenting the action in a conventional middle-class environment similar to the one the audience would retire to after the event, she hoped to ensure that the images of injured, suffering or dead beings would no longer be that easily accepted and would 'give rise to new, undoubtedly changed, behaviour'.[79]

Self-Portrait(s) (Galerie Stadler, Paris, 11 January 1973) continued Pane's exploration of the theme of the wound and used the image of the mixing of blood and milk, which she had first employed in *Hot Milk* (private apartment in Paris, 31 May 1972). The performance consisted of three parts. 'The Conditioning' showed Pane lying on an iron bed-frame, under which fifteen candles burned, only five centimetres away from her body. She suffered the pain in silence, but communicated her state of discomfort to the audience by facial contortions and wringing her hands in pain. Half an hour later she stood up and made herself feel comfortable again by caressing her own body. For the second part, 'Contraction', she moved to a room next door and leaned against a wall, her back towards the audience, while slides of women applying red nail varnish were being projected onto adjacent walls. Pane began cutting her fingers around the nails with a razor blade, but concealed the action under a white handker-chief. Still turned away from the audience, she then made a cut on her inner lip. In front of her she had a microphone, but she was unable to communi-cate with the people behind her, apart from whispering some incomprehen-sible phrases. All the while, a video camera filmed the audience's reactions and displayed them on monitors distributed in the hall. For the third part, 'Rejection', she turned around, and kneeled in front of an empty bowl and a litre of milk. She started drinking the milk, gargling with it and swallow-ing it, but in increasingly violent spasms her stomach regurgitated the liquid back into the bowl. During this process, the wound in Pane's mouth had opened up again and blood mixed with the milk.

Pane discussed her performance in several interviews, saying that it 'was criticizing women for remaining aesthetic objects in society, for becoming conscious of themselves, for not trying to surpass their image'.[80] The mute microphone and television images referred to the media in a soci-ety that fades out the suffering of women. The archetypal images of the wound, of milk and blood recalled childhood memories and the connection between nurturing and pain.[81]

Sentimental Action (Galleria Diagramma in Milan, 1973; see Illustration 16) was for Pane another battle against her physical limits when suffering pain. Before reaching the room where the action was to take place, the audi-ence had to pass through a gallery space in which black velvet drapes were laid out on the floor. Sewn into the centre was an image of a white rose, and on the walls hung three photographs of a rose in a silver vase. A second gallery had a close-up image of Pane holding a bunch of red roses projected onto the walls. In a third space a chalk circle had been drawn on the floor, with the word *DONNA* (woman) written at its centre. The audience was asked to take a seat in this circle. The performance that followed had a highly ritualistic quality with strong mystical and erotic undertones. When Pane entered the room, she held a bunch of red roses and took up different positions on the floor (lying prone, leaning forward, curled up like a foetus). Slowly but determinedly she began to flagellate herself with the roses. After a while she rolled up one sleeve, extended her arm to the spectators and

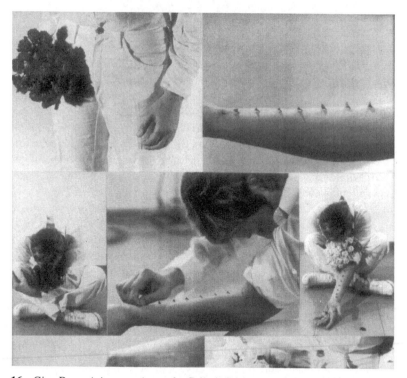

16   Gina Pane: *Azione sentimentale*, Galleria Diagramma, Milan, 1973

drove eight thorns into her skin. She then took a razor blade and cut the outlines of a rose into the palm of her hand. Simultaneously with the action, two women read some letters exchanged between an Italian and a French woman. Pane repeated the action of the first part with a bunch of white flowers, again changing positions three times, while over a loudspeaker Frank Sinatra could be heard singing 'Strangers in the Night'.

In the 1970s, Pane performed over thirty actions, until an accident in 1980 convinced her that she had to stop doing live events. She continued to write scenarios and scores to be performed by other people, but her main medium was from now on sculpture, and her main theme the life of saints and martyrs. Of course, in her previous performances she herself had often appeared like a saint and martyr, carrying out acts of self-castigation and spiritual exercises. Always dressed in white, she almost looked like a vestal virgin marked by the blood flowing from her self-inflicted wounds. The other role she seems to have identified with was that of a healer, medicine woman or shaman. She once stated that these holy men and women would only be able to heal a wound if they themselves had been wounded.[82] This allowed them to identify with the sick or injured person, to *incarnate* their affliction and then bring about their convalescence. A modern artist taking on this role may no longer engage with physical illness, but could still become 'a catalyst of social and moral change'.[83] For this reason it is misguided to regard Pane as a masochist. A meticulous preparation of each performance allowed her to experience pain more on a psychic and emotional than a physical level. Pain had a clearly assigned role in her work: 'I love life and I hate pain and suffering – it gives me no pleasure. But I undergo it because I feel it's necessary in order to reach an anaesthetized society.'[84]

The theme of anaesthesia runs through most of her performance work of the 1970s and was regularly referred to in her interviews. In her opinion, people build up defence mechanisms against aggression from their social and physical environment, which eventually makes them blind and deaf towards their own suffering and that of other people. Modern mass media play a particularly negative role in desensitizing people and making them oblivious to the horrors of the world. Pane often found that modern audiences had been manipulated to such a degree that it took them a long time before they could take in and relate to her performances. 'I feel I'm touching a totally anaesthetized and conformist society,' she once stated in an interview.[85] Many people found the images in her work too perturbing or terrifying to engage with, but the majority felt deeply touched by the experience. They sensed that with her wounds Pane opened up fragile body memories, but also made them aware of the values of 'real' life, as opposed to mechanical, routine existence.[86]

Pane's performances could be understood on various levels, and with her statements, programme notes and interviews she tried to deflect any narrow interpretation of her works. She did not undervalue the political, social and feminist aspects of her actions, but at the same time she encouraged people to open themselves up to the deeper and more universal concerns behind them ('mythological politics that are connected with man's subconsciousness'[87]). It was her intention 'to unveil natural states that are otherwise repressed'[88] and to 'uncover reality through my body'.[89] Every viewer's relatedness to his or her own biological body guaranteed a certain level of understanding of her actions. For example, when in *Hot Milk* she lifted a razor blade and approached her cheek, even those who had previously watched and accepted her inflicting a wound on her back started yelling 'No! Not the face, no!' Blood, milk, and wounds are archetypal images with universal resonance. They belong to archaic aspects of the human species and form a universal vocabulary that links one person's experience and subconscious to the rest of humankind: 'My self-portrait is the portrait of others in general. My elements of expression are universal – they are not autobiographical. "Je suis les autres".'[90] However, it would be misleading to portray Pane as an essentialist Body Artist. Her work focused on the body not only as a biological organism, but also as being 'invaded and fashioned by society',[91] or as 'an attitude in its social and political context'.[92] This is why she continued to address environmental issues and the ecological imbalances that have been brought about by human intervention in Nature.

From the many associations prompted by Pane's work, two stand out as particularly important: the wound as a metaphor of the female sex, and of Christ's passion. Drawing on feminist theology and martyrology, she actively embraced her 'passion' and turned stigma into charisma,[93] while at the same time questioning a culture that destroys Nature (seen to be feminine) in the name of progress and technological development. Pane's shift from Land Art to Body Art was primarily caused by her desire to communicate directly with her audience. When she entered a performance space, she felt that she 'was making a true contact with the body of others and that [her] body became part of a communal body'.[94] Her first live actions gave her a strong sense of establishing 'a communication with other bodies' and showed her that 'the problems I was enacting became their problem – there was a very real contact with my work which provoked a behavioural assessment in them'.[95] Asked whether this work could also have been done in the theatre she is adamant: 'This would have been absolutely impossible. Theatre is neither my purpose nor my language. . . . A body artist and a theatre actor have entirely different ways of organizing the signs of body language.'[96] But it was not only that. For Pane, every action was an unrepeatable event that produced a lasting change in her.[97] There was no pretence, no acting, no dissimulation involved, only a heightened awareness of self and of the issues she addressed. Pane prepared herself for a performance by fixing her actions in precise scenarios and scoring gestures and movements in a series of preparatory drawings. She extracted herself from the sphere of everyday life and lived through the action long before it actually took place. There was never any rehearsal or repeat performance. Each event was like 'a liberation from oneself and from all constraints normally imposed by life'.[98] After the performance, she felt totally drained, and it took her a long time before she could insert herself back into normal life.

Marina Abramović

Abramović began her career as a painter in Belgrade, Yugoslavia, in the 1960s and became an independent performance artist in 1973. Like other artists discussed in this chapter, she felt a strong need to communicate with her audiences directly, rather than via an art object. This immediate contact in a live situation produced an exchange of energy that was qualitatively different from responses prompted by a gallery exhibition. She defined the purpose of her actions as 'using body as material . . . pushing my body to its physical and mental limits'.[99] She regularly used pain and danger to intensify her experience of reality. When she met Ulay (Uwe Laysiepen) on 30 November 1975, their respective birthdays, she left her native Serbia and moved to Amsterdam. Together they created some 68 performances over a period of twelve years. In 1980, they undertook a journey to Tibet and Australia, which resulted in a new phase of their work: 'I saw that all these cultures pushed the body to the physical extreme in order to make a mental jump. . . . Performance was the form enabling me to jump to that other space and dimension.'[100] After their last joint action – a ninety-day walk on the Great Wall of China in 1988 – the couple separated. A year later Abramović began a new cycle of solo performances, again using her body as prime material; but the risk and pain elements were now replaced by Eastern techniques, which she employed to reach a heightened aware-ness of Being and to establish a harmonious balance of body and mind.

Abramović's early performance work was characterized by the use of danger and physical ordeals. In a society obsessed with comfort and cocooning people from aspects of reality that were considered abject, unpleasant or horrifying, Abramović came to the conclusion that 'the subject of my work should be the *limits* of the body. I would use perfor-mance to push my mental and physical limits beyond consciousness.'[101] This was literally the case in *Rhythm 5* (Studenski Kulturni Centar, Belgrade, 1974), where she poured petrol over a five-pointed star – a polit-ical emblem of Yugoslav Communism – lit it and lay down in its centre. As the flames used up all oxygen, she lost consciousness and was only saved by a doctor in the audience, who realized what was happening and pulled her out of the fire. Abramović's creations in this early phase were partly influenced by her knowledge of the West European and American avant-garde (she entertained close contacts with Joseph Beuys, admired Gina Pane, Vito Acconci and Chris Burden, and performed in Nitsch's *Orgies-Mysteries-Theatre*[102]), but also by her desire to find a spiritual grounding (in 1968 she discovered Zen Buddhism, and in the mid-1970s she joined the Theosophical Society). Her interest in Eastern concepts of time and in the Buddhist perspective on life and death became apparent in a cycle of ten *Rhythm* pieces. For example, in *Rhythm 10* (Richard Demarco Gallery, Edinburgh, 1973) she sat at a table, her left hand resting on a white sheet of paper and ten knives lying in front of her. She took a knife and stabbed it, as fast as possible, into the space between her fingers. Each time she injured herself, she changed the knife until she had used them all. The sound of the knife cutting into wood or flesh was documented on a tape recorder. Abramović then listened to the recording and repeated the action, including all the injuries, in exactly the same manner as before. In *Rhythm 0*, her last performance of this series (Galleria Studio Morra, Naples, 1974), she presented herself as a totally passive object and informed the audience on a placard: 'There are 72 objects on the table that can be used on me as desired.' As the day progressed, people took an increasingly violent stance towards her. They cut all clothes from her body, touched her in intimate places and assaulted her sadistically. After standing motionless for six hours, Abramović had completed her perilous performance.

Three more performances, *Freeing the Voice* (Studenski Kulturni Centar, Belgrade, 1975), *Freeing the Memory* (Galerie Dacić, Tübingen, 1975) and *Freeing the Body* (Künstlerhaus Bethanien, Berlin, 1975) tested her physical and mental stamina to the limits. The actions were carried out with all the rigour of Eastern performance systems and allowed her to 'empty' herself in order to reach a higher plane of consciousness and a sense of freedom that cannot otherwise be known. *Thomas Lips* (Galerie Krinzinger, Innsbruck, 1975; see Illustration 17) drew on shamanic techniques and archetypal symbolism as integral parts of a ritual, in which she sat naked at a table drinking a litre of honey and a litre of red wine. She then crushed the glass with her hand, took a razor, and cut a five-pointed star on her stomach. Subsequently she whipped herself until she could no longer feel any pain, lay on a block of ice under a heater suspended from the ceiling, and waited until the audience intervened and rescued her.

In 1976 she began a series of 'Relation Works' with Ulay, which was strongly informed by Eastern traditions of ritual and meditation, shamanism, Tibetan Buddhism, Tantric and Sufi philosophies, etc. The couple's total immersion in each other and their attempt at overcoming gender and ego barriers operated with concepts of male and female energy derived from ancient Chinese, Indian, Sumerian and Greek sources. In her first phase as a performance artist, Abramović had taken 'a completely male approach',[103] pushing herself relentlessly and risking death in the process; now she 'went back to a female energy because he was the male. Then there was the idea of the hermaphrodite as the perfect human being . . . and of two bodies coming into one.'[104] Their attempt at establishing harmony

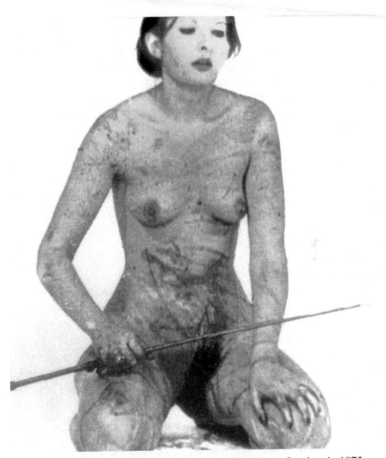

17   Marina Abramović: *Thomas Lips,* Galerie Krinzinger, Innsbruck, 1975

between mind and body, human being and natural environment, man and woman often bordered on obsessive behaviour and expressed an impossible longing for total fusion.[105] Meditative introspection alternated with travels to faraway cultures, which were both physical and spiritual journeys and often arduous vision quests.

Their first joint performance was *Relation in Space* (July 1976), where for an hour they walked into each other, naked, and increased the speed until their bodies collided violently and painfully. *Talking about Similarity* (30 November 1976) had Ulay sewing his mouth shut and Abramović taking his place and answering spectators' questions for him. When she made the mistake of answering a question for herself, the performance came to an end. In *Breathing In, Breathing Out* (April 1977) the couple blocked their noses with cigarette filters, took a deep breath, and engaged in a kiss which for the next nineteen minutes pushed the inhaled carbon dioxide from the lungs of one into the other. *Relation in Time* (October 1977) was a seventeen-hour performance in which they sat back to back with their hair braided into a thick plait. In *Light/Dark* (October 1977) the couple kneeled on the floor facing each other and slapped each other's face until one of the two decided to stop. *Balance Proof* (December 1977) showed the couple holding up a two-metre high, double-sided mirror by leaning their naked bodies against it. When after thirty minutes they intuitively and nearly simultaneously left the room, the mirror fell to the floor without breaking. In *Caesarean Section* (April 1978), the couple was linked to a horse by means of a rope that ran through a ring in the wall and was attached to their arms. Each movement of the horse became a separating force for the lovers. *Three* (30 November 1978) was performed with a snake that was constrained by a steel wire in a space about eight by eight metres square. Lying on the floor, Ulay and Abramović each blew into a bottle and produced a steady sound that was conducted through the vibration of the steel wire to the snake. The intention was to see which of the two sound sources the snake would slither towards.

During her early career, Abramović had sought enlightenment from reading Zen, Vedic and Theosophical scriptures, by studying Eliade's account of Siberian shamanism and Jung's theory of archetypes. She extended her knowledge of esoteric spiritual techniques during a series of journeys that took her to Australia, the Sahara, the Gobi Desert and China. This allowed her to tap a vast reservoir of mystic wisdom and equipped her with new experiences and techniques that had not been accessible to her in Communist Yugoslavia or capitalist Europe. The immersion into the living praxis of Eastern religion and the ancient culture of indigenous Australians gave Abramović and Ulay's work an increasingly mystical direction and led to what they called Motionless Work. The most important of this was *Nightsea Crossing* (1981–7), which had as its motto: 'Presence. Being present, over long stretches of time, until presence rises and falls, from material to immaterial, from form to formless, from instrumental to mental, from time to timeless.'[106] The slightly enigmatic title referred to 'crossing the ocean of the unconscious . . . [and] surfing different mental states'.[107] As Abramović explained, the performance was the fruit of their experiences in the Australian desert:

They say that Mohammed, Moses and Jesus all went to the desert as a nobody and they came back as somebody special. Why? Because the desert is the place where you are really confronted with yourself, nothing but yourself. You can't move. If you take three steps, your heart thumps. You can't take the heat, your body temperature is lower than the temperature around you. It is like pushing a hot wall all the time. All this makes you sit. That sitting is doing nothing, and that doing nothing is essential. . . . When you empty yourself, you can connect with the natural flow of energy of our planet, of vibrations, magnetism. And when you connect with the natural flow of energy, then you come to be at peace with reality.[108]

The first version of *Nightsea Crossing* had the two artists sitting motionless at opposite ends of a table for sixteen days throughout the opening hours of the Art Gallery of New South Wales (seven hours per day). They were dressed in colour combinations derived from Vedic texts; in front of them on a table lay 250 grams of gold nuggets found in the Australian desert, a boomerang covered with gold leaf, and a live python serving as a shamanic power animal to guide their journey. In a state of emotional and physical emptiness they communicated to their audience the inner peace and freedom that resulted from this long meditative-ceremony. The programme contained the following explanation, taken from Franz Kafka: 'You don't need to leave your room. Remain sitting at your table and listen. Don't even listen, simply wait. Don't even wait. Be quiet, still and solitary. The world will freely offer itself to you . . . it will roll in ecstasy at your feet.'[109] The work was performed 22 times in a variety of venues with different objects, using six colour variations and lasting between one and twelve days (the whole series lasted 90 days altogether). Although some visitors looked at the *tableau vivant* for only a few minutes, others stayed for hours and experienced not only the tangible sensation of a positive energy flow, but also a sedimentation of the striking image in their subconscious mind, where it often prompted unforeseeable effects. Ulay and Abramović saw these performances as a useful contribution they could make to a society that had lost its connections with the past, the earth, the cosmos: 'Decadent societies need art; in big cities, where mankind has completely lost its connection with nature, the main role of the artist is to make that connection visible again and to re-establish it if necessary.'[110]

Ulay and Abramović's final project was *The Great Wall Walk*, a ninety-day performance which, after a five-year preparation period, started on 30 March 1988 and was originally intended to end with a wedding ceremony. As they set off from opposite ends of the Wall, the couple unknotted their symbiotic ties, and when they met in the middle of a bridge in Shaanxi

Province they embraced and walked their separate ways. Abramović's subsequent solo performances were an attempt to come to terms with the accumulated experience, personal and professional, of her previous life. It still focused on her body as a medium of expression, combining cathartic with meditative techniques, but it also began to employ elements that are more typical of theatre. *Biography* (Hebbel Theatre, Berlin, 1993) was a collaboration with the designer Charles Atlas and chronicled her life and performance history in an open-ended performance that was updated every time she presented it in a new venue. *Delusional* (1994) was a five-part, autobiographical performance at the Theater am Turm in Frankfurt, dealing with her youth and family problems in Belgrade. She explained her sudden infatuation with the theatre in an interview:

> With this piece, *The Biography*, it is the first time that I perform in the theatre. As performance artists, we absolutely hated the structure of theatre. . . . *Biography* that I'm doing now really only works in a theatre set-up. Because you're playing a kind of a past, your past.[111]

The piece was performed in conventional proscenium-arch theatres with plush seats, crystal chandeliers and gilded fittings; however, within this environment where everything is fake and make-believe, Abramović undermined her audience's expectations by not playing another character, and instead carrying out, in an unfeigned manner, some of the body lesions of previous performances, such as cutting a star with a razor blade into her stomach. It was not astonishing that 'the public started fainting in the front row because first they thought it was a fake and then they saw it was real'.[112] The scenes presented were all taken from Abramović's life in art, and the fact that she herself played her own life, or rather, certain aspects of it, distinguished it from theatre. It still involved her in an act of transformation, of entering into 'another state', but it was not to imitate another person. In some ways it continued what she had previously explored with Ulay: in their Relational Work, audiences did not see their private life as a couple, but only certain facets of it expressed symbolically through their 'performance body'.[113] Compared with conventional theatre, their performances made art and life converge to a considerable degree, but fusing the two domains proved to be impossible. In fact, by the time they performed *The Great Wall Walk* they had separated as a couple, but it was none the less possible to 'stage' this ultimate metaphor of union:

> We have been working a lot with the male and female principle – not just presenting our egos or our real relationship, but acting as a kind of example for

the principle itself. . . . The Dragon-Head [of the Great Wall] is the male and the Dragon-Tail is the female. So that, actually, I will be walking as a female on the male part, and Ulay will be a male walking on the female part of the Wall, and the coming together is the unifying of the principle of the mental and the spiritual.[114]

Abramović saw herself as a medium and believed that her shamanic vision quests could empower her audience to find peace of mind and enlightenment through connecting with the forces that spoke through her. Her increasingly mystical introspection and spiritual concerns led her to the conclusion that all audiences have the potential to be creative and 'connected', but that this ability needs to be opened up and developed in them. Abramović called the technique to achieve this aim ''Boat emptying, stream entering." This means that you have to empty the body/boat to the point where you can really be connected with the fields of energy around you.'[115] This became the central idea of *Between* (1998), a piece that could not be 'seen' in the conventional manner. Before being allowed to enter the room, the 'spectators' had to make a contract with the artist and give her their word of honour that they would spend forty minutes in the space without moving. When they had done so, they were blindfolded and for 25 minutes they could 'watch' the installation on their 'interior screens'. Similarly revelatory were her workshops called *Cleaning the House*, which demanded an even greater commitment from the participants: five days of no food, five days of no talking, five days of heavy physical exercises and ten-kilometre walks in the forest in a blindfolded state, and on the sixth day looking at oneself in the mirror for an hour and then making an object with materials found during the workshop.

In all of her performances, Abramović used her body as a vehicle or agent to effect a transformation of the self[116] and to transmit impulses to the audience. In her early Body Art she reached a state of trance through physical ordeals; in her middle period with Ulay she connected with the deeper layers of her self, the earth's energy and flow of Nature; her later work was more akin to a cleansing process. But in each of her live performances the audience provided her with a tremendous energy and helped her to push herself deeper and deeper into a process of discovery. 'That energy only happens if I am relating to the public; it doesn't happen if I'm alone in my studio doing something by myself. The public become like an electric field around me. And then the communication is possible because they can project on me like a mirror.'[117] On the whole, she found a great deal of understanding from her audiences: 'They performed with you and gave you the necessary support.'[118] Some people were scared and found it difficult to cope with the elements of danger and pain. But when they stayed and accompanied her on her journey, they, too, were touched by the experience. They were enfolded by an energy field and put into a trance-like state where the archetypal actions and symbols used in the performance could sink into their subconscious mind and effect subtle changes there. The result of this process Abramović described thus: 'The deeper you go into yourself as an artist, the more universal your work becomes. You should be like a mirror, so the spectators can project themselves on you. Every moment, every symbol you use as a performer, is actually the tool to a universal language.'[119] By putting her whole life into her performances, Abramović could communicate to her audiences profound experiences that opened up new aspects of human existence. Thus, she was able 'to push them through an opening and give them a key to something'.[120] She could act like 'a bridge' that allowed spectators to connect with 'a higher self' and with the source of energy she herself was 'plugged into'.[121]

6

Video and Multi-media Performance

From Video Art to Video Performance

The technology for capturing and preserving moving images and sound on electro-magnetic tape was first developed in the 1950s for television broadcast purposes (see Chronology 6.1). Whereas film fixes images chemically on an oxide-coated plastic carrier and makes them visible to the naked eye, the video camera encodes and transmits pictures electronically, directly and without time delay, onto monitors. As there is no laboratory processing involved, these images can be simultaneously recorded and played back. In the 1960s, the technology became widely used by television companies in an expensive and cumbersome two-inch format. For many years to come, the term 'video' continued to be used as a technical term for the television picture signal. Only with the development of half-inch helical scan equipment in the mid-1960s did video make its first inroads into the domestic market. In the late 1960s, after the release of the first portable video recorder, Sony's 'Portapak', it also became an important new tool of expression for artists.

The triumphant advance of television as the most influential popular medium of the electronic age caused many artists to reflect on this new cultural force and to explore alternatives to its aesthetics and prevalent forms of discourse. The early video art of the 1960s was largely excluded from established exhibition outlets and found only small niches in specialized galleries and film festivals. Although television served as a model for the video medium, the latter defined itself in opposition to its 'older brother' and incorporated from the very beginning aspects of other media such as theatre and fine arts. In the 1970s, with the explosion of so-called 'Media Arts', video finally entered the privileged domains of High Art and came to be used principally in five types of production set-up:

179

1   Video tapes that explored the technical possibilities and limitations of the medium.

2   Real-time, closed-circuit situations, where the artist engaged in an interactive dialogue with the video camera and recorded this on tape for future distribution.

3   Video performance, where in a live event the artist confronted physical presence with mediated presence, and encouraged the audience to reflect on the representational qualities of the electronic medium.

4   Interactive or participatory events, where the electronic media of video and television were manipulated and transformed by the audience, following scores or instructions provided by the artist.

5   Video sculptures, single- or multi-monitor installations and environments where gallery visitors viewed an assembly of monitors playing pre-recorded tapes.

Many of the early video tapes were produced by painters and sculptors who had switched to time-based art in the wake of the Happening and Fluxus movement. The production of electronic images offered an alternative to canvas and easel, just as celluloid film had challenged previous generations of artists. Videomakers continued the process of 'dematerialization of art' (L. Lippard), which had been started by the Dadaists and developed further by the Action Painters of the 1950s. In the 1970s, video art was often related to Conceptualism, as electronic images were considered 'art ideas' rather than physical 'art objects'.

Most early video art followed two dominant trends and can principally be divided into tapes that continued the Modernist traditions of formalist experimentation, or works that focused on the production and reception process as a social praxis. A number of factors influenced this development:

- McLuhan's theory of mass communication;
- theories of semiotics, poststructuralism, deconstruction and postmodernism;
- counter-cultural theories on television as a form of social manipulation;
- feminism and the Women's Movement challenging traditional forms of representation and deconstructing gender-biased imagery on television and in other mass media.

Most of the tapes produced during this early period were self-reflexive exercises examining the nature of the new electronic medium. Avant-garde video, like Modernist painting, sculpture or film, had little to do with the meaning or representation of reality, but rather focused on the material properties of the medium and the structural laws of the signifying process. In the 1970s, a less formalist examination of the expressive and social potential of video gained prominence. As the medium did not require any operating crews, it afforded a strong sense of intimacy and became particularly attractive to artists working in an 'expressionist' environment, where immediacy and spur-of-the-moment creativity were highly rated. Here, video replaced the canvas as the medium on which to 'imprint' creative 'gestures'. Another approach could be observed amongst artists who had been politicized by the 1968 rebellion and who placed video and television in a broader social context. Twenty-five years of television had given rise to new perceptions and representations of the world and had programmed a whole generation's way of seeing and understanding life. The so-called 'video guerrillas' used video as a tool to deconstruct the myth of television as a 'window onto the world'. They examined TV as 'a way of life', criticized the pervasive influence of television and the mass media, and revealed the skewed picture of reality that dominated commercial television broadcasts. Integrating art and social change became the objective of many radical video producers, who explored the possibilities for setting up counter-structures for the democratization of the television medium. Instead of relying on galleries or TV stations, the guerrilla groups worked in community centres or with political groups, were active in educational settings and generally contributed to making video an accessible and versatile medium of social practice.[1]

The situation began to shift again in the mid-1970s. Television with its endless flow of images and multi-level information gave rise to postmodern vernaculars. This was helped, no doubt, by new editing equipment becoming available for home use and thus opening up new possibilities for synthesizing and transforming images. This trend was reinforced in the early 1980s with the advent of new computer software and digital animation devices. Furthermore, radically improved camcorder equipment could now produce broadcast-compatible colour tapes; and small-scale TV stations, which had sprung up with the deregulation of TV networks, developed an interest in the new languages of electronic communication employed in experimental video programmes.

These opportunities allowed many video artists to get out of the gallery circuit, exploit their work commercially, and have it shown on public broadcast channels. However, TV's potential as a useful showcase was counterbalanced by the detrimental effect of its bureaucratic hierarchies, commercial imperatives and conventional aesthetics. Some video artists managed to establish a special relationship with certain TV channels that took an interest in a new visual culture, and were able to preserve their integrity and maintain control over the production and distribution of their ideas. But others became absorbed by the institutions, or moved into the even more commercial market of music videos. The compromises forced upon artists by commercial outlets were vehemently opposed by the video purists. Some of them distributed their products via mail, others switched to cable broadcast as an alternative to conventional TV networks, and others again returned to exhibiting their works in galleries and art centres.

Whereas video art in the 1970s was characterized by a dichotomy of formalist avant-garde and political video culture, the aim of the Media Generation in the 1980s was to dismantle the distinctions between popular and High Art. Many of these artists had graduated from art academies, where Live Art and video art had found their way into the curriculum and were taught as legitimate art forms beside the more traditional media of painting and sculpture. Many of these young video artists pursued their careers in a thoroughly professional manner. They adapted some of the avant-garde techniques of the 1970s, combining them with new narrative forms and televisual vocabularies. Not least because of this aesthetic fusion and the complex technologies at their disposal (often better than those of television studios back in the 1960s), their products possessed commercial viability and found release opportunities outside the gallery circuit. In a manner that was typical of the 1980s, avant-garde video artists entered into a dialogue with the broader public and created an unusual amalgamation of art and commerce. Television, advertising companies and the music industry were the prime customers for this lucrative, yet still experimental practice; but galleries and museums, who increasingly relied on private sponsorship for their shows, were equally keen to provide showcases for major video artists. The proliferation of video production in the 1980s, both in the artistic and commercial domains, created a large catalogue of slick, high-tech productions that was equally suited to gallery or broadcast exhibition. This complex pluralism, where the avant-garde merged with the mainstream, was seen by many critics to be a typical trait of postmodernism.

However, apart from this proliferating and increasingly ill-defined middle-ground, where a large number of artists found profitable employment, there existed also a purely commercial sector producing an endless string of advertising clips, pop videos and wall-decorations for discotheques. On one end of the scale, video jockeys in night-clubs and programmers at MTV[2] turned video art into 'vuzak', a genre of popular entertainment devoid of any critical intention; at the opposite end of the spectrum there were avant-garde artists, who did not lose sight of the social and political dimensions of the electronic media and refused to 'sell out' to the culture industry. Some of these switched from 'guerrilla video' or critical television to experimenting with new formalist devices that had become available through computers and digital image processors. Others worked with associatively structured visual narratives of a postmodern kind, multi-layered collages of sounds and images, or developed the novel format of video sculpture and installation. The main features of video as a medium are summarized in Box 6.1

BOX 6.1: SOME KEY CHARACTERISTICS OF THE VIDEO MEDIUM

- Electronic (magnetic) recording.

- Immediate live feedback (no time-lag between the recording and viewing of images; the recording and playback of the image occur simultaneously).

- Continuous flow of electromagnetic signals (as opposed to individually framed images on celluloid film).

- The monitor image is a picture and light source in one (as opposed to the projected celluloid image that is reflected from the film screen).

- Unlimited possibilities for image transformation and manipulation in the recording or post-production process.

- Storage of images on inexpensive cassettes that can be erased and reused.

- Images can be read as electronic signals and transmitted via cable for long-distance broadcasts.

- Simplicity and flexibility of the portapak renders recording crews and operators superfluous (individual work replaces team work).

This chapter will not be concerned, in the first instance, with video art, but with the use of video in live events, for which at the time the new term 'video performance' was coined. As the expression was widely used by artists of the period without necessarily denoting the same phenomenon, I shall begin my discussion with a clarification of how I am employing it on the following pages.

In a video performance, a stage action is confronted with an electronically mediated image of the same event, and both are exhibited simultaneously to the audience. Two separate, but interconnected, discourses take place at the same time, enabled by the instant-relay property of the video camera (see Illustration 18). The monitor displays sequences of images that are an objective refraction or a distorted manipulation of the live performance. The discourse of the body is combined with the discourse of the electronic medium. The juxtaposition of the two information systems allows the audience to compare and critically assess the two simultaneous presentations of an organic body and its artificial image.

A different category of video performance was developed by artists who substituted the live events with electro-magnetic tapes. These videos were not conceived as an element of a live event, but rather, a performance was

---

CHRONOLOGY 6.1:   EARLY HISTORY OF VIDEO

1951   Bing Crosby Enterprises launch a magnetic video tape for broadcast use.

1956   Ampex Corporation develops a two-inch quadruplex videotape of broadcast standard.

CBS in New York broadcasts first TV programme via videotape (30 November 1956).

1960s   Black and white video equipment becomes widely used in the television industry.

1963   Nam June Paik, 'Exposition of Music. Electronic Television', at the Galerie Parnass in Wuppertal.

First video exhibition by Wolf Vostell at the Smolin Gallery in New York.

Vostell presents an Electronic TV décollage, 'Sun in Your Head', at the Galerie Parnass, Wuppertal.

1964   Sony releases a half-inch, reel-to-reel, helical scan, monochrome VTR, designed for home use.

1965   First video portapak released by Sony.

Nam June Paik shows 'Electronic Video Recorder' at the Café A Go Go in New York (first gallery exhibition of a video tape).

→

→

1968   First public TV broadcast of a video-art tape ('Black Gate Cologne' by Otto Piene and Aldo Tambellini), by WDR Cologne.

1969   WGBH-TV Boston broadcasts video-art tapes produced by six artists in its experimental studio.

First video exhibition ('TV as a Creative Medium'), at the Howard Wise Gallery in New York.

Gerry Schum opens the first Television Gallery in Berlin, followed in 1971 by a first Video Gallery in Düsseldorf.

1970   Paik/Abe video synthesizer.

1971   Sony launches a helical scan, three-quarter-inch video recorder, the 'U-Matic', with the tape enclosed in a cassette.

First video department established at Everson Museum in Syracuse, NY.

1972   Philips launches the first half-inch video cassette recorder (VCR).

First Annual National Video Festival at Minneapolis College of Art and Design.

First Women's Video Festival at The Kitchen in New York.

1973   First videodiscs released.

1975   Betamax, as the first half-inch consumer video cassette recorder, introduced.

'Video Art', the first comprehensive video survey, at the ICA in Philadelphia.

Computerized image processors become commercially available.

1977   Half-inch VHS (video home system) cassettes introduced as a consumer format.

WDR Cologne broadcasts nine instalments of video art from the documenta 6 exhibition in Kassel.

1980   Portable recorder and camera combinations (Camcorders) introduced.

1995   Sony, Philips, and Toshiba agree on a standard for a digital video disc.

18 Ulrike Rosenbach: *Die einsame Spaziergängerin*, video performance in Folkwangmuseum Essen, 1979

devised to be viewed on a video monitor. The resulting images had a theatrical origin, but they were specifically generated for the video camera. They were processed, filtered, manipulated and designed to establish an objectifying distance between performer and spectator. The physical reality of the body was turned into an electronic discourse that was specific to the video medium. Since the artist was at once performer and editor of the tape, he or she could control the primary material (i.e. his or her body) and the secondary images generated from it. Through the use of montage and editing techniques the artist arrived at a re-arrangement of the material, a re-structuring of the time nexus and a re-composition of the imagery. The video tape became an autonomous creation in which the performance was subsumed without losing its intrinsically performative quality.

The first performances that combined body-centred live art with an electronic mediation through the video camera took place around the year 1970. Vito Acconci and Dan Graham can be regarded as the fathers of this new genre, but it was soon taken up by women artists, and in the course of the 1970s it developed into a favourite genre of feminist Performance Art. There was a general tendency amongst women artists to be drawn towards body-centred video performances, whereas male artists were more actively concerned with exploring the formal and material characteristics of the new electronic medium. Video performances offered an ideal outlet for feminists who sought to confer value upon women's experiences and achievements, expose and subvert the traditional images and roles assigned to women in the mass media, and develop a new identity outside the constraints of patriarchal society.

As discussed above in the chapter on Body Art, many women artists concerned themselves with problems of representation. They saw in the mass consumption of gender-specific imagery a major obstacle to establishing an emancipated female identity, and sought to reclaim the body as a site of female subjectivity instead of having it serve as a canvas for the projection of male desires. It was therefore paramount to disrupt and subvert the accepted languages of representation in advanced information societies. Both Body Artists and female video artists demonstrated in their works that just as gender was not biologically determined but socially constructed, there existed no 'natural sign' of the body but only ideologically charged representations of it. Video turned out to be a useful tool for deconstructing the dominant discourses of femininity because the displayed images on the monitor resembled those on the television screen. The picture frame of the television was regarded as an electronic equivalent to the proscenium arch in the theatre and the wooden frame around a painting. In all three forms of representation, the female human being was objectified in principally the same manner: she occupied the same status, she was subjected to the same distortions, she was denied her own voice. The advantage of video performances over Body Art or painting was its ability to juxtapose 'woman as subject' with 'woman as object' in the same live event. The synchronous feedback of video technology offered a unique means for making the viewing process a focus of attention. It problematized the relationship between the real woman in the performance area with the image of the woman on the video monitor, and thereby fostered new types of spectatorship.

I have refrained in this chapter from discussing video installations that uphold the ontological distinction between audience and stage (here a sculpted or architectural setting with electronic actors) and therefore set up a viewing situation that is not principally different from the cognitive experience of looking at a play, painting or sculpture. It is my view that museums and galleries have so readily accepted video installations because this new art form bore close resemblance to traditional presentational formats such as sculpture or the classical triptych, not to mention the multimedia display techniques at trade fairs etc. Although multi-monitor video installations have often been described as 'electronic theatre' that requires the viewer to be 'operative' and 'subjective' in the site, standing both inside and outside the installation, I would still maintain that their interaction with the display is extremely limited. The performative quality of a piece of sculpture (even if it fills a whole room and contains electronic images that introduce a time dimension into the arrangement) is different from that of a human actor.

The exploration of the frontiers between theatre and fine art is undoubtedly a task that is pertinent to avant-garde experimentation. I have therefore included some borderline cases, such as Paik's *Exhibition of Music – Electronic Television*.[3] However, I do not share the view of some scholars, who regard video installations as performance *per se*. The curatorial initiatives in the 1980s that made Installation Art a popular medium[4] rarely provided the audience with a creative role or any particularly challenging tasks. In most cases, the live feed-ins of the electronic apparatus only triggered fairly basic stimulus-response mechanisms. If the machine used a tree of options, the tasks set to users rarely went beyond the complexity of multiple-choice questions. In the best cases, this could create some startling effects and reactions, but it did not add up to a fully participatory involvement. Even very successful works such as Gary Hill's *Tall Ships* (1992), where the viewer was led through a dark corridor and sixteen video projections reacted in response to his or her movements,[5] gave visitors only a minimal input role. True, *Tall Ships* exists only as a virtual artwork until an active participant ('user') completes the creation process; but when I visited the installation, I felt like a Pavlovian dog, who was forced to *re*act rather than *inter*act. I was not given many choices by the (very simple) parameters of the apparatus and could not assume any particularly creative input roles. On the other hand, when artists employed computer technology to widen the range of participatory options, visitors could feel overtaxed. Annette Hünnekens summed up the problem in her study of interactive media art, in the following manner: 'The experiences gathered on media festivals made it clear that visitors were generally unable to handle the computer-directed installations without being given a conventional instruction manual.'[6] It is only when we move into the domain of electronic media arts and include video games and Virtual Reality theatres, that we can speak of proper performances and extended concepts of performativity (see Chapter 7).

The same can be said about the numerous multimedia spectacles, where artists employed video technology to create a bridge between theatre and the mediatized culture of the postmodern information society. These works brought Brecht's demand for a 'theatre for the scientific age' up to date and created performances for the televisual age by introducing elements of mass media into a conventional playhouse setting. In the 1920s, before electronic images could be employed in stage shows, there were numerous attempts to integrate actors with filmed décor. Eisenstein pioneered this method at The Proletkult First Workers' Theatre,[7] and Erwin Piscator developed it to perfection at the Theater am Nollendorfplatz.[8] In 1931, Marinetti made concrete suggestions for a *teatro aeroradiotelevisivo*,[9] but as far as I am aware, the first major theatrical spectacle that used the full spectrum of electronic media was Wolf Vostell's *Hamlet*. It was produced in 1979 in collaboration with Hansgünther Heyme at the Cologne municipal theatre, and included an electronic stage design and actors playing their roles in conjunction with 120 video monitors (see Illustration 19).

In the 1980s, video became a ubiquitous ingredient of experimental theatre productions, with several companies, such as the Wooster Group, George Coates' Performance Works, Dumb Type, Gaia Scienza, Studio Azzurro, Magazzini Criminali, etc., specializing in such shows. Other large-scale works where video technology played a dominant role, but was displayed in a conventional theatrical setting, were Steve Reich and Beryl Korot's Video Opera, *The Cave* (Vienna, 1993), and Philip Glass and Robert Wilson's 3-D computer-animation extravaganza, *Monsters of Grace* (Los Angeles, 1998). Also, in the area of dance, there were many initiatives to incorporate computer-aided imaging technologies into live performances. But before discussing such experiments, I shall examine the works of some early pioneers in the domains of video and multimedia

19 Wolf Vostell: Stage, costumes and media conception for Hansgünther Heyme's production of *Hamlet*, Bühnen der Stadt Köln, 1979.

performance, discuss their relation to the fine arts, Body Art, music and performing arts of the period, and focus in particular on the contribution made by women artists to this development.

Vito Acconci's Video Works

Vito Acconci's early interest in film and video was closely related to and grew out of his Body Art experiments of the 1960s (see above, Chapter 5). In his trajectory from solipsistic activities via relational work to social performances, Acconci felt that an exclusive focus on the artist's body 'became kind of a trap after a while'.[10] In the 1970s, Acconci produced over 30 video works, some as self-contained tapes, some as documents of live performances, some as elements of an installation, and some 'video performances', in which the camera and monitor were indispensable ingredients of a live event. It is especially these latter works which I shall discuss in this section.

In 1969, Acconci began to use still photography to record some of his activities for exhibition purposes. In 1970, he made his first films, again primarily to preserve the ephemeral gestures of the body's occupancy of time and space, but also to transform private acts into public exhibitions for a wider audience. Others, however, were self-contained works that reflected on the problem he experienced with his self-reflexive body-exercises (see above, Chapter 5). For example, *Hand and Mouth* (1970) presented the performer's feeling of being closed off from his audience: 'Pushing my hand into my mouth until I choke and am forced to release my hand . . . I am taking myself in, the viewer is an outsider.' *Openings* (1970) showed him pulling hairs out of the skin around his navel area until a pristine white skin with a deep dark hole, looking like a vagina, appeared. Opening himself up to viewers and making his body penetrable to their gaze addressed a whole series of issues that formed part of a topical debate at the time, especially in feminist film criticism. Other films tied in with his exploration of physical boundaries and the problematics of gender identity. For example, in *Conversions* (1970–1) he worked on the idea of sex-change by hiding his penis between his legs, burning off the hair on his chest, and pulling his skin to give it the appearance of female breasts. As this was not a live performance in front of an audience, or a private ritual of a would-be transsexual, but rather a super-8 film for public consumption, the notions of masculinity and femininity and their representation, particularly in popular mass media, were exposed to scrutiny. *Conversions* showed the construction of gendered images, their sources and history. By 'feminizing' himself in front of the viewer, Acconci parodied the traditional object position of women in the media and revealed the bi-polar model of male/female as a dubious construction. Other films of this period addressed the issues of masochism and sadism, submissive and authoritarian behaviour, hetero- and homosexuality, questions of identity and social interaction, the relationship between viewing and being viewed, inner and outer space. etc.

Acconci's first video tape, *Corrections* (1970), tied in with his live performances dealing with the theme of 'observing the self as the other'. He used the instant relay propensity of video technology to look at himself 'in the round'. Having the camera positioned behind his back, he felt as if he had a third eye that could observe what would otherwise go unnoticed. In this case it was a tuft of hair at the nape of his neck, which he regarded as an imperfection. He therefore lit some kitchen matches and singed off the unwanted hairs.

Several of Acconci's early videos addressed the mechanisms of visual communication. He firmly rejected the disembodied, gender-neutral concept of the gaze that dominated formalist criticism of the Late-Modernist period and anchored vision in a spatial and social matrix. For him the gaze had to do with desire, power, aggression, voyeurism. Video was a means of analysing the process not only of representation, but also of personal interaction with the viewer. Acconci accentuated the limitations of this encounter, emphasized the formal separation of viewer and performer, and made the spectator aware of the power that is inscribed in the process of viewing:

> The film frame . . . separates my activity from the outside world, places me in an isolation chamber (a meditations chamber, where I can be – have to be – alone with myself). . . . I've turned myself into a self-enclosed object: the viewer is left outside, the viewer is put in the position of a voyeur.[11]

Undertone (1973) was an attempt to use the director's ability to manipulate the viewer's gaze. We see Acconci sitting at the end of a long table, which is framed in such a manner that the camera/viewer cannot see what is underneath it. He places his arms under the table and begins an obsessive monologue, suggesting that there is a woman under the table rubbing his thighs. He then places his hands on the table, looks straight into the camera and addresses the viewer: 'I need someone to confess to.' He then places his hands again under the table and says: 'I want you to believe that there is nobody under the table. It is me who is caressing my thighs.' The two scenes are repeated six times with the suggested action under the table getting increasingly explicit: Acconci/the girl caresses the inside of his thighs, reaches inside his underpants, touches his penis. Acconci makes a masturbatory movement under the table, followed by a description of the girl taking the penis into her mouth and a direct address to the viewer: 'I need you . . . I need to know that I can depend on you . . . I need you to filter out my lies . . . Don't turn your back on me . . . I need you to force me to confess . . . I need you to look into my eyes to prove that I am not deceiving you.'

Acconci had a strictly Catholic upbringing, and his experiences at a Jesuit school undoubtedly formed an autobiographical background to many of his videos. Acconci denied to the viewer, who acts like a confessor, an 'under-the-table perspective' and played a perverse game with his/her desire to find out what exactly is happening under the table. He coerced the viewer into a position of both voyeur and accomplice and used the tension between what is shown and what is hidden to establish a 'power field' between himself and the spectator. He assumed the role of power and superior knowledge and undermined the 'feminine' position of the object as something to be looked at, thereby frustrating the spectator's voyeurism and defusing the power of his or her gaze.

Several of Acconci's early videos were centred on the theme of isolation, which he was also exploring in his live performances at that time. *Theme Song* (1973), for example, showed him lying on the floor and talking to the camera: 'I know you have a beautiful face. . . . Come close to my body. . . . Come over to me. . . . You can't leave me alone. . . . How long I'll have to wait for you?' However much identification this may have induced in the viewer, his following actions underlined the limitations of the medium: bending his legs around the camera cannot produce the effect of wrapping himself around the viewer. A tape recorder may play a romantic song about love and friendship while Acconci continues talking seductively to the viewer, but the interaction is doomed to failure as the artist remains trapped behind the screen. A similarly futile attempt at interaction with an audience is demonstrated in *Open Book* (1974), which showed a close-up of Acconci's open mouth and his desperate attempts at forming sentences while keeping his mouth open: 'I'm not closed, I'm open. Come in.' When the strain on his muscles is too strong and he closes his mouth, he immediately begs for forgiveness: 'That was a mistake. I won't close. I won't close you off. I won't close you in. I'm open to everything.' However, the viewer will never be able to accept the invitation. Videos such as this one made it clear that building a relationship through camera and monitor has strict limitations that cannot be overcome.

For *Claim* (1971), Acconci invited the audience to visit him in the basement of a building, where he sat at the bottom of the stairs, blindfolded and armed with a crowbar and an iron rod. Acconci claimed possession over this terrain and treated it as a power field that was connected to the outside world by way of a video instant-relay installation. The visitors knocking on the door were greeted by his voice and image on the monitor, warning them: 'I am alone in this basement. I want to stay alone here. I'll stop anybody from coming down here.' Initially people thought that this was only a video tape, but when they opened the upper door they realized that there was a real person behind the monitor screen, in fact an immensely violent one, who was ranting and raving when he heard any noise at the top of the stairs, and scared visitors off by hitting the walls with his weapons.

Other videos from this phase focused on Acconci's private life, his persona and relationships (especially with his partner Kathy Dillon). The camera was not only used here to document an action and relay it to an outer world, but became a power tool to dominate or manipulate the other (the co-performer, or the audience). *Pryings* (1971) was a video performance at the Loeb Center of New York University. He placed a video monitor on stage and performed an action with Dillon in the front of the auditorium, leaving it to the audience to decide whether they wished to observe the live action or the relayed images. Dillon was subjected to a long and violent struggle, where Acconci tried to force her tightly shut eyes open. The male aggressor was shown to be doubly obnoxious as Dillon offered only muted resistance and repeatedly pressed her face against his chest as if to seek protection from him. Acconci's sadistic coercion of his partner acted as a metaphor for his forceful attempt to make the viewer see what he wants them to see. The spectator always assumes a voyeuristic position in the theatre. But placing a monitor on stage and feeding it with video images (*video* = Latin for 'I see') that show a face with eyes permanently closed, undermines the whole circuit of 'seeing/being seen', and the social matrix of the 'voyeuristic gaze/exhibitionist display'. I would therefore disagree with the criticism that Acconci's work legitimized violence and spectatorial norms. Rather, he employed video as a powerful tool to unveil and demonstrate the ingrained structures behind cultural practices, which surely must be the first step towards altering them. Soliciting spectatorial desire while at the same time making it the subject of the performances allows viewers to reflect on their relation to the displayed body and to transform an otherwise subliminal act into conscious experience.

The live performances of 1970–3 brought Acconci to the realization that his attempts at undermining the status of the artist and the dominant practices of the distribution system had been seriously flawed. Removing the art object from its altar and replacing it with the artist's body still adhered to the ideology of art's uniqueness and required audiences to come to a particular place (gallery, theatre, exhibition hall or whatever) in order to view a product or process. To change the monodirectional gaze he withdrew his presence from sight and communicated using his voice alone. He then realized that if he could not be seen, there was no reason why he should be present in the space at all. He therefore replaced his physical presence with an installation of video tapes and monitors.

Command Performance (1974) at 112 Greene Street, Manhattan, operated with such a mediated presence in a very site-specific installation (see Illustrations 20 and 21). Two monitors (A and B) and a camera pointing towards a spotlit stool were placed between three columns, which separated the room into different sections. If a visitor sat on the stool, he could view a pre-recorded tape on monitor A standing in front of him. In front of monitor B lay a carpet, on which the audience could gather and observe the viewer's actions and reactions on the stool. The pre-recorded tape showed Acconci lying on his back, projecting his desires, dreams and fears onto the viewer, giving instructions or asking the viewer to take the lead. The tape began with a hypnotic incantation: 'Dream myself out of here, into you.' Cajoling, pleading, insulting, fantasizing, Acconci tried to seduce the viewer into taking his or her place in the spotlight: 'You're there where I

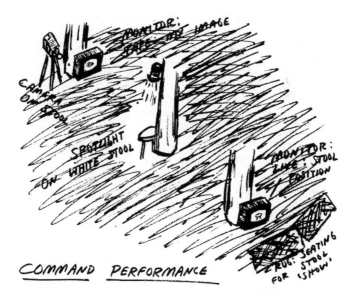

20   Vito Acconci, drawing of *Command Performance*, 112 Greene Street, January 1974

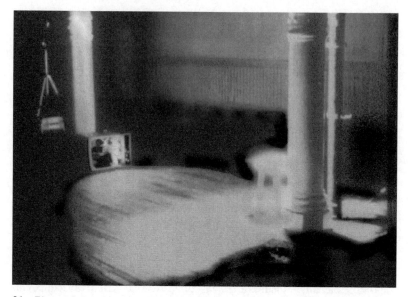

21   Photo of *Command Performance*, 112 Greene Street, January 1974

used to be . . . I don't have to be there any more . . . You can do it for me now . . . Oh, you didn't expect this, did you baby?' As the tape progressed, Acconci became more and more obsessed with his fantasies: 'Like a little dog . . . jump up on the stool . . . show them your ass . . . it's your turn to play the fool for them . . . the stool is all yours . . . take it baby . . . give it to them.' After ten minutes, he sought to compel the viewer to perform a striptease or table dance. After twenty minutes, he imagined the viewer to be male, to exhibit his penis, and to punish him by penetrating his mouth and anus. After 45 minutes, his voice became softer and he confessed that his work had always been too private, as he had been afraid to come out of his shell, and he pleaded with the viewer to help him find contact in the wider social world: 'I admit . . . my work has always been too private . . . I've never been able to break out . . . but you can do it . . . be a model for me . . . show me how to get out of it . . . teach me how to be there, strong, in public . . . take me out of myself . . . take the lead . . . they want you to be the leader too.' After 50 minutes, he imagined being in a military camp and suggesting to his comrades efficient methods of fighting the enemy. The scene ended with a romantic vision of the group having won the battle and everyone wanting 'to follow you, join you, be with you'.

When Acconci realized that he was returning to art as a mediated form of communication – a practice he had tried to move away from in the late 1960s – he decided to employ the gallery or museum as 'a meeting place, a place to start a relationship',[12] i.e. a social space in which people would gather, talk and entertain each other as in a plaza. From then on, he moved further and further away from performing in any institutional settings and instead embraced architecture, interior design, street furniture, landscape gardening, construction of public amenities, and other activities in the civic arena, as his media.

Nam June Paik

In Chapter 4 I discussed Paik's early career as a musician and performer and some of the basic premises behind his œuvre of the 1960s. Throughout the 1960s and 1970s, he engaged in a wide spectrum of experiments in various electronic media and explored some of the performative potentials of video sculptures, video installations, video projections and video environments. From these I have selected for discussion his early interactive television/video work, as it stands closest to the concept of performance that I have been using throughout this volume.

Nam June Paik was a multi-talented 'jack of all trades': a composer, pianist, performer, video artist, scientist, sculptor, theoretician. It may be an exaggeration to call him an 'uomo universale', but he certainly had many of the qualities required for a latter-day Renaissance man, a cross between a postmodern Mozart and a cybernetic Leonardo. This artist from Korea arrived in central Europe at a time when Modernism had reached a stage of terminal decline. Having been taught to admire Western music, he was struck to find composers like Cage turning to Eastern cultures for inspiration. His intention had been to complete his studies in art and music with a PhD, and he soon found that as a creative artist he had nothing to add to the traditions of Western arts as they had developed over the last 500 years.

> Instead of being just another 'successful' artist in commercial galleries and concert halls, I want to dedicate the next year to academic and fundamental studies, which may radically change art and the status of art in society in the decades to come.[13]

> I learned from Arnold Schoenberg to dig up the root and shake the tree from the root on.[14]

Paik's early installations and video tapes operated with a strategy that ran counter to the ever-increasing flood of electronic imagery. The guiding aim behind his video work of the past forty years has been to convert television from 'a passive pastime to an active creation'.[15] He countered the one-way communication structure of the mass media by highly creative interventions into the operative heart of the medium. The motto of Paik's early video œuvre was: 'Television has attacked us for a life time, now we strike back!!'[16] He had a love–hate relationship with technology ('I use technology in order to hate it better'[17]) and both used and abused the electronic media to achieve his aims ('TV tortured the intellectuals for long time . . . it is about the time that the intellectuals torture TV'[18]). He showed live broadcasts on 'prepared' television sets, and manipulated and controlled the images by tampering with the TV tube, thus revealing that television does not present a natural but rather a distorted view of the world. ('High INfidelity. TV became TV art through all technical mal-functions.'[19])

As he pursued avant-garde ideas with the showmanship of an entertainer ('I come from a very poor country and I am poor. I have to entertain people every second'[20]), he found a following across a wide spectrum of communities. He has often berated video art for being boring and accessible only to the producing artists' closest friends. Compared with the often tedious tapes of the 1960s and 1970s, Paik's works had instead considerable flair, wit and humour. His works have been broadcast on commercial television channels; he appeared on prime-time chat shows and his face graced the front page of mass-circulation magazines. Yet, at the same time he had major retrospectives in some of the most prestigious museums of the world. He managed to bridge the gap between the gallery world of High Art and the commercial world of popular culture in a manner that only Picasso and Warhol achieved before him.

Paik eschewed any kind of techno fetishism, yet at the same time he did not share Vostell's negative attitude towards the electronic mass media. Of course, Paik deplored the social and psychological effects of the information overkill in a media-sodden society; but he was also a great optimist who believed in technology's potential for being a positive force in human life. In some of his works he criticized the present state of human–machine interaction, but he also attempted to revert the electronic media to their creative origins and explored different ways of developing their technical and artistic potential. The idea behind this was to turn television into an innovative vehicle of communication and to stimulate viewers to look for 'new, imaginative and humanistic ways of using our technology'.[21]

Paik found that TV was a widely accessible medium because of its global visual language. He therefore employed these universal discourses and combined them with a thoroughly modern syntax based on the editing techniques of TV commercials as well as materialist avant-garde film. His video tapes, sculptures and installations had a strongly carnivalesque quality: they were subversive, yet fun to watch. Intellectual and artistic seriousness was paired with entertainment, critical comments with frivolous fun, popular culture with High Art. I have rarely attended a screening or visited an exhibition of his works where people were not smiling. This stands in marked contrast to other occasions, where only a handful of dedicated aficionados could muster the staying power to watch a given work to its very end. Paik's creations certainly never belonged to the type of artists' videos which cause a mass exodus from a viewing theatre.

In the late 1950s, Paik had been introduced by Karlheinz Stockhausen to the infinite possibilities of electronic means of sound production. He recalled in an interview of 1974: 'I was working with electronic music at the Radio Station of Cologne every day, which also transmits TV. It was natural for me to think that something similar to electronic music could also be done on the TV screen.'[22] However, in those days Paik was not considering the use of cameras and videotapes, as they were out of his reach, and he had to wait until the arrival of the Sony Portapak in 1965. He made use of the equipment he could find at low cost (second-hand TV sets) and played around with its electronic entrails, changing circuits, manipulating the signal flow, etc., thereby discovering an unlimited range of possibilities for creating new and startling images. These 'prepared TV sets' were an equivalent to Cage's 'prepared piano' and were born out of a similar attitude, i.e. don't accept instruments as they are; alter them and engage creatively with the tools of creativity.

Through his Fluxus activities, Paik became acquainted with Joseph Beuys, whose colleague at the Düsseldorf Academy of Arts, Karl Otto Goetz, had experimented in the late 1940s with radar and the Braun tube to produce electronic images on television screens:

Television technology opened up new ways of generating and manipulating kinetic forms and structures . . . which can be called de-materialized kinetic light paintings. . . . The ephemeral character of electronic paintings stands in contrast to the stored images on film, but the American 'Ampex' equipment allows us nowadays to preserve electronic impulses of a television broadcast on tape.[23]

Paik talked to Goetz about his experiments, which at that time also included computer technology. Paik had studied enough electronics and cybernetics to understand that an IBM 7090 with an output of 400,000 bits per second was far too slow to programme the 12 million dots which appear every second on a TV screen. But when comparing the piano's 88 keys with the

TV's 12 million pixels, the TV suddenly assumed an amazing potential and provoked in Paik the idea of 'composing a piano concerto using a piano equipped with 12 million keys'.[24] He saw in the TV screen 'an electronic canvas for an artist whose brush consists of light'.[25]

So, in the 1960s he switched from music theory to electronics. The shelves full of technical literature in his studio bore witness to his scientific interests. Although he acquired considerable technical expertise, in the end he had to leave much of the construction process to competent collaborators and concentrate on exploring the artistic potential of the technology put at his disposal. In the laconic style that is so typical of him, he commented: 'I didn't have any preconceived idea. Nobody had put two frequencies into one place, so I just do that, horizontal and vertical, and this absolutely new thing comes out. I make mistake after mistake, and it comes out positive. That is story of my whole life.'[26]

Paik had shown with his early concerts that he was moving far beyond the traditional boundaries of music. He employed sculptorial and visual elements, but integrated these into his sound structures in a manner that gave them a temporal dimension. An as yet underdeveloped component in this process was film. His work at the WDR (West German Broadcast Station) provided him with opportunities to take this a stage further, but as his specialization was electronic music, he developed an interest in the latest broadcast technology: electronic recording and editing devices (video). While this technology was unavailable for private use, Paik focused his attention on the television set as the final link in the communicative chain. He began to collect second-hand TV cabinets and to undertake 'research into the boundary regions between various fields, and complex problems of interfacing these different media and elements, such as music and visual art, hardware and software, electronics and humanities in the classical sense'.[27]

After his first performances in Cologne (see above, Chapter 4), Paik was invited to give a 'concert' of his *Symphony for 20 Rooms* (1961) at the Galerie Parnass in Wuppertal. For various reasons, the event had to be postponed from November 1961 to March 1962, and Paik changed his score for the sixteen rooms he was offered by the owner of the gallery. He transported twelve TV sets, four prepared pianos, two record players and various *objets sonores* to Wuppertal and set them up for an *Exposition of Music – Electronic Television*.[28] The events of 11–20 March 1963 became a landmark event in postwar art, as they exhibited, for the first time, television art in a gallery space. Televison was removed from its customary context and function, transformed into a tool that could be handled and manipulated in an infinite variety of ways in order to generate an aesthetic text that questioned the discourses and the social dimensions of the medium. The audience entered the large villa through an entrance that was ornamented with the head of a freshly slaughtered cow, and stepped into a room that contained a prepared piano decorated with barbed wire, photographs, dolls etc. At the opening, Joseph Beuys 'played' on it with a hammer and an axe. Another piano had the keys converted into switches that could be used to set off a transistor radio, a film projector or fan heater, or to switch off the lights. A third piano was turned on its back and could be played with the feet while people walked over it. *Sex Piano* was a toy grand piano with the keys hammering on condoms instead of strings. *Schallplatten-Schaschlik* ('Records on Spits') allowed the visitors to select their own piece of music. *Random Access* had strips of audio tape hanging on the wall and audiences were encouraged to rub magnetic tape heads over the tapes in order to produce short sequences of 'Do it yourself' music. One record player had a pickup arm in the form of a dildo, which had to be taken into the mouth and then lowered onto the record. *Zen for Walking* consisted of eight tins on a string, which could be dragged along the floor. In another room, chimes made from buckets, tubs, cans and various metal objects were hung from the ceiling and a golf club was provided to make them sound.

At the heart of the exhibition was a room with eleven prepared television sets. Five of these played 'electronic music' by K. O. Goetz, others showed a negative image, a one-line scanning pattern, deformed sine curves, or simply the broadcast of the day, with Paik manipulating, scrambling and deforming the images. While some of the unusual visual patterns were controlled by Paik, others were created by the audience (and according to Tomas Schmit's testimonial, 'they were keenly utilized, since they were mightily exciting'[29]). *Points of Light* connected a radio to a television monitor and allowed the audience to change the images by turning the volume knob on the radio. *Kuba TV* had a television set linked to a tape recorder, and depending on the sound signal, the image on the television screen changed as well. *Participation TV* translated sounds spoken into a microphone by the visitors into explosive visual patterns on the monitor.

These and various other sound-producing objects went indeed a stage beyond *Symphony for 20 Rooms*, which was intended to give the audience only the choice of either listening or not listening as they moved around the rooms. [30] *Exposition of Music*, on the other hand, implemented Paik's concept of 'indeterministic music'[31] and gave the visitors the freedom to handle the *objets sonores* in a manner they saw fit. This transformed the role of the composer – to use Paik's phrase – from 'cook to delicatessen dealer' and produced 'music from the people through the people to the people'.[32] In a text written after the exhibition he reflected on the variability and participation strategies employed in the show and found that they had indeed produced a fundamental change: here, the mass media functioned not just as a one-way system, but as one in which the audience could 'perceive SIMULTANEOUSLY the parallel flows of many independent movements'. At this point, the composer/artist had finally relinquished his role of expressive–creative genius trying to produce a work of art that approximated as much as possible to a premeditated ideal. Rather, his role was to put the means of creativity into the hands of the audience and to suggest ways of using them, without determining the results of the operation.[33]

In the following years, Paik continued to develop his concept of Participation TV. During a visit to Japan in 1963/64, he met Shuja Abe, who became his most important collaborator and technical expert for the next decade and who informed him about the possibilities of manipulating the flow of electrons by means of strong magnets. The result was *Magnet TV* (1965), which allowed visitors to create their own images on the TV screen by moving a magnet along the picture tube. A similar construction was used in *Dancing Patterns* (1966), where a cathode ray was fed with acoustic signals and produced pulsating images of an abstract nature. This integration of visual and musical elements was highlighted in the titles of several other, yet similar constructions: *Electric Blues, Tango Électrique, Rondo Électrique*, etc.

With the emergence of colour TV and affordable video cameras, Paik's experiments became more and more complex. *Participation TV II* (1969), for example, worked with several video cameras in a closed-circuit installation where signals were modulated by acoustic means and displayed on colour monitors, and where viewers/operators could see their distorted mirror-images floating through electronic clouds, fog or water.[34] In 1969/70, Paik progressed a stage further in this attempt to turn the television viewer into an artist. Together with Shuja Abe he developed the video synthesizer, which allowed the creation of an infinite range of sounds, colours and forms. The images generated by it were not only displayed as electronic 'paintings', but also juxtaposed or overlayed with commercial TV footage. The result was a dazzling display of what Paik called 'electronic art. Polyphonic painting à la Freud'.[35] The synthesizer was an artistic tool that could be operated by just about anybody and, as such, functioned as an 'anti-machine machine' in the service of 'participation TV (the one-ness of creator, audience, and critic)' and 'instant TV making'.[36] Given the price and the size of the instrument, it was not a commercial proposition on the electronics market (for years, Paik dreamt of a miniature version in the form of a pocket calculator that people could use while sitting in their television armchair). But it served a useful function in the training of visual artists and became a favourite gadget at the California Institute of Arts and in Otto Piene's Center for Advanced Visual Studies in Cambridge, Massachusetts. Paik himself demonstrated a wide range of possible applications on WGBH-TV in Boston, at gallery exhibitions, and in 'concerts' such as *Boston Symphony Video* at the Mercer Art Center in New York (1972). Some of these creations, such as *Electronic Opera No 2* (1972), were also recorded on video tape and exhibited in multi-monitor installations, which became a key aspect of his work from the mid-1970s onwards.

This is not the place to discuss in any more detail those aspects of Nam June Paik's œuvre that did not involve him as a performer or that excluded the audience as an active participant. Suffice it to state that after 1970 he worked predominantly in the domains of video sculpture and installation and became a figure of major influence in this and related fields. Being a musician and composer, Paik's approach to the dimension of time was different from that of video artists who came from a painting or sculpture background. Working with magnetic tapes in a sound studio prepared him for the structuring of video tapes according to rhythmic principles. When these tapes were incorporated into single- or multi-monitor installations, the static quality of the television hardware (often very early, Baroque-looking cabinets) offered a strange contrast to the fleeting images displayed in them. Another theme that ran through many of his video installations was the correlation between different layers of reality and the issue of TV as a 'second Nature'. For example, in *TV Garden* (1974), he 'planted' thirty television monitors, on which images of plants were displayed, in a garden-like environment. In *Video Fish* (1975), he played a similar game with the dichotomy of reality and the image of reality by placing monitors showing footage of swimming fish inside an aquarium with living fish in it. Such juxtapositions and witty metaphors removed television from its customary context, commented on its discourses and showed how Nature (reality) was appropriated by the medium of television.

The ultimate aim behind such tactics and formal interventions was, of course, to question dominant production and reception practices in a media-saturated society. Paik shared with many artists of the 'Media Generation' a critical attitude towards modern mass media and people's habits of using of them. At the same time, he pursued a Utopian vision of the democratic potential of the new electronic media and saw the role of the artist as a humanizing agent in a world that was increasingly dominated by technology:

Underground outlet is my safety valve. I like being the world's most famous bad pianist. But I also like to do NET [i.e. TV broadcasts] because it is important, is where I can maybe influence society. . . . Like McLuhan say, we are antenna for changing society. But not only antenna – we also have output capacity, capacity to humanize technology. My job is to see how establishment is working and to look for little holes where I can get my fingers in and tear away walls. And also try not to get too corrupt.[37]

Paik was a social critic and subversive visionary, who questioned television's function as a medium that instils a passive acceptance of dominant ideologies and societal structures by dispensing an opiate of mindless entertainment and low-brow information. Anyone who unintentionally zapped into the programmes he produced for WNET in New York or WGBH in Boston was likely to stop and wonder what on earth was going on there. There was no way of mistaking these images for a continuation of life in another medium, or using them as 'electronic wallpaper'. Paik set up alternative uses of modern electronic media so that people would become aware of what they were watching. A typical gesture that says much about Paik's subversive strategies was his appearance, in 1975, in Tom Snyder's popular talk show *Tomorrow*. In a video link-up, Paik led the host through his studio and demonstrated to him the use of his recently made *TV Chair*, a sculpture fitted with a TV screen to sit on. As he was bantering politely with the TV star, he switched on a video recording of Snyder's last talk show, connected it to the TV chair, and then sat on Snyder's 'face'.[38]

In his writings, Paik outlined many concrete projects concerned with transforming television from a one-way delivery system into a medium of active exchange ('Participation TV'). The ubiquity and universal accessibility of TV made it an ideal medium for reaching the masses, and he hoped that high-frequency technologies would lead to the creation of 'thousands of large and small TV stations. This will free us from the monopoly of a few TV channels.'[39] He foresaw the creation of a 'global university', where data banks were put at the disposal of educational institutions so that people all over the world could access the stored information and pursue their education at their own pace. Furthermore, the universal intelligibility of TV images would enable educators to use them, for example, for introducing family planning to Indian villages with a predominantly illiterate population.[40]

Unfortunately, the global development of the information society took a different course. The information flow became even more mono-directional and non-participatory. Although satellite and cable TV connected homes to hundreds of TV channels, the commercial hold on these channels meant that the dominant values of Western, and predominantly US-American, society came to reign supreme all over the world. Slum dwellers watch soap operas rather than family planning programmes, and information monopolies control (and usually charge for) access to educational networks.

In the course of his long and distinguished career, Paik published over 200 essays and statements,[41] which are full of insightful comments on contemporary media culture and contain many alternative suggestions. Yet, taken as a whole, they do not add up to a consistent theory. In Paik's dual function of artist and educator, the former certainly prevailed, in an instinctual rather than an intellectual manner. ('Artists, generally, have not profound theories, you know – we have instincts, and then practical methods afterwards.'[42]) None the less, Paik was a sharp-minded and witty thinker, who tackled complex issues in an imaginative manner, asked many pertinent questions and demonstrated how much of the creative potential of modern media lay neglected and unused. But he hardly ever dwelled on the political causes behind the media structures he condemned, and rarely focused his attention on social and economic matters unless they impinged directly on the realms of art and media. His works contain a judicious balance of aesthetic enjoyment and social critique; but he left it to the audience to decide what conclusions to draw from these elements. As Leigh Landy and Antje von Graevenitz rightly pointed out, this was not necessarily a sign of political naivety, but rather rooted in the Zen method of teaching: opening the eye to phenomena by asking questions about concrete examples, not by offering abstract precepts and instructions.[43]

Joan Jonas

Joan Jonas was one of the early female pioneers of video performance and a major influence on many younger artists who converted to the medium in the course of the 1970s. She featured prominently in several of the early video showcases and since then has been honoured with three major retrospectives. She was a sculptor by profession and studied art history and fine arts in Massachusetts and New York (1954–64). In the early 1960s, she had occasion to observe the burgeoning Happenings scene and became an enthusiastic follower of the Judson Church Dance Theatre. From Bernini to Boccioni, there have been many sculptors who attempted to overcome the static quality of sculpture and introduced into their creations the aspect of time and the transitory dynamics of the human body in motion. Joan Jonas followed their lead and shifted her interests from sculpture to working with the moving body in space. She joined the wider ambits of the Judson group, took classes and workshops with Trisha Brown and received a great deal of inspiration from Lucinda Child and Yvonne Rainer. This led to her first choreographies and performances with the Judson dancers, *Jones Beach Dance* (1970) and *Nova Scotia Beach Dance* (1971).[44]

Parallel to these outdoor pieces, she engaged in a series of small-scale interior performances that used mirrors as a structural component: *Oad Lau* (1968), *Mirror Piece I* (1969), *Mirror Piece II* (1970), *Choreomania* (1971) and *Mirror Check* (1970). For many years, these mirrors became a signature prop of Jonas's performances and the also featured prominently in her first video performances. Some of these works were inspired by Jorge Luis Borges's short story, 'The Library of Babel',[45] which described a maze-like library with mirrors doubling a myriad of hallways and creating an illusion of infinite space.[46] Lacan has written extensively on the role of the mirror in the infant's development of an identity and self-image. In a similar way, Jonas established her subject position on stage with the use of the mirror (and subsequently with the video camera as a reflective tool and mirror substitute). She commented on *Oad Lau*, in which she wore a dress with a variety of mirrors pasted on it, reciting excerpts from Borges's short story:

> The mirror provided me with a metaphor for my reflective investigation. It also provided a device to alter space, and to fragment it. I could mix reflections of performers and audience, thereby bringing all of them into the same time and space of the performance. In addition to creating space, a mirror also disturbs space, suggesting another reality through the looking glass. To see the reflection of Narcissus; to be a voyeur. To see one's self as the other.[47]

In *Mirror Piece I* and *Mirror Piece II*, she had fifteen performers carrying large mirrors, 45 × 150 cm, around on stage. As the spectators saw themselves reflected in the mirrors, they became conscious of their role in the reception process; thereby the act of seeing as a constitutive component of theatre was made 'visible' to them. Similarly, in *Choreomania*, the viewers saw themselves reflected in a wall that looked like a flipped-up stage floor. Part of it was covered with mirrors, part of it had brackets, ropes and handles attached to it, allowing the performers to climb up the wall and make it swing from side to side. In *Mirror Check*, Jonas stood naked in the empty space of the Leo Castelli Gallery and used a small, hand-held mirror to investigate parts of her body that otherwise would remain hidden from her view. In this performance, she came closest to the self-discovery aspect of Body Art. Although this dialogue with herself was an attempt at constructing her identity and authenticating her presence by means of external agents, it resulted in showing the impossibility of perceiving one's body as a whole or integrated unity. And, more significantly, by staging a double action of looking and being looked at, she emphasized how the refractive mirror imposed an object status on the body, which the viewing subject could not escape from. This insight became a guiding principle of her subsequent video performances, which established her reputation in the international art world.

In 1970 Jonas brought a Sony Portapak back from a visit to Japan and began to explore the self-reflexive properties of the closed-circuit, live-relay setup. Like many artists of her generation, she was fascinated by the possibility of recognizing oneself and of communicating with oneself by means of camera and monitor. In 1972, she gave the first presentations of *Organic Honey's Visual Telepathy* and *Organic Honey's Vertical Roll*. These two key works in her early œuvre were performed in different configurations until 1980 and involved video in a variety of capacities, establishing what Rosalind Krauss later called a 'video aesthetics of narcissism'.[48] *Vertical Roll* was also released as a video-art tape and shown at many festivals. Organic Honey was Joan Jonas's glamorous alter-ego and a product of her adolescent infatuation with the illusionary world of theatre, circus and magic shows. Both works showed a woman as she existed in real life and how she made use of media-based images to construct herself as a beautiful, available object. Jonas's transformation of her everyday self into an 'electronic sorceress'[49] by means of costume, mask and props problematized the definition and representation of female identity in art and life. The performances juxtaposed the masquerade of femininity and the subject position of the person behind the mise-en-scène. The video camera and monitor played a crucial role in breaking through the conventions of representation, as they showed 'the discrepancy between the camera's view of the subject – seen in the monitor, a detail of the whole – and the spectator's'.[50] They transmitted selected aspects of the performance, made details larger than life, and forced the audience into a distanced position from which they could compare and critically assess the two simultaneous discourses. Jonas explained: 'The audience sees in fact the process of image-making in a performance simultaneously with a live detail. I was interested in the discrepancies between the performed activity and the constant duplicating, changing, and altering of information in the video.'[51] She set up the stage like a film set and performed to a camera, with the images being relayed to a monitor, a wall projector and a small control monitor on the set. She also used pre-recorded tapes, and subsequent performances incorporated taped and edited documentation of previous performances into the piece.

In *Organic Honey's Vertical Roll*, the live images relayed to the monitor were disturbed by decoupling the video and monitor frequencies, thereby making the images roll vertically over the screen rather than producing a stable picture. The slight jerk each time when a line scanner jumps into the next frame was emphasized by the synchronized sound of a spoon hammering on a mirror. The seemingly 'organic' nature of an eroticized female body was permanently disrupted by literally breaching the frame of the picture and juxtaposing live presence with mediated image. Joan Jonas's ambivalent double function as both subject and object of the show dismantled the unity of the picture even further. The audience had to glance from live body to monitor to projection, and could only perceive partial impressions of the action on stage. Such disruption of the spectacle of femininity had a variety of effects on the audience: it destroyed the illusion of Jonas's eroticized body and 'electronic-fairy' identity; it revealed the ambiguities of selfhood and showed identity to be rooted in a complex web of alternating personas; it questioned the essentialist concept of womanhood and showed femininity to be a mask that can be worn or taken off; it demonstrated the sign 'woman' to be a socially determined construct or a combination of set pieces selected for their specific signifying functions.

However, it would be misleading to see in *Organic Honey's Vertical Roll* only a feminist exercise in semiosis. Jonas was an artist with a strong interest in ancient Greek, Chinese, Indian and Native-American cultures and possessed sufficient art-historical training to interpret the remains of prehistoric civilizations. She was greatly fascinated by Minoan sculptures of earth goddesses, by the masks in Japanese Noh theatre, and by the symbolic function of mirrors in Semitic and Mayan rituals. Her studies of Shamanism and Buddhist mysticism contributed further components to her performances and gave them a dimension that went far beyond their purely aesthetic and political qualities. Although these elements were more noticeable in her second creative phase in the late 1970s and 1980s, their roots could already be discerned in her early video performances.

Following the two *Organic Honey* pieces, Jonas produced one further real-time, closed-circuit video performance, *Funnel* (in 1974). Instead of Organic Honey's glamorous green chiffon dress, she used a white satin suit, a red shadri and a blue silk shirt, which placed her firmly in another, this time a-sexual, role. The stage set of this magic show was strewn with a variety of personal objects that triggered associations with childhood and animal taming. The funnel served as a shape for the stage layout as well as a real prop. Its symbolic significance may have been the gathering of free energy and forcing its flow into the increasingly narrow passage. The video images displayed on a monitor, placed in a downstage-right position, were often highly abstract and not always easy to relate to Jonas's stage actions.[52]

In 1978, Jonas began a three-year-long collaboration with the Wooster Group, performing in their adaptations of Eliot's *Cocktail Party* and Chekhov's *Three Sisters*. This experience reinforced her shift towards more narrative structures based on sagas, fairy tales and ritual enactments of archetypal representations of women. *Upside Down and Backwards* (1979), *Double Lunar Dogs* (1981), *He Saw Her Burning* (1982), *Volcano Saga* (1985), and *Revolted by the Thought of Known Places* (1994) still operated in a multi-media vein, but were shows of a distinctly theatrical nature and employed professional actors and stage technicians. Her own role was predominantly that of a director and designer, but she also appeared on stage as a performer. These later shows formed part of a wide spectrum of multi-media performances which became popular in the late 1970s and 1980s, and found a positive response from audiences and critics, but lacked the unique and pioneering quality of Jonas's early video work.

Joan Jonas came on the scene when the traditional concept of art as object was being dissolved in favour of more fluid arrangements of art as process, which brought the artist into an immediate live contact with the audience. Therefore, her move into dance and performance, and subsequently into composing transitory images on screen, was a natural progression from being a sculptor and visual artist. In parallel with her group dances and choreographies she also explored the medium of solo performances in intimate, indoor settings. But rather than moving in the direction of Body Art, she experimented with the technical properties of the video camera and integrated this into works that were rooted in her autobiography without, however, revealing much about her life. She was interested, as she said, in 'exploring the female psyche and the possibilities of a visual language without being too obvious about it'.[53]

The objectifying lens of the video camera transformed her personal or individual self into something of a more universal significance. The hybrid genre of video performance allowed her to stand outside herself, to objectify her being and present her female identity with all its physical, psychological and social ramifications. This juxtaposition of personal self and mediatized image of self was the key aspect of her early video art. Combining a subject and object position for the duration of a performance pointed out some fundamental principles of representation in live and electronic media. After 1975, she updated the intermedia elements of her work and incorporated the latest video technology; but rather than moving in the direction of Media Art (see Chapter 7), she remained committed to video and live performance. She increased the visceral appeal of her works by collaborating with accomplished sound and lighting designers and gave her performances an unusual intellectual and spiritual edge by drawing on archetypal narratives and ritual structures.

Valie Export

Waltraud Höllinger, née Lehner, began her artistic career in the late 1960s in the wider ambit of the Viennese Actionists. She participated in several actions of the Vienna Institute for Direct Art under the name VALIE EXPORT ('The name Export indicates that I am exporting what is inside me'[54]), which since then has become her artist name. At the same time, she was an active member of the Austrian Filmmakers Cooperative and soon combined her interests in film, video and performance art, thus creating a series of works that focused on the body, in both a direct and a mediated fashion. As I suggested above in Chapter 5, the Viennese Actionists opened up a fertile field of experimentation in an extremely conservative cultural landscape. Export shared with them an interest in the representation and use of the body in performance; but instead of taking a painterly approach to Body Art she linked it with her media practice. Her Action Art was complemented by works in other media such as photography, video, installation and, more recently, CD-ROM.

Valie Export's early contacts with the feminist movement made her increasingly critical of the Actionists' use of the female body as a passive object;[55] but rather than repudiating the tactics of her male colleagues she opted for developing a 'corrected' form of Actionism.[56] The only person on the Viennese art scene who supported her in this 'Feminist Actionism' was Peter Weibel. She remembered her isolation in Vienna at that time: 'In the 1960s there existed no Women's Movement in Vienna. Not a single woman occupied herself with feminism or the new media as artistic expressions of the avant-garde. All the information I received on the feminist movement came from American magazines and books.'[57]

Export introduced her concept of Feminist Actionism in a 'Body Action for Expanded Cinema', *Cutting* (1967–8), where she examined bodily sign codes in a social and aesthetic environment. In *Tap and Touch Cinema* (1968), performed in Vienna, Munich, Zurich, Cologne, Essen and various international venues, Export encased her nude upper body in a cardboard box. At the front, there were two large holes covered with a mock-theatrical curtain. As she walked through the streets, she encouraged passers-by to reach into the box and get in touch with her *cinéma véritée*. Here, the body was not used merely to provide a spectacle, but served as a medium capable of eliminating the formal boundaries between art and life.[58] In Vienna, on the occasion of the Second Marais Festival, the Action was carried out in a cinema as a substitute for her prize-winning film *Ping-Pong*, and caused a riot. In Munich, Weibel accompanied her with a mega-phone through the streets and encouraged passers-by to 'grasp' the meaning of 'mani'-pulation in the cinema. Export commented on her performance practice at that time: 'Feminist Actionism seeks to transform the object of male natural history, the material "woman", subjugated and enslaved by the male creator, into an independent actor and creator, subject of her own history.'[59]

Export attacked sexual taboos and the authoritarian politics of the Austrian government in several other controversial actions. For example, in 1968 she performed together with Peter Weibel *From the Portfolio of Doggedness*, where she led Weibel on a leash through Vienna's shopping district. In 1969 they engaged in a *War Theatre Campaign*, which took them to Munich, Cologne, Zurich and Essen and was documented, like the previous action, in photographs. Export entered a cinema wearing blue jeans with the crotch cut out to show her genitalia. She provoked the view-ers to give up their passive voyeurism and engage actively with a 'real' woman. Export explained her artistic approach at that time: 'It is important for me to create a perceptual space of experiencing reality and to represent the mise-en-scène of the experience of reality by means of technical media, so as to intervene in the temporal–spatial structure we call reality.'[60] Whereas in *Tap and Touch Cinema* she appeared like a shy and gentle *Wiener Madl*, the photographs of her *Action Pants: Genital Panic* made her look like a guerrilla fighter sporting a machine gun.[61] Such contradictions were also common in her photographic works called Body Configurations, where she juxtaposed her body with urban landscapes and showed how internal states force a body into accommodation with, or resistance to, the environment.

Export's main medium of expression in the late 1960s was Expanded Cinema. Just as the Actionists had felt a need to extend Action Painting beyond the canvas, Export wanted to extend cinema beyond the screen. She experimented with film as material, and with the technical apparatus of film projection (often replacing projector and screen with other materials). For example, *Abstract Film no. 1* (1967–8) had a spotlight pointed at a mirror covered with running water, which made the reflections produce abstract patterns on a screen. In *Ars Lucis* (1967–8), she extended the mirror projec-tions into the environment. The light beams issued by film projectors on rotating disks were intercepted by prisms, refracted, distorted and reflected from various projection surfaces in the room. *Untitled xn* (1968) gave the audience a more active role by immersing them in an environment filled with large three-dimensional objects and film projections of nature scenes. In *Instant Film* (1968, with Peter Weibel) she sought to break down the distinction between production and consumption of film by giving the audience sheets of transparent film, and sending them home with the instruction to look through them and create a film of their own invention. In *Auf+Ab+An+Zu* (1968) she gave the audience the task of completing missing lines in the projected film by drawing directly onto the screen. *The Magic Eye* (1969, with Peter Weibel) used a projection screen fitted with light–sensitive cells, which triggered sound effects that depended on the amount of light or shadow falling on the screen. The film projection was fragmented by the audience's movements in the hall, and these interactions between audience and projected images created a 'sound picture'.

In her experiments with Expanded Cinema, Export examined not only the material characteristics of film and the dynamic relationship between screen and audience; she also introduced aspects of Body Art and began to perform Actions in a live situation with camera (8-mm, 16-mm, video) and audience. In several of these Film Actions and Video Performances she examined the mute language of the female body as an alternative to male-dominated verbal language. She was influenced in this undertaking by the Viennese tradition of language scepticism, stretching from Karl Kraus and Ludwig Wittgenstein to the Wiener Gruppe; it also reflected contemporary debates on Merleau-Ponty's phenomenology (the body as the last refuge for the confirmation of lived experience), and Lévi-Strauss's structuralism (the body as a projection screen and surface for social inscription). The fusion of Body Art with technology was for Export a way of escaping the biological determination of the female body and of examining the historical and social determinants of female body language. She viewed her media practice as 'a way to continue expanded cinema in my performances in which I, as the center point for the performance, positioned the human body as a sign, as a code for social and artistic expression'.[62] By re-examining the body in a concrete social environment and re-presenting it in a natural and in a mediated context, she encouraged her viewers to take a critical stance towards the signifying functions of the body: 'The skin is a site of social conflict and belonging. . . . Through the body, the human being is imbedded in a social community; the body is fraught with social signification.'[63] She understood this critical discourse of the body to be 'a revolutionary action that contributes towards the construction of a new society', confirming Hegel's dictum that 'history is primarily a history of liberation', in which 'art plays the role of medium of self-determination and progressive individuation'.[64]

Eros/ion (performance and video, 1971) was an action in which the naked performer first rolled over a glass plate, then over broken glass, and finally over a large sheet of paper. The wounds caused by the broken glass left traces of blood on the glass and paper. Here, the body surface, which is always a projection screen, was lacerated and opened up to reveal the intimate architecture behind the image. The title, it has been suggested,[65] refers to the fact that the eroticizing of the female body, for example in mass media and pornography, also leads to the erosion of female identity. However, the rationale of this performance can also be related to the fact that 'ecstasy and pain are the two forms of experience where we apperceive the body most distinctly and directly, and we develop from this binary polarity strategies of ego development, of physical awareness and of the relationship to the outside world'.[66]

In *Hyperbulie* (performance and video, 1973), Export used electrical wire to indicate socially determined barriers and restrictions. She had to walk, crouch and crawl through a narrow corridor defined by the live wires, and every time her naked body touched them she received an electric shock. By the end of the performance, her body was covered with 'the stigmata of a social matrix',[67] and only by an act of extreme willpower ('hyperbulia') was she able to overcome the pains caused by the enclosure and to liberate herself. Some of these motifs Export took up again in *Movement Imaginations* (video performance, 1974–5), where she investigated the forces of inertia and ways to overcome them, as well as the role of willpower to endure and resist hostile conditions. The actions included: standing on her toes inside a small circle of barbed wire, which dug into her skin whenever the weight of her body forced her to lower her heel onto the floor; resting on the floor in a push-up position until her strength waned and her face sank into a pile of broken glass; using her mouth to suck a nail out of a plank of wood.

I am Beaten (video performance, 1973) took as its theme a phrase from Freud's essay 'A Child is Being Beaten'. Export lay flat on the floor in the middle of a room with a mirror suspended from the ceiling and a tape recorder standing next to her, listening to an endlessly repeated phrase, 'I am beaten'. Initially, she repeated the phrase in a very different intonation, as if to argue against the text. But gradually, she gave up her resistance until in the end her voice was in absolute synchronization with the tape. A video camera took the reflected image from the mirror and relayed it to the audience via two monitors.

Kausalgie (1973) was a four-part performance whose first part consisted of an anthropological slide show of a scarification ceremony, accompanied by a taped voice which explained that 'the body is a site of civilization . . .

marked with social signals, with signs of belonging to gender, tribe, terri-tory'.[68] In the second part, Export used a hammer and chisel to break a hole in the wall that had just served as a projection surface for the slides. She then cut open the dress of another woman, while a taped text explained that clothes are a second skin underlying social regulation and that the house is a third skin subject to similar prescriptive conventions. Export suggested that the social deformation of consciousness (the 'tattooing of the mind') was the main hurdle for an individual's liberation and self-determination. In the third part, Export projected a slide of her *Body Sign Action* of 1970, which showed her having a garter tattooed onto her upper thigh.[69] A text was read out, explaining that women in phallocratic societies are carriers of fixed sexual symbols, which are imposed on their bodies, and that they can only escape this system of repression by rejecting the manners in which society defines femininity.[70] In a more general sense, the scene showed 'the surface of the human body as a canvas or screen, as a battle ground, as a site and carrier of inscriptions'.[71] The fourth part signalled the transition from object to self-determining subject. The stage floor had been divided into zones and furnished with a 'verbal scaffolding for the action'. A man standing on a swastika cast a shadow onto a plate covered with wax and indicated his desire to form her image according to his imagination. With a blow torch, Export burned the outlines of the shadow into the wax. She then undressed and lay on the wax until her body heat had melted a negative mould into the wax. At the same time, the man erected a fence around her with electrical wire connected to a battery. After a while, Export escaped the man's shadow by rolling underneath the red-hot wire, and pressed her body onto a large, virgin-white sheet of paper. She then filled the wax mould with lead and covered it with a tombstone. The words drawn onto the floor commented on the action: 'Order – chaos, freedom – imprison-ment. Body traces. The human body as a medium of communication, as a symbol and carrier of information.'

Asemie, or the Impossibility to Express Oneself through Facial Expression (performance and video, 1973) referred to the medical condi-tion of being unable to communicate with the outer world through words, gestures or signs. On a raised platform surrounded by a ring of nails, Export tied a budgie onto a plank, kneeled in front of it and poured hot wax over the creature, and over her own hands and feet. When the wax had stiffened, she picked up a knife with her mouth and cut herself free. In an accompa-nying text she explained that the bird, usually a symbol of freedom and fantasy, turned into a symbol of torpidity when paralysed by the stiffened wax. Likewise, human desire for communication is stifled when being cast in predetermined forms, and a potentially agile mind is reduced to inertia.

Homometer I and *II* (performance and video, 1973 and 1976) dealt with woman being weighed down by her reproductive and nurturing functions, symbolized here by loaves of bread. In the first part, performed on the Belgian coast, Export emerged from the sea weighed down by the soaked loaves, which had become as heavy as millstones and only allowed her the barest minimum of movement. In the second version, a loaf was tied to her belly and she walked through a shopping district in Vienna, asking passers-by to cut off slices of the bread. *I [(Beat) It]* (performance and video, 1978) took up ideas from the performance *I am Beaten* (1973), and developed them further to show how woman can emancipate herself from the impositions of society and find her own inner voice. In the original performance (see Illustration 22) at the Edinburgh Festival, Export showed how sadistic treatment can be transformed into masochistic pleasure. A second version in Cologne, in 1974, involved two cameras, two monitors and various mirrors, illustrating how images inscribe an attitude onto a woman's body. In the 1978 version, three monitors showing barking dogs were arranged in a triangular position and like the watchful eyes of God the Father, Son and Holy Ghost (or the unholy trinity of State, Nature and ideology) looked down on a life-size photograph of a woman lying in its centre. Export, wearing leaden bandages on her knees and arms, spilled a lubricant from a container, moved in a spiral towards the image, and finally lay on top of it. A pre-recorded voice on tape drowned out the barking of the dogs and spoke the phoneme <mer>, meaning both *mehr* (more) and *Meer* (sea). She commented on the action:

> a woman machinist, who, as an extension of the machine, moves like a marionette to the beat of the machine, is it still her body that is moving? her body acts dependently, literally dependently, the weights of the machine are hanging from her, the body works for the machine, not for itself. The woman works selflessly in the (social machinery).[72]

The lubricating oil was an ambivalent metaphor, as the substance could both facilitate a smooth running of the action and cause the performer to skid and fall. Similarly, the <mer> sound was ambiguous as it could indicated that more pain was to be endured, or that the sea was to wash the performer out of the quagmire and allow her to evolve and liberate herself as a human being.

Valie Export occupied an important position at the cutting edge of performance, video art and feminism. From the very beginning of her career, she worked as a media artist, but her concerns intersected with those of Actionism and shared many features of Body Art. Expanded Cinema

22 Valie Export: *I [(Beat) It]*, video performance, Edinburgh Festival (1978)

allowed her to encounter and engage with live audiences. The instant relay properties of video 'expanded' this terrain even further and caused her to switch over to that new medium once it became available to her. Furthermore, video images displayed on monitors bear a close resemblance to television pictures, which by the 1970s had become the most powerful medium of popular culture and a major influence on social codes of behaviour.

Export's work was paradigmatic for the feminist struggle to overcome the narrow spectrum of images portraying women in the media. Her interrogation of the body as a site of formalized social inscription was linked to a systematic deconstruction of the coded language employed by the mass media. Her video performances, photo actions and films broke out of the semiotic conventions and standardized discourses of the culture industry; yet at the same time her method of presenting the discourses of the body undermined the impositions of society and opened up a critical awareness that fostered social change. Her work demonstrated, to use Chrissie Iles's words, how 'the autonomy of the female body is achieved through the construction of a third space, in which the fractured self can transcend the trauma of technological control and heal itself'.[73]

Laurie Anderson

Before becoming one of the most celebrated performance artists of the 'Media Generation', Laurie Anderson established herself in the 1970s as a sculptor and installation artist. As a teenager, she had been a gifted musician, playing the violin with the Chicago Youth Orchestra, and a talented draftswoman, who also took painting classes at the Chicago Art Institute. But in a late-adolescent revolt she rejected her classical training and became a student of art history at Barnard College, New York. She took a Master's degree at Columbia University, and taught for a while at City College, New York. She also worked as a journalist on magazines such as *ArtNews*, *Art in America* and *Artforum* and became an acute observer of the New York art scene, which at that time was making the transition from Happening and Fluxus to Performance Art, from postmodern dance to dance theatre, from aleatoric and electronic music to systems music, from video art to media arts. In 1970, she had her first exhibition at Barnard College, and throughout the 1970s she continued to show her sculptures, drawings and photographs in a variety of New York galleries.[74]

Anderson's participation in the New York Minimalism scene exposed her to a heavy dose of hyper-intellectual art rooted in abstract theory rather than corporeal expression. Much of her own production at the time (mainly language objects in the Duchampian mode) had a similar bias, although there were also excursions into sound sculptures, filmmaking, illustration of children's books, and political caricature. Her fine art œuvre had a solid, but not outstanding quality, and when she was given a retrospective exhibition at the Queens Museum in 1984, Kim Levin praised her high degree of craftsmanship, but found the works lacking in innovative drive.[75] Similarly, her early attempts at establishing herself as an 'electronic cabaret star' showed her to be well informed about contemporary trends in Performance Art, but she did not exactly venture into virgin territory.

Boundaries between the different arts were very fluid at that time in the downtown New York art scene. Painters mixed with dancers, musicians with poets, etc., and it was easy for Anderson to combine her varied skills as sculptor, musician and performer. Yet, at the same time, it was difficult to find a clear direction and a role for herself in this fluid and multifaceted environment. Janet Kardon rightly observed that Anderson's 'performances evolved as a context which would superimpose these layers of media on layers of meanings'.[76]

In 1972, following an exhibition of sound sculptures, Anderson staged in Rochester, Vermont a concert for car horns, called *Automotive*.[77] Around that time, Vito Acconci was organizing his Street Works series[78] and he invited Anderson to participate. This resulted in *O-Range* (1973), an exhibition at the Artists' Space and a sound performance at the Lewisohn Stadium at City College, New York,[79] and *As:If* (1974), a performance presented again at the Artists' Space in SoHo. The latter combined very personal stories about her past life with projections of words on an overhead screen. Anderson's concern with language, her juxtaposition of spoken and written words, and the way she contrasted narrative and imagery, all became characteristic traits of her later works.

As Mel Gordon has rightly pointed out, Anderson's early performance practice was closely linked to her teaching experience as an art historian.[80] Just as literary scholars operate with two simultaneous narratives in texts and footnotes, art historians communicate through slide projections and verbal commentary on the images presented. Anderson developed an interest in this combination of verbal and visual imagery and explored it in several artist's books and conceptual word paintings. For a while, she operated with the concept of words as sound, and letters as pictorial signs, but then she found that performance was a more appropriate medium for her concerns.

Anderson's performance works of the mid-1970s explored the dimension of time as a central feature that separates print from performance media. In *Duets on Ice* (1974–5), she performed on ice skates with the blades embedded in blocks of ice. The length of the performance was determined by the time it took for the ice to melt. *Duets on Ice* contained another element, which became a trademark of her later work: a violin connected to a tape recorder. The sounds she produced on the instrument coincided with sequences of pre-recorded hillbilly music triggered with every stroke of the bow, allowing her to perform a duet with herself.

Another piece, called *Engli-SH*, first performed in 1976 in Berlin, had a vocal narrative related through a microphone, and a simultaneous translation projected onto a screen. After a while, the projection went out of sync. As the spoken text used a lot of 's' and 'sh' sounds, the projection turned into long 'zzz' signs. Anderson was running back and forth between two microphones, playing the violin and trying to bridge the barriers between language and communicative media. *For Instants* (1975–8) explored the relationship between space, time and light by projecting a filmed image of a window onto a wall. Anderson told the audience two stories, the first lying on the floor, the second in the corridor between light source and projection screen. Her live narratives were combined with taped stories and music played on her violin.[81]

For years she worked on the development of a 'tape-bow violin', a device that allowed her to demonstrate the liquid nature of language. It was first introduced in *Like a Stream* (1978), a collection of autobiographical scenes and dreams in conjunction with the sounds of her violin. A great deal of technical expertise went into the construction of this instrument, whose bridge had been replaced with a playback head. The bow was fitted with magnetic tape rather than horsehair, and could reproduce pre-recorded speech when drawn across the audio head (for example, 'no' became 'one', 'yes' turned into 'say', depending on the direction of the bow movement). The electronic sounds were combined with Anderson's solo talking (quirky little vignettes delivered in a very non-theatrical manner) and images (slides), thereby creating a multi-layered text with multiple meanings.[82]

Many of Anderson's performances in the 1970s were designed to accompany exhibitions of her artworks. In the 1980s, the relationship reversed and the performances became her prime medium of expression. The progression from short and simple conceptual performances to increasingly complex multimedia shows reached a new phase in 1979, when she presented *Americans on the Move*. This work was not premièred in a gallery or alternative performance space, but in a proscenium arch theatre, the Carnegie Recital Hall, with members of the Fast Food Band she had formed in 1975.[83] Over the next two years, she focused increasingly on her musical work, added material to the highly compartmentalized structure of *Americans on the Move*, and turned it into *United States Part I* (ICA

Boston, 10 March 1980), followed by *United States Part II* (Orpheum Theatre, New York, 20–6 October 1980), and *United States Part III* (Seattle Art Museum, 26 July 1981). The final version, *United States I–IV*, premièred 3–10 February 1983 at the Brooklyn Academy of Music, was a compendium of previous performances, which had expanded over the years and in the end become a seven-hour multimedia event. As John Howell observed, much of her material was recycled from former shows, 'blown up to epic proportions rather than developed' and given a form of 'almost total musicalization'.[84] It involved five other musicians, a complex projection apparatus (video, computer graphics, slides, animation), her famous tape-bow violin, a synclavier, which triggered sounds from a computer memory, and a vocorder, which transformed her vocal register from female to male and allowed her to switch between different intonations. *United States* was certainly not the 'poor theatre' of her early Performance Art years. She worked on the show as a visual designer, composer, musician, singer and storyteller, set up a complex electronic apparatus that embraced all the devices of multimedia arts, and produced a cornucopia of visual and acoustic effects.

United States was a kaleidoscopic montage of texts and images, monologues and songs, which focused on the themes of travelling and communication. Dozens of intertwining segments formed a mosaic picture of the information society and combined minute observations from everyday life with apocalyptic visions of a Western world dominated by technology and the media. Much of this material was assembled from the debris of the media jungle and fragments of postmodern culture. Clichés of television chat shows and popular magazines were mixed with the arcane phraseology of science; anecdotes alternated with lyrical passages, word games with social satire, autobiographical vignettes with philosophical reflections, etc. The context of music and visuals added further layers to the narratives and created a dense and richly textured collage about 'learning to live in a world of electronics'.[85] Recurring leitmotifs expressed as sounds, words, phrases and images provided a certain pattern of continuity, but the overall impression of the sprawling arrangement of the show was disjunctive, fragmented and, one might say, typically postmodern.

Anderson gave the media employed in the production considerable independence. Rather than harmonizing the different semiotic systems she made them counteract each other, thereby creating multimedia dialogues full of ambiguity and contradictions. The audience was encouraged to navigate its own path through this forest of signs, which was partly located in a country called the United States of America and partly taken from 'a great jumble of "states" – state of mind, state of feeling, state of the art'.[86]

Numerous scenes dealt with situations of attempted communication, with the dialogue usually ending in some kind of linguistic breakdown or semantic short-circuit.[87] Anderson was very suspicious of language and presented various forms of non-communication, where instead of sharing ideas and feelings people get drowned in a sea of codes. Words were estranged from the speaker through their mediated form, led an autonomous life in various 'cans' (e.g. voice-mail machines or in-flight announcements) and brought about a triumph of the signifier over the signified:

> For Anderson, the crux of this breakage in communication is that the media of interpersonal communication have taken on a life of their own generally: not just language, but all its mediations have solidified into protocols whose sheer presence overwhelms their communcative purpose. . . . Anderson's constantly remodulated vocals not only enact the decay of individuality that accomplishes its ossification; they also continue the estangement of the voice from the body in which we can recognize the theft of knowledge under the guise of information.[88]

At a time when the popular arts were borrowing freely from the avant-garde, it could no longer be frowned upon when an artist adopted techniques and state-of-the-art equipment from the entertainment industry. Laurie Anderson, more than any performance artist of the 'Media Generation', exemplified the crossover from the 'élite' world of Performance Art, centred on lofts and small galleries, into the 'Pop' world of theatres and concert halls. She was extremely successful in merging High and Low Art, reached mass audiences and sold 800,000 copies of 'Oh Superman', which in 1980 reached no. 2 in the British pop charts. In the eyes of many critics, this disqualified her from being considered any longer a performance *artist*. A *performer*, maybe, or even an *artiste* (i.e. a skilled craftswoman). But not an artist in the Modernist tradition.

These critics may be right, because in a postmodern age these distinctions no longer make sense. At least, they need to be examined more closely. In Late-Modernism, mass culture became a key element and central focus of artistic discourses. But these tended to be critical discourses of *high* artists on *low* art. A first shift towards a different, i.e. postmodern, attitude occurred with the Pop Artists, who elevated mass-produced artefacts to the status of works of art and exhibited them in privileged institutions such as galleries and museums. What distinguished Warhol from Duchamp, who had also placed everyday objects such as a pissoir or a bicycle wheel into exhibition spaces, was the fact that Pop Art was not a protest against the pretensions of the bourgeois art world, but rather, an attempt at incorporating new materials into artistic discourses.

Many postmodern artists focused on the problematic status of art and non-art and the value system that underpins it. As a well trained art historian, Laurie Anderson was intimately familiar with the theories and practices of the Modernist period, and as a political artist she took a critical attitude towards the 'American Way of Life' and the culture of a post-industrial information society. In her political and artistic philosophy, a number of recurring themes and concerns can be distinguished: language and face-to-face communication; man–machine communication; the mass media and their influence on the way we perceive reality; the individual *versus* corporate institutions. In the way she approached these subjects, Anderson pursued a strategy of (a) describing selected and highly typical facets of the American Way of Life; and (b) offering a commentary on these anecdotes. This Brechtian device of taking incidents out of their normal context and making the ordinary look strange through unexpected juxtapositions created in the audience an awareness of the incidents as being not at all natural, but odd, artificial, or simply false.

This strategy was supported by the sleek, high-tech lustre of her performances, which employed the whole gamut of multimedia technology: voice filters, electronic instruments, video and film projection, slide shows, synthesizers, TV monitors, etc. In contrast to this massive apparatus of technical machinery and the epic size of the stage events, a small, frail-looking woman talked about her personal experiences and incidents from her past. The juxtaposition of these two main components of the show – technology and human body – created a synthesis that was contradictory on many levels: on the one hand, the personal, subjective element was objectified through the apparatus and made to appear cool and distanced; on the other, the electronic element was given a highly sensual and visceral character.[89]

Anderson eschewed all received notions of 'theatre', of acting or simulating reality. She did not act out characters and did not inhabit a fictitious world. The stage events had a high degree of physical presence – the presence of the human body, of the technical apparatus, of the interaction between them. What audiences saw on stage was a reality, yet at the same time also a comment on reality. Anderson's performance style was crucial to the success of her shows. 'Without her graceful body language, this magnum opus would seem rigid and programmatic,' one reviewer commented on *United States*.[90] Already in *Duets on Ice* she had displayed her talent as a professional entertainer. *Americans on the Move* had a certain rock 'n' roll-biz flair and incorporated elements of stand-up comedy. It was therefore not astonishing that *United States Part II*, with its increased technical apparatus and elements of a large-scale entertainment show, moved into an old Variety hall, the Orpheum Theater. So on the one hand she used a theatricality that had long been eschewed by avant-garde performance artists, but on the other hand she also undercut traditional role concepts and techniques of theatrical presentation. Despite the autobiographical nature of many scenes in her shows, the narcissism and pretentiousness that would have been typical of 'self-expressive' Performance Art of the early 1970s were removed by the cool, distancing device of the vocoder and the slick precision of the back-projections. Her transformation from white-gowned hippy to spiky-haired punkette indicated that the 'Laurie Anderson' she presented to her audiences was not a true self, but rather an assumed persona created for public consumption. Recalling Ervin Goffman's book *The Presentation of Self in Everyday Life*, Anderson once remarked that her different vocal styles reflected her need to use as many as eight different voices in a single day, depending on whom she talked to.[91] Consequently, the concept of personality became just as liquid as the concept of language. Anderson excelled at using an autobiographic *style* that did not necessary have any roots in the *reality* of her own, private, and intimate life.

This juxtaposition of futuristic high-tech modernity and very personal feelings, of cool factualness and surreal dreamscapes, of paranoia and comedy led the audiences into a precarious, disjointed postmodern space that reflected the contradictions inherent in contemporary Western society. Contrasts, tensions and conflicts were a central component of Laurie Anderson's performances. Whatever she presented was 'filtered', i.e. given an appearance that contradicted the 'natural' appearance of things. Everything became relative and contingent on the context in which it appeared. The juxtaposition of different media commenting on the same thing, enabled the audience to distinguish between image and reality and to become aware of their perception of the world. Anderson's gestures, movements and vocal delivery 'performed' her lyrics in a manner that gave them a resonance and meaning which otherwise could not have been deduced from a reading of the printed text. Although full of precise observations, her stories were also laden with ambiguity 'so they can resonate differently and leave lots of room for people to make connections'.[92]

Anderson never imposed her messages on her audiences but rather revealed her ideas in an indirect manner, leaving it up to the individual spectator to make up his or her mind. She analysed the predicament of a society where communication is mediated by a technical apparatus, and questioned the present state of the relationship between individual and technology. This is not to say that she wished to return to a pre-industrial state of existence. Rather, she aimed at establishing a positive balance between these two elements – a new marriage of mankind and the machine, where technology is employed for the benefit of humankind. Poised between the positions of critic and prophet, she pointed out the dangers of technology, but also its positive potential. If her work was ambivalent, this was ultimately because her subject matter was so.

As an artist and critic who had moved freely in various fine art and Performance Art circles in New York, Laurie Anderson had become aware that the classic concept of the avant-garde had outlived its usefulness. The structuralist/minimalist/conceptualist art of the 1970s had lost touch with social and political reality, and she realized that as a sculptor, performer and musician she had to pursue a different path. Although primarily concerned with deconstructing the myths of the Information Age and critiquing the routines of (non-)communication in a media-sodden society, she avoided dry political commentary and hyper-intellectualized 'discourses'. Instead, she brought a rare emotional sensibility to her performances and imbued them with a raconteur's delight in storytelling. Her typically postmodern hybridization of narration, music and electronic pyrotechnics enjoyed a brief period of artistic and commercial success. However, the fusion of popular and élite cultures in a techno-performance art attracted mass audiences only with *United States* and *Empty Places* (1989) and rapidly declined in popularity with *Voices from the Beyond* (1991) and *Halcion Days* (1992). Subsequent shows, such as *Stories from the Nerve Bible* (1995) and its interactive CD-ROM version, *The Muppet Motel*, offered little more than a Laurie Anderson pastiche, and headed towards a direction which in the final section of *United States Part II* Anderson had laconically summed up as 'Melting Pot. Meltdown. *Shutdown.*'[93]

Videodance and Cyberdance

From the very inception of the motion picture, the 'seventh art' entered into a creative coexistence with the theatre. Many pioneers of the silver screen were competent theatre directors, and vice versa: theatre directors tried their hand at being film directors. The early avant-garde, too, was characterized by such collaborations and mutual influences. Marinetti sought to submit the theatre to the same montage techniques that had become prevalent in the cinema. Meyerhold and Piscator employed projected film sequences in their theatre productions, and Moholy-Nagy developed an artistic practice that merged theatre and cinema in a unique fashion.

Similarly, in the early Modernist period one can observe a mutual enrichment between cinema and dance. Some of the best documents we possess of early Modern Dance are recordings on film, either as self-contained shorts or as interludes in feature films.[94] Many Variety theatres mixed dance performances with cinema presentations, and Fernand Léger's *Ballet mécanique* was one of the first experimental dance productions to employ film projections on the ballet stage. Film musicals became serious outlets for dancers and choreographers such as Fred Astaire and Busby Berkeley, and narrative dance films, from *The Red Shoes* (1948) to *Saturday Night Fever* (1977), delighted audiences throughout the postwar period. Maya Deren was a filmmaker who seriously concerned herself with an integration of the two media and produced several works that are considered masterpieces in the genre of cinedance. Finally, one needs to mention the intermedia experiments of artists belonging to the Happening and Expanded Cinema movements, where film and dance were conjoined in live performances of a truly avant-garde nature. But after 1970, when electronic recording devices became generally available, the emphasis shifted away from film to video.

In the dance world, it was Merce Cunningham who first came to use video as a tool in the rehearsal process and he soon recognized the aptitude of the medium for the exploration of kinesthetic–visual correspondences. In spring 1974, he created *A Video Event* for a CBS broadcast, and subsequently teamed up with Charles Atlas for further 'screen choreographies', such as *Westbeth* (1974), *Blue Studio* (1975), *Squaregame Video* and *Fractions* (both 1977), and *Locale* (1979).[95] Whereas previously, directors of dance films had usually remained faithful to the original stage productions and had tried to adapt these only slightly for the transfer to the two-dimensional TV screen, Cunningham created new dances with the visual facilities of the video medium. Together with his collaborators – they included Merrill Brockway, Nam June Paik, Shigeko Kubota and Elliot Caplan – he explored the kinetic qualities of two dynamic systems and engaged the camera in an active dialogue with the moving body.

In the mid-1970s, the term 'videodance' came into currency for these dances that could only be viewed through the 'proscenium frame' of the video monitor. It served as a kind of shorthand for a whole range of productions that employed electronic recording and editing devices, but was also used for other creations which originally existed as stage works, but had been radically recontextualized so that the resulting creations became fully-fledged video works. In either case, they overcame the restrictions of the physical body and the spatial constraints of the stage; movements and movement sequences were composed in a manner that was determined by image flow rather than physical impulse. The dancing body was a raw material for the generation of images that were rhythmically ordered according to montage principles.

In the 1970s, videodance became an independent creative field adjacent to dance theatre and postmodern dance. Its origins and initial development took place in the USA, but by the mid-1980s funding through the National Endowment of the Arts dried up and the hub of activities shifted towards Europe, where State-subsidized television companies and other cultural institutions provided a more proactive network of producers and sponsors. This was greatly aided by the creation of specialist festivals such as Grand Prix Vidéo Danse (from 1988), Dance Screen (from 1990), Dance on Camera (from 1972) and Danza & Video (from 1992). But also, film and video festivals regularly screened videodance programmes, as did some dance and theatre festivals. These outlets appealed in the first instance to specialized audiences, who were often professionally involved in the making of dance and/or video. The makers of video tapes also generated their own distribution networks, with companies such as 235 Media, Montevideo, Heure Exquise, or Electronic Arts Intermix hiring tapes to educational and cultural institutions, and many museum and theatre book-shops offering them for sale. In addition, the general public was catered for in television series such as the BBC's *Dance for the Camera 2* or Channel Four's *Dance on 4*, which reached audiences of over one million viewers.[96]

Expanding financial resources and growing markets meant that experi-mental videodance tapes of the 1970s were soon supplanted by sophisti-cated and costly productions made for television, theatres, or dance companies. Consequently, the spectrum of the material that could be encountered on video became very wide-ranging indeed. It encompassed Modernist and postmodern styles, ballet, *butoh*, *bharata natyam*, flamenco, jazz dance, hip-hop etc. The filmic rendering could be highly experimental and akin to video art, or a fairly straightforward multi-camera recording. Some videos contained dramatic narratives whilst others were visual mosaics devoid of any recognizable meaning. Increased financial resources compelled directors to shoot on the visually superior 16-mm or 35-mm formats and then transfer the footage onto video for electronic postproduc-tion. Claudia Rosiny's examination of 444 entries for the Dance Screen award revealed that although 72 per cent of them were video productions, amongst the prize winners 71 per cent were made on film, and 60 per cent of these as 35-mm productions. However, in the category 'experimental production', 81 per cent were made on video, and very few of these had been produced by a television company.[97] This indicates that television had a significant role in shaping the development of videodance and in raising its aesthetic quality; but being essentially a conservative medium that favours documentary or narrative productions, it also tended to foster quality in rather more conventional formats.

Although my viewing of videodance has not been anything like as extensive as Rosiny's, I can offer some observations on the characteristic features of the avant-garde end of the spectrum. One of the key criteria of videodance and one that distinguishes it from dance films and dance videos is the fact that direction, camera work and montage do not aim at producing clever adaptations of stage works, but try to create original works of art that make use of the dynamics of the moving body in time and space. If these defining criteria are fulfilled, it becomes relatively unimportant whether the recording process is undertaken on celluloid or magnetic tape. In the 1980s, it was usually the production budget that determined the choice of film or video; in the 1990s, the increased sophistication of video electronics, combined with their drastic decrease in cost, caused many producers to opt from the start for one of the better video formats such as Betamax or U-matic.

Many of the videastes' concerns in this genre overlap with what has been discussed earlier in this chapter: the human body and the way it is represented in the media; the self-conscious and self-reflexive use of pastiche and collage; the fragmentation of narrative and visual compositions; the parodic appropriation of material from different cultures and periods; the mixing of high and low art; the ambiguity of meaning, and so on. Stylistically, one can observe many borrowings from avant-garde cinema, electronic media arts and postmodern visual culture. Some of these traits I should like to discuss under the headings 'camera work', 'editing', 'sound design' and 'electronic postproduction'.

Camera work tends to be highly subjective and to reflect the dynamics of the dance movements. The use of zoom lenses, tracking devices and steadycam creates the impression of the camera being a partner of the dancer rather than a recording device. The video tape adapts to the fragmented, discontinuous choreography that is so typical of postmodern dance and replicates the performer's free treatment of space. The camera can also be a key device for the construction of spectatorship. Instead of the frontal view commonly found in stage dance and documentary recordings, the camera assumes positions that cannot be experienced in the theatre and invites an active participation of the viewer (rather than passive contemplation, as is usually the case in television and ballet). Furthermore, the camera lens creates views of the dancer's body that are impossible to experience in a theatre setting. Especially the ability to record minute details opens up for the choreographer an unlimited choice of possibilities not available on stage. For example, John Burrows' *Hands* (1996), made in collaboration with the director Adam Roberts for the Arts Council of England, focused on a gestural vocabulary that would have been entirely lost in a playhouse. A whole range of subtle, small-scale movements that are important in the everyday language of non-verbal communication, suddenly became available for artistic exploration in the medium of video-dance.

Editing avoids the conventional visual narratives to be found in commercial television and cinema. The montage is conspicuous, plays with time continuity, breaks up linear developments, and produces fragmentary mosaics that defy expectations. It seeks to influence the viewer's sense of duration and distorts the chronological flow of images by means of slow motion, stop trick, fast motion, repetition etc. The rhythm of the montage is a vital means of finding an equivalent to the dynamics of the dancer's body. From jump cuts to slow dissolves, from intercutting to shot/reverse shots, the 'beat' of the images has to be finely attuned to the dancer's motions in time and space.

The *sound design* provides the director with many tools to support this undertaking. Since in most postmodern productions music no longer provides the rhythmic structure of a dance but functions as an independent unit sharing the same time frame, the editor is free to use the soundtrack as a means of reinforcing the rhythm of the montage and to emphasize (or contradict) the emotional climaxes of the dance. Between these two poles, of heightening visual impact and providing emotional resonance for a scene, one may encounter other functions such as the creation of mood and atmosphere, and the use of leitmotifs to provide a subtext or to tell an inner story. Rather than employing ambient sound to anchor an image or sequence in a realistic setting, acoustic effects tend to act as an independent medium used to support the visual interpretation of the dance.

Electronic postproduction provides a wide range of further possibilities, which because of their relatively low cost gives video a great advantage over film. Sophisticated computer software allows images not only to be ordered sequentially but to grow out of and merge into each other. Chroma Key, Blue Screen, Matte shots, etc. permit the overlaying and amalgamation of sequences; solarization merges positive and negative images; various electronic techniques are available to produce colour shifts and textures that let images stand out or fade into the background: the possibilities are unlimited and have sometimes been employed to the point of saturation. The danger of such videos is that the dancer's body is dissolved into malleable pixels and reconfigured into an electronic painting that adheres, more often than not, to the short-lived aesthetics of pop videos and the fashionable rhetorics of the mass media. Dancers rightly object to such technological distortion of their bodies, and deplore the extraneous interventions into their art that make the dancer's movements the least significant element of a video. However, on the positive side, choreographers acknowledge the wide range of possibilities that have become available for the creation of original video works. Some of the best creations in the genre have demonstrated how filmic conventions, video technology and dance aesthetics can be joined in a convincing fusion. These works have given dance a dimension that could not be experienced prior to the electronic age, and they have confirmed that videodance is indeed a vibrant new departure and a major step ahead from the dance films of the 1950s.

In the following chapter, I shall examine the transition from electronic to digital media and how it affected the world of performance. As this development also had a major impact on the dance world and led to choreographies initiated and controlled by cybernetic means, I shall, for the sake of convenience, discuss this type of performance in this section.

In the 1960s, a large number of experiments were carried out to link the computer to the world of the arts. In 1964, Paul Le Vasseur at the University of Pittsburgh began to collaborate with Jeanne Hays Beaman on the creation of solo dances, whose key parameters (sequence of actions, path, direction, speed and duration) were determined by an IBM 7070.[98] A few years later, during the 1968 *Cybernetic Serendipity* show at the ICA in London, a range of other possibilities in the cooperation between dance and computer was demonstrated.[99] This inspired the architect John Landsdown and a London-based dance company, Another Dance Group, to develop a special software programme for computer-generated dances. Simultaneously, the New York choreographer Twyla Tharp used a computer to determine the movement choices in one of her choreographies, *History of the Up and Down*.[100]

The artists mentioned above felt attracted to the computer for reasons that were similar to those that compelled Merce Cunningham to develop his techniques of chance operations. But whereas, in the 1950s, Cunningham had to establish long and cumbersome score sheets and then spend days on manually correlating elements from these lists, the computer could calculate all the possibilities within a few minutes. It does not come as a surprise then that once the technology became available with an affordable price tag attached, Cunningham was one of the first to try it out in his company.[101] In 1989, he availed himself of LifeForms, a computer animation programme that had been developed in 1984–6 by Thomas Calvert and was commercially marketed by Kinetic Effects Inc., later to be renamed Credo-Interactive.[102] Cunningham used the equipment provided by Simon Fraser

University in Vancouver, and the training he received from Thecla Schiphorst, to create *Trackers* (1991), *Enter* (1992) and *Ocean* (1995). His first computer-generated dances were the result of a creative relationship he established with the computer, and hence a far cry from the popularized fear of 'the computer taking over', or 'the human being becoming an adjunct to a machine'.

For Cunningham, the computer is a tool that allows him to overcome the conventions that dancers acquire through their training. The computer can suggest movement possibilities and choreographic patterns that have never been considered before. Just as videodance opened up choreographic possibilities that could not be achieved in the theatre, cyberdance defeats the hurdles of gravity and anatomy and take the artist into unknown territory.

The first tentative experiments with linking the oldest artform, dance, with the latest technological invention, the computer, revealed that the digital media could be more than a tool in the hands of a choreographer. The explosive growth of digital technologies and improved storage media allowed choreographers to develop cyberdances and distribute them via CD-ROM. The advent of motion-capture software allowed the transformation of a dancer's movements into data that could be processed, recomposed, or mixed with other graphic layers. The resulting 'dancing images' can then be projected or viewed via a monitor.

In the 1990s, when personal computers had sufficiently increased their speed and memory capacities, live interaction between dancer and computer became a new area of exploration. Mixing dance with the latest technologies was, of course, not an entirely new undertaking. From Loïe Fuller's Light Dances to the Futurist Machine Dances, many relationships between the dancer's body and the machine world had been explored in the first part of the twentieth century. At the dawn of the electronic age, Billy Klüver's E.A.T. initiative (from 1965) included several dance projects in his industrial laboratory designed to bring artists and engineers together, and Merce Cunningham, in *Variations V* (1965), used a system designed by Gordon Mumma and David Tutor that translated the dancers' proximity to strategically placed photoelectric cells and antennae on stage into musical signals.[103] Edouard Lock's company, Lalala Human Steps, and the electronically enhanced dances of the Nikolais Dance Theater and of William Forsyth's Frankfurt Ballet greatly stimulated the interest in live interactions between dancers and computers. Here, the interconnected flow of information between different cybernetic systems – one of which is the dancer – was controlled by software usually written specifically for this purpose. This enabled the performer to elicit responses from the other scenic systems, to which he or she then had to react again. Major proponents of this new stage art were the Palindrome Dance Company (est. 1982 by Robert Wechsler), Dumb Type (est. 1984 by Teiji Furuhashi), Alien Nation (est. 1993 by Johannes Birringer), Troika Ranch (est. 1993 by Mark Coniglio and Dawn Stoppiello), and the Electronic Dance Theater (est. 1995 by Julie Wilson and Mark Bromwich), to name but a few.[104]

Subsequently, processing movement via computer software became easier through the availability of devices for gestural sampling, body mapping, video motion tracking, etc. The basic idea behind the experiments in the 1990s was to have dancers perform in a scenic environment that reacts to their movements. The physical dynamics of the dancer on stage are read by detection devices using motion capture, touch lines, laser triggers, etc. and are then channelled into a computer-controlled feedback system. The best known of these is probably David Rokeby's Very Nervous System, which has a sophisticated, computer-controlled motion-sensing mechanism and translates the dancers' movements via MIDI (Musical Instrument Data Interface) software into compositional algorithms.[105] Other systems work with electrodes attached to the dancer's limbs and joints. Heartbeat, muscle contractions etc. send signals to a computer, which translates these into light, sound or video impulses. Thus, the dancer can control various multimedia extensions of his or her body (lighting board, music files, video playback, images stored on laser discs, etc.) and explore an infinite range of possibilities for improvisation using such response loops.

In the 1990s, many composers worked with electronic procedures to convert motion signals via MIDI systems into sound designs. Initially, these were simple trigger devices that effected a tight correlation between dance and music. However, soon it became apparent that these creations possessed a rather retrogade character: considering that John Cage and Merce Cunningham had dismantled the chain between dance and music, did one really want to go back to what in the film industry is known as 'Mickey-Mouse Effect', i.e. an on-the-cut synchronization of sound and image? Therefore, composers became engaged in devising more complex strategies to overcome the simple one-to-one relationship between sound and movement.[106] Todd Winkler, for example, treated the whole environment of the stage as a musical instrument to be manipulated by the movements of the dancer.[107] Just as a violinist uses his fingers to manipulate the sound-producing components of his instrument, the dancer's moving body can employ weight, force, pressure, speed, effort or energy to exercise a sound-producing effect. The violin's strings are here replaced with photo-electric sensors, laser beams, or force-sensing resistors on the dance floor, which generate a multitude of signals that are subsequently filtered, scaled and processed by the software, and then used to produce complex musical sounds.

The explosive development of the world-wide-web in the 1990s opened up a wide array of further creative possibilities. Just as actors seized upon the opportunities offered by webcam and internet-conferencing software, dancers created online performances, sometimes with other dancers in remote geographical locations. Motherboard (directed by Amanda Steggell and Per Platou), for example, created with *M@ggie's Love-Bytes* (1995) a 'post-modem' dance theatre performance occurring in virtual space. Realtime video-conferencing facilities connected Motherboard with geographically dispersed dancers and musicians via the Internet. Equipped with a 'plunger', the 'lovers' interacted with M@ggie, and the resulting images were projected onto a wall behind her (see Illustration 23). New

23   Amanda Steggell and Per Platou: *M@ggie's Love-Bytes*, Internet performance (1995)

participants were allowed to enter the project at any time during the performance and to deposit audio or visual presents in M@ggie's Giftbox via her homepage.[108]

To many companies, an Internet website is just a promotional platform; but some groups and individuals, often working together with universities and cultural institutions, began to explore the unique interactive possibilities of the new medium and introduced concepts for a dance-oriented web art. Their work was greatly aided by international web-based organizations such as Dance and Technology Zone (D&TZ), DanceOnline, and Association for Dance and Performance Telematics (ADaPT). A pioneer in these matters was the Australian artist and performer, Stelarc, who soon adopted the term 'dance' for his net-based creations (see Chapter 7). Around the same time, John Vincent began to work in virtual studios, linking his group Very Vivid, in Canada, with other dancers who were physically present in Europe, and making the results visible to his audiences in the form of digitalized images on a screen. In *Ghosts and Astronauts* by Susan Kozel and Gretchen Schiller, the audience of the 1997 Dance Umbrella Festival could view projected images of a dance created in two telematically linked London theatres, Riverside Studios and The Place. Similarly, Wayne McGregor joined dancers in London and Melbourne in an Internet performance entitled *Trial by Video* (1999).

Other choreographers seized upon the technology of Virtual Reality (VR) when, in the 1990s, it became available for artistic experimentation. For example, Yacov Sharir's *Dances with the Virtual Dervish* (1994) was an attempt to let a VR user perform a *pas de deux* with a virtual dancer.[109] A large-scale, virtual body was created and programmed to remain permanently in motion. The sensuously undulating VR body became an immersive architecture for the body of a human agent. The user's movements in physical space were transcribed onto the virtual plane, where the VR dancer began to interact with the real dancer. The user lived in two worlds simultaneously and experienced a simulation of himself as a kind of mirror effect to his actual being. Sharir comments:

> As my perception accommodates itself to a 3-D illusion, I experience a sense of being in another, additional skin – I feel immersed. At the same time, I have this sense of heightened anxiety, caused by the doubling of my own body image. The sensation of disembodiment cannot be disconnected from the sensation of embodiment; that is, I feel the physicality, the groundedness of gravity simultaneously with the sense of immersion and altered abilities, such as the ability to 'fly' through the simulation.[110]

24   Yacov Sharir: *Hollow Ground II,* Virtual performance (1997)

Blurring the distinctions between the virtual and the real world and making the one contingent on the interactions of the other was also the theme of Sharir's second experiment, *Hollow Ground II* (1997), and his most recent, *Automated Body Project.* Again, he paired cyberdancers with their human counterparts and intersected the two spaces in which they moved (see Illustration 24). But this time he sought to develop a model for the collaboration between several individuals in local and distributed sites, and to investigate various methods of expression in virtual space. He arrived at interesting results regarding the schizophrenic nature of the fragmented self, the duality of virtual and real worlds, and the collective identity of virtual and physical interactors.

The media hype and popular discussion centred on virtual technologies, cyborgs, the post-organic body, etc. could not but effect the dance world, which for millennia had explored and challenged body boundaries. The partnership established between scientists and dancers at the early stage of the cybernetic revolution became more common in the 1990s, when nearly every household in the Western hemisphere had become connected to digital networks. The London Dance Umbrella, a major annual dance festival, in 1995 introduced Techno Dance Bytes, followed in 1997 by Digital

Dancing, to reflect the growing interest in digital technologies amongst the dance community. The key significance of these computer-aided dances is similar to what I discussed above, namely that interactivity destroys the object character of art and transforms a product into an open-ended process of creativity. In the dance world, this meant that repeatable performances with clear, linear narratives were replaced with strategies linking a variety of interactive modules, each of them contingent upon the input of human and cybernetic agents.

As is the remit of avant-garde creativity, works shown at festivals dedicated to the 'cutting edge' of fusing dance and the newest electronic technologies were predominantly experiments and not always convincing on a conceptual and artistic level. Many performances I watched over the past decade were technically underdeveloped. In other cases, audiences were fascinated by the technological wizardry, but once the novelty value had worn off, little stayed in one's memory except some clever visual effects and at most some haunting images and metaphors of the 'human machine' forming part of larger cybernetic environment. At the beginning of the twenty-first century, digital technologies are still in their infancy and collaborations between art and science remain an exception rather than a rule. Although it would be tempting to end this chapter with an outlook on some of the possibilities that begin to emerge on the horizon, it is likely that such predictions will already be out of date by the time this book has passed through the press. Just as people who saw the first Lumière or Meliès films could not have foreseen the shape of present-day Hollywood or Bollywood cinema, it would be equally premature for me to make any forecasts about future interchanges between dance and digital technologies.

7

Performances in Cyberspace

From Electronic to Digital Culture: the Emergence of a Second Modernity?

In the long course of human civilization, a variety of media have been employed to communicate and store knowledge. Until fairly recently, all of these used analogue paradigms to transcribe an image or idea and capture it for posterity. Modern technology made it possible to shift from physical objects to electro-magnetic carriers. These media are not immediately accessible to our senses, as a process of inscription and decoding is necessary to store the information and make it available to users.

With the advent of the computer, an entirely different system came into common use. A digital medium does not contain a physical palimpsest of a message, but is merely a resource for the processing of information. Similarly, the stored or processed information has no corporeal existence, and no intrinsic material alliance is formed between message and carrier. Each picture, sentence, sound, etc. exists only as a sequence of numbers, which algorithmic procedures can modify, rearrange and combine in an infinite number of permutations and then convert back into legible images or scripts.

The first encounters between the cybernetic and artistic communities took place back in the 1950s, when artists attempted to understand and harness the latest technological developments for their creative activities. People treated the computer as a design tool and began to create electronic 'paintings' by cybernetic means. The electronic 'brain' was employed as an 'autonomous' creator of synthetic images and visual effects. In the 1980s, pictures began to move and to be combined with sound. Scanners and digitalized image processing widened the range of computer art even further, and in the 1990s a viable market had been created for electronic artworks stored on videodisk or compact disk, displayed on high-definition monitors, or projected onto screens.

The late twentieth century became the age of Media Arts, of interactive, multimedia installations that could be explored, modified and transformed by the visitor to (or 'user' of) an exhibition. Improved telecommunication networks and electronic visualization techniques produced a large number of interactive possibilities onsite and online, for individuals or groups. With the rapid expansion of the world-wide-web in the 1990s,[1] the ideal of global connectivity seemed to have become a reality and Net-Art came to be added to the already wide spectrum of digital, interactive arts. So, by the turn of the millennium, the computer had established itself as the most important tool for the creation of new visual and performative languages and of new roles for artists and viewers. Dozens of festivals and exhibition centres provided showcases for thousands of artists who had abandoned the easel or stage in order to focus their creativity on cyberart.

For a while, critics filed the Media Arts under the rubric 'postmodernism'. But as people's living and work environment became more and more saturated with electronic and digital technologies, and as the scale and range of New Media responding to this development increased, some cultural historians suggested that the turn of the millennium may have functioned as a threshold for a Second Modernity. Heinrich Klotz, for example, promoted the idea that 'Modernism was not a style that comes and goes like fashion, but a concept which over a course of time finds multifarious realizations and explications.'[2] The electronic and digital media ushered in a new age of avant-garde experimentation, which helped to overcome the long phase of postmodern stagnation. Rather than recycling trends and fashions of the First Modernity, the Media Arts of the *fin-de-millennium* moved into genuinely new terrain and reflected upon the altered modes of communication, their aesthetic and social implications, and people's radically changed modes of interacting with the world around them. In this respect, the Second Modernity is similar to its predecessor in the earlier part of the century; but whereas the historical avant-garde both promoted an aesthetic and social Utopia and sought to overcome the dichotomy of art and life, artists of the Second Modernity were much more sceptical of the revolutionary potential of creative discourses. Therefore, their socio-political engagement relinquished the 'grand narratives' of former decades, and a more pragmatic, yet still critical, appropriation of the New Media became the norm.

Interactive Cyberart as a Performative Medium

Throughout history, there has always been a lively exchange between art and science. Brunelleschi, Leonardo da Vinci, and Buontalenti – to mention just a few familiar names – were engineers who invented remarkable machines for military, civic and artistic purposes. The technologies of the industrial age gave birth to photography, the panorama, cinema, radio and many other mechanical means of reflecting the world. The Futurists and Constructivists made the integration of art and science a fundamental principle of their aesthetics. But many of their Utopian concepts had to wait until the invention of the computer before they could become reality.

In the 1960s, interactivity was a topical issue in the performing and visual arts. It became an 'in thing' in avant-garde circles to give the spectators more active agency and to integrate them into participatory performances (see, for example, the Happening movement, theatre companies such as the Living Theatre, the Bread and Puppet Theatre, Chaikin's Open Theatre or Schechner's Performance Group, and special initiatives such as Billy Klüver's Experiments in Art and Technology or Otto Piene's Center for Advanced Visual Studies). The first generation of artists who had a chance to experiment with the new electronic equipment coming on the market felt an enormous excitement about their potential for building bridges between art and life in the information age: 'The work of art is not to point to itself exclusively, it is to encourage the recipient to become active. This is the seed of dialogue that can be developed further, if the work of art becomes the interface of a dialogue of thoughts and perhaps also of common creation.'[3] Consequently, artists such as Peter Weibel, Roy Ascott, Jeffrey Shaw or Fred Forester, who had their roots in these interactive forms of theatre, quickly realized the potential of the New Media to create new types of performance.

However, early interactive Media Art was rather basic in concept and execution. Like Nam June Paik's manipulations of TV monitors, discussed in Chapter 6, these works possessed only a limited range of operational possibilities. This was due partly to the limitations of the hardware and partly to the inexperience of the practitioners. Artists required time to complement their artistic education and acquire – usually in an autodidactic fashion – the necessary technical know-how to produce media artworks that truly explored the inner logic of the digital world. In the 1960s and 1970s, training facilities for such tasks were rarely available. This may explain why so many early media installations only demonstrated a *potential*, rather than a *fully developed* accomplished work of art.

It was only in the 1980s that simple stimulus-response mechanisms were replaced with more sophisticated interactive models. Media artists created non-linear and open-ended works that made use of hypermedia to allow users to navigate through a wide array of possible paths. Thus, the media artwork offered a scenario of possibilities which only became realized through the user's interactions.[4] Each encounter produced different interventions and allowed the creation of different works, not dissimilar to what Kandinsky had demanded of an open artwork. But whereas the early Modernists had still been thinking in terms of art objects, the interactive artwork of the cybernetic age was more akin to a theatrical performance: the work of art existed only as long as the user/performer engaged in the creative act. However, this still leaves two questions unresolved: How can a user be considered a free and creative co-producer of a work of art when the interactions are predetermined by the author of the software? And is every interaction with a media artwork indeed a performance?

David Saltz rightly suggested that 'we must stop considering computer interaction as a unified phenomenon and draw some distinctions between various kinds of interactive systems'.[5] Triggering devices, hypermedia and VR interfaces assign a variety of performative roles to users, and not all of these become fully fledged performances. If a media user 'performs' a task just for himself, he gives a concrete 'form' to an otherwise virtual work of art. The artwork that requires such interactive input can be described as performative, but it knows only one actor and no audience. Thus, it is different from a presentation specially laid on for an audience (as in the theatre), and from an activity, which other people can watch (as is often the case at Media Art festivals or in game arcades).

In the course of the 1980s, new developments in the game industry overtook media artists, who were still trying to improve the creative potential of computers. A commercial market exploited existing technology and turned serious users into frivolous consumers; the 'Information-Super-Highway' became congested with 'data-trash', and 'web-surfers' found their brain addled with 'info-smog'. So if Media Art was not going to be submerged in the electronic toy market, it had to rise above the facile attractions of the telematic world and engage the user on more sophisticated intellectual levels. In 1990, the Prix Ars Electronica introduced the new category of Interactive Media Art. Roy Ascott defined the medium thus:

> Interactive art presents a flow of data (images, text, sound) and an array of cybernetic, adaptive and, one might say, *intelligent* structures, environments and networks (as performances, events, personal encounters and private experiences) in such a way that the observer can affect the flow, alter the structure, interact with the environment or navigate the network, thus becoming directly involved in the acts of transformation and creation.[6]

Unfortunately, only a small minority of enthusiasts ever had a chance to experience the works singled out for awards at the Ars Electronica festival in Linz. The new digital media produced 'art beyond art', which fell outside the established categories of artistic expression and transformed the traditional concepts of author, spectator and work of art. Although occasionally exhibited in museums and galleries, Media Art was not generally admitted to the permanent collections of these institutions as it was considered to belong to the performing rather than the fine arts.[7] It took until the 1990s before this attitude began to change. A new generation of artists, who had grown up with computers and video games as part of their everyday life, produced ever more complex and artistically challenging works, in which interactivity was no longer a gimmick, but an integral component of an artistic concept.

The artistic merit of these media artworks hinged on their ability to facilitate experiences that were impossible to achieve in any other medium. At one end of the spectrum one could find an emphasis on purpose-free, ludic creativity; at the other a radical questioning of the social ramifications of new technologies, a philosophical reflection on their influence on the human psyche, and suggestions for an emancipatory use of advanced technologies. Many of the most convincing works showed how the media have altered human experience of reality and our consciousness of being, how they have influenced our identity and psychology, how they have transformed our relationships with our bodies and environment, etc. And these works not only *reflected* on these changes, but also allowed users to experience them and develop a critical attitude towards them.

In the last decade of the twentieth century, the use of interactive scenic elements also entered the theatrical domain and updated experiments already undertaken in the earlier part of the century. However, until fairly recently, few of these works attempted to link the realm of dramatic theatre with the cybernetic world.[8] It was only when the game industry developed an interest in more interactive, multi-player software that large computer research laboratories began to invest in cybernetic theatre projects. An example of this was the support and funding MIT's Media Laboratory provided to Claudio Pinhanez's *Computer Theater*. Pinhanez rightly deplores the limited creative input offered to users of video games or media installations. His attempts at widening their repertoire of actions/reactions, at turning interaction into acting and the users into performers, has led him to study the latest developments in virtual scenography, the existing patterns in interactive music and the use of responsive environments in dance. Consequently, he has come up with programmes for action-based, rehearsed and improvised performances that involve a real-life actor, a cyber-actor (i.e. a computer, which he calls a 'hyper-actor'), and a fully-computerized stage that can map movements and correlate them to sound and lighting design. The computer-actor assumes the role of a character in a play and interprets the behaviour of the human partner by using speech recognition and visual-action recognition of emotional states as indicated through facial expressions, gestures and motions. In his responses he projects emotions via synthesized facial expression and modulated speech, thus arriving at a true dialogue between cybernetic and organic actor.[9]

The Virtual Body in Cyberspace

Cyberspace is a symbolic space, an electronically produced immaterial realm that occupies a hybrid position between the real and unreal. Its real aspect is linked to the hardware, the engineering skill of the software developers, the workers in the Third World who assemble the micro chips, etc. In this respect, cyberspace is not an alternative to the everyday sphere, but is firmly rooted in the political and economic realities that control cyberspace: the companies who produce the workstations, the providers who give access to information, the global corporations who transmit the binary codes, the institutions who regulate public access, the censors who filter out undesirable contents, etc. Left-wing activists often saw in the new electronic networks an opportunity for collective, creative initiatives and a means to 'ignite a real democratic change'.[10] But like other early interactive tools, these soon became consumer items dependent on commercial software and hardware developed by companies interested in money rather than political liberation. As Simon Penny aptly formulated:

> It is difficult to understand how a digital utopia of freedom of expression can be proposed, without acknowledging its dependence upon millions of dollars worth of (mostly privately owned) computers, fibre-optics, satellites, and dishes. . . . Virtuality builds a class structure based on access to information. The new under-class are the virtual homeless, those who cannot afford virtual bodies.'[11]

The virtual aspects of cyberspace link it to the world of imagination. All works of fiction conjure up alternative worlds, but in the past they were either mental constructs (stories, fairy tales, dramas) or physical representations of these constructs (such as paintings, sculptures, dances, photographs, films). Whereas conventional performance acted out myths in a make-believe, yet still real world, the fractal dreams of cyberia have no grounding in physical space. None the less, the characters who reside in this world are experienced as actual, because in Virtual Reality systems the barriers of the screen or proscenium arch have been abolished and the multi-dimensional stage has been opened up to sensory and cognitive inhabitation by the user.

These cybernetic constructs of virtual worlds are only the last stage in the development of modern visual media. The nineteenth century saw the first deluge of mechanically produced representations of the world. The lithographed images in the illustrated press – *Saturday Evening Post* (from 1821), *Magasin pittoresque* (from 1833), *Illustrated London News* (from 1843), *L'Illustration* (from 1843), *Illustrierte Zeitung* (from 1843), *La Vie parisienne* (from 1863), *La Vie moderne* (from 1879), etc. – played a particularly important role in conditioning the minds of the big-city dwellers and determined their experience of modernity. Diorama, panorama, photography and cinema intensified the thrill of travelling in alternative spaces. Baudelaire captured the immense attraction of these voyages into a virtual world when he wrote: 'A madness and unusual fanaticism took possession of these new sun-worshippers. . . . Thousands of eager eyes leaned over the holes of the stereoscope as if they were gable-windows into the infinite.'[12] The development from still photography to moving pictures, from contemplative to interactive media gave users an increased sense of freedom, which was further enhanced by the most recent cybernetic simulations of the material world.

Given the technical complexity of VR equipment, most users fail to understand the internal working of the machines they are using and develop a relationship to cyberspace that is akin to our early ancestors' admiration (or fear) of the magical forces of Nature. Many observers of cyberculture have noted the ritualistic use of VR equipment and have reported on the shamanic experiences afforded by it. I have discussed above in Chapter 3, the seemingly astonishing convergence of New Age mentality and cyber-spiritualism; now we can probably understand why the widely pursued quest for transcendence, trance states and ecstatic abandonment could find a new application in the 'magical reality' of cyberspace.[13]

The oneiric world of video games and fully immersive VR equipment is a realm that delivers users from the limitations and imperfections of Nature and the prison policed by the Reality Principle. But when the Pleasure Principle escapes the control of the Super Ego and promises realization of the omnipotent fantasies of the infantile mind, then this can have cata-strophic consequences for the development of an individual's personality. Infants need to develop a capacity to see beyond the world created by their fantasies and to relate to others as actual humans with a will of their own. Cyberspace as an environment that connects internal with external worlds enables the virtual self to fuse with the machine and allows the Ego to inter-act with its mental representations as if they were malleable, internal objects. Here, the fantasies of mastery and control, the unconscious quest for magical power and the desire to suspend the constraints of the social environment are given free rein.

Cyberspace's inherent immateriality promises redemption from the shackles of mundane everyday existence. It appeals to young (or not so young) adults who, like Jaron Lanier, 'always wanted to transcend the unfair boundaries of the physical world, which seemed very frustrating and contrary to the infinity of imagination'.[14] When we become players in cyberspace, the flesh body, our 'home' in the material world, is 'parked' in front of the computer. Cyberidentity is not rooted in a physical body but functions as an extension of the mind. The 'multi-user dungeons' and 'chat-rooms' of the Internet provide simulacra of intimacy that encourage its users to overcome personal inhibitions and to transcend the limitations of their social position. People often use this opportunity to redefine their subjectivity and undergo a process which Tim Jordan has called 'online individuation'.[15] By choosing different avatars for their online existence, they dissolve the boundaries of the old identity and fashion for themselves new and often multiple 'selves'. This allows them to live out aspects of their personality that otherwise would lie dormant in the inner recesses of their mind. Fantasy and imagination determine the choice of identity and of how to live out the new role(s). What is variously referred to as 'conscious dreaming' or 'lucid dreaming' comes close to acting out scenarios of an alternative life and bears close resemblance to conventional theatre, except that there the virtual is real .

Virtual Reality: from Video Games to Immersive Environments

Most people will have encountered Virtual Reality systems for the first time in arcades, where players can interact with characters in computer-animated games. As all the actions are determined by his or her decisions, the player is always the leading character in the scenario, which makes VR equipment much more attractive than television, even though the visual quality of the graphics leaves much to be desired.

Historically, one needs to distinguish between video games and fully immersive VR environments, although since the mid-1990s these have coexisted and influenced each other. Video games had their origin at the Massachusetts Institute of Technology, way back in the early 1960s, when students of engineering and mathematics explored the existing facilities on the large-scale mainframe computers and tried to enhance them for no other reason than having fun with dismantling and rearranging existing software.[16] Steven Levy, who has chronicled these experiments on Boston's

---

BOX 7.1   CYBERNETICS, TELEMATICS, CYBERSPACE, CYBORG, AVATAR, AND VIRTUAL REALITY

Cybernetics
The science of automated communication in self-regulated systems (Gr. *kybernē* = steersman). In the 1950s, it became the name of a large mainframe computer and from then on it connoted the computer and its operations.

Telematics
New technologies resulting from the convergence of computers and telecommunicative systems.

Cyberspace
The storage space of data in a computer, into which the user 'enters' when 'navigating' through the information system.

Cyborg
Contraction of cyb[ernetic] org[anism], a hybrid of a human and a machine, which has been popularized in science fiction as a creature who lives in cyberspace but is indistinguishable from a human being.

Avatar
A digital alter ego in cyberspace, or assumed identity used in online chat environments. Some people use several avatars related to different aspects of their off-line personality.

Virtual Reality (VR)
A computer-generated, three-dimensional environment with the operator as an interactive agent. The human perceptual system is stimulated in a manner that creates the impression of being immersed in virtual space. Cybernetic feedback and control systems allow the user to interact with the artificially created world and to experience it as real.

Tech Square, emphasized that 'to qualify as a hack, the feat must be imbued with innovation, style and technical virtuosity'. However, this was done 'not solely to fulfil some constructive goal, but with some wild pleasure taken in mere involvement'. Successful 'hacks' led to the invention of new interactive programmes, e.g. for playing chess or solving puzzles. Subverting the 'serious' image of computers and treating these high-performance machines as if they were toys became a popular pastime in computer clubs and hacker communities.

The first commercial game that grew out of these experiments was *Spacewar* (1962).[17] It took about ten years before chip prices had fallen sufficiently to introduce such games into the arcades. They were an immediate success and, from 1972 onwards, Atari produced some twelve new video games every year. In 1975, they were modified for home use on games consoles and micro computers. A simplified technology and an extended narrative framework made the games extremely popular with young audiences. By 1982, 30 million games had been sold in the USA, producing something of a saturation point in the 35 million households with children aged 6 to 16. Another upsurge of sales figures came in 1986, when Nintendo introduced a new generation of games. Within three years, 18 million of these had been sold, grossing $3.4 billion for the Corporation.

In the 1980s, video games in their home or arcade versions formed the largest sector of the entertainment industry (see Table 7.1[18]), surpassing the market for pop music (worth up to $4 billion) and for Hollywood films ($3 billion). By 1990, twenty-five of the thirty best-selling toys in the USA were video games' hard- or software (with Nintendo cornering 80 per cent of the market), amounting to some 30 per cent in the overall volume of toy sales.[19] It has been estimated that 95 per cent of all software produced for home computers fell into the genre of video games.[20]

Although home video games were viewed on a flat television screen, they created in children's minds the feeling of getting inside the box.

Table 7.1 **Annual sales figures for video game industry in the USA, 1979–97 (in US$)**

1979	1980	1981	1982	1983	1984	1985
330 million	446 million	1 billion	3 billion	2 billion	800 million	100 million

1986	1987	1988	1989	1990	1991	1992
430 million	1.1 billion	2.3 billion	3.4 billion	4 billion	3.6 billion	3.9 billion

1993	1994	1995	1996	1997		
4.2 billion	4.5 billion	4.5 billion	5.1 billion	5.6 billion		

Instead of watching passively images flickering on a monitor, they feel like becoming one with the world created by the software. The active involvement and sense of control over the images offered a degree of identification that was much higher than in watching movies or videos.

Skirrow proposes a psychoanalytic reading of the attraction and immense success of video games: they represent a journey into the maternal womb. The images produced on the monitor suggest an inexhaustible flow of nourishment and promise endless consumption. The child therefore wants to force its way into the mother's body and take possession of its contents. The operations with the joystick promise a path of fulfilment towards this ultimate objective.[21]

In the 1970s, television became the most significant sparetime activity for children. Daily viewing times increased from 2.8 hours in 1967 to 3.1 hours in 1976, rising to 4.7 hours in 1983. This means that between the ages of 6 and 18, the average amount of time spent in front of a TV screen had risen from 12,000 to 20,000 hours! In the early 1980s, 73 per cent of US-American children owned a home video game and spent an average of two hours a day playing with it. More than half of the boys also went to the video arcades at least once a week.[22] This added a further 10,000 hours of interactive video time to the already impressive 20,000 hours of television time which children will have spent in front of a TV set by the time they have grown up.

These viewing habits explain why multimedia games, VR systems and other cyberspace equipment had such a captivating appeal for young adults in advanced information societies. Experiences made at an early age with simulated worlds leave a lasting mark on a child's cognitive development, interactive behaviour and communicative competence. Traditional games stimulate the child's imagination, but video games with their narrow bandwidth of narratives and interactive roles restrict the child's creativity and social competence. Users have to surrender their freedom to the machine, accept the rules of the game and follow its logic. Imaginative capacities are reduced in favour of functional skills (such as hand–eye coordination) and instrumental thinking (e.g. how to overcome an obstacle). Video games are competitive and do little to encourage lateral and contextual thinking, or foster a critical mind. Furthermore, the emotive power of the stereotypical plots, the superhuman qualities of the heroic characters, and the fixed rules of the game foster an intimate attachment to electronic machines and set up unrealistic expectations when it comes to interacting with human beings. Until recently, there existed no video game that could be played in a team. As an investigation into arcade games found out, children and adolescents are caught up in an almost autistic fantasy world which makes them withdraw from their social environment: 'Videogames rate higher than human companions – the games were viewed as more exciting and more fun than human companions.'[23]

The virtual world of video games is easy to fall in love with and holds an almost hypnotic fascination for its users. Children are easily trapped in the worlds created by computer programmers, which ultimately cripple rather than foster their mental development. A child interacting with these machines learns nothing about history, psychology, society. There is little time to reflect, only to act. The key attraction of video games lies in its interactivity, but it is the parameters of the software that control the actor; he (or she) is only *re-acting*; he performs a function assigned to him or her by the machine; and in the end the game *forms* him, his mind, his behaviour.

This becomes most apparent when considering the dominant theme of nearly all video games: violence. There are basically two schools of interpretation of games that require the child to accept violence not only as an acceptable but also a necessary means to achieve a goal: one regards it as cathartic and therapeutic, the other believes that it stimulates aggressive patterns of behaviour in the real world. Certainly, the stress of puberty and adolescence has always found a release in violent games. But whereas the fights between youngsters teach them many useful lessons about the rules of social interaction, the violent resolution of conflicts in video games has no repercussions in the real world and hence no pedagogic value. Interviews with video game players suggest that the games establish behavioural models that induce children to interact with their social environment according to similar patterns. Such desensitization is purposely employed in some military training designed to overcome a natural reticence towards taking the life of other human beings, even when they are considered enemies.[24] As a military psychologist, Dave Grossman has studied the training methods that increased the firing rates from 15 per cent in World War I to 20 per cent in World War II, 55 per cent in the Korean War and 90 per cent in Vietnam. His subsequent investigation of video games revealed that they employ the same strategies that have quadrupled the firing rates of modern soldiers. They therefore contribute towards a 'systematic process of defeating the normal individual's age-old psychological inhibition against violent, harmful activity toward one's own species'. He concludes: 'If we had the clear-cut objective of raising a generation of assassins and killers who are unrestrained by either authority or the nature of the victims, it is difficult to imagine how we could do a better job.'[25]

As yet, it is difficult to predict in which direction commercial Virtual

Reality systems are likely to develop. However, it is obvious that software producers will respond to the immense opportunities VR offers for the arousal of some very primitive urges. Margaret Morse gave a good description of the sensations felt by a user on her first contact with the virtual world:

> The allure of this cyberspace was the impression that it was responsive to me, as if my gaze itself were creating (or performing) this world and that I was to some extent enunciating it according to my own desire. . . . I had a sense of the weight-lessness and superpower that I had imagined in childhood and had read about in myths and comic books, but had never before experienced, not even in my dreams. . . . It is this feeling of transcendence of the mortal body and the grav-ity of the earth that for me is the key to the desire and media attention which have been focussed on 'cyberspace' and the subculture that has grown around it. . . . I was fascinated with being both *in* the picture and having *control* over it.[26]

VR systems are machines for generating dynamic worlds of enchant-ment that allow the dreamer to enter his or her dreams. As such, they are different from narrative scenarios of an epic or dramatic kind. Theatre, also, has the potential of being an interactive medium, but the Western tradition that evolved since the Renaissance has been a closed system (a rehearsed stage show visible at a distance through a proscenium opening). VR systems are a further phase of development from previous experiments with opening up the black box called theatre (participatory and environ-mental Performance Art) or the small box called television (interactive Media Art). Introducing the spectator as an active agent *into* the scenic space turns him or her into the principal actor, as only his or her physical and psychological operations make the performance possible.

The consumer equipment provided by the electronic entertainment industry usually consists of a head-mounted, stereoscopic display unit ('eyephones'), a tracking device to monitor head movements, and a feed-back glove to manipulate perceived objects and create haptic sensations. The HMD (head-mounted display) helmet, and even more so a datasuit, isolates the user from the surrounding world and gives him or her the feel-ing of entering an enclosed, alternative world. VR is like a theatre of simu-lation, an interactive representational apparatus that allows immersion into a synthetic, three-dimensional environment. The VR tools exploit the perceptual mechanisms and cognitive apparatus, which have evolved in the course of human evolution for the understanding of and interaction with the world, in order to stimulate perceptual experiences that are similar to the information processed by our sense apparatus when confronted with a physical reality. As a result, the sensory experience triggered by the virtual environment makes the user experience the artificial world as if it were real.

The first VR systems were developed in the 1960s and 1970s for military, scientific and industrial purposes. The apparatus used for flight simulation in the training of aircraft pilots or for virtual operations in medical training came very close to the 'real thing', whereas those used in architecture or engineering were more functional and did not rely on high-resolution graphics or high-fidelity audio effects. The version used on the Holodeck of Starship Enterprise in the popular *Star Wars* series, and the general hype in the media, set up inflated expectations in the general public, which consumer systems that were presented in the early 1990s never lived up to. The human body is a holistic entity, which, over millions of years, has developed a complex system for relating to the outside world. In a VR environment, such interactive possibilities are very limited, as two of our five senses – smell and taste – are entirely switched off, and the sense of touch is only partially engaged in a simulated experience.

Despite the strong emphasis on vision, the quality of VR graphics is still so poor that it quickly causes simulation sickness. The only high-fidelity component employed is sound, and even that is not much better than a medium-priced personal stereo. The system's interactive qualities can be most impressive; equally, some of the applications in the field of engineering, where machines can be tested before they have been built, clearly demonstrate the value of investing a million dollars in a test programme rather than, for example, wasting billions on recalling faulty cars from unhappy customers.[27] But nevertheless, the 'bandwidth' of reality that can be found in cyberspace is still very narrow.

Given these limitations, it seems rather astonishing that multi-billion-dollar industries can be based on such an underdeveloped technology. The potential for further growth is staggering, especially if VR conquers the market currently occupied by pornographic video tapes and disks. This will, no doubt, bring a new dimension to the old discussion about sex and violence in the media, and about the mind–body duality in the realm of imagination.

The cyberbody is a rather one-dimensional extension of the human mind and, some psychologists would say, only of great attraction to those who have a disturbed relationship to their physical body. Virtual existence in cyberspace is constituted through discourses that are firmly rooted in a body-hostile culture.

One does not take one's body into VR: one leaves it at the door. VR reinforces Cartesian duality by replacing the body with a body image, a creation of mind (for all 'objects' in VR are the product of mind). As such, it is a clear continuation of the rationalist dream of the disembodied mind, part of the long Western tradition of the denial of the body. Augustine is the patron saint of cyberpunks.[28]

Katherine Hayles has described the person attracted to a disembodied existence as one who treats his or her body like a flawed and unwieldy vehicle and/or seeks to transcend the body in order to achieve immortality. Psychologists are, of course, very familiar with the related phenomenon of the masochistic identification with a source of repression. Seen from that angle, the datasuit can be interpreted as being not a gateway to a liberated state of existence but a straitjacket for cybernauts. To believe in a disembodied existence in cyberspace one has to erase awareness of the technological interfaces and perceptual processes that bring this 'alternative' world into existence: 'Our bodies are no less involved in the construction of virtuality than in the construction of real life. It is obvious that we can see, hear, feel, and interact with virtual worlds only because we are embodied.'[29]

Even before leisure industry VR systems became commercially available (in 1991), artists such as Myron Krueger, Fred Brooks, Jill Scott, Jeffrey Shaw and Peter Weibel were already experimenting with interactive varieties of the new technology, focussing on the users' receptive behaviour and confronting them with unexpected choices in order to stimulate their creative imagination. Here, the VR apparatus provided an interactive 'stage' and the digital mise-en-scène, but in the actual 'performance' the user had to make creative use of the tools placed at his or her disposal. Jeffrey Shaw summed up a common sentiment amongst media artists working with such systems: 'Virtual space is for me a kind of surreal or imaginative meditation of reality onto which imaginative worlds can be projected.'[30]

Such innovative, stimulating and activating scenarios were, however, a far cry from the seductive quality of commercial VR systems. Regular exposure to these constructed realities, which appeal predominantly to the lower instincts, have a lasting effect on the individual's ability to interpret exterior reality and distinguish fact from fiction. Many of the topical issues of the modern information society (political manipulation, racial stereotyping, degradation of women, corruption of social and cultural values) are likely to become more acute by the influence of VR systems on users' cognitive development, socialization, and personality structure. The new technology produced for a mass consumer market transports the values and ideologies of the dominant social groups. VR is not a neutral technology; its positive or negative effects will depend on how society uses it. Given the fact that the cyberindustry is a lucrative enterprise with aims similar to those of the Hollywood dream factory, it is safe to predict that VR products will not be used primarily to promote human values and educational principles but will be determined by the forces of profit maximization. The short history of the VR medium demonstrates that its products do not foster mature ludic creativity but cater to basic instincts and infantile desires. Therefore, their long-term effect is likely to resemble those of the older media of television, video and computer games.

Stelarc and Virtual Performances of the Post-human Age

By the end of the twentieth century, some 10 per cent of the Western population were, technically speaking, cyborgs. They were kept alive by electronic pacemakers and drug implants, made mobile by prosthetic limbs and synthetic joints, could only interact with the world by means of hearing aids, ophthalmic accessories and artificial larynxes. The body, colonized by technology, had become a 'post-human body'. Ever more powerful human–machine interfaces, together with biotechnology and genetic engineering, gave rise to visions of conquering the physical and mental limitations of the human species by means of direct mind–machine connections (e.g., chip implants into the brain or neurological pathways connecting human and computer). At the same time, these technical developments produced fears of the organic body becoming reduced to mere 'wet-ware' in a mind–machine symbiosis.

> Posthuman bodies are the causes and effects of postmodern relations of power and pleasure, virtuality and reality, sex and its consequences. The posthuman body is a technology, a screen, a projected image; it is a body under the sign of AIDS, a contaminated body, a deadly body, a techno-body; it is, as we shall see, a queer body. The human body itself is no longer part of the 'family of man' but of a zoo of posthumanities.[31]

The dawn of a biocybernetic age not only launched a wide range of new possibilities for humans to control virtual bodies and for machines to regulate the human body; it also launched innovative developments in artistic media based on digital technology and prompted new departures in the performing arts. In past centuries, actors concerned themselves daily with the task of imagining themselves as a different person, and novelists conjured up travels to imagined lands. But in the age of 'telepresence' in 'artificial life-worlds', technological apparatuses and sophisticated software allowed every person with access to Virtual Reality equipment to slip into the minds of other people, borrow their personality, act out alternative lives, etc. Or vice versa, the human mind could become part of a feedback system controlled by exterior forces. The resulting schizoid condition – an ambiguous state of being two persons at once, of having more than one body, or of being an external part of a cybernetic system which can 'steer' our body – has bewildering consequences for traditional concepts of personality and identity.

One of the first artists to explore in a practical way the consequences of a body being accessed and acted upon by cybernetic means and caught in a maelstrom of post-isms was Stelarc (artist name of Stelios Arcadiou, a Greek Cypriot who lived in Japan and Australia for most of his life). He trained as a sculptor in Melbourne and was principally interested in the body as an architectural structure, an object in various magnetic, electrical and gravitational states, or a container of rhythms and flows of energy. He began his career as a performer in 1968 with multimedia works, moved into 'body events' in 1970 (amplification of blood-flow, brain-waves, muscle signals and various body functions by means of EEG, ECG and EMG), and sensory–deprivation events in 1972. In 1973–5, he filmed the inside of his body (stomach, colon, lungs), and then made himself a name with spectacular body suspensions. Twenty-five of these were carried out between 1976 and 1988, of varying length and in different types of location. These 'Events for Stretched Skin' usually involved the insertion of 18 hooks into his skin, and his body being hoisted up into a horizontal position. Only a small number of spectators were admitted to these events and they watched him hanging suspended between trees, over the sea, in a Japanese Temple, or in an art gallery.[32] The general public was able to witness his work in 1984, when he hung from a mobile pulley system between high-rise blocks in New York.[33] He commented on his suspension work:

> Having done 6 years of suspensions with harnesses I became intrigued about the possibilities of using less support for the body, minimizing the support for the body. At that time I became aware of the ritual suspensions of the Hindu Indians. . . . Having read about the suspensions by insertions into the skin, I really became taken by the idea of the body becoming its own support structure.[34]

He also performed the 'Sun Dance', a trance technique practised for centuries by Native Americans, which had been reawakened by the Modern Primitives community in the USA.[35] But Stelarc was adamant that his motivation was entirely different: 'I've never meditated before an event. I've never had any sort of out-of-body experiences. I've never felt a sense of being a shaman, or an S&M situation. To me those notions are largely irrelevant.'[36] In a programmatic statement in *Flash Art*, Stelarc explained that his hyper-engagement with the body was a response to the neglect of corporeal existence in Minimalism, Concept Art and electronic culture: 'In this age of information overload, only physical commitment is meaningful.'[37] As a sculptor-turned-performer, Stelarc concerned himself with issues that are entirely proper to his profession: space, movement, weight. What makes it unusual is that his explorations of the inner space and outer boundaries of the body, of the skin as a membrane separating the body from surrounding space, were conducted with the aim of redesigning the human body. This technological, genetic, and cybernetic project to liberate the body from its physical confinement pushed him increasingly into domains which no other artists before had probed in such a systematic and dedicated manner.

Already in the 1970s, Stelarc had introduced high-tech components into some of his performances and gave lectures on artificial intelligence, robotics and prosthetics. His explorations of the limits of the body went hand in hand with experiments investigating how the physical capacities of the body could be extended, and in the 1980s, he gradually shifted his focus from the suspension events to an examination of new relationships between technology and the body.

In a number of interviews, Stelarc has suggested that the time has come to escape the tyranny of biology and evolutionary development. Unlike the critics of Western techno-civilization, who conjure up visions of humanity's descent into electronic incarceration (the postmodern equivalent to Dante's hell), Stelarc does not believe that the human race is enslaved by technology. Rather, he deems technology to be the root of our existence, with humanity's future depending on its creative interaction with technology. In Stelarc's anthropology, the human species has evolved from the animal kingdom because bipedalism gave it an ability to handle tools. The production of instruments and artefacts is intimately connected to our speciation and must be considered a defining criterion of humanity. The technologies of the past millennia allowed humans to exploit and master their natural environment. But since the planet Earth cannot guarantee the survival of the species, we may well need to find habitats outside the terrestrial sphere. However, our five senses currently function on an electromagnetic spectrum that is too narrow for operating effectively in macro- and micro-worlds. Our biological hardware is ill-equipped for the infosphere of cyberspace, and our body is not flexible and durable enough for extraterrestrial existence. Only successful body–machine symbiosis can release us from our biological and ecological containment. Therefore, our move into cosmic and cybernetic worlds forces us into an amalgamation of the visceral and the mechanical, of carbon chemistry and silicon-chip technology.

As an artist, Stelarc was particularly interested in the human–machine interface and the hybridization of the body with new technologies. His aim was to fuse man and machine, to make the machine a component of the body and the body a component of the machine: 'Machines, bits of technology, will inhabit the internal tracts and soft tissues of the body, and the human body will become the landscape of machines.'[38] He calls the human being, augmented, extended and enhanced by technology, a 'bionaut'. In his most radical visions he literally translates Deleuze's 'body without organs' into a hollowed-out body where biological functions are performed by computer software and technological life-support systems. The redesigned body will have extended connectivity and will link up with intelligent machines 'as a kind of external nervous system that motivates and manipulates and modulates the body, both in its muscular motions and its acoustical and optical inputs'.[39] Thus supplemented by computer-directed sensors directly implanted into the skin, the body will multiply its operational range.

Stelarc's ultimate aim is to 'redesign the body to function in this intense information realm of faster and more precise machines'.[40] Once the neuro-logical network that coordinates our senses can be connected to the global telecommunication network, and once brain-chips make our thoughts compatible with computer memory, then a two-way communication system can be set up: humans entering electronic space, and the telematic world accessing, interfacing and uploading its terrestrial hosts. An operational system of spatially distributed but electronically interfaced bodies will be able to interact with remote agents. The Internet will not only be a means of transmitting information, but become an instrument of transduction, of effecting physical action between bodies. Electronic space will function as a realm of action, rather than information, allowing intimacy without prox-imity, intercourse with humans and machines. Once bionautics and cyber-nautics have completed our evolutionary development, 'the body falls behind like a rocket stage as *Homo sapiens* accelerates into "pan-planetary" posthuman evolution'.[41]

More recently, Stelarc has described his works as choreographies or dances: 'These performances have always been concerned with the dynam-ics of body and machine movement and how to choreograph and counter-point them. . . . In *Ping Body*, the body does a data dance. . . . Internet activity composes and choreographs the performance'.[42] Of course, any kind of movement requires feedback loops of sensory and perceptual data that coordinate the articulation of the jointed body. But performing with electronic sensors, video goggles, chip implants and machine attachments augments the body's capabilities, heightens physical awareness and disrupts the habitual sense of position and orientation. Moving involuntarily by remote prompting and muscle stimulation also generates feelings of alienation.

Stelarc's performances force us to reconsider what constitutes self and identity, but he does so as an artist, not as a scientist or philosopher. His career as a sculptor and performer brought him into contact with very advanced technologies, but his use of these facilities has always been determined by artistic considerations. He has approached the converging realms of science and aesthetics on a purely intuitive, creative level, and he believes that his artistic sensibilities enable him to act as a 'pioneer of a new Renaissance' and 'evolutionary guide', exploring new trajectories and alternative practices that may transform humanity and prepare it for a different life in new environments.

In the course of the 1990s, Stelarc has given an average of eighteen performances a year, including lecture-demonstrations which are often just as impressive as his techno-performances. From these latter, I have selected a handful of generic categories (the titles varied with each performance) to give the reader a better idea of what could be observed on stage.[43]

The Virtual Body (*Le Corps amplifié*, 1993) was a computer-generated surrogate body activated by an electro-magnetic motion-capture system connected to Stelarc's head, upper and lower back, arms and legs. These position-orientation sensors mapped his body motions onto a virtual body, and to make the choreography more interesting, virtual cameras switched angles from an ants-eye view to a birds-eye view of the virtual body. Movements were accompanied by amplified body signals and the sounds of a Third Hand.

Third Hand was a project developed over five years (1976–81) and centred on a manipulator attached to Stelarc's right arm. It was controlled by EMG signals from electrodes positioned on four sites on the abdominal and leg muscles. By contracting the appropriate muscles, he could activate the desired mechanical hand motion. After many years of using it in performances, Stelarc was able to operate the third hand effortlessly and intuitively. Performances in the 1980s were also complemented by amplified body sounds and interactive video and described by Mark Dery in the following manner:

A welter of *thrrrups*, squeals, creaks, and *cricks*, most of them originating in Stelarc's body, whooshes around the performance space. The artist's heartbeat, amplified by means of an ECG (electrocardiograph) monitor, marks time with a muffled, metronomic thump. The opening and closing of heart valves, the slap and slosh of blood are captured by Doppler ultrasound transducers, enabling Stelarc to 'play' his body. . . . A kinetic-angle transducer converts the bending of his right knee into avalanches of sound; a microphone, placed over the larynx, picks up swallowing and other throat noises . . . The Third Hand chirrs frantically, its stainless steel fingers clutching at nothingness.[44]

After a series of performances using a left arm automated with single-channel muscle stimulators, a new category, *Involuntary Body*, with a six-channel muscle stimulation system and a computer-interface, was developed. The first version, called *Fractal Flesh*, was presented at Telepolis 1995, where audiences in Paris (the Pompidou Centre), Helsinki (the Media Lab) and Amsterdam (the Doors of Perception Conference) were given remote access through the Internet to the main performance site in Luxembourg and could view and actuate Stelarc's body via a touch-screen interface. The feedback-loops allowed one side of Stelarc's body to be guided by the audience while the other was steered by himself, effecting a split physiology controlled by local and remote agency. Stelarc could watch part of his body move without having to contract any muscle.

Stimbod (1995) was a related experiment that allowed audiences to direct Stelarc's body either by touching the muscles on the computer model or by pasting together a series of gesture icons. Video screens at the different locations allowed the artist to see the face of the person who, through a six-channel muscle stimulation system, sent electric currents of 0–60 volts to the muscle sites (deltoids, biceps, flexors, thigh and calf muscles) to choreograph his movements. The remote programmers also composed sound sequences and video images, as the body had been fitted with sensors, electrodes and transducers that triggered sampled body sounds and functioned as a video switcher and mixer. The system allowed simulation of the programmed movement for analysis and evaluation before transmitting it to actuate the body. Stelarc commented on the performance:

> This is not about remote control of the body, but rather of constructing bodies with split physiologies, operating with multiple agency. Was it Wittgenstein who asked if in raising your arm you could remove the intention of raising it what would remain? Ordinarily, you would associate intention with action .... With *Stimbod*, though, that intention would be transmitted from another body elsewhere.[45]

> Imagine two dancers in different locations wired up with transmitting and receiving systems. It would be possible for the two connected dancers to be in control of a half of each other's bodies.[46]

Ping Body (1996) was an Internet-actuated and uploaded performance, where Stelarc's body was telematically scaled up and stimulated by reverberating signals to over 30 global Internet domains. The Pings[47] were mapped to his deltoid, biceps, flexors, hamstring and calf muscles and used to determine his movements (see Illustration 25). So instead of having his body prompted by the internal nervous system or by people in other locations (as in *Stimbod*), it was the external ebb and flow of cyberactivity itself that choreographed and composed the performance. A more sophisticated version was *ParaSite* (1997), where a customized search engine was constructed to scan the world-wide-web to select and display images through a video headset. Computer analyses of the graphics (JPEG) files provided data that were mapped to the muscles, so that Stelarc effectively performed the images he was seeing without having control over the movements they were inducing in him. His body, optically stimulated and electrically activated, became a 'parasite' sustained by an external nervous system operating in a global electronic space of information and images.

Stelarc's aesthetics of prosthetics, his redesign of the human body, his practical experiments with mechanical extensions of the body and with electronic link-ups to the nervous system, have their origin in an old dream: 'A synthesis of organic and synthetic to create a new hybrid human, one that can evolve with Larmarckian speed.'[48] This suggests that by the 1990s, the avant-garde had gone full circle and returned to its Futurist beginnings, when Lamarck could also serve as a model for Marinetti in his manifesto *Man Extended and the Reign of the Machine*.[49] Stelarc's experiments, together with those of other media artists at the start of the twenty-first century, point towards certain similarities between the cultures that emerged from the Industrial Revolution and the Information Revolution. Stelarc, as a latter-day Futurist, committed himself to a Modernist advancement of a techno-society. Like Marinetti, he became the prophet of a machine god and propagated a Utopian belief that technology would allow humans to transcend themselves and reach happiness in a radically transformed existence.[50] This suggests that postmodernism was only an intermittent phase in the transition from the twentieth to the twenty-first century and that the avant-garde might still have some lifeblood left, in a period that may turn out to have been a 'Second Modernity'.

25 Stelarc: *Ping Body* (1996)

8

Epilogue: the Future of the Avant-garde

Looking back at the history of twentieth-century avant-garde performance, one notices periods of great artistic explosion, such as 1909–28 and 1965–85, interspersed with periods of relative lull, and within each period a succession of trends and counter-trends. Received opinion has it that the last quarter of the twentieth century was a period of stasis again. It should be apparent from Chapters 6 and 7 that I do not share this view and regard the new developments in the electronic media as having opened up novel and untried possibilities for performing artists. Although these new media were anticipated by concepts of virtuality in photography and cinema as far back as the nineteenth century, I would disagree with Richard Schechner's estimation that the electronic media were only an extension and globalization of visioning and communication technologies that had already been in existence for fifty years.[1] Rather, I side with Heinrich Klotz, who regards the turn of the millennium as a threshold of a Second Modernity that ushered in a new age of avant-garde experimentation.

Much of twentieth-century avant-garde experimentation was characterized by various swings of the pendulum between the two poles of technophilia and primitivism. Whole histories of twentieth-century art have been constructed from pitting Futurism against Surrealism, Dada against Constructivism, Expressionism against New Objectivity, High-Abstraction against New Realism, electronic Media Art against spiritualist Neo-Shamanism. However, such models of interpretation can be rather deceptive. From the Futurists to the cybernauts there was a primitivist and even spiritual undercurrent in technophile thinking, and vice versa, primitivists such as the Expressionists availed themselves of the latest technologies, and much of their success depended on it. The same may be said of the Neo-Shamans who nowadays populate the Internet, or of cybergurus such as Stelarc, who also slip into the role of Body Artists. Although categories such as primitivism/technophilia, abstraction/construction, body/media art offer some useful paradigms for analysis, they should not make us overlook the considerable overlap that existed between them, or their mutual dependence on each other.

The explosion of electronic and digital technologies in the late twentieth century has led to fundamental changes in our communicative behaviour. I shall leave it to future generations to judge whether IBM, Hewlett Packard and Microsoft were to the cyber-age what Gutenberg was to the Renaissance. But there can be little doubt that we are standing at the beginning of a new era and that the arts, including the performing arts, will be deeply affected by it. The trends discussed in Chapter 7 are only at an early stage of development, both technically and conceptually. Yet, one can already discern a counter-trend in the making, inspired, predominantly, by pre-modern practices. Ancient rituals in particular are invoked as counter-measures to the detrimental effects of modernity (or a Second Modernity) and the over-emphasis given to cerebral aspects in the arts. A new generation of artists, acting in opposition to the institutional art world, seeks a return to a mythical Ur-art, where aesthetic and social processes were not yet separated from each other. Thus, the proliferation of digital technologies and their integration into artistic fields goes hand in hand with a withdrawal into quasi-sacred realms outside the constraints of a commercialized art market and globalized economy. Such attempts at returning to a non-instrumentalized art by linking it to personal, social and aesthetic concerns, are complemented by a re-auratization of artistic products and processes in those quarters still linked to the circulation of intellectual capital. The postmodern equivalents to Benjamin's art in the age of mechanical reproduction have prompted a desire to transcend the object character of art and the fixation with 'safe products' in the theatre. A society characterized by an abundance and overproduction of goods, images, works of culture and so on encourages the rise of avant-garde élites that reinstate the values of singular experiences and unrepeatable acts. Vacuity of existence in a mundane and normed world, crisis of identity, loss of spiritual certainties etc. foster the search for compensations in intensely personal and distinctly transcendental art 'events', which by definition are performative and in many cases ritualistic.

What concerns us here is the question whether any of these trends – those at the 'cutting edge' of exploring the frontiers of a digitally based civilization or those that reinstate the aura of presence, individuality and performativity in art – are to be classified as 'avant-garde'. As far as I can observe, the old concepts of the avant-garde have lost their relevance to twenty-first-century artists. The speed of information exchange in a media-dominated society has shortened the shelf life of avant-garde schools to such a degree that an endless cycle of -isms have exhausted their *raison d'être*. When nothing new can be produced any longer, and the grand narratives of progress and development have been thoroughly deconstructed, there is nothing left to be 'ahead of', and the pressure to produce something fundamentally different from preceding movements no longer imposes itself on the new generation. Artists of the twenty-first century cannot make the same claims to originality or heterology as their colleagues a hundred years ago. An avant-garde that has become absorbed into the fabric of bourgeois culture cannot be recuperated to fulfil its old functions.

Yet, writing off the history of twentieth-century avant-garde creativity as old hat would ignore the fact that without the pioneering work of Futurists and Constructivists, Expressionists and Surrealists etc. we would still have to battle against the constraints of Realism or Classicism. One does not have to be an advocate of a Hegelian concept of progress to acknowledge that present experiences do not cancel out previous developments but rather sublate them in a new synthesis. The old battlecry 'Let's Destroy the Academies'[2] has not brought down any such institution, but rather led to the exhibition of works inspired by these sentiments in the very same temples of the arts. Hence, the new avant-garde (or post-avant-garde, or whatever it may be called) must be the result of a *critique* of the old avant-garde; but such a dialectic opposition also recoups substantive components of its predecessor and transforms them into a new gestalt. A productive relationship between old and new artistic practices would include the use of historical paradigms in order to comment on present conditions in the culture industry. It would, as Foster suggests, '*re*connect with a lost practice in order to *dis*connect from a present way of working felt to be outmoded, misguided, or otherwise oppressive'.[3] Such strategies of historical appropriation do not equate with a recycling of the historical avant-garde (something Peter Bürger censures the Neo-avant-garde for), but rather acknowledge the fact that there is no way out of the process of cultural confluence and that two streams, which may have started from opposite directions, will in the end always flow into the same wide ocean.

Artists have already begun to adopt attitudes to the masters of the historical and postmodern avant-garde that are different from those the Futurists or Dadaists were forced to assume *vis-à-vis* their predecessors. The avant-garde, or what remained of it in the late twentieth century, was no longer characterized by an attitude of opposition. Rather, artists used the appellation 'avant-garde' as a marketing device to promote their works on the market; they applied for grants from the very same institutions, that their predecessors had regarded as nests of incorrigible conservatism; they established their careers on the strength of their avant-garde style of creativity. A large number of the artists mentioned in Chapters 4 to 7 became professors at art schools or universities and taught their strategies and methods of creation to the next generation. Similarly, art centres and festivals with the avowed aim of fostering avant-garde expression in the arts have sprouted everywhere in the world. The avant-garde, in short, has become an economic force and one of many hues in a wide palette of cultural manifestations.

From these facts one might conclude that a central objective of the avant-garde has actually been fulfilled: rather than having been simply absorbed by the mainstream, it has widened the spectrum of Western culture and has compelled the conservative majority to give recognition to innovative and untested forms of expression. Whereas, a hundred years ago, Europe counted hardly two handfuls of art theatres, every capital nowadays possesses dozens of them. There are probably more performers employed now in fringe theatres and experimental companies than in national, state or municipal theatres taken together, and a considerable portion of productions presented in these mainstream houses aim to be innovative rather than derivative.

These fundamental changes in the cultural landscape of most Western countries make anarchical attacks on 'the establishment', as promoted by the former avant-garde, an anachronism. This is not meant to justify blind acceptance of mainstream production methods, but to acknowledge that the stream has become very wide indeed and no longer consists solely of a commercialized culture industry. Does this intimate that there is no longer any need for an avant-garde? Some artists (and critics) would certainly agree; others insist that as long as there are hegemonic élites and dominant ideologies, artists must continue to produce work that falls outside established structures and systems. The impulse not to be restricted by traditions, canons and conventions makes them venture into unexplored territories (although these may no longer be virgin soils as in the nineteenth and twentieth centuries). It will propel them to work in areas that are not occupied by the mainstream and have not been traversed by the historical avant-garde. But what has changed is the vision of artists marching heroically under the banner of progress (exemplified by their ever more innovative techniques) into a brighter future, or the belief that they can overthrow the status quo in artistic matters and achieve autonomy from the institution of art.

I would therefore disagree with Paul Mann's assessment that 'without exception art that calls itself art, that is registered as art, that circulates within art contexts can never again pose as anything but systems-maintenance.'[4] It does not seem to me that art has reached a ground-zero point beyond which there is only no-art, or withdrawal from art. Poised between 'daydreams of escape' and 'unprecedented silence',[5] artists will escape discursive suicide by exploring a third path. Dietrich Scheunemann, Hal Foster, Peter Weibel, Heinrich Klotz and others have questioned the mantra-like proclamations of the death of the avant-garde and reopened a chapter, which Bürger had so forcefully closed in 1974.[6] Hal Foster, in looking at developments since 1974, suggested that 'the neo-avant-garde has produced new aesthetic experiences, cognitive connections, and political interventions, and that these openings may make up *another* criterion by which art can claim to be advanced today'.[7] Ben Highmore has taken on one of these criteria, which Bürger thought to have dismissed once and for all: the sublation of art into life. Drawing on Lefebvre's theory of modern everyday life, he has shown that Bürger's 'life' is not at all as homogeneous and monolithic as suggested. By restricting himself to a discussion of an avant-garde economy within the institution of 'art',[8] Bürger failed to recognize the potential for avant-garde interventions in the conflicts between the repressive and liberating aspects of everyday life. It is common for individuals to play out the tensions between the colonization of life by capitalist forces and the tenacity of a festive, refreshing and invigorating enjoyment of life. Similarly, artists develop a precarious and ambiguous relationship with quotidian existence and find space for creative operations in the interstices between alienation and jubilation. He concludes from this: 'What Bürger misses, and what makes his thesis less than adequate for an account of avant-gardism, is the sense of ambivalence with which the avant-garde figured modern everyday life.'[9]

Scheunemann adds a further criticism and amplifies views here that have been elaborated at an earlier stage by the theorists of the ZKM Center for Art and Medium in Karlsruhe. Whereas Bürger's account ends with the Neo-Expressionists and Neo-Dadaists, Scheunemann suggests a revised concept of the avant-garde based on the impact of technological innovations and the challenges of the new media. It is the avant-garde's mission to bridge the gap not only between art and life, but also between art and technology. A history of the avant-garde focused on the interaction between art, literature, theatre and music on the one hand, and photography, cinema, telephone, television, video, and computers on the other, will not arrive at the same periodization as Bürger did in 1974. It will place at centre stage such techniques as montage and collage, which Bürger only discussed at arm's length, and incorporate deconstructive methods, which Bürger did not mention at all. It will examine the connections between the avant-garde and anti-hegemonic forces such as feminism, the Green movement, NGOs, anti-globalism, post-colonialism, etc.

This epilogue, written three years into the new millennium, is both look-ing back and looking ahead, and suggests that the art of the early twenty-first century – an art that has, as yet, no prefix and I prefer avoiding the term avant-garde here – will be both a critique of the historical avant-garde and its safeguarding under changed conditions. It incorporates in a dialectic manner some substantive components of its predecessors, and merges them with forces that belong to the new age. Many of these, I have no doubt, will not stem from Western traditions, but will arise from developing countries. In a globalized world, new energies will emerge from quarters which currently play only a minor role in the market economy (artistic markets included). Artists from those countries, that are now undergoing transfor-mations similar to those the West experienced some 100 to 150 years ago, will find opportunities to learn from history and avoid some of the worst mistakes made by their colleagues in the preceding century.

What kind of artistic scenario will eventually materialize from an enlightened modernity is impossible to predict. It may be a transformed avant-garde, or a practice for which the term 'avant-garde' has lost all significance. It certainly will be the result of a critical examination of the structural and discursive parameters of twentieth-century art production and reception, and not just a simple continuation of old trajectories.

Notes

Notes to the Introduction

1. Martin Lüdke's influential collection of essays responding to Peter Bürgers book on the avant-garde (*'Theorie der Avantgarde': Antworten auf Peter Bürgers Bestimmung von Kunst und bürgerlicher Gesellschaft*, Frankfurt-am-Main: Suhrkamp, 1976) occupied more of my time than reading the little red Suhrkamp volume that prompted it.

2. Richard Schechner in an interview with James Harding, in Harding (ed.), *Contours of the Theatrical Avant-garde: Performance and Textuality* (Ann Arbor, MI: University of Michigan Press, 2000), p. 212.

3. Most of my teaching took place in the Department of Drama at the University of Bristol. Guest lectures and visiting professorships at other universities in Britain, Europe, Latin America and the USA often led to a different range of responses to my teaching and made me all the more aware that my scholarship was not acting in a socio-political or ideological vacuum!

4. Paul Mann, *The Theory Death of the Avant-garde* (Bloomington, IN: Indiana University Press, 1991), p. 6.

5. The only exception to this rule that I can think of is a pure 'theatre of the mind' as suggested by Ben Vautier, Dick Higgins et al.

6. Edward Braun, *The Director and the Stage: From Naturalism to Grotowski* (London: Methuen, 1982), p. 201.

7. See the still tentative definition given by its curator, Joachim Diederichs, 'Zum Begriff "Performance"', *documenta 6*, Kassel 1977, vol. 1, pp. 281–3. Other important deliberations on the concept took place at the *Settimana Internazionale della Performance* in Bologna (1977), curated by Franco Solmi, Renato Barilli and Giovanni Accame, and at *Concepts in Performance* in Cologne (1977), curated by Elisabeth Jappe. See the catalogue *La performance oggi: Settimana internazionale della performance, Bologna, 1–6 giugno 1977*; the special section of *Kunstforum International* 24 (1977) on 'Performance', edited by Georg W. Schwarzbauer; and Massimo Mininni, *Arte in scena: La performance in Italia, 1965–1980* (Ravenna: Montanari, 1995).

8. Elisabeth Jappe, 'Das Recht, fliegen zu können: Performance – Ritual und Haltung', *documenta 8* (Kassel 1989), vol. 1, pp. 115–22, here p. 116. She compiled the volume *Performance, Ritual, Prozeß: Handbuch der Aktionskunst in Europa*, based on her curatorial experience of 1977–89.

9. The Benjaminian concept of the aura in contemporary live performances has

been discussed by Dieter Mensch, 'Ereignis und Aura: Radikale Transformation der Kunst vom Werkhaften zum Performativen', *Kunstforum International* 152 (October–December 2000), pp. 94–103.

10 On the role of photography in Live Art exhibitions see Barbara Fischer, 'A Cyclopean, Evil Eye: On Performance, Gender and Photography', *Canadian Theatre Review* 86 (Spring 1996), pp. 9–14; and Catherine Grant, 'Private Performances: Editing Performance Photography', *Performance Research* 7:1 (March 2002), pp. 34–44.

Notes to Chapter 1: The Genesis of Modernity and the Avant-garde

1 For a general introduction to the history of urbanization in Europe see Lewis Mumford, *The City in History: Its Origins, its Transformations, and its Prospects* (New York: Harcourt Brace Jovanovich, 1961); Jan de Vries, *European Urbanization 1500–1800* (London: Methuen, 1984); Paul M. Hohenberg and Lynn Hollen Lees, *The Making of Urban Europe, 1000–1950* (Cambridge, MA: Harvard University Press, 1985); Gary Bridge and Sophie Watson (eds), *A Companion to the City* (Oxford: Blackwell, 2000).

2 Statistics are taken from B. R. Mitchell, *International Historical Statistics: Europe 1750–1993*, 4th edn (London: Macmillan, 1998).

3 Catherine Gore, *Paris in 1841* (London: Longman, Brown, Green and Longmans, 1842), p. 267.

4 See Mitchell, *International Historical Statistics*, pp. 673–7.

5 See Anthony Sutcliffe, *The Autumn of Central Paris: The Defeat of Town Planning, 1850–1970* (London: Arnold, 1970), pp. 80–4, 155.

6 Henry T. Tuckerman, *Papers about Paris* (New York: Putnam, 1867), pp. 25–6.

7 See Keith Tester (ed.), *The Flâneur* (London: Routledge, 1994).

8 A colourful impression of life on the boulevards is given in the exhibition catalogues, *Les Grands Boulevards* (Paris: Musée Carnavalet, 1985); and *Les Grands Boulevards: Un parcours d'innovation et de modernité* (Paris: Action Artistique de la Ville de Paris, 2000); and the monograph by Patrice de Moncan, *Les Grands Boulevards de Paris: De la Bastille à la Madeleine* (Paris: Les Éditions du Mécène, 1997).

9 Edward King, *My Paris: French Character Sketches* (Boston, MA: Loring, 1868), p. 45.

10 Jules Janin, *Un hiver à Paris* (Paris: Curmer & Aubert, 1843), p. 192. I quote from the English edition, *The American in Paris* (London: Longman, Brown, Green and Longmans, 1843), pp. 162–3.

11 Anon., 'Le Flâneur, par un Flâneur', in *Paris, ou Le Livre des cent-et-un*, vol. 6 (Paris: Ladvocat, 1832), pp. 95–110, here pp. 96–7.

12 See Walter Benjamin's *Passagen-Werk*, a unique collection of material translated as *The Arcades Project* (Cambridge, MA: Harvard University

Press, 1999); and the more recent studies of Johann Friedrich Geist, *Arcades: The History of a Building Type* (Cambridge, MA: MIT Press, 1983); Bertrand Lemoine, *Les Passages couverts en France* (Paris: Délégation à l'Action Artistique, 1989); Patrice de Moncan, *Le Guide des passages de Paris: Guide pratique, historique et littéraire* (Paris: SEESAM-RCI, 1991); Jean-Claude Delorme, *Passages couverts parisiens* (Paris: Parigramme, 1996).

13 See H. Pasdermadjian, *The Department Store: Its Origins, Evolution and Economics* (London: New Books, 1954); Jeanne Gaillard, *Paris, la Ville, 1852–1870: L'Urbanisme parisien à l'heure d'Haussmann* (Paris: L'Harmattan, 1997), pp. 524–58; Alison Adburgham, *Shops and Shopping 1800–1914* (London: Allen and Unwin, 1964); Michael B. Miller, *The Bon Marché: Bourgeois Culture and the Department Store, 1869–1920* (Princeton, NJ: Princeton University Press, 1981); Philip G. Nord, *Paris Shopkeepers and the Politics of Resentment* (Princeton, NJ: Princeton University Press, 1986).

14 Émile Zola, *Au Bonheur des Dames* (1883), in *Œuvres complètes*, vol. 4 (Paris: Cercle du Livre Précieux, 1967), p. 888.

15 Auguste Luchet, 'Les Passages', in *Nouveau Tableau de Paris aux XIXe siècle*, vol. 6 (Paris: Charles-Béchet, 1835), pp. 97–113, here p. 107.

16 King, *My Paris*, p. 271. Other marketing devices were described by Auguste Luchet, 'Les Magasins de Paris', in *Paris, ou Le Livre des cent-et-un*, vol. 15 (Paris: Ladvocat, 1834), pp. 237–68.

17 *Das Passagen-Werk* A4, 1, in *Gesammelte Schriften*, vol. 5 (Frankfurt-am-Main: Suhrkamp, 1982), p. 93.

18 Henri Lefebvre, *Everyday Life in the Modern World* (New Brunswick, NJ: Transaction, 1984), p. 90. See also Judith Wechler, 'The Spectator as Genre in Nineteenth-Century Paris', in Marc Bertrand (ed.), *Popular Traditions and Learned Culture in France* (Saratoga, CA: Anma Libri, 1985), pp. 227–36; Martin Roberts, 'Mutations of the Spectacle: Vitrines, Arcades, Mannequins', *French Cultural Studies*, vol. 2 (1991), pp. 211–49; Christopher Prendergast, *Paris and the Nineteenth Century* (Oxford: Blackwell, 1992), pp. 31–45; Vanessa R. Schwarz, *Spectacular Realities: Early Mass Culture in Fin-de-siècle Paris* (Berkeley, CA: University of California Press, 1998).

19 Zola described the 'splendeur féerique d'apothéose, sous cet éclairage nouveau' in his novel *Au Bonheur des Dames*, in *Œuvres complètes*, vol. 4, p. 1038.

20 The parallels between these two types of exhibition have been elaborated in Rémy G. Saisselin, *The Bourgeois and the Bibelot* (New Brunswick, NJ: Rutgers University Press, 1984), pp. 41–9.

21 See Ann Martin-Fugier, *La Bourgeoise: Femme au temps de Paul Bourget* (Paris: Grasset, 1983), pp. 157–79. The opposite can be observed in rural areas, where the bourgeois woman became more restricted to reproductive and domestic functions than before. See Bonnie G. Smith, *Ladies of the Leisure Class: The Bourgeoises of Northern France in the Nineteenth Century* (Princeton, NJ: Princeton University Press, 1981).

22   Camille Debans, *Les Plaisirs et les curiosités de Paris: Guide humoristique et pratique* (Paris: Kolb, 1889), p. 14.

23   *Cassell's Illustrated Guide to Paris* (London: Cassell, 1884), p. 65.

24   On the female *flâneuse* see Saisselin, *The Bourgeois and the Bibelot*, chs 2 and 3; Rachel Bowlby, *Just Looking: Consumer Culture in Dreiser, Gissing and Zola* (New York and London: Methuen, 1985), ch. 2; Janet Wolff, 'The Invisible *flâneuse*: Women and the Literature of Modernity', *Theory, Culture and Society* 2:3 (1985), pp. 37–48; Anne Friedberg, *Window Shopping: Cinema and the Postmodern* (Berkeley, CA: University of California Press, 1993), chs 1 and 2; Anke Gleber, 'Female Flanerie and the *Symphony of the City*', in Katharina von Ankum (ed.), *Women and the Metropolis: Gender and Modernity in Weimar Culture* (Berkeley, CA: University of California Press, 1997), pp. 67–88; Deborah L. Parson, *Streetwalking the Metropolis: Women, the City, and Modernity* (Oxford: Oxford University Press, 2000); Rita E. Täuber (ed.), *Femme flâneur: Erkundungen zwischen Boulevard und Sperrbezirk*, exhibition catalogue (Bonn: August Macke Haus, 2004).

25   See Michael Robert Marrus (ed.), *The Emergence of Leisure* (New York: Harper and Row, 1974); Peter Bailey, *Leisure and Class in Victorian England: Rational Recreation and the Contest for Control, 1830–1885* (London: Routledge and Kegan Paul, 1978); Hugh Cunningham, *Leisure in the Industrial Revolution c. 1780–c. 1880* (New York: St. Martin's Press, 1980); Rosalind H. Williams, *Dream Worlds: Mass Consumption in Late Nineteenth-Century France* (Berkeley, CA: University of California Press, 1982); Alain Corbin (ed.), *L'avènement des loisirs, 1850–1960* (Paris: Aubier, 1995).

26   Walter Benjamin, 'Paris, die Hauptstadt des XIX. Jahrhunderts', in *Passagen-Werk*, p. 50.

27   See C. W. Ceram, *Archaeology of the Cinema* (New York: Harcourt, Brace and World, 1965); Richard Altick, *The Shows of London* (Cambridge, MA: Harvard University Press, 1978); Ralph Hyde, *Panoramania: The Art and Entertainment of the 'All-Embracing-View'* (London: Trefoil, 1988); Vanessa R. Schwartz, *Spectacular Realities: Early Mass Culture in Fin-de-Siècle Paris* (Berkeley, CA: University of California Press, 1998); Bernard Comment, *The Panorama* (London: Reaktion, 1999).

28   Maxime du Camp, *Paris, ses organes, ses fonctions et sa vie dans la seconde moitié du XIXe siècle*, vol. 6 (Paris: Hachette, 1876), p. 233. Edward King, *My Paris*, pp. 333–5, also speaks of 40 regular theatres, but adds that they offered mainly 'glittering spectacles and trashy melodramas' (p. 333).

29   These figures are given by James Jackson Jarves, *Parisian Sights and French Principles, Seen through American Spectacles* (New York: Harper & Brothers, 1852), pp. 192–4.

30   James Dabney McCabe, *Paris by Sunlight and Gaslight* (Philadelphia: National Publishing Company, 1869), pp. 64–5. This author also compiled a number of other useful statistics on Parisian social life.

31   Gore, *Paris in 1841*, p. 259.

32 Jarves, *Parisian Sights*, p. 143.

33 Jules Vallès, 'Le Tableau de Paris: Les Foires, I', *Gil Blas*, 6 April 1882, reprinted in *Œuvres complètes*, vol. 3 (Paris: Livre Club Diderot, 1969), p. 774.

34 See the chapter 'The Ancients and the Moderns' in Ernst Robert Curtius, *European Literature and the Latin Middle Ages* (London: Routledge and Kegan Paul, 1963), pp. 251–4.

35 *Œuvres du Sieur Théophile, Seconde Partie* (Paris: Billaine, 1632), p. 18; reprinted in Théophile de Viau, *Œuvres*, ed. Guidi Saba, vol. 2 (Rome: Ateneo & Bizzarri, 1978), p. 14.

36 There are no less than 150 such entries in his notebooks of 1797–1803. See the *Kritische Friedrich-Schlegel-Ausgabe*, ed. Ernst Behler, vol. 16: *Fragmente zur Poesie und Literatur. Teil I* (Paderborn: Schöningh, 1981), especially fragments 44 (p. 114), 92 (p. 79), 104 (p. 236), 110 (p. 307), 127 (p. 512), 159 (p. 866), 332 (p. 925), 375 (p. 106); and 242–4 on p. 82 of vol. 17 (Paderborn: Schöningh, 1991).

37 *Von Emile Zola bis Gerhard Hauptmann: Erinnerungen zur Geschichte der Moderne* (Leipzig: H. Seemann Nachfolge, 1902).

38 *Die Bilanz der Modern* (Berlin: Cronbach, 1904).

39 *Der Ausgang der Moderne: Ein Buch der Opposition* (Dresden: Reissner, 1909).

40 Arthur Rimbaud, 'Adieu (Une Saison en enfer)', *Œuvres complètes* (Paris: Gallimard, 1972), p. 116.

41 Kurt Pinthus (ed.), *Menschheitsdämmerung: Ein Dokument des Expressionismus* (Berlin: Rowohlt, 1920), p. X (in the reprint of 1959, p. 25).

42 Étienne Pasquier, *Des Recherches de la France* (Paris: Longis and Le Manier, 1560), quoted in Matei Calinescu, *Five Faces of Modernity: Modernism, Avant-Garde, Decadence, Kitsch, Postmodernism* (Durham, NC: Duke University Press, 1987), p. 98.

43 See 'L'Organisateur' (1819), in *Œuvres de Saint-Simon*, vol. 4 (Paris: Dentu, 1869) [this forms vol. 20 of the *Œuvres de Saint-Simon et d'Enfantin*, 47 vols (Paris: Dentu, 1865–78)], pp. 24, 42 and 184; and *Lettres de Henri Saint-Simon à Messieurs les Jurés* (Paris: Corréard & Pélicier, 1820), reprinted in *Œuvres de Claude-Henri de Saint Simon*, vol. 6 (Paris: Éditions Anthropos, 1966), pp. 399–433, here p. 422.

44 [Olinde Rodrigues], 'L'Artiste, le savant et l'industriel', in Henri, Comte de Saint Simon, *Opinions littéraires, philosophiques et industrielles* (Paris: Galerie de Bossange Père, 1825), pp. 331–92, here p. 341. In *Œuvres de Saint-Simon*, vol. 10 (Paris: Dentu, 1875) [this is vol. 39 of the *Œuvres de Saint-Simon et d'Enfantin*], pp. 210–11.

45 G.-D. Laverdan, *De la mission de l'art et du rôle des artistes* (1845). Excerpts from the essay have been reprinted in Manfred Hardt (ed.), *Literarische Avantgarden* (Darmstadt: Wissenschaftliche Buchgesellschaft, 1989), pp. 17–25.

46   This was predominantly the case in Romance countries. In Germany and England one was more likely to find the expressions 'highly advanced', 'ultramodern', 'far-out', 'extremist' etc. See Jean Weisgerber, *Les Avantgardes littéraires au XXᵉ siècle*, vol. 1 (Budapest: Akamémiai Kiadó, 1984), pp. 7–72.

47   The *Foundation and Manifesto of Futurism* and *Let's Kill Off the Moonlight* abound with military metaphors, the most potent being the equation of Futurism with a 'purgative war'. Emilio Settimelli applied this to the theatre in *Inchiesta sulla vita italiana* (Rocca San Casciano: Cappelli, 1919), p. 97. See Günter Berghaus, *Italian Futurist Theatre, 1909–1944* (Oxford: Clarendon Press, 1998), pp. 45–50, 219, 398–99.

48   Richard Huelsenbeck, *Reise bis ans Ende der Freiheit* (Heidelberg: Schneider, 1984), p. 120.

49   Umberto Eco, *A Theory of Semiotics* (Bloomington, IN: Indiana University Press, 1976), p. 272.

50   George Steiner, *After Babel: Aspects of Language and Translation* (London: Oxford University Press, 1975), p. 465.

51   F. T. Marinetti, 'Fondazione e manifesto del futurismo', in *Teoria e invenzione futurista* (Milan: Mondadori, 1968), p. 12; 'Founding and Manifesto of Futurism', *Selected Writings* (London: Secker & Warburg, 1972), p. 43.

52   See Michel Sanouillet, *Dada à Paris* (Paris: Pauvert, 1965), p. 155.

53   Hardekopf in a letter of 13 May 1917 to Olly Jacques, in Richard Sheppard, 'Ferdinand Hardekopf und Dada', *Jahrbuch der Schillergesellschaft* 20 (1976), p. 135.

54   Huelsenbeck, 'En avant Dada', in Robert Motherwell, *The Dada Painters and Poets*, 3rd edn (Cambridge, MA: Harvard University Press, 1989), p. 45.

55   Albert Gleizes and Jean Metzinger, 'Cubism, 1912', in H. B. Chipp, *Theories of Modern Art* (Berkeley, CA: University of California Press, 1970), p. 214.

56   Rimbaud, in his letters to Georges Izambart of 13 May 1871 and Paul Demeny of 15 May 1871, in *Œuvres complètes*, ed. Antoine Adam (Paris: Gallimard, 1972), pp. 249 and 250.

Notes to Chapter 2: Towards an Avant-garde Performance Practice, 1896–1919

1   This applies in the first instance to the Futurist *serate* and Dada *soirées*. However, the historical avant-garde did not abolish the concept of 'production' altogether. There are many examples of performances that were rehearsed and designed, but not for the sake of arriving at a fixed 'product' organized for passive consumption, but rather to create events that might provoke, challenge or rouse an audience.

2   See the testimonies in Noël Arnauld, *Alfred Jarry* (Paris: La Table Ronde, [1974]), pp. 216–21.

3   See Jarry's critical writings on the theatre, collected in Alfred Jarry, *Œuvres*

complètes, ed. M. Arrive, 3 vols (Paris: Gallimard, 1988), vol. 1, pp. 399–423, and partly translated in *Selected Works of Alfred Jarry*, ed. R. Shattuck and S. W. Taylor (London: Methuen, 1965; 2nd edn 1980), pp. 65–90.

4 His demands were very similar to those of the Futurists some fifteen years later. See the *Futurist Playwrights' Manifesto* and the *Manifesto of Dynamic and Synoptic Declamation*, discussed in Günter Berghaus, *Italian Futurist Theatre, 1909–1944* (Oxford: Clarendon Press, 1988), pp. 157–61 and 172–5. Like Jarry, Marinetti gave a first foretaste of this style of acting in the soirées of the *Mercure de France*.

5 See Jarry's letters to Lugné-Poë of 29 July and 1 August 1896, in *Œuvres complètes*, vol. 1, pp. 1049–50.

6 Alfred Jarry, 'Questions de théâtre', *Œuvres complètes*, vol. 1, p. 416.

7 For primary sources see the Folio edition of 1978, the summaries provided by Arnauld, *Alfred Jarry*, pp. 312–22; P. Lié, 'Comment Jarry et Lugné-Poe glorifièrent Ubu à l'Œuvre', *Cahiers du Collège de 'Pataphysique* 3–4 (27 October 1950); and Lié, 'Notes sur la seconde représentation d'Ubu Roi', *Cahiers du Collège de 'Pataphysique* 20 (29 June 1955), pp. 47–52.

8 See the testimonial of Georges Rémond, 'Souvenirs sur Jarry et autres', *Mercure de France* 323:1099 (1 March 1955), pp. 426–46; 323:1100 (1 April 1955), pp. 656–77, here pp. 664–5.

9 See Rémond, 'Souvenirs sur Alfred Jarry', pp. 664–5. This appears to have developed into a constituent feature of many avant-garde performances, as I demonstrate in the sections on Futurism and Dada.

10 Henry Fouquier in his review of 13 December 1896, quoted in Keith Beaumont, *Alfred Jarry: A Critical and Biographical Study* (Leicester: Leicester Press, 1984), p. 102. A detailed analysis of the press response has been given by Henri Robillion, 'La Presse d'Ubu Roi', *Cahiers du Collège de 'Pataphysique* 3–4 (27 October 1950), pp. 73–88.

11 See Berghaus, *Italian Futurist Theatre*, p. 30.

12 For a detailed analysis see Günter Berghaus, *The Genesis of Futurism: Marinetti's Early Career and Writings 1899–1909* (Leeds: Society for Italian Studies, 1995), pp. 58–72.

13 Oskar Kokoschka, *My Life* (London: Thames and Hudson, 1974), p. 29.

14 Kokoschka, *My Life*, p. 30.

15 See Werner J. Schweiger, *Der junge Kokoschka* (Pöchlarn: Oskar Kokoschka-Dokumentation, 1983), p. 106.

16 Kokoschka, *My Life*, p. 28.

17 Kokoschka, *My Life*, p. 29.

18 The newspaper notices can be found in Schweiger, *Der junge Kokoschka*, pp. 111–13.

19 Kokoschka, *My Life*, p. 28.

20 Kokoschka, *My Life*, pp. 28–9.

21 F. T. Marinetti, 'Prime battaglie futuriste', *Teoria e invenzione futurista* (Milan: Mondadori, 1968), p. 201. A similar idea was expressed in an inter-

view with *L'avvenire* of Messina, 23 February 1915: 'When I created this effective propaganda in the form of the Futurist *serate*, Futurism became a sign of war bursting into the field of art.'

22   See F. T. Marinetti, 'In tema del futurismo', *La diana*, vol. 1, no. 1, January 1915, pp. 27–9, here p. 28.

23   Marinetti, 'In tema del futurismo'.

24   'The destructive gesture of freedom-bringer' (*il gesto distruttore dei libertarî*) he called it in 'Foundation and Manifesto of Futurism'. See Marinetti, *Teoria e invenzione futurista*, p. 10; F. T. Marinetti, *Selected Writings* (London: Secker & Warburg, 1972), p. 42.

25   F. T. Marinetti, 'The Pleasure of Being Booed', in *Teoria e invenzione futurista*, p. 267; *Selected Writings*, p. 114.

26   See the manifesto, 'Dynamic and Synoptic Declamation', in Marinetti, *Teoria e invenzione futurista*, pp. 104–11; *Selected Writings*, pp. 142–7.

27   F. T. Marinetti, 'Un movimento artistico crea un Partito Politico', in *Teoria e invenzione futurista*, p. 298.

28   F. T. Marinetti, 'Gli sfruttatori del futurismo', *Lacerba* 2:7 (1 April 1914), pp. 106–7, reprinted in *Teoria e invenzione futurista*, pp. 92–4.

29   F. T. Marinetti, Preface to *Mafarka il futurista*, reprinted in *Teoria e invenzione futurista*, p. 217.

30   A list of source material on which my descriptions are based can be found in Berghaus, *Italian Futurist Theatre*, p. 152, n. 126.

31   Alberto Viviani, *Giubbe rosse* (Florence: Vallecchi, 1983), p. 66.

32   Ardengo Soffici, *Fine di un mondo* (Florence: Vallecchi, 1955), p. 328.

33   Francesco Cangiullo, *Le serate futuriste* (Pozzuoli: Tirena, 1930), pp. 160–1.

34   F. T. Marinetti, 'Discorso del Teatro Verdi', in *Teoria e invenzione futurista*, p. 499.

35   Ottone Rosai, 'Pagine di memorie', unpublished manuscript in the Gabinetto Vieusseux, Archivio Contemporaneo, Fondo Rosai, Cassetta 17, Inserto 8, pp. 112–15.

36   Soffici, *Fine di un mondo*, p. 330.

37   Carlo Carrà, *Tutti gli scritti* (Milan: Feltrinelli, 1978), p. 663.

38   F. T. Marinetti, 'Il teatro futurista sintetico', *Teoria e invenzione futurista*, p. 98; *Selected Writings*, p. 123.

39   G. Papini, 'Contro il futurismo', *Lacerba* 1:5 (15 March 1913), p. 45.

40   Hugo Ball, *Briefe 1911–1927* (Einsiedeln: Benziger, 1957), pp. 34–5.

41   Hugo Ball, *Flucht aus der Zeit* (Lucerne: Stocker, 1946), p. 14 (Nov. 1914).

42   Letter of 18 December 1914 to August Hofmann, in Ball, *Briefe 1911–1927*, p. 36.

43   The manifesto was first published by Gerhard Schaub, '*Dada avant la lettre*: Ein unbekanntes "literarisches Manifest" von Hugo Ball und Richard Huelsenbeck', *Hugo Ball Almanach* 9–10 (1985/86), pp. 63–180, here p. 86.

44   Hennings had led a gypsy-like existence for many years, performing in road

shows, operettas and nightclubs in Moscow, Budapest and Cologne. She met Ball in 1913 while performing at the Café Simplicissimus in Munich and joined him in Berlin in November 1914.

45 F[ritz] St[ahl]: 'Expressionisten-Abend', *Vossische Zeitung* [Abendausgabe], 14 May 1915.

46 Ball, *Flucht aus der Zeit*, p. 71.

47 Richard Huelsenbeck, *Reise bis ans Ende der Freiheit* (Heidelberg: Schneider, 1984), p. 114.

48 See the chapter 'Publikum und Presseberichte', in H. Bolliger et al., *Dada in Zürich* (Zurich: Arche, 1985), pp. 54–63; and Richard Sheppard (ed.), *Dada Zürich in Zeitungen: Cabaret, Ausstellungen, Berichte and Bluffs* (Siegen: Universität-Gesamthochschule, 1992).

49 Kurt Guggenheim, *Alles in allem*, vol. 2 (Zurich: Artemis, 1953), p. 184.

50 Hans Arp, *On My Way* (New York: Wittenborn, Schultz, 1948), p. 45.

51 Richard Huelsenbeck, *Memoirs of a Dada Drummer* (New York: Viking Press, 1974), p. 19.

52 See his description in Huelsenbeck, *Reise bis ans Ende der Freiheit*, p. 121; and Ball, *Flucht aus der Zeit*, pp. 77–8 (11 March 1916).

53 Ball, *Flucht aus der Zeit*, p. 78 (12 March 1916).

54 Huelsenbeck, *Reise bis ans Ende der Freiheit*, p. 115.

55 Hans Arp, *On My Way* (New York: Wittenborn, Schultz, 1948), p. 48.

56 Marcel Janco, 'Dada at Two Speeds', in Lucy R. Lippard (ed.), *Dadas on Art* (Englewood Cliffs, NJ: Prentice-Hall, 1971), p. 36.

57 Ball, *Flucht aus der Zeit*, p. 85 (14 April 1916).

58 Hans Richter, *Dada, Art and Anti-Art* (London: Thames and Hudson, 1965), p. 77.

59 The *National-Zeitung* of 14 April 1919 mentioned 'townsfolk and ladies in elegant attire', and the *Basler Nachrichten* of 30 April 1919 wrote that 'the upper echelons of society were particularly well represented'.

60 'Chronique Zurichoise', in Tristan Tzara, *Œuvres complètes*, ed. Henri Béhar, 6 vols (Paris: Flammarion, 1975–91), vol. 1, p. 567.

61 Richter, *Art and Anti-Art*, pp. 78–9.

62 'Chronique Zurichoise', in Tzara, *Œuvres complètes*, vol. 1, p. 564.

63 Sanouillet, *Dada à Paris* (Paris: Pauvert, 1965), p. 132.

64 Theo van Doesburg, El Lissitzky and Hans Richter, 'Erklärung der internationalen Fraktion der Konstruktivisten', *De Stijl* 5:4 (April 1922), pp. 61–4.

65 See *Dada and Constructivism: The Janus Face of the Twenties*, exhibition catalogue (London: Juda Fine Art, 1984; Hanne Bergius, *Das Lachen Dadas: Die Berliner Dadaisten und ihre Aktionen* (Giessen: Anabas, 1989), pp. 302–9, 380–5; Maria Müller, 'Dada–Merz–Konstruktivismus: Versuch einer Annäherung', in *Raumkonzepte*, exhibition catalogue (Frankfurt am Main, Städel, 1986), pp. 373–9.

66 Theo van Doesburg, 'Vers une construction collective', *De Stijl* 6:6–7 (1924), pp. 89–92, here p. 92.

67 'L'arte meccanica: Manifesto futurista', *Noi*, series II, vol. 1, no. 2 (March 1923), pp. 1–2.
68 R. Banham, *Theory and Design in the First Machine Age* (New York: Praeger, 1960), p. 153. *De Stijl* published essays, manifestos and art work by Marinetti, Prampolini, Severini, Carrà, Sant'Elia, and regularly reported on Futurist activities.
69 Enrico Crispolti, *Storia e critica del futurismo* (Rome: Bulzoni, 1986), pp. 247–57.
70 *Bulletin de l'effort moderne*, no. 4 (April 1924).

Notes to Chapter 3: From Late-Modernism to Postmodernism

1 See Alan S. Milward, *The Reconstruction of Western Europe, 1945–51* (London: Methuen, 1984); David W. Ellwood, *Rebuilding Europe: Western Europe, America and Postwar Reconstruction* (London: Longman, 1992); John Killick, *The United States and European Reconstruction 1945–1960* (Edinburgh: Keele University Press, 1997; 2nd edn, Chicago, IL: Fitzroy Dearborn, 2000).
2 The term 'Fordism' relates to an automated assembly-line production of standardized goods and a scientific system of labour management and control. It was introduced in 1914 to increase the output of mass-produced goods and to secure discipline of the labour force and reproduction of man-power. The five-dollar, eight-hour work-day in Ford's car factory provided workers with income and leisure time, which in turn was used for an increased consumption of goods and thereby provided further growth and development in the industry at large.
3 Charles Jencks, *What is Post-Modernism?*, 4th edn (London: Academy Editions, 1996), p. 50.
4 The statistics are taken from James R. Beniger, 'The Information Society: Technological and Economic Origins', in Sandra J. Ball-Rokeach and Muriel G. Cantor (eds), *Media, Audience, and Social Structure* (Newbury Park, CA: Sage, 1986), pp. 51–70, here p. 67. See also Liam Bannon, Ursula Barry and Olav Holst (eds), *Information Technology: Impact on the Way of Life* (Dublin: Tycooly, 1982); and Ian Mackintosh, *Sunrise Europe: The Dynamics of Information Technology* (Oxford: Blackwell, 1986).
5 See Eugene B. Skolnikoff, 'Computers, Armaments, and Stability', in Denis P. Donnelly (ed.), *The Computer Culture: A Symposium to Explore the Computer's Impact on Society* (Rutherford, NJ: Fairleigh Dickinson University Press, 1985) pp. 124–35; David Lyon, *The Information Society: Issues and Illusions* (Cambridge: Polity Press, 1988) pp. 26–30; Les Levidow and Kevin Robins (eds), *Cyborg Worlds: The Military Information Society* (London: Free Association Books, 1989); Manuel de Landa, *War in the Age of Intelligent Machines* (New York: Zone Books, 1991); Paul N. Edwards, *The*

Closed World: Computers and the Politics of Discourse in Cold War America (Cambridge, MA: MIT Press, 1996).

6 In the 1950s, nearly all of the American semiconductor production was for military purposes. Ernest Braun and Stuart MacDonald quote a study of 1952 that showed that 60 per cent of naval electronic equipment was unreliable because of valve problems. Consequently, of the 90,000 transistors produced in 1952, nearly all were bought by the military. In 1960, the military still had a 50 per cent share of the market; in 1972 this had fallen to 24 per cent. See Ernest Braun and Stuart MacDonald, *Revolution in Miniature: The History and Impact of Semiconductor Electronics* (Cambridge: Cambridge University Press, 1982), pp. 70–71, 159.

7 See Lev Manovich, 'The Automation of Sight: from Photography to Computer Vision', in Timothy Druckrey (ed.), *Electronic Culture: Technology and Visual Representation* (New York: Aperture, 1996), pp. 228–39.

8 Mackintosh, *Sunrise Europe*, p. 41.

9 *Electronic Market Data Book* (Washington: Electronic Industries Association, Marketing Services Association, 1974), pp. 79, 87, 89. To give an idea of more recent developments: The *Electronic Market Data Book* for 1998, p. 66, gives a figure of 1.4 billion dollars for US factory sales of transistors, which by then had been far surpassed by other semiconductors (\$ 10.7 billion) and integrated circuits (\$54 billion). The global figure for semiconductor sales in 1998 was \$134.6 billion (ibid., p. 71).

10 *Electronic Market Data Book*, 1974, pp. 95–7.

11 See Michael Orme, *Micros: A Pervasive Force. A Study of the Impact of Microelectronics on Business and Society, 1946–90* (London: Associated Business Press, 1979).

12 Figures taken from Frank Webster and Kevin Robins, *Information Technology: A Luddite Analysis* (Norwood, NJ: Ablex, 1986) pp. 282–83.

13 The exclusive and exploitative nature of late twentieth-century globalization practices has been poignantly demonstrated in Dan Schiller, 'Translational Telecommunications and the Global Reorganization of Production', in T. Druckrey and P. Weigel (eds), *Net Condition: Art and Global Media*, exhibition catalogue (Graz: Steirischer Herbst; Karlsruhe: ZKM/Zentrum für Kunst und Medientechnologie, 1998–2000; Cambridge, MA: MIT, 2001), pp. 336–44.

14 See Howard Rheingold, *The Virtual Community: Finding Connections in a Computerized World* (London: Secker and Warburg, 1994); Steven G. Jones, 'Understanding Community in the Information Age', in Steven G. Jones (ed.), *CyberSociety: Computer-mediated Communication and Community* (Thousand Oaks, CA: Sage, 1998), pp. 10–35.

15 Kevin Robins, 'Cyberspace and the World we Live in', in Jon Dovey (ed.), *Fractal Dreams: New Media in Social Context* (London: Lawrence & Wishart, 1996), pp. 1–30, here p. 11.

16   Robert Dunn, *Identity Crises: A Social Critique of Postmodernity* (Minneapolis, MN: University of Minnesota Press, 1998), p. 65. See also Douglas Kellner, 'Popular Culture and the Construction of Postmodern Identities', in S. Lash and J. Friedman (eds), *Modernity and Identity* (Oxford: Blackwell, 1992), pp. 141–77.

17   See Milton W. Brown, *American Painting from the Armory Show to the Depression* (Princeton, NJ: Princeton University Press, 1955); Judith K. Zilczer, 'The Armory Show and the American Avant-garde: a Re-evaluation', *Arts Magazine* 54 (September 1978), pp. 126–30; *The Shock of Modernism in America: The Eight and the Artists of the Armory Show*, exhibition catalogue (Roslyn, NY: Nassau County Museum of Fine Arts, 1984); Milton W. Brown, *The Story of the Armory Show* (New York: Abbeville Press, 1988).

18   Sheldon Cheney, *The Art Theater* (New York: Knopf, 1927), p. 10.

19   Milton W. Brown, 'After Three Years', *Magazine of Art* (Washington) 39:4 (April 1946), pp. 138 and 166.

20   Clement Greenberg, 'Review of the Second Pepsi-Cola Annual', *Nation*, 1 December 1945, p. 604, reprinted in Clement Greenberg, *The Collected Essays and Criticism*, vol. 2 (Chicago: University of Chicago Press, 1986), pp. 42–4, here p. 44.

21   For the subsequent impact of US-American culture on Europe see C. W. E. Bigsby (ed.), *Superculture: American Popular Culture and Europe* (London: Elek, 1975); and Rob Kroes et al. (eds), *Cultural Transmissions and Receptions: American Mass Culture in Europe* (Amsterdam: VU University Press, 1993).

22   Editorial Statement on the Symposium 'Our Country and Our Culture', *Partisan Review* 19:3 (May–June 1952), pp. 282–326, here p. 284.

23   John Hunt, officer for the Congress for Cultural Freedom, in an interview with Frances Stonor Saunders, July 1997, quoted in Frances Stonor Saunders, *Who Paid the Piper? The CIA and the Cultural Cold War* (London: Granta Books, 1999), p. 158.

24   See Walter Goodman, *The Committee: The Extraordinary Career of the House Committee on Un-American Activities* (New York: Farrar, Straus & Giroux, 1968); David Caute, *The Great Fear: The Anti-Communist Purge under Truman and Eisenhower* (New York: Simon and Schuster, 1978); Larry Ceplair and Stephen Englund, *The Inquisition in Hollywood: Politics in the Film Community, 1930–1960* (Garden City, NY: Doubleday, 1980); Cedric Belfrage, *The American Inquisition* (New York: Thunder's Mouth Press, 1989); Jeff Broadwater, *Eisenhower and the Anti-Communist Crusade* (Chapel Hill, NC: University of North Carolina Press, 1992); Ellen Schrecker, *Many are the Crimes: McCarthyism in America* (Boston, MA: Little, Brown, 1998).

25   See Caute, *The Great Fear*, p. 112.

26   National Security Council Directive NSC-10/2, quoted in Saunders, *Who Paid the Piper?*, p. 39.

27   All figures are taken from Saunders, *Who Paid the Piper?*, pp. 41, 97, 106.

28 The USIA, created in 1953, was an 'independent' government agency and developed out of the Office of International Information and Cultural Affairs (OIC), attached to US diplomatic missions, and the Office of International Information and Educational Exchange (USIE). At the height of the Cold War it commanded a budget of $131 million. See John W. Henderson, *The United States Information Agency* (New York: Praeger, 1969); and Fitzhugh Green, *American Propaganda Abroad* (New York: Hippocrene Books, 1988).

29 Apart from the art exhibitions discussed below, there were huge showcases of the American way of life, seen by some 15 million Europeans. See Robert H. Haddow, *Pavilions of Plenty: Exhibiting American Culture Abroad in the 1950s* (Washington, DC: Smithsonian Institute Press, 1997).

30 See *United States of America Congressional Record. 84th Congress, First Session*, vol. 101, part 11: Index, House Bills and Resolutions (Washington, DC: United States Government Printing Office, 1955), p. 878 (House of Representative Bills nos. 5040 and 6874).

31 Saunders, *Who Paid the Piper?*, p. 129.

32 Dondero in an interview with Emily Genauer, published by the *New York World Telegram* and quoted in William Hauptman, 'The Suppression of Art in the McCarthy Decade', *Artforum* 12:2 (October 1973), pp. 48–52, here p. 58. The other quotes are taken from Dondero's congressional speeches, the most important of which can be found in the *United States of America Congressional Records*, especially *81st Congress, First Session*, vol. 95, part 2, pp. 2317–18 (11 March 1949); *81st Congress, First Session*, vol. 95, part 5, pp. 6372–5 (17 May 1949); *81st Congress, First Session*, vol. 95, part 9, pp. 11584–7 (16 August 1949); *82nd Congress, First Session*, vol. 97, part 4, pp. 4920–5 (4 May 1951); *82nd Congress, Second Session*, vol. 98, part 2, pp. 2423–7 (17 March 1952); *84th Congress, Second Session*, vol. 102, part 8, pp. 10419–25 (14 June 1956); *84th Congress, Second Session*, vol. 102, part 10, pp. 13774–9 (20 July 1956). See also the documents compiled from the Dondero papers in Jane de Hart Mathews, 'Art and Politics in Cold War America', *American Historical Review*, 81:4 (October 1976), pp. 762–87.

33 Quoted in *The New York Times Magazine*, 26 October 1952, p. 32. See Gary O. Larson, *The Reluctant Patron: The United States Government and the Arts, 1943–1965* (Philadelphia, PA: University of Pennsylvania Press, 1983), p. 60; and Taylor D. Littleton and Maltby Sykes, *Advancing American Art: Painting, Politics, and Cultural Confrontation at Mid-Century* (Tuscaloosa, AL: University of Alabama Press, 1989), p. 55 and p. 151, n. 42.

34 George A. Dondero, 'Modern Art Shackled to Communism', speech of 16 August 1949, in *81st Congress, First Session*, vol. 95, part 9, pp. 11584–7, here p. 11585–6.

35 See the citations from Motherwell's file in David Craven, *Abstract Expressionism as Cultural Critique: Dissent during the McCarthy Period* (Cambridge: Cambridge University Press, 1999), p. 98, and his chapter on FBI surveillance of Abstract Expressionists due to their former political engagement, pp. 80–96.

36   Letter of Richard M. Nixon to Charles E. Plant, 18 July 1949, published in the San Francisco weekly *Argonaut*, 14 November 1949, quoted in George V. Sherman, 'Dick Nixon: Art Commissar', *Nation* 176:2 (10 January 1953), p. 21.

37   Editorial of the *Baltimore American* in October 1946; letter of protest to the Department of State by the American Artists Professional League, dated 6 November 1946 and printed in the *Art Digest* 21 (1946), pp. 32–3; and front-line report in the *Journal-American* of 4 April 1947. The controversy over the exhibition has been documented in Littleton and Sykes, *Advancing American Art*.

38   See, for example, the arguments of Alfred H. Barr in 'Is Modern Art Communist?', *New York Times Magazine*, 14 December 1952, pp. 22–3, 28–30, reprinted in *Defining Modern Art: Selected Writings of Alfred H. Barr, Jr.*, ed. Irving Sandler and Amy Newman (New York: Abrams, 1986), pp. 214–19. This article should be read alongside his introduction to an exhibition catalogue, *The New American Painting as Shown in Eight European Countries 1958–1959* (New York: The Museum of Modern Art, 1959), pp. 15–19, where he describes modern American art as 'symbolic demonstrations of freedom in a world in which freedom connotes a political attitude' (p. 16; in *Selected Writings*, p. 231).

39   See Saunders, *Who Paid the Piper?*, pp. 252–78; Max Kozloff, 'American Painting during the Cold War', *Artforum* 11:9 (May 1973), pp. 43–54; Eva Cockroft, 'Abstract Expressionism, Weapon of the Cold War', *Artforum* 12:10 (June 1974), pp. 39–41; David and Cecile Shapiro, 'Abstract Expressionism: the Politics of Apolitical Painting', *Prospects: An Annual of American Cultural Studies* 3 (1977), pp. 175–214.

40   See Annette Cox, *Art-as-Politics: The Abstract Expressionist Avant-Garde and Society* (Ann Arbor, MI: University of Michigan Press, 1982); Serge Guilbault, *How New York Stole the Idea of Modern Art: Abstract Expressionism, Freedom, and the Cold War* (Chicago, IL: University of Chicago Press, 1983); Nancy Jachec, *The Philosophy and Politics of Abstract Expressionism, 1940–1960* (Cambridge: Cambridge University Press, 2000).

41   Kozloff, 'American Painting during the Cold War', p. 44. See also Cockroft, 'Abstract Expressionism, Weapon of the Cold War'; and the rebuttal given on behalf of the Museum of Modern art by Michael Kimmelman, 'Revisiting the Revisionists: the Modern, its Critics, and the Cold War', *Studies in Modern Art 4: The Museum of Modern Art at Mid-Century* (New York: MoMA, 1994), pp. 38–55. For a more recent assessment of the touring exhibitions sponsored by MoMA and USIA, see Jachec, *The Philosophy and Politics of Abstract Expressionism*, pp. 157–224.

42   Russell Lynes, *Good Old Modern: An Intimate Portrait of the Museum of Modern Art* (New York: Atheneum, 1973), p. 385.

43   'Tachism' (*taches* = stains, blots or patches) was a type of painting characterized by spontaneous, intuitive treatment of the canvas. It was also known as 'Art Informel', a term coined in 1950 by the French critic Michel Tapié.

Both methods were meant to offer a seismographic reflection of the artist's subconscious states and to overcome the intellectually controlled forms of abstract art.

44 See Harold Rosenberg, *The Tradition of the New* (New York: Horizon Press, 1959).

45 Allan Kaprow, 'Should the Artist Become a Man of the World?', *Art News* 63:6 (October 1964), pp. 34–7, 58–9, here p. 35.

46 See Eric Hodgins and Parker Lesley, 'The Great International Art Market', *Fortune* 52:6 (December 1955), pp. 118–20, 150, 152, 157–8, 162, 169; 53:1 (January 1956), pp. 122–5, 130, 132, 134, 136. This essay was first pointed out to me by Stuart Hobbs, who dedicated a large chapter in *The End of the American Avant-garde* (New York: New York University Press, 1997), to the domestication of the avant-garde in the 1950s.

47 Lawrence Alloway, 'The Arts and the Mass Media', *Architectural Design* 28:2 (February 1958), pp. 84–5.

48 'A Symposium on Pop Art', *Arts Magazine* (New York) 37:7 (April 1963), pp. 36–44, here p. 37.

49 Quoted in C. Tomkins, *The Bride and the Bachelors* (London: Weidenfeld & Nicolson, 1965) pp. 193–4.

50 See Susan Hapgood (ed.), *Neo-Dada: Redefining Art, 1958–1962* (New York: American Federation of Arts and Universe Publishing, 1994); and the chapter 'Existentialism in the USA' in Jachec, *The Philosophy and Politics of Abstract Expressionism*, pp. 62–104.

51 Jean Baudrillard, 'The Implosion of Meaning in the Media and the Implosion of the Social in the Masses', in Kathleen Woodward (ed.), *The Myths of Information: Technology and Postindustrial Culture* (Madison, WI: Coda, 1980), pp. 137–48, here p. 139.

52 Kellner, 'Popular Culture and the Construction of Postmodern Identities', p. 147.

53 Paul Mann, *The Theory Death of the Avant-garde* (Bloomington, IN: Indiana University Press, 1991), p. 69. See also George T. Noszlopy, 'The Embourgeoisement of Avant-garde Art', *Diogenes* 67 (Fall 1969), pp. 83–109; Miklós Szabolcsi, 'Avant-garde, Neo-avant-garde, Modernism: Questions and Suggestions', *New Literary History 3* (1971), pp. 49–70; Matei Calinescu, 'Avant-garde, Neo-avant-garde, Post Modernism: the Culture of Crisis', *CLIO* 4:3 (June 1975), pp. 317–40; Richard Bolton, 'Enlightened Self-Interest: the Avant-garde in the 80s' *Afterimage* 16:7 (February 1989), pp. 12–18; Donald Kuspit, 'The Good Enough Artist: Beyond the Mainstream Avant-garde Artist', in Donald Kuspit, *Signs of Psyche in Modern and Postmodern Art* (Cambridge: Cambridge University Press, 1993), pp. 292–9; Hobbs, *The End of the American Avant Garde*; Chin, 'The Avant-garde Industry', *Performing Arts Journal* 9:2&3 (PAJ no. 26/27, 1985), 59–75.

54 Octavio Paz, *Los hijos del limo: Del romanticismo a la vanguardia* (Barcelona: Seix Barral, 1974), p. 195.

55   See Hans-Magnus Enzensberger, 'Constituents of a Theory of the Media', *New Left Revue* 64 (November–December 1970), pp. 13–37, reprinted in Hans-Magnus Enzensberger, *Critical Essays* (New York: Continuum, 1982), pp. 46–76; and 'The Industrialization of the Mind', in Enzensberger, *Critical Essays*, pp. 3–14.

56   For some of the positions in this attempt to reach a higher level of consciousness by cybernetic means, see Celia Pearce and Erik Davis, 'The Soul of the Machine: the Search for Spirituality in Cyberspace', *Siggraph '96* (New York: ACM Press, 1996), pp. 503–4.

57   See, for example, Christopher Innes, *Avant-garde Theatre, 1892–1992* (London: Routledge, 1993); Theodore Shank, *Beyond the Boundaries: American Alternative Theatre*, 2nd rev. edn (Ann Arbor, MI: University of Michigan Press, 2002); John L. Styan, *Modern Drama in Theory and Practice*, 3 vols (Cambridge: Cambridge University Press, 1981); Arnold Aronson, *American Avant-garde Theatre: A History* (London: Routledge, 2000).

Notes to Chapter 4: Happening and Fluxes

1   William Fetterman compiled the most complete documentation of the event and suggests that the Black Mountain calendar entry of 16 August for a 'concert by John Cage' is most likely to have been the date of the event.

2   See Michael Kirby and Richard Schechner, 'An Interview with John Cage', *Tulane Drama Review* 10:2 (Winter 1965), pp. 50–72, here pp. 52–3; William Fetterman, *John Cage's Theatre Pieces: Notations and Performances* (Amsterdam: Harwood, 1996), pp. 97–104; Richard Kostelanetz, *The Theatre of Mixed Means: An Introduction to Happenings, Kinetic Environments and Other Mixed-Means Performances* (New York: Dial Press, 1968; London: Pitman, 1970), pp. 56–7; Mary Emma Harris, *The Arts at Black Mountain College* (Cambridge, MA: MIT Press, 1987), pp. 226–8; Martin B. Duberman, *Black Mountain: An Exploration in Community* (New York: Dutton, 1972), pp. 348–58; Calvin Tomkins, *Off the Wall: Robert Rauschenberg and the Art World of Our Time* (Garden City, NY: Doubleday, 1980), pp. 71–5; Walter Hopps and Susan Davidson (eds), *Robert Rauschenberg: A Retrospective*, exhibition catalogue (New York: Guggenheim Museum, 1999), pp. 229–30.

3   Michael Kirby, *Happenings: An Illustrated Anthology* (New York: Dutton, 1965; London: Sidgwick & Jackson, 1967), p. 45.

4   'Conversation with Allan Kaprow', Kostelanetz, *The Theatre of Mixed Means*, pp. 109–10.

5   'Conversation with Allan Kaprow', Kostelanetz, *The Theatre of Mixed Means*, p. 107.

6   'Conversation with Allan Kaprow', Kostelanetz, *The Theatre of Mixed Means*, p. 109.

7   All quotes are taken from Kostelanetz, *The Theatre of Mixed Means*, pp. 118, 119, 121 and 128.

8   Artist's statement, printed in *Claes Oldenburg: An Anthology* (New York: Guggenheim Museum, 1995), p. 130.

9   Kostelanetz, *The Theatre of Mixed Means*, pp. 154-5.

10 Artist's statement printed in *Claes Oldenburg: An Anthology*, p. 130.

11 Kostelanetz, *The Theatre of Mixed Means*, p. 146.

12 Artist's statement, printed in *Claes Oldenburg: An Anthology*, p. 130.

13 See Gail B. Kirkpatrick, *Tanztheater und bildende Kunst nach 1945* (Würzburg: Königshausen & Neumann, 1996) pp. 36–106.

14 Kostelanetz, *The Theatre of Mixed Means*, p. 94.

15 Kostelanetz, *The Theatre of Mixed Means*, p. 88.

16 See his copious writings on Nouveau Réalisme, a few of which have been listed in the Bibliography.

17 See Pierre Restany, 'The New Realism', *Art Since Mid-century,* vol. 2: *Figurative Art* (Greenwich, CT: New York Graphic Society, 1971), pp. 247–8 and his comments in Pierre Restany, *Une Vie dans l'art* (Neuchâtel: Ides et Calendes, 1983, pp. 49–58.

18 Many of these projects, together with documents and Klein's theoretical statements, have been described in the catalogue of the Yves Klein exhibition at the Nationalgalerie Berlin in 1976.

19 See his memoir of the event in Pierre Restany, *Yves Klein: Le Monochrome* (Paris: Hachette, 1974), pp. 93–4, and the photographs in the illustrated edition, *Yves Klein* (Paris: Chêne, 1982).

20 Some of these were outlined in *Dimanche: Le journal d'un seul jour*, 27 November 1960. See Günter Berghaus, 'Happenings in Europe: Trends, Events and Leading Figures', in Mariellen Sandford (ed.), *Happenings and Other Acts* (New York: Routledge, 1995), p. 315.

21 Germano Celant, 'Piero Manzoni, an Artist of the Present', in Germano Celant (ed.), *Piero Manzoni*, exhibition catalogue (Paris: Musée d'Art Moderne de la Ville de Paris, 1991), p. 13.

22 See Manzoni's comments on the action in his essay 'Progetti immediati', *Zero* 3 (July 1961); in the MIT reprint of 1973, on pp. 212–3

23 P. Manzoni, 'Libera dimensione', *Azimuth* 2 (1960).

24 See Celant, *Piero Manzoni* (Paris, 1991), pp. 21 and 36.

25 'Per la scoperta di una zona di immagini' (1956), in *Piero Manzoni: Catalogo generale*, ed. Germano Celant (Milan: Praero, 1975), p. 73.

26 See Otto Piene, 'The Development of the Group Zero', *Times Literary Supplement*, 3 September 1964; Anette Kuhn, *Zero: Eine Avantgarde der sechziger Jahre* (Frankfurt-am-Main: Propyläen, 1991); Heiner Stachelhaus, *Zero: Heinz Mack, Otto Piene, Günther Uecker* (Düsseldorf: Econ, 1993); Klaus Gereon Beuckers (ed.), *Zero-Studien: Aufsätze zur Düsseldorfer Gruppe Zero und ihrem Umkreis* (Münster: LIT, 1997); Renate Damsch-Wiehager (ed.), *Zero Italien, Zero und Paris*, and *Zero aus Deutschland* (for further details see the Bibliography), and the catalogues *Zero: Eine europäi-*

sche Avantgarde; *Zero: Bildvorstellungen einer europäischen Avantgarde*; *Zero: Vision und Bewegung*.

27 Piene, 'The Development of the Group Zero', p. 812.

28 Otto Piene, 'Position Zero', in *Zero: Eine europäische Avantgarde*, exhibition catalogue (Essen: Galerie Neher, 1992), pp. 7–9, here p. 8.

29 Piene, 'The Development of the Group Zero', p. 812.

30 Otto Piene, *More Sky* (Cambridge, MA: MIT, 1973), p. 73

31 See the descriptions and photographs in Kuhn, *Zero*, pp. 39–40; Malte Feiler, 'Aktionen bei ZERO-Happenings', in Beuckers, *Zero Studien*, pp. 135–48; Wieland Schmied (ed.), *Heinz Mack, Otto Piene, Günther Uecker*, exhibition catalogue (Hanover: Kestner-Gesellschaft, 1965), pp. 10–14; and Karl Ruhrberg, *Alfred Schmela, Galerist* (Cologne: Wienand, 1996), pp. 33–45.

32 See also Otto Piene's essay 'Lichtballett', *Theatre Heute* (May 1965), pp. 26–7 and the interview with him in *Kunst: Magazin für moderne Malerei, Graphik, Plastik* 4:3 (September 1964), pp. 63–6.

33 Lawrence Alloway, 'Viva Zero', in *Zero* reprint (Cambridge, MA: MIT Press, 1973), p. X.

34 See his interview statements in Jürgen Wissmann, *Otto Piene* (Recklinghausen: Bongers, 1976), pp. 11–13; the descriptions of the various formats of the light ballet in Kuhn, *Zero*, pp. 80–1; and the catalogues *Piene – Light Ballet* (New York: Howard Wise Gallery, 1965); *Otto Piene: Lichtballett und Künstler der Gruppe Zero* (Munich: Galerie Heseler, 1972).

35 See *Otto Piene – Sky Art* (Ingolstadt: Kunstverein, 1974); *Otto Piene Retrospektive 1952–1996* (Düsseldorf: Kunstmuseum im Ehrenhof, 1996); *Otto Piene: Sky Art 1968–1996* (Cologne: Wienand, 1999).

36 For a more extended discussion see my essay 'Happenings in Europe' in Sandford, *Happenings and Other Acts*; Jürgen Schilling, *Aktionskunst: Identität von Kunst und Leben? Eine Dokumentation* (Lucerne: Bucher, 1978); and the documentation in Jürgen Becker and Wolf Vostell (eds), *Happenings, Fluxus, Pop Art, Nouveau Réalisme: Eine Dokumentation* (Reinbek: Rowohlt, 1965).

37 Wolf Vostell, 'Genesis and Iconography of My Happenings', in Wolf Vostell, *Miss Vietnam, and Texts of Other Happenings* (San Francisco: Nova Broadcast Press, 1968), p. 3.

38 Vostell, *Miss Vietnam*, p. 4. On the early décollages see also the essay by Jörn Merkert, 'Pre-Fluxus-Vostell', *Kunstforum* 2:10 (1974), pp. 195–204.

39 Reprinted in Wolf Vostell, *Happening und Leben* (Neuwied: Luchterhand, 1970), pp. 327–8.

40 See his essay of 1965, 'Das Bewußtsein der de-coll/age', in Vostell, *Happening und Leben*, pp. 198–200.

41 The score is reprinted in Vostell, *Happening und Leben*, pp. 308–15. For an English translation see Allan Kaprow, *Assemblage, Environments and Happenings* (New York: Abrams, 1966), pp. 244–5.

42 Vostell, *Happening und Leben*, p. 269.

43 See Vostell, *Happening und Leben*, pp. 321–2. The score was written for a

WDR broadcast and subsequently performed as a live event in Cologne. Edith Decker has questioned the date of the score in *Paik Video* (Cologne: DuMont, 1988; English edn, New York: Barrytown, 1997), pp. 40–52, suggesting that Vostell pre-dated it in order to gain precedence over Paik's work with prepared television (see below, Chapter 6). For a similar work see *TV-Dé-coll/age and Morning Glory. 2 Pieces by Wolf Vostell* (New York: Third Rail Gallery, 1963).

44 Vostell, *Happening und Leben*, p. 321.

45 See Vostell, *Happening und Leben*, pp. 170–2. The score for the Happening has also been translated in Vostell, *Miss Vietnam*, pp. 8–9.

46 Wolf Vostell, 'Neun Nein Decollagen von Wolf Vostell', in Vostell, *Happening und Leben*, p. 270. An English translation is contained in Kaprow, *Assemblage*, pp. 248–53.

47 He stayed there from November 1961 to February 1962, holding an exhibition at the March Gallery on 10th Street, giving poetry readings at the Living Theater, and participating in Claes Oldenburg's Happening *Store Days* at the Ray Gun Theater.

48 See the detailed description of the Happening by E. C. Nimmo, in John Calder (ed.), *New Writers IV: Plays and Happenings* (London: Calder & Boyars, 1967), pp. 50–2, the review by Elena Guicciardi, 'L'uomo-televisore annuncia la rivoluzione', *Il Giorno* (18 December 1962), reprinted in *Jean-Jacques Lebel: Le Retour d'exil. Peintures, dessins, collages, 1954–1988*, exhibition catalogue (Paris: Galerie 1900–2000, 1988), pp. 66–7. The report in Kaprow, *Assemblage*, p. 234, relates to a repeat performance in Boulogne. There are several photographs in *Le Happening*, nos. 27–8, and in Kaprow, *Assemblage*, pp. 235–40.

49 For other descriptions of the Happening see Jean-Jacques Lebel, *Le Happening* (Paris: Denoël, 1966), pp. 71–3; *Le Retour d'exil*, pp. 68, 70, 72 and 73–4. There is a set of five photographs of the show in Charles Dreyfus, *Happenings & Fluxus* (Paris: Galerie 1900–2000, 1989), p. 6, another one in Jean-Jacques Lebel, 'On the Necessity of Violation', *The Drama Review* 13:1 (1968), pp. 89–105, and in *Le Happening*, no. 32.

50 Jean-Jacques Lebel, 'Notes on Political Street Theater', *The Drama Review* 13:4 (T44) (Summer 1969), pp. 111–18, here p. 112

51 'Zwei Briefe von Jean Jacques Lebel, Paris, an Wolf Vostell, Köln 1968', in Wolf Vostell, *Aktionen: Happenings und Demonstrationen seit 1965* (Reinbek: Rowohlt, 1970), s.p.

52 Quoted in Alexandra Munroe, *Japanese Art after 1945: Scream Against the Sky* (New York: Abrams, 1994), p. 42.

53 Ichiro Hariu, 'Progressive Trends in Modern Japanese Art', *Reconstructions: Avant-garde Art in Japan 1945–1965*, exhibition catalogue (Oxford: Museum of Modern Art, 1985), pp. 23–7, here p. 24.

54 Munroe, *Japanese Art after 1945*, p. 22. See also her essay '*Circle*: Modernism and Tradition' in the same volume.

284 *Notes*

55 Printed in *Document Gutai 1954–1972*, exhibition catalogue (Ashiya: Ashiya Shiritsu Bijutsu Hakubutsukan, 1993), p. 362.

56 These are preserved in the Gutai archive in Ashiya. For an assessment of the actions, see the catalogues listed in the bibliography and the essays on the Gutai in Munroe, *Japanese Art after 1945*, and Paul Schimmel (ed.), *Out of Action: Between Performance and the Object, 1949–1979* (London: Thames & Hudson, 1998).

57 See the perceptive review by Yoshiaki Inui, 'Fine Arts as a Theatrical Act: Jiro Yoshihara and the Gutai', in *Yoshihara Jiro to Gutai 1954–1972*, exhibition catalogue (Ashiya: Civic Gallery, 1985), reprinted in Shinichiro Osaki et al., *Giappone all'avanguardia: Il gruppo Gutai negli anni cinquanta*, exhibition catalogue (Rome: Galleria Nazionale d'Arte Moderna, 1990–1; Milan: Electa, 1990), p. 147.

58 A detailed description of the show is given by Jiro Yoshihara, 'Gutai Art on the Stage', *Gutai 7* (15 July 1959), reprinted in Osaki et al., *Giappone all'avanguardia*, pp. 158–60, *Japon des avant gardes 1910–1970*, exhibition catalogue (Paris: Centre Georges Pompidou, 1986), p. 299; Barbara Bertozzi and Klaus Wolbert (eds), *Gutai: Japanische Avantgarde/Japanese Agant-garde 1945–1965*, exhibition catalogue (Darmstadt: Mathildenhöhe, 1991), pp. 425–9; Françoise Bonnefoy et al. (eds), *Gutai*, exhibition catalogue (Paris: Galerie Nationale du Jeu de Paume, 1999), pp. 212–13.

59 'Manifest of the Neo-Dada Organizers at Their First Exhibition, April 1960', quoted in Genpei Akasegawa, 'The 1960s: the Art which Destroyed Itself. An Intimate Account', *Reconstructions: Avant-garde Art in Japan 1945–1965*, pp. 85–90, here p. 85, and in *Japon des avant gardes*, p. 336.

60 The actions of Neo-Dada Organizers have been documented in the catalogues *Ryudo-suru bijutsu III: Neo Dada no shashin / Art in Flux III: Neo-Dada Witnessed. Photo Documents* (Fukuoka City: Fukuoka Art Museum, 1993); *Shinohara Ushio-ten* (Hiroshima: City Museum of Contemporary Art, 1992) and Rand Castile (ed.), *Shinohara* (New York: Japan House Gallery, 1982). See also Yoshiaki Tono, 'Neo Dada et Anti-Art', *Japon des avant gardes*, pp. 328–37; Schimmel, *Out of Action*, pp. 141–42, 149–54; Munroe, *Japanese Art after 1945*, pp. 157–9; *Dada in Japan: Japanische Avantgarde, 1920–1970*, exhibition catalogue (Düsseldorf: Kunstmuseum, 1983), pp. 26–7, 106–9; Yoshiaki Tono, 'Artists in the Early Sixties', in Shuji Takashina et al. (eds), *Art in Japan Today* (Tokyo: Kinskuniya Books, 1974), pp. 16–21.

61 See Shigeko Kubota (ed.), *Hi Red Center* (New York: Fluxus, 1965); Genpai Akasegawa, *Tokyo mikisa keikaku: Haireddo senta chokusetsu kodo no kiroku (Tokyo Mixer Plans: Documents of Hi Red Center's Direct Actions)* (Tokyo: PARCO Shuppankyoku, 1984). See also Schimmel, *Out of Action*, pp. 77–8, 142, 149–55; Munroe, *Japanese Art after 1945*, pp. 77–81, 159; *Reconstructions: Avant-garde Art in Japan 1945–1965*, pp. 88–90; *Dada in Japan*, pp. 28–9, 110–13; *Japon des avant gardes*, pp. 356–8.

62 This is the version of the movement's origin given in Emmett Williams and

Ann Noël (eds), *Mr Fluxus: A Collective Portrait of George Maciunas 1931–1978* (London: Thames & Hudson, 1997), p. 32. Maciunas liked to adopt the legendary origins of Dada by saying that he found the name Fluxus by flicking randomly through a dictionary and sticking his finger on the word 'fluxus'. This caused Emmett Wiliams to comment sarcastically: 'Did George know in advance where his index finger was going to land?' *My Life in Flux and Vice Versa* (London: Thames & Hudson, 1992), p. 164.

63 Invitation flyer reproduced in Achille Bonito Oliva (ed.), *Ubi Fluxus ibi motus 1990–1962*, exhibition catalogue (Venice, 1990; Milan: Mazzotta, 1990), p. 108. See also ibid., p. 206; René Block and Anne-Marie Freybourg (eds), *Wiesbaden Fluxus 1962–1982: Eine kleine Geschichte von Fluxus in drei Teilen*, exhibition cagalogue (Wiesbaden: Museum Weisbaden, 1983), p. 112; and Thomas Kellein, *'Fröhliche Wissenschaft'. Das Archiv Sohm*, exhibition catalogue (Stuttgart: Staatsgalerie, 1987), p. 78.

64 Henry Flynt, 'Mutations of the Vanguard: Pre-Fluxus, During Fluxus, Late Fluxus', in Bonito Oliva, *Ubi Fluxus ibi motus*, pp. 99–128, here p. 112.

65 Maciunas in a letter to Emmett Williams, printed in Williams and Noël, *Mr Fluxus*, p. 38.

66 See Günter Berghaus, 'Tomas Schmit: A Fluxus Farewell to Perfection', *Drama Review* 38:1, T141 (Spring 1994), pp. 95–6.

67 Letter of 18 November 1962, in Williams and Noël, *Mr Fluxus*, p. 41.

68 Letter of 7 March 1962 from Wiesbaden to La Monte Young, reproduced in Bonito Oliva, *Ubi Fluxus ibi motus*, p. 119.

69 See Stephan von Wiese et al. (eds), *Brennpunkt Düsseldorf: Joseph Beuys, die Akademie, der allgemeine Aufbruch, 1962–1987*, exhibition catalogue (Düsseldorf: Kunstmuseum Düsseldorf, 1987); Manfred de la Motte, 'Jean-Pierre Wilhelm und die Galerie 22, Düsseldorf', *Kunstforum International* 104 (November–December 1989), pp. 225–8; Karl Ruhrberg (ed.), *Alfred Schmela, Galerist: Wegbereiter der Avantgarde* (Cologne: Wienand, 1996).

70 See *Das Atelier Mary Bauermeister in Köln, 1960–62* (Cologne: Emons 1993). Several other catalogues have explored the art scene of the Rhineland: Georg Jappe (ed.), *Der Traum von der Metropole: Vom Happening zum Kunstmarkt. Kölns goldene sechziger Jahre* (Cologne: Kölnischer Kunstverein, 1979); Manfred Leve, *Aktionen, Vernissagen, Personen: Die Rheinische Kunstszene der 50er und 60er Jahre* (Cologne: Rheinland-Verlag, 1982); Wulf Herzogenrath and Gabriele Lueg (eds), *Die 60er Jahre: Kölns Weg zur Kunstmetropole. Vom Happening zum Kunstmarkt* (Cologne: Kölnischer Kunstverein, 1986).

71 See Will Baltzer and Alfons W. Biermann (eds), *Treffpunkt Parnass Wuppertal, 1949–1965*, exhibition catalogue (Wuppertal: Von der Heydt-Museum, 1980; Cologne: Rheinland-Verlag, 1980) and Günter Bär et al. (eds), *Crossroads Parnass: International Avant-garde at Galerie Parnass, Wuppertal 1949–1965*, exhibition catalogue (Paris: Goethe Institut, 1982).

72 See the chapters on Brock and Spoerri in Berghaus, 'Happenings in Europe',

and Williams, *My Life in Fluxus*, p. 102. Darmstadt was also the city where the Ferienkurse für Musik, an annual gathering of the international avant-garde in experimental music, were held. See Rudolf Stephan (ed.), *Von Kranichstein zur Gegenwart, 1946–1996: 50 Jahre Darmstädter Ferienkurse / Internationale Ferienkurse für Musik* (Stuttgart: Daco, 1996); Gianmario Borio and Hermann Danuser (eds), *Im Zenit der Moderne: Die Internationalen Ferienkurse für Neue Musik Darmstadt 1946–1966. Geschichte und Dokumentation in vier Bänden* (Freiburg im Breisgau: Rombach, 1997).

73 Undated letter, quoted in Historisches Archiv der Stadt Köln (eds), *Intermedial, Kontrovers, Experimentell: Das Atelier Mary Bauermeister in Köln* (Cologne: Emons Verlag, 1993), p. 142.

74 See the revised programme of the event in Baltzer and Biermann, *Treffpunkt Parnass*, p. 192. A sound recording of the event from the estate of Rolf Jährling is preserved in the Zentralarchiv des Internationalen Kunsthandels in Cologne.

75 George Maciunas, 'Neo Dada in den Vereinigten Staaten', in Becker and Vostell, *Happenings*, pp. 192–5, here p. 192. An English draft version was published in Bonito Oliva, *Ubi Fluxus ibi motus*, pp. 214–16.

76 Maciunas, 'Neo Dada in den Vereinigten Staaten', p. 193.

77 Maciunas, 'Neo Dada in den Vereinigten Staaten', p. 194.

78 The programme-poster of the fourteen events, reproduced in many catalogues and critical studies, lists only the works Maciunas *intended* to see presented. Many of these were never performed, and others, not listed on the poster, were given instead. See, for example, Ludwig Gosewitz's list of works he actually saw performed, in Block and Fresbourg, *Wiesbaden Fluxus 1962–1982*, p. 101.

79 Dick Higgins, *Postface / Jefferson's Birthday* (New York: Something Else Press, 1964), p. 69.

80 'Musik und Antimusik: Konzert der "Fluxus"-Festspiele in Wiesbaden', *Allgemeine Zeitung / Mainzer Anzeiger*, 3 September 1962. See also 'Musikalisches Variété: "Internationale Festspiele neuester Musik" in Wiesbaden', *Wiesbadener Tagblatt*, 4 September 1962; and 'Das Stemmeisen im Resonanzkasten', *Wiesbadener Kurier*, 4 September 1962.

81 'Das Stemmeisen im Resonanzkasten', *Wiesbadener Kurier*, 4 September 1962.

82 George Maciunas in a letter to Wolf Vostell of 3 November 1963 (Archiv Sohm), printed in Williams and Noël, *Mr Fluxus*, pp. 41–2.

83 Tomas Schmit in an interview with Günter Berghaus, 'Tomas Schmit: A Fluxus Farewell to Perfection', p. 92. Schmit's comment that Maciunas was 'more orthodox than Leftist thinking ought to be' is corroborated in Williams and Noël, *Mr Fluxus*, pp. 102, 104 and 107–9; Bonito Oliva, *Ubi Fluxus ibi motus*, pp. 112–28; Dieter Daniels (ed.), *Fluxus: Ein Nachruf zu Lebseiten*, special issue of *Kunstforum* 115 (September–October 1991), p. 175; Henry Flint, 'George Maciunas and My Work with Him', *Flash Art* 84–5 (Oct–Nov. 1978), p. 49.

84 Williams and Noël, *Mr Fluxus*, p. 73.

85 'Proposed Propaganda Action For Nov. Fluxus in N.Y.C.', *Fluxus News – Policy Letter*, no. 6 (April 1963), reproduced in Bonito Oliva, *Ubi Fluxus ibi motus*, p. 120; and Williams and Noël, *Mr Fluxus*, pp. 93–4.

86 See the documents in Williams and Noël, *Mr Fluxus*; and Ken Friedman (ed.), *The Fluxus Reader* (London: Academy Editions, 1998), and an interpretation of these events in Kristine Stiles, 'Between Water and Stone', Elizabeth Armstrong and Joan Rothfuss (eds), *In the Spirit of Fluxus*, exhibition catalogue (Minneapolis, MN: Walker Art Center, 1993), pp. 63–99.

87 Jean-Pierre Wilhelm reported on this decisive influence in his opening speech to the performance festival *Neo-Dada in der Musik* (Kammerspiele, Düsseldorf, 16 June 1962). Other major sources of influence mentioned here are Luigi Russolo, Edgar Varèse and John Cage. See p. 6 of the manuscript, preserved in the Archiv Sohm, Stuttgart.

88 See Michael Nyman, 'Nam June Paik, Composer', *Nam June Paik*, exhibition catalogue (New York: Whitney Museum, 1982, pp. 79–90.

89 See *Nam June Paik: Werke 1946–1976. Musik–Fluxus–Video*, exhibition catalogue, ed. Wulf Hertzogenrath (Cologne: Kölnischer Kunstverein, 1976–7), pp. 39–43; *Das Atelier Mary Bauermeister*, pp. 30–3; *Nam June Paik Fluxus, Video*, exhibition catalogue, ed. Wulf Herzogenrath (Bremen: Kunsthalle, 1999–2000), pp. 24–8. A first draft of the piece, then conceived of as a Gesamtkunstwerk in the Wagnerian tradition, was mentioned in 1959 in a letter to John Cage (see Cage, *A Year from Monday: New Lectures and Writings* (London: Calder and Boyars, 1969), p. 90.

90 Paik uses the terms 'théâtre pure' and 'a piece of sounding Schwitters' in a letter to Wolfgang Steinecke, printed in *Niederschriften eines Kulturnomaden: Aphorismen, Briefe, Texte*, ed. Edith Decker (Cologue: DuMont, 1992), p. 49. See also ibid., p. 52: 'I want to complement Dadaism with music.'

91 Paik in a letter of 2 May 1959 to Wolfgang Steinecke in *Nam June Paik: Werke 1946–1976*, p. 40.

92 Ibid.

93 Interview with G. M. König, in *Das Atelier Mary Bauermeister*, p. 51.

94 This act has often been referred to as the first use of the telephone as an artistic medium (e.g. by Herzogenrath in the catalogue *Nam June Paik: Video Works 1963–88*, p. 11). This, however, ignores an even more creative employment of it in a performance by Marinetti in 1914, when the technology was truly new. See Günter Berghaus, *Italian Futurist Theatre, 1909–1944* (Oxford: Clarendon Press, 1998), p. 175.

95 Nam June Paik, *About the Exposition of the Music*. Invitation sheet to the planned exhibition in January 1963 at the Galerie Parnass, reproduced in *Nam June Paik: Fluxus, Video*, p. 53.

96 N. J. Paik, 'Postmusic', *The Monthly Review of the University of Avant-garde Hinduism* 1 (1963), p. 1. The essay has been reproduced in *Nam June Paik: Videa 'n' Videology 1959–73*, exhibition catalogue, ed. Judson Rosebud (Syracuse, NY: Everson Museum of Art, 1974), p. 3, and *Niederschriften*

eines Kulturnomaden, pp. 93–5. The performance score of *Symphony for 20 Rooms* can be found in *The Worlds of Nam June Paik*, exhibition catalogue (New York: Guggenheim Museum, 2000), p. 41. For his realization of these works see below, Chapter 6.

97   See N. J. Paik, 'Charlotte Moorman: Zufall und Notwendigkeit', in *Niederschriften eines Kulturnomaden*, pp. 186–91.

98   See the very informative letter to Mary Bauermeister of 12 April 1967, in *Niederschriften eines Kulturnomaden*, pp. 69–71.

99   Further information can be found in Barbara Moore (ed.), *The World of Charlotte Moorman: Archive Catalogue* (New York: Bound and Unbound, 2000); David Bourdon, 'A Letter to Charlotte Moorman', *Art in America* 88:6 (June 2000), pp. 80–5, 135–7; Peter Frank, 'TV-Body: Die Zusammenarbeit von Paik-Moorman', in *Nam June Paik: Werke 1946–1976*, pp. 96–102; 'Charlotte Moorman: Die Kunstfigur Paiks', in W. Herzogenrath, *Nam June Paik: Fluxus-Video*, pp. 58–65; 'Humanisierte Technik: Die Videoobjekte für Charlotte Moorman', in Edith Decker, *Paik Video* (Cologne: DuMont, 1988; English edn, New York: Barrytown, 1997), pp. 121–40.

100   Paik in an interview with Paul Schimmel, *Arts Magazine* 49:4 (December 1974), pp. 52–3, here p. 52.

101   Letter to George Maciunas of 27 May 1970, printed in Hans Sohm (ed.), *Happening und Fluxus*, exhibition catalogue (Cologne, 1970), s.p.

102   Interview with Robert Filliou, in *Robert Filliou – Commemor*, exhibition catalogue (Aachen: Neue Galerie im Alten Kurhaus, 1970), s.p.

103   Filliou sometimes used the metaphorical term 'mind-opener' for this. Art was for him a tool just as a tin-opener is a tool for more mundane purposes.

104   Quoted in Johannes Cladders, 'Fröhliche Einsamkeit', in *Robert Filliou 1926–1987: Zum Gedachtnis*, exhibition catalogue (Düsseldorf 1988), p. 27.

105   See Berghaus, 'Happenings in Europe', p. 341.

106   The text of *Yes* and *Le Filliou idéal* are reprinted in *A Filliou Sampler*, pp. 5–10 and in *The Eternal Network Presents: Robert Filliou* (Hanover: Sprengel-Museum, 1984), pp. 70 and 88.

107   See the Filliou catalogue of Galerie Buchholz, 1973.

108   Interview in *Robert Filliou – Commemor* (n.p.).

109   Interview in *Robert Filliou – Commemor* (n.p.).

110   Ben Vautier, 'Mon actuelle position en art (1974)', in *Ben, pour ou contre: Une rétrospective*, exhibition catalogue (Marseilles: Galeries Contemporaines des Musées de Marseille, 1995), p. 164.

111   See the interview with E. Giraud, printed in the communiqué *Le Théâtre Total* of 1964; reprinted in *Ben, pour ou contre*, p. 69.

112   Reprinted in Sohm, *Happening und Fluxus*, exhibition catalogue, s.p.; and Charles Dreyfus (ed.), *Happening & Fluxus* (Paris: Galerie 1900–2000, 1989), p. 178.

113   See *Art = Ben* (Amsterdam: Stedilijk Museum, 1973), p. 29.

Notes to Chapter 5: Body Art, Ritualism and Neo-Shamanic Performances

1 Tomas Schmit, in an interview with Günter Berghaus, 'Tomas Schmit: A Fluxus Farewell to Perfection', *The Drama Review* 38:1, T141 (Spring 1994), p. 89.

2 See the excellent survey in Tracey Warr and Amelia Jones (eds), *The Artist's Body* (London: Phaidon, 2000); and the revised, updated edition of Lea Vergine, *Body Art and Performance: The Body as Language* (Milan: Skira, 2000).

3 Bojana Pejić, 'Bodyscenes: an Affair of the Flesh', *Marina Abramović: Artist Body: Performances 1969–1998* (Milan: Charta, 1998), pp. 26–40, here p. 28.

4 Jorge Glusberg, 'Introduction aux langages du corps: L'art corporel et les performances', in *Journées interdisciplinaires sur l'art corporel et performances, Paris, du 15 au 18 février 1979* (Buenos Aires: Centro de Arte y Comunicación, 1979), fols. 4r–9v, here 9v.

5 See Günter Berghaus, 'Ritual and Crisis: Survival Techniques of Humans and Other Animals', and several other essays in Günter Berghaus (ed.), *On Ritual*, special issue of *Performance Research* 3:3 (Winter 1998).

6 See *Modern Primitives: An Investigation of Contemporary Adornment and Ritual*, special issue of *Re/Search* 12 (1989); Ted Polhemus and Housk Randall, *Rituals of Love* (London: Picador, 1994); and *The Customized Body* (London: Serpent's Tail, 1996); Ted Polhemus, 'The Performance of Pain', in Berghaus, *On Ritual*, pp. 97–102; Judith Squires (ed.), *Perversity*, special issue of *New Formations* 19 (Spring 1993); Paul Sweetman, 'Only Skin Deep? Tattooing, Piercing and the Transgressive Body', in Michelle Aaron (ed.), *The Body's Perilous Pleasures: Dangerous Desires and Contemporary Culture* (Edinburgh: Edinburgh University Press, 1999), pp. 165–87; Eric Gons, 'The Body Sacrificial', in Tobin Sievers (ed.), *The Body Aesthetic: From Fine Art to Body Modification* (Ann Arbor, MI: University of Michigan Press, 2000), pp. 159–78.

7 Amelia Jones, *Body Art: Performing the Subject* (Minneapolis, MN: University of Minnesota Press, 1998), p. 122

8 Interview with Hans Ulrich Obrist, in *Marina Abramović: Artist Body*, pp. 41–51, here p. 46.

9 Interview, in Nick Kaye (ed.), *Art into Theatre: Performance Interviews and Documents* (Amsterdam: Harwood, 1996), pp. 25–39, here pp. 34–5.

10 I fully agree here with Kristine Stiles's assessment in 'Schlaget Auf: the Problem with Carolee Schneemann's Painting', in the exhibition catalogue *Carolee Schneemann: Up to and Including Her Limits* (New York: New Museum of Contemporary Art, 1996), pp. 15–25. It also seems symptomatic that Schneemann has not been honoured with large-scale exhibitions and weighty catalogues like the ones granted to her male colleagues from this

period, and that often announced monographs such as the ones by Stiles and Jay Murphy have still not appeared in print.

11   Carolee Schneemann, 'Form is Emotion' (1960–2), in Carolee Schneemann, *More than Meat Joy: Complete Performance Works and Selected Writings*, ed. Bruce McPherson (Kingston, NY: Documentext/McPherson, 1997), p. 13.

12   Schneemann, *More than Meat Joy*, p. 52.

13   Dan Cameron, 'In the Flesh', *Carolee Schneemann: Up to and Including Her Limits*, pp. 7–14, here p. 12.

14   Schneemann, *More than Meat Joy*, p. 63. The volume also contains the score of the piece and some twenty pages of photographs.

15   Schneemann, *More than Meat Joy*, p. 230.

16   Schneemann, in an interview with Andrea Juno in *Angry Women*, special issue of *Re/Search*, no. 13 (1991), p. 72.

17   The text has been reprinted in *More than Meat Joy*, pp. 238–9. She later admitted that the person referred to was actually a female critic, Annette Michelson. See Scott MacDonald (ed.), *A Critical Cinema: Interviews with Independent Filmmakers* (Berkeley, CA: University of California Press, 1988), pp. 134–51, here p. 143.

18   'Carolee Schneemann: Working Against Existing Taboos', *The Soho Weekly News*, 31 May 1979, pp. 29–30.

19   Marcia Tucker in her introduction to the exhibition catalogue *Carolee Schneemann: Up to and Including Her Limits*, 1996–97.

20   Carolee Schneemann, 'Istory of a Girl Pornographer' (1974), in *More than Meat Joy*, p. 194.

21   Schneemann, 'Istory of a Girl Pornographer', p. 192. Confessing a personal trait in public was less an act of self-revelation for him than an impetus for the audience to confront issues such as the constitution of private and public spheres.

22   Schneemann, in an interview with Andrea Juno in *Angry Women*, p. 69.

23   Schneemann, in an interview with Linda Montano, in *Sex, Performance, and the 80's*, special double issue of *The Flue / Franklin Furnace*, 1982, pp. 6–8, here p. 7.

24   Interview with Nick Kaye, in *Art into Theatre*, p. 38.

25   Lawrence Alloway, 'Carolee Schneemann: the Body as Object and Instrument', *Art in America* 68:3 (March 1980), pp. 19–20, here p. 20.

26   Schneemann, 'Istory of a Girl Pornographer' p. 194.

27   'Vito Acconci', *Avalanche* 6 (Fall 1972), pp. 3–4, here p. 4. Unfortunately there is no collected edition of Acconci's writings. Scripts and scenarios of his performances (often written after the event) were published in a variety of contemporary journals and catalogues. I have mainly relied on the *Avalanche* special issue on Acconci, the scenarios printed in *Interfunktionen*, the Chicago retrospective of 1980 and the collection of statements in W. M. H. Kaiser, *Vito Acconci: Poetry, Activities, Sculpture, Performances, Installations, Video* (Amsterdam: n.p., 1977).

28 Interview with Martin Kunz in *Vito Acconci*, exhibition catalogue (Lucerne: Kunstmuseum, 1978), n.p.

29 He acknowledged his debt to the Judson Church Dancers in an interview recorded for Video Data Bank in Chicago and published as an Acconci issue of *Profile*, Summer 1984.

30 See James T. Hindman, 'Self-Performance: Allan Kaprow's Activities', *The Drama Review* 23:1 (T81) (March 1979), pp. 95–102.

31 In Vito Acconci, 'Biography of Work 1969–1981', published on the occasion of the *documenta 7*, he divided his work into eight phases, of which the first four are of relevance here. They can be summarized thus: (1) private activity made public at a later point; (2) self-sufficient actions exhibited to an audience; (3) the 'agent' (artist) establishes through the performance an exchange point with spectators; (4) the 'agent' projects himself into an exhibition space by means of slides, tapes, videos.

32 *Profile* interview, p. 28.

33 'I was very involved with [politics]. . . . I probably saw that I could do some analogue of what was going on in politics . . . The only work I wanted to do was work that brought in politics.' *Profile* interview, pp. 4–5.

34 See Acconci's documentation, *Street Works*, published as a supplement to his magazine *0 to 9*, no. 6 (1969).

35 *Profile* interview, p. 8.

36 Acconci, Note on *Following Piece* (1969), in *Avalanche* 6 (Fall 1972), p. 31.

37 *Profile* interview, pp. 12–13.

38 *Profile* interview, pp. 16–17.

39 See Vito Acconci, 'Power Field – Exchange Points – Transformations', *Avalanche* 8 (Fall 1972), pp. 62–69.

40 *Profile* interview, p. 17.

41 Interview with Effie Stephano, 'Image Changes', in *Art and Artist* 8:1 (no. 95) (February 1974), pp. 24–7, here p. 25

42 *Profile* interview, p. 32.

43 V. Acconci, 'Some Notes on Activity and Performance', *Interfunktionen* 5 (November 1970), p. 138, reprinted in *Art and Artist* 6:2 (May 1971), p. 68. See also his comments on Brecht in the *Profile* interview, p. 41.

44 See V. Acconci, 'Steps into Performance (and out),' in A. A. Bronson and Peggy Gale (eds), *Performance by Artists* (Toronto: Art Metropole, 1979), pp. 27–40.

45 Acconci, *Profile* interview, p. 32.

46 See Jones, *Body Art: Performing the Subject*, pp. 135 and 148.

47 Günter Berghaus, 'Happenings in Europe: Trends, Events and Leading Figures', in Mariellen Sandford, *Happenings and Other Acts* (New York: Routledge, 1995), pp. 310–88.

48 A rare exception was the Destruction in Arts Symposium in London, where they gave several performances at the Africa Centre (10 and 15 September 1966), the Conway Hall (12 September) and the St Bride's Institute (13 and 16 September).

49   See *Hermann Nitsch: Das früheste Werk, 1955–1960*, ed. Otmar Rychlik (Vienna: Sonderzahl, 1986); and *Hermann Nitsch: Aktionsmalerei 1960–1963/1989–1990*, exhibition catalogue (Düsseldorf: Galerie Heike Gurtze, 1990).

50   See H. Nitsch, *die wortdichtung des orgien mysterien theaters*, and H. Nitsch, *das orgien mysterien theater: die partituren aller aufgeführten aktionen, 1960–1979*. His theoretical writings have been collected in *könig oedipus: eine spielbare theorie des dramas*; *das orgien mysterien theater 2: theoretische schriften*; *Das Orgien Mysterien Theater: Manifeste, Aufsätze, Vorträge*; *Zur Theorie des Orgien Mysterien Theaters: Zweiter Versuch*. A few of these texts have been translated in the bi-lingual edition, *Orgien Mysterien Theater. Orgies Mysteries Theatre* (Darmstadt: März, 1969).

51   The ancient Greek dramatists felt that a staged action revives in the spectator the memory of experiences that have been long forgotten or repressed, thus leading to a curative release of emotions. Freud and Breuer adopted the idea in their *Studies on Hysteria* (1893), in which they describe how re-experiencing a past traumatic event results in a discharge of the emotions originally attached to that event.

52   See Hermann Nitsch, *Die Architektur des Orgien Mysterien Theaters / The Architecture of the O.M. Theatre*, 2 vols (Munich: Jahn, 1987–93).

53   For a description of these myths and the cults that accompanied them, see Eddehard Stärk, *Hermann Nitschs 'Orgien Mysterien Theater' und die 'Hysterie der Griechen'* (Munich: Fink, 1987), pp. 31–6.

54   Hermann Nitsch, *Das Orgien Mysterien Theater: Manifeste, Aufsätze, Vorträge* (Salzburg: Residenzverlag, 1990), pp. 15–19, here p. 15.

55   Hermann Nitsch, 'Rudolf Schwarzkogler', in *Rudolf Schwarzkogler*, exhibition catalogue (Innsbruck: Galerie Krinzinger, 1976), unpag. For a critical assessment of Nitsch's psychoanalytic concepts see Josef Dvorak, 'Die Blutorgien des Hermann Nitsch: Zur Psychologie des o.m. theaters', *Neues Forum* 20:239 (November 1973), pp. 50–4.

56   Otto Mühl, 'Die Materialaktion', *Ausstellung Brus–Muehl–Nitsch: Vom Informel zum Aktionismus*, exhibition catalogue (Zurndorf: Archiv des Wiener Aktionismus, Friedrichshof, 1984), p. 40, reprinted in Jürgen Becker and Wolf Vostell (eds), *Happenings, Fluxus, Pop Art, Nouveau Réalisme: Eine Dokumentation* (Reinbek: Rowohlt, 1965), pp. 362–3.

57   Otto Mühl, 'Kalender 1964', p. 7, unpublished typescript in the Archiv des Wiener Aktionismus, Friedrichshof.

58   See Otto Mühl, *Mama & Papa: Materialaktion 63–69* (Frankfurt-am-Main: Kohlkunstverlag, s.d. [1969]).

59   However, they were represented in the first representative anthology of Happening documents, Becker and Vostell's *Happenings, Fluxus, Pop Art, Nouveau Réalisme* of 1965, and the first major retrospective of Happening art, held in Cologne in 1970.

60   Karl Rosenkranz's *Ästhetik des Häßlichen* (Königsberg: Bornträger, 1853), reads in part like a philosophical comment on Viennese Actionism.

61 Hermann Nitsch, 'Vortrag an der Hochschule für Film und Fernsehen, München, 1970', in *Das Orgien Mysterien Theater: Manifeste, Aufsätze, Vorträge*, p. 41.

62 Hermann Bahr, 'Elektra', in H. Bahr, *Glossen zum Wiener Theater 1903–1907* (Berlin: Fischer, 1907), p. 276.

63 Mühl, *Papa und Mama: Materialaktion 63–69*, p. 9.

64 See Hermann Nitsch (ed.), *Das rote Tuch: Der Mensch das Unappetitlichste Vieh*, (Vienna: Friebord, 1988); and Gerhard Jaschke (ed.), *Reizwort Nitsch*, 2 vols (Vienna: Friebord, 1993, 2nd edn, Vienna: Sonderzahl, 1995).

65 Nitsch represented Austria at the Expo 1992 in Seville and had a major catalogue published for the event by the Bundesministerium für Unterricht und Kunst; his production of Massenet's *Herodiade* in 1994/95 was a major event in the Viennese cultural diary and was documented for State television; he participated in the exhibition *Lost Paradise Lost: Kunst und sakraler Raum*, presented in 2000 in thirteen churches in Hanover (the catalogue contains two interesting essays on Nitsch as a religious artist).

66 See Uwe M. Schneede, *Joseph Beuys, die Aktionen: Kommentiertes Werkverzeichnis mit fotografischen Dokumentationen* (Ostfildern: Hatje, 1994), pp. 8–67; Johannes Stüttgen, 'Fluxus und der "Erweiterte Kunstbegriff" ', *Kunstmagazin* 20:2 (August 1980), pp. 53–63; Thomas Kellein, 'Zum Fluxus-Begriff von Joseph Beuys', in Volker Harlan (ed), *Joseph-Beuys-Tagung Basel 1–4 Mai 1991* (Basle: Wiese, 1991), pp. 137–42.

67 Interview with Caroline Tisdall, in *Joseph Beuys*, exhibition catalogue (New York: Guggenheim Museum, 1979; London: Thames and Hudson, 1979), p. 95.

68 J. Beuys, quoted in G. Adriani, W. Konnertz and K. Thomas, *Joseph Beuys*, 3rd rev. edn (Cologne: DuMont, 1994), p. 72.

69 J. Beuys, 'und in uns . . . unter uns . . . landunter', in *Vierundzwanzig Stunden*, s.p., reprinted in Schneede, *Joseph Beuys: Die Aktionen*, p. 89. In the right-hand corner he wrote the formula 'PAN XXX ttt', which may be translated as 'Urgent message: Save the Earth!', assuming that throughout the text 'h' stands for *homo* and 't' for *terra*. (During the Second World War, Beuys trained as a radio operator before becoming a pilot and had therefore a clear understanding of international emergency signals.)

70 For a detailed analysis of the performance see Friedhelm Mennekes, *Manresa: Eine Fluxus-Demonstration als geistliche Übung nach Ignatius von Loyola* (Frankfurt/M: Insel, 1992).

71 Interview with Caroline Tisdall, in Caroline Tisdall, *Joseph Beuys: Coyote* (Munich: Schirmer-Mosel, 1976; 2nd edn, 1980), p. 113.

72 Statement by Beuys, in Tisdall, *Joseph Beuys: Coyote*, p. 16.

73 See Botho Strauß, 'Joseph Beuys: Die Identität um Zeit und Form', *Theater Heute*, special issue, 1969, pp. 102–3; and Marlene Baum, 'Joseph Beuys und der Schimmel', *Pantheon* 52 (1994), pp. 167–72.

74 In the period of the student rebellion he founded the German Student Party

(1967), followed by the Organization of Non-Voters/Free Referendums (1970), the Organization for Direct Democracy (1971), and the Free International School for Creativity and Interdisciplinary Research (1973). He became a candidate for the ecological Green Party in the European Parliament election in 1979.

75 From a description of the aims of the Organization for Direct Democracy, translated in Tisdall, *Joseph Beuys: Coyote*, p. 268

76 The text has been reproduced in Anne Tronche, *Gina Pane: Actions* (Paris: Fall, 1997), p. 65.

77 'Performance of Concern: Gina Pane Discusses her Work with Effie Stephano', *Art and Artist* 8:1 [no. 85] (April 1973), pp. 20–7, here p. 22.

78 Interview with Effie Stephano, *Art and Artist*, April 1973, p. 22.

79 Pane, in a statement distributed before the performance, reprinted in Gilbert Gatellier, 'Gina Pane: Un humanisme du corps', *Chroniques de l'Art vivant* 41 (July 1973), pp. 10-11, here p. 10.

80 Interview with Effie Stephano in *Art and Artist*, April 1973, p. 26.

81 See the interview with Irmeline Lebeer, 1975, in *L'Art au corps: Le corps exposé de Man Ray à nos jours*, exhibition catalogue (Marseille: Musée de Marseille, 1986), pp. 347–52, here p. 351.

82 Interview with Irmeline Lebeer in *L'Art au corps*, p. 352.

83 Interview with Effie Stephano in *Art and Artist*, April 1973, p. 24.

84 Interview with Effie Stephano in *Art and Artist*, p. 23.

85 Interview with Ephie Stephano in *Art and Artist*, p. 26.

86 See Pane's interview with Ezio Quarantelli, 'Travels with St. Francis', *Contemporanea* 4 (November–December 1988), pp. 44–7: '[The body] is the irreducible core of the human being, its most fragile part. . . . And the wound is the memory of the body; it memorizes its fragility, its pain, thus its "real" existence' (p. 46). See also her interview with Helena Kontová, 'The Wound as Sign: An Encounter with Gina Pane', *Flash Art* 92–3 (October–November 1979), pp. 36–7.

87 Interview with Kirsten Martins, in Kirsten Martins and Peter P. J. Sohn (eds), *Performance: Another Dimension*, exhibition catalogue (Berlin: Frölich & Kaufmann, 1983), pp. 155–7, here 156

88 Interview with Irmeline Lebeer in *L'Art au corps*, p. 349.

89 Interview with Effie Stephano in *Art and Artist*, April 1973, p. 26.

90 Interview with Effie Stephano in *Art and Artist*, April 1973, p. 26.

91 G. Pane, 'Lettre à un(e) inconnu(e)', *Artitudes international* 15–17 (October–December 1974), p. 34.

92 Interview with Kirsten Martins in *Performance: Another Dimension*, p. 155.

93 For a detailed examination of the Christian undertones in Pane's work, see Karoline Künkler, 'Die Künstlerin als "Schmerzensfrau": Selbstverletzungs-aktionen von Gina Pane', in Kathrin Hoffmann-Curtius and Silke Wenk (eds), *Mythen von Autoschaft und Weiblichkeit im 20. Jahrhundert* (Marburg: Jonas, 1997).

94 Interview with Irmeline Lebeer in *L'Art au corps*, p. 348.
95 Interview with Effie Stephano in *Art and Artist*, April 1973, p. 21.
96 Interview with Irmeline Lebeer in *L'Art au corps*, p. 347.
97 See her statements in the interviews with Leeber, p. 375, and Stephano, p. 24.
98 Interview with Irmeline Lebeer in *L'Art au corps*, p. 349.
99 M. Abramović, 'Biography', in *Marina Abramović: Artist Body. Performances 1969–1998* (Milan: Charta, 1998), p. 390.
100 See Abramović's interview with Johan Pijnappel, in L. Wijers and J. Pijnappel, *Art Meets Science and Spirituality*, special issue of *Art & Design* 6:5/6 (London: Academy Editions, 1990), pp. 54–63, here p. 59.
101 Abramović in an interview with Thomas McEville, 'States of Energy: Performance Art Ground Zero', in *Marina Abramović: Artist Body*, p. 15. In an interview with Helena Kontová, conducted in Milan, in October 1977, she expressed the idea thus: 'We, who live in cities, protected by clothes, houses, bath with warm water, are in fact protected by everything which makes a confrontation with nature almost impossible.' *Flash Art*, 80–1 (February–April 1978), pp. 43–4, here p. 44.
102 She heard about these early pioneers of Body Art, but while living in Yugoslavia she could not experience their work at first hand. See her interviews with Nick Kaye in his *Art into Theatre: Performance Interviews and Documents* (Amsterdam: Harwood, 1996), p. 182, and Hans Ulrich Obrist in *Marina Abramović: Artist Body*, pp. 43–4.
103 Abramović in an interview with Thomas McEville, in *Marina Abramović: Artist Body*, p. 16.
104 Abramović in an interview with Nick Kaye in *Art into Theatre*, p. 185. She expressed some similar ideas in an interview with *Flash Art*, where she stated that with her performances in the early 1970s she had reached a point near to self-destruction: 'If I hadn't met Ulay, they would have destroyed my body. . . . My body couldn't take it any more. I was really at the end. If I hadn't stopped, I wouldn't be here any more. Now with Ulay my work is more constructive in an optimistic way. . . . We're a man-and-woman. I am half, he is half and together we are one. And one can do more than half.' *Flash Art* 80/81 (February– April 1978), pp. 43–4, here p. 43.
105 A brief glimpse into their private life is given in the interview with Paul Kokke in *Ulay/Abramović: Performances 1976–1988*, exhibition catalogue (Eindhoven: Stedelijk Van Abbemuseum, 1997), pp. 117–24.
106 *Marina Abramović: Artist Body*, p. 258.
107 *Marina Abramović: Artist Body*, p. 410.
108 Marina Abramović in an interview with Johan Pijnappel, in Wijers and Pijnappel, *Art Meets Science and Spirituality*, pp. 54-63, here p. 61.
109 *Marina Abramović: Objects, Performance, Video, Sound*, exhibition catalogue, ed. Chrissie Iles (Oxford: Museum of Modern Art, 1995), p. 15.
110 *Marina Abramović: Artist Body*, p. 410.

111   Ilse Kuijkens, 'Catching the Moment: an Interview with Marina Abramović, *Theaterschrift 3: Border Violations* (March 1993), pp. 104–21, here p. 106.

112   Interview with Hans Ulrich Obrist in *Marina Abramović: Artist Body*, p. 46.

113   See Paul Kokke's interview with Abramović and Ulay in *Ulay/Abramović: Performances 1976–1988*, p. 120.

114   Interview with Nick Kaye in 1983, in *Art into Theatre*, pp. 179–92, here p. 189.

115   Abramović in an interview with Bernard Goy, Paris, June 1990, *Journal of Contemporary Art* 3:2 (Spring/Summer 1990), pp. 47–54, here p. 48.

116   She describes some of the transformational effects in each performance in her interview with Elisabeth Jappe, *Performance, Ritual, Prozeß: Handbuch der Aktionskunst in Europa* (Munich: Prestel, 1993), pp. 141–2; and how the accumulative effect of her performances changed her life, in *Marina Abramović: Artist Body*, p. 413.

117   Interview with Thomas McEvilley in *Marina Abramović: Artist Body*, p. 18.

118   *Ulay/Abramović: Performances 1976–1988*, p. 123.

119   *Ulay/Abramović: Performances 1976–1988*, p. 120.

120   *Ulay/Abramović: Performances 1976–1988*, p. 122.

121   See her conversation with Velimir Abramović in *Marina Abramović: Artist Body*, p. 409.

Notes to Chapter 6: Video and Multi-media Performance

1   See Michael Shamberg, *Guerrilla Television* (New York: Holt, Rinehart and Winston, 1971), and Deirdre Boyle, *Subject to Change: Guerrilla Television Revisited* (New York: Oxford University Press, 1997).

2   The international broadcast channel Music Television was founded in 1981 as a joint venture between Warner Communications (which included Warner Bros Records) and American Express to feature music videos. It operated as a cable/satellite company in the United States, Latin America, Asia and Europe and defined the 'look' of music for a whole generation.

3   For a wider discussion of these definitional quandaries see Johannes Birringer, 'Video Art/Performance: a Border Theory', *Performing Arts Journal* 13:3 (September 1991); and Ann-Marie Duguet, 'Does Interactivity Lead to New Definitions in Art?', in Hans Peter Schwarz and Jeffery Shaw (eds), *Media Art Perspectives: The Digital Challenge – Museums and Art Sciences Respond* (Ostfildern: Cantz, 1966), pp. 146–50.

4   Several surveys have dealt with this phenomenon: *Time/Space/Performance/Installation*, exhibition catalogue (Dublin: Project Arts Centre, 1978); Andrew Benjamin (ed.), *Installation Art*, special issue of *Art and Design* 30 (London: Academy, 1993); Nicolas de Oliveira, *Installation Art* (London: Thames and Hudson, 1994); Barbara London (ed.), *Video Spaces: Eight Installations* (New York: Museum of Modern Art, 1995); Hugh Marlais

Davies (ed.), *Blurring the Boundaries: Installation Art, 1969–1996*, exhibition catalogue (San Diego: Museum of Contemporary Art, 1996); Nicky Childs and Jeni Walwin (eds), *A Split Second of Paradise: Live Art, Installations and Performance* (London: River Oram Press, 1998); Julie H. Reiss, *From Margin to Center: The Spaces of Installation Art* (Cambridge, MA: MIT Press, 1999); Erika Suderburg (ed.), *Space, Site, Intervention: Situating Installation Art* (Minneapolis, MN: University of Minnesota Press, 2000).

5 A detailed description of the installation can be found in *Gary Hill*, exhibition catalogue (Amsterdam: Stedelijk Museum, 1993), pp. 98–108.

6 Annette Hünnekens, *Der bewegte Betrachter: Theorien der interaktiven Medienkunst* (Cologue: Wienand, 1997), p. 117.

7 In *The Wise Man* (1923), Eisenstein presented his concept of a Montage of Attractions and incorporated a brief film montage specially shot for the production, entitled 'Glumov's Diary'. See Edward Braun, 'Futurism in the Russian Theatre, 1913–1923', in Günter Berghaus (ed.), *International Futurism in Arts and Literature* (Berlin: DeGryter, 2000), pp. 75-99, here pp. 94–9.

8 Piscator's productions of *Sturmflut* (1926), *Gewitter über Gottland* (1927), *Hoppla wir leben* (1927), *Rasputin* (1927), *Schweijk* (1927) and *Der Kaufmann von Berlin* (1929) have been described in John Willett, *The Theatre of Erwin Piscator* (London: Eyre Methuen, 1978); and Knut Boeser and Renata Vatková (eds), *Erwin Piscator: Eine Arbeitsbiographie*, vol. 1 (Berlin: Hentrich, Frölich & Kaufmann, 1986).

9 See the manifesto *Il teatro aeroradiotelevisivo* (April 1931), trans. Günter Berghaus (ed.), *F. T. Marinetti: Critical Writings* (New York: Farrar, Straus & Giroux, 2005).

10 Vito Acconci, interview in special issue of *Profile* (Chicago) 4:3–4 (Summer 1984), p. 16.

11 V. Acconci, 'Steps into Performance (and out)', in A. A. Bronson and Peggy Gale (eds), *Performance by Artists* (Toronto: Art Metropole, 1979), p. 30. See also 'Some Notes on Film (Performance as Concentration', no. 4: 'Film as Chamber', in *Interfunktionen* 8 (January 1972), p. 26.

12 Acconci, 'Steps into Performance (and out)', p. 34.

13 N. J. Paik, 'Meine Projekte für 1966 bis 1967', *Niederschriften eines Kulturnomaden: Aphorismen, Briefe, Texte*, ed. Edith Decker (Cologne: DuMont, 1992), p. 117.

14 Paik in an interview with Paul Schimmel, *Arts Magazine* 49:4 (December 1974), pp. 52–3, here p. 53.

15 N. J. Paik, 'Projects for Electronic Television' (1965), in *Videa 'n' Videology 1959–1973*, exhibition catalogue, ed. Judson Rosebud (Syracuse, NY: Everson Museum of Art, 1974), p. 11, and *Niederschriften eines Kulturnomaden*, p. 113.

16 Wulf Herzogenrath, *Nam June Paik: Fluxus, Video* (Munich: Schreiber, 1983), p. 79.

17   N. J. Paik, 'Video Synthesizer Plus', *Radical Software* 1:2 (Fall 1970), p. 25; reprinted in *Videa 'n' Videology*, p. 59, and *Niederschriften eines Kulturnomaden*, pp. 130–1.

18   Untitled essay in *Sonsbeek 71*, exhibition catalogue, ed. Loorje Kapteyn (Arnheim: Sonsbeek, 1971); reprinted in *Videa 'n' Videology*, p. 62, and Herzogenrath, *Nam June Paik: Fluxus, Video*, p. 147.

19   N. J. Paik, 'Vision and Television' (1970), in *Videa 'n' Videology*, p. 59. As this catalogue is unpaginated, I count pages starting with the Foreword as p. 1.

20   Calvin Tomkins, 'Profiles: Video Visionary – Nam June Paik', *New Yorker* 51:11 (5 May 1975), pp. 44–79, here p. 77.

21   N. J. Paik, 'TV Bra for Living Sculpture', Programme of performance at Howard Wise Gallery, New York, 1969, reprinted in *Videa 'n' Videology*, p. 47

22   N. J. Paik in an interview with Paul Schimmel, *Arts Magazine* 49:4 (December 1974), pp. 52–3, here p. 52.

23   K. O. Goetz, 'Gemaltes Bild – Kinetisches Bild', *Blätter und Bilder* 5 (1959), pp. 45–7, here p. 47. Paik acknowledged the inspiration he received from Goetz in the flyer for the Galerie Parnass exhibition, later published in *dé-Coll/age* 3 (December 1963) and *Videa 'n' Videology*, p. 90, and 'Electronic TV & Color TV Experiment', invitation to a show at the New School for Social Research in New York, January 1965, reprinted in *Videa 'n' Videology*, p. 8. See also Edith Decker, *Paik Video* (Cologne: DuMont, 1988; English edn, New York, Barrytown, 1997), pp. 21 and 38, and Herzogenrath, *Nam June Paik: Fluxus, Video*, p. 46.

24   N. J. Paik, in an interview with Jud Yalkut, 'Art and Technology of Nam June Paik', *Arts Magazine* 42:6 (April 1968), pp. 50–1, here p. 51.

25   Tomkins, 'Profiles: Video Visionary – Nam June Paik', p. 45.

26   Tomkins, 'Profiles: Video Visionary – Nam June Paik', p. 46.

27   N. J. Paik, 'New Projects' (1973), in *Videa 'n' Videology*, p. 79–81, here p. 79.

28   For a general introduction to Paik's installations see John J. Hanhardt, 'Paik's Video Sculptures', in *Nam June Paik*, Whitney catalogue 1982, pp. 91–100; 'Die Video Installationen', in Decker, *Paik Video*, pp. 60–120. The Wuppertal exhibition was documented in *Videa 'n' Videology*, pp. 4–6; *Nam June Paik: Werke 1946–1976*, pp. 67–92; Decker, *Paik Video*, pp. 31–9; *The Worlds of Nam June Paik*, pp. 42–52; Herzogenrath, *Nam June Paik: Fluxus, Video*, pp. 60–77. Paik's reflections on the exhibition can also be found in *Niederschriften eines Kulturnomaden*, pp. 100–9.

29   Tomas Schmit, 'Exposition of Music', *Nam June Paik: Werke 1946–1976*, pp. 67–73, here p. 69.

30   See *The Worlds of Nam June Paik*, exhibition catalogue, ed John Hanham (New York: Guggenheim Museum, 2000), p. 41.

31   N. J. Paik, 'Über die Ausstellung der Musik', *Dé-coll/age* no. 3 (December 1962), reprinted in *Niederschriften eines Kulturnomaden*, pp. 100–2, here p. 100.

32 Paik, 'Über die Ausstellung der Musik', p. 102.

33 See N. J. Paik, 'Afterlude to the Exposition of Experimental Television', *Fluxus cc fiVe ThReE*, June 1964, reprinted in *Videa 'n' Videology*, pp. 5–6, and *Niederschriften eines Kulturnomaden*, pp. 103–9.

34 See Herzogenrath, *Nam June Paik: Fluxus, Video*, pp. 54–7; and Decker, *Paik Video*, pp. 60–6.

35 N. J. Paik, 'Electronic Art', in *Electronic Art*, exhibition catalogue (New York: Gallery Bonino, 1965); reprinted in *Videa 'n' Videology*, p. 13.

36 N. J. Paik, 'Video Synthesizer Plus', in *Radical Software* 1:2 (1970); reprinted in *Videa 'n' Videology*, p. 59, and *Niederschriften eines Kulturnomaden*, pp. 130–1.

37 Tomkins, 'Profiles: Video Visionary – Nam June Paik', p. 79.

38 The anecdote is reported in David Ross, 'Truth or Consequences: American Television and Video Art', in John G. Hanhardt (ed.), *Video Culture: A Critical Investigation* (New York: Smith, 1986), pp. 167–78, here pp. 173–4.

39 N. J. Paik, 'Utopian Laser TV Station' (1965), in Dick Higgins (ed.), *Manifestos* (New York. Something Else Press, 1966), p. 25, reprinted in *Videa 'n' Videology*, p. 17.

40 See N. J. Paik, 'Expanded Education for the Paper-less Society', *Magazine of the Institute of Contemporary Arts* 6 (September 1968), and *Interfunktionen* 7 (September 1971); reprinted in *Videa 'n' Videology*, pp. 31–9 and Herzogenrath, *Nam June Paik: Fluxus, Video*, pp. 148–9.

41 Only a few of these are available in the collections *Videa 'n' Videology* and *Niederschriften eines Kulturnomaden*. For a complete list, see Herzogenrath, *Nam June Paik: Fluxus, Video*, pp. 348–50

42 'Nam June Paik: an Interview by Nicholas Zurbrugg, Sydney, 10th and 13th April 1990', *Lund Art Press* 2:2 (1991), pp. 131–9, here p. 131.

43 Leigh Landy and Antje von Graevenitz, ' "I Make Technology Ridiculous": The Unusual Dialectics of Nam June Paik', *Avant Garde* 7 (1992), pp. 93–4.

44 On her early performances see Douglas Crimp, 'Joan Jonas's Performance Works', *Studio International* 192:982 (July/August 1976), pp. 10–12 and Joan Jonas, 'Seven Years', *The Drama Review* 19:1 (T65) March 1975), pp. 13–17.

45 Jorge Luis Borges, 'La biblioteca de Babel' first appeared in the collections of short stories *El jardín de senderos que se bifurcan* (Buenos Aires: Sur, 1941), and *Ficciones* (Buenos Aires: Sur, 1944).

46 See Jonas's interview with Nick Kaye, 'Mask, Role and Narrative', in *Performance* 65–6 (Spring 1992), pp. 49–59, here p. 50; and the essays by Howard Junker, 'Joan Jonas: The Mirror Staged', and Anja Zimmermann, 'The (Im)Mobile Trap of the Reflecting Surface: Self-Construction and Image Construction in the Work of Joan Jonas', in *Joan Jonas: Performances, Video, Installations 1968–2000*, exhibition catalogue (Stuttgart: Galerie der Stadt Stuttgart, 2000–1; Stuttgart: Hatje Cantz, 2000), pp. 97–103.

47 Artist's statement in *Joan Jonas: Performance, Video, Installation 1968–2000*, p. 70. See also her comments in *Art and Artist* 8:7 (October 1973), p. 15.

48   Rosalind Krauss, 'Video: the Aesthetics of Narcissism', *October* 1 (Spring 1976), pp. 51–64, and reprinted in many anthologies.

49   Joan Jonas in an interview with Nick Kaye, 'Mask, Role and Narrative', p. 53.

50   Joan Jonas in an interview with Joan Simon in *Art in America* 83:7 (July 1995), pp. 72–9, 100–1, here p. 76; reprinted in *Joan Jonas: Performance, Video, Installation 1968–2000*, pp. 25–35, here p. 28.

51   *Joan Jonas: Performance, Video, Installation 1968–2000*, p. 108.

52   See Noel Carroll, 'Joan Jonas: Making the Image Visible', *Artforum* 12:8 (April 1974), pp. 52–3.

53   Joan Jonas in an interview with Joan Simon, in *Art in America*, 83:7 (July 1995), p. 100; *Joan Jonas: Performance, Video, Installation 1968–2000*, p. 34.

54   Valie, or Wally, is a common short form for Waltraud; Export was the name of a popular cigarette brand in Austria.

55   See the interviews with Danièle Roussel in D. Roussel, *Der Wiener Aktionismus und die Österreicher: Gespräche* (Klagenfurt: Ritter, 1995) pp. 117–22 and with Anita Prammer in A. Prammere, *Valie Export: Eine multimediale Künstlerin* (Vienna: Wiener Frauenverlag, 1988), p. 97.

56   See 'Mediale Anagramme: Valie Export im Gespräch mit Sara Rogenhoffer und Florian Rötzer', *Kunstforum International* 97 (November–December 1988), p. 159.

57   Interview in Roussel, *Der Wiener Aktionismus und die Österreicher*, p. 120.

58   By presenting the work herself in a street environment, Export achieved an entirely different reaction from that to Yves Klein's *Tactile Sculture* (exhibited on 14 January 1961 at the Museum Haus Lange in Krefeld), which consisted of a cube with four ruche-covered holes and a nude woman inside.

59   V. Export, 'Aspects of Feminist Actionism', *New German Critique* 47 (Spring–Summer 1989), pp. 69–92, here p. 71. See also her reflections on the Action in 'tapp & tast kino etc.', *Neues Forum* 20: 234–5 (June–July 1973), p. 57.

60   V. Export, 'Medial Anagrams: a Lecture Based on Ideas and Images. Early Works', in *White Cube/Black Box*, exhibition catalogue, ed. Sabine Breitwieser (Vienna: EA-Generali Foundation, 1996), pp. 99–127, here p. 107.

61   In a text published on the occasion, she referred to her performance as a 'paramilitary action' and 'art that understands itself as war' ('war art riot', 'krieg kunst aufruhr', 'kriegskunst kunstkrieg'). See Pteer Weibel and Vali Export (eds), *Wien: Bildkompendium Wiener Aktionismus und Film*, (Frankfurt-am-Main: Kohlkunstverlag, 1970), p. 266.

62   V. Export, 'Expanded Cinema as Expanded Reality', *JAM* 1:4 (July 1991), p. 7; quoted in Roswitha Mueller, *Valie Export: Fragments of the Imagination* (Bloomington, IN: Indiana University Press, 1994), p. 31

63   'Tapp & tast kino etc.', p. 57. See also her manifesto 'Woman's Art', in *Neues Forum* 20:228 (January 1973), p. 47, where she defines this 'social

reality' as a 'male reality' that needs to be transformed into 'a human reality'. She understands her art to be a contribution towards this aim.

64   V. Export, 'Vorwort', in Silvia Eiblmayr, Valie Export, and Monika Prischl-Maier (eds), *Kunst mit Eigen-Sinn: Aktuelle Kunst von Frauen. Texte und Dokumentation*, exhibition catalogue (Vienna: Museum Moderner Kunst/Museum des 20. Jahrhunderts, 1985; Vienna: Löcker, 1985), pp. 7–8, here p. 7.

65   See Kristine Stiles' essay in *Valie Export: Ob/De+Con(Struction)* (Philadelphia, PA: Goldie Paley Gallery at Moore College of Art and Design, 2001), p. 23.

66   V. Export, 'The Real and Its Double: The Body', *Discourse: Journal for Theoretical Studies in Media and Culture* 11 (Fall–Winter 1988–9), pp. 3–27, here pp. 4–5.

67   Artist's statement in 'Film und Videos von Valie Export', *White Cube/Black Box*, p. 345. This text refers to Mircea Eliade's chapter 'The Bridge and the 'Difficult Passage' in his classic volume on *Shamanism: Archaic Techniques of Ecstasy*, trans. W. R. Trask (New York: Pantheon Books, 1964), in which the passage through a narrow and dangerous conduit is described as a common element of initiation rites.

68   Export Personal Archive, quoted in Mueller, *Valie Export*, p. 36. The German text can be found in Andrea Zell, *Valie Export: Inszemierung von Schmerz. Selbstverletzung in den frühen Aktionen* (Berlin: Reimer, 2000), p. 140.

69   *Body Sign Action*, of 2 July 1970 in Frankfurt-am-Main, worked with the analogue 'parchment–skin' and presented the human body as if inscribed like a book. The photograph of the tattoo and a related text ('The human being as codex. The human being as carrier of signals and information') was published in *Die Schastrommel* 7 (April 1972), s.p.

70   Export Personal Archive, quoted in Mueller, *Valie Export*, p. 36. The German text can be found in Zell, *Valie Export*, p. 141.

71   V. Export, Statement, in Bernhard Bürgi (ed.), *Körperzeichen Österreich*, exhibition catalogue (Winterthur: Kunstmuseum, 1982), p. 74.

72   V. Export, 'I (BEAT – it –) PERFORMANCE', in Bronson and Gale, *Performance by Artists*, pp. 260–3, here p. 261.

73   *Valie Export: Ob/De+Con(Struction)*, p. 40.

74   See *Laurie Anderson: Works from 1969 to 1983*, exhibition catalogue, ed. Janet Kardon (Philadelphia, PA: Institute of Contemporary Art, University of Pennysylvania, 1983); Roselee Goldberg, *Laurie Anderson* (New York: Abrams, 2000); and the interview with William Duckworth in *Talking Music* (New York: Schirmer, 1995), pp. 368–85.

75   See Kim Levin, 'O Superwoman', *The Village Voice*, 24 July 1984; reprinted in Kim Levin, *Beyond Modernism* (New York: Harper & Row, 1988), pp. 187–9.

76   Janet Kardon, 'Laurie Anderson: A Synesthesic Journey', in *Laurie Anderson: Works from 1969 to 1983*, pp. 6–31, here p. 7.

77   See 'Laurie Anderson: Interview by Robin White at Crown Point Press, Oakland, California, 1979', *View* 2:8 (January 1980), p. 13; Goldberg, *Laurie Anderson*, p. 37.

78   See Vito Acconci (ed.), *Street Works*, supplement to *0 to 9*, issue no. 6 (July 1969); and my analyses above, Chapter 5.

79   See Goldberg, *Laurie Anderson*, p. 40.

80   See Mel Gordon, 'Laurie Anderson: Performance Artist', *Drama Review* 24:2 (T86) (June 1980), pp. 51–64.

81   See Laurie Anderson, 'For Instants – Part 3', *Studio International* 192:982 (July–August 1976), pp. 20–1, and 'For Instants – Part 4: Songs'; 'For Instants – Part 5', *documenta 6*, vol. 1 (Kassel, 1977), p. 286. Anderson performed various instalments of the 12-part series between 1975 and 1978.

82   See Laurie Anderson, 'Notes from "Like a Stream" ', in Bronson and Gale, *Performance by Artists*, pp. 42–8.

83   In fact, there was a preview of the show on 1 December 1978 at the Nova Convention at the Entermedia Theater in New York. After the Carnegie Hall performance on 11 February 1989 it went to The Kitchen (13–14 April 1979) and then toured Europe and the Americas.

84   John Howell, 'Laurie Anderson', *Artforum* 21:10 (June 1983), pp. 79–80. However, when Phil Smith interviewed her on the show, Anderson maintained: 'Early on the music was almost background and now it has become more important, although the most important thing is the words.' Philip Smith, 'A Laurie Anderson Story', *Arts Magazine* (New York) 57:5 (January 1983), pp. 60–1, here p. 61.

85   L. Anderson, quoted in Roger Copeland, 'Laurie in Wonderland: Anderson's "Altered Egos" Confront Culture in the Age of High Technology', *Theater Communications* 5:4 (April 1983), pp. 14–17, here p. 15.

86   Jack Kroll, 'An Electronic Cassandra', *Newsweek*, 21 February 1983, p. 77.

87   For a detailed analysis of her use of language see Jessia Prinz, ' "Always Two Things Switching": Laurie Anderson's Alterity', in Marjorie Perloff (ed.), *Postmodern Genres* (Norman, OK: University of Oklahoma Press, 1988).

88   Sean Cubitt, 'Laurie Anderson, Myth, Management, and Platitude', in John Roberts (ed.), *Art Has No History* (London: Verso, 1994), p. 286

89   I disagree here with Stephen Melville's concept of synthesis, largely derived from Wagner's *Gesamtkunstwerk* and ignoring Kandinsky's alternative proposal, which is more applicable to Anderson's work as it is much more than a sprawling accumulation of unrelated vignettes. See his essay, 'Between Art and Criticism: Mapping the Frame in *United States*', *Theatre Journal* 37 (1985), pp 31–43, here p. 35.

90   Milo Miles, 'The Romance of Robots: Laurie Anderson Re-creates America', *Boston Phoenix*, 22 March 1983.

91   Laurie Anderson, quoted in *Performance Art 2* (New York: Performing Arts Journal, 1979), p. 16.

92   L. Anderson, quoted in Michael Walsh, 'Post-Punk Apocalypse', *Time*, 21 February 1983, p. 68.

93   L. Anderson, *United States* (New York: Harper & Row, 1984), s.p.

94   See John Mueller (ed.), *Dance Film Directory: An Annotated and Evaluative Guide to Film on Ballet and Modern Dance* (Princeton, NJ: Princeton Book Co., 1979); and Jane Pritchard, 'Movement on the Silent Screen', *Dance Theatre Journal* 12:3 (Winter 1995/96), pp. 26–30.

95   See Richard Lorber, 'Experiments in Videodance', *Dance Scope* 12:1 (Fall–Winter 1977–8), pp. 13–16; David Vaughan, 'Locale: the Collaboration of Merce Cunningham and Charles Atlas', in Richard Kostelanetz (ed.), *Merce Cunningham: Dancing in Space and Time* (Pennington, NJ: A Cappella, 1992), pp. 151–5; Nancy F. Becker, 'Filming Cunningham Dance: A Conversation with Charles Atlas', *Dance Theatre Journal* 1:1 (1983), pp. 22–5; Cunningham, *The Dancer and the Dance: Merce Cunningham in Conversation with Jacqueline Lesschawe* (London: Boyard, 1985), pp. 190–2; Peter Z. Grossman, 'Talking with Merce Cunningham about Video', *Dance Scope* 13:2–3 (Winter–Spring 1979), pp. 56–8. For a complete list and a summary description of the videos see the company's website at http://merce.org.80/filmvideo.html.

96   See Sherril Dodds, *Dance on Screen: Genres and Media from Hollywood to Experimental Art* (Basingstoke: Palgrave, 2001), p. 145. A choreographer could only hope to reach similar audience ratings if s/he created dance sequences for a pop video of a major music star. On the 1980s series on British television see also Sarah Rubidge, 'Recent Dance Made for Television', in Stephanie Jordan and David Allen (eds), *Parallel Lines: Media Representations of Dance* (London: Libbey, 1993), pp. 185–215.

97   See Claudia Rosiny, *Videotanz: Panorama einer intermedialen Kunstform* (Zurich: Chronos, 1999), pp. 87–93.

98   See Paul Le Vasseur, 'Computer Dance: the Role of the Computer', *Impulse: The Annual of Contemporary Dance* (San Francisco), 1965, pp. 25–7; Jeanne Hays Beaman, 'Computer Dance: Implications of the Dance', *Impulse: The Annual of Contemporary Dance*, 1965, pp. 27–8.

99   See Jasia Reichardt (ed.), *Cybernetic Serendipity: The Computer and the Arts*, 2nd rev. edn (London: Studio International, 1968), p. 33.

100   See A. William Smith, 'A Dance Historian Looks at Computers and their Applications for the Art of Dancing and Dance Education', in A. W. Smith (ed.), *Dance and Technology I: Moving Toward the Future* (Westerville, OH: Fullhouse, 1992), pp. 52–9.

101   Some earlier attempts, by Michael Noll in 1966 and by Carol Withrow in 1969, have been described by Smith, 'A Dance Historian Looks at Computers', pp. 55–7.

102   The programme is described on http://fas.sfu.ca/uilo/publications/rp/evolv.htm and its commercial distributor, http://www.credo-interactive.com/. Thecla Schiphorst, who worked with the programme in the Merce

Cunningham Dance Company, described it in '*LifeForms*: Design Tools for Choreography', in Smith, *Dance and Technology I*, pp. 46–52. There is also a webpage dedicated to it under www.merce.org. Other useful descriptions of the programme can be found in Max Wyman, 'Computer Program Aids Dance Makers', *Dance Magazine* 65:3 (March 1991), pp. 12–13; Anne Pierce, 'Cunningham at the Computer', *Dance/USA Journal* 9:1 (Summer 1991), pp. 14–15; Max Wyman, 'This Computer Loves to Dance', *New York Times*, 27 June 1993, sect. 2, p. 24; Thecla Schiphorst, 'Merce Cunningham: Making Dance with the Computer', *Choreography and Dance* 4:3 (1997), pp. 79–98.

103   For a detailed description of the performance see Gordon Munna, 'Technology in the Modern Arts: Music & Theatre', *Chelsea* 20–1 (1967), pp. 99–105; Merce Cunningham's description in 'Choreography and the Dance', in Stanley Rosner and Lawrence E. Abt (eds), *The Creative Explosion* (New York: Grossman, 1970), 175–86, here pp. 184–5, and the comments in Michael Nyman, *Experimental Music: Cage and Beyond* (New York: Schirmer, 1974), pp. 82–3.

104   Information on their works and those of other artists working at the cutting edge of art and electronic technologies can be accessed at websites such as www.ntticc.or.jp, http://art.net/~dtz, http://dpa.ntu.ac.uk.

105   See Douglas Cooper, 'Very Nervous System', *Wired Magazine* 3:3 (March 1995), pp. 134, 170.

106   See Robert Rowe, *Interactive Music Systems* (Cambridge, MA: MIT Press, 1993).

107   See Todd Winkler, 'Making Motion Musical: Gesture Mapping Strategies for Interactive Computer Music', *Proceedings of the International Computer Music Conference (ICMC '95: The Banff Centre for the Arts)* (San Francisco: International Computer Music Association, 1995), pp. 261–4; Todd Winkler, 'Motion-sensing Music: Artistic and Technical Challenges in Two Works for Dance', *Proceedings of the International Computer Music Conference* (San Francisco: International Computer Music Association, 1998), pp. 471–4; Todd Winkler, *Composing Interactive Music: Techniques and Ideas Using Max* (Cambridge, MA: MIT Press, 1998).

108   My description is taken from Stegell's website www.notam02.no/~amandajs/what.html. By 1999, the piece had been performed nine times.

109   See Yacov Sharir, 'Im Sturzflug durch die Simulation', *Ballet International/Tanz aktuell*, August 1997, pp. 28–9.

110   Yacov Sharir, 'Virtually Dancing', available at Dance and Technology Zone, art.net/~dtz/links. An earlier version of the essay appeared in Mary Anne Moser and Douglas MacLeod (eds), *Immersed in Technology: Art and Virtual Environments* (Cambridge, MA: MIT Press, 1996), pp. 283–5. See also Diana Gromala, 'Pain and Subjectivity in Virtual Reality', in Lynn Hershman-Leeson (ed.), *Clicking In: Hot Links to a Digital Culture* (Seattle, WA: Bay Press, 1996), pp. 222–37.

Notes to Chapter 7: Performances in Cyberspace

1 The statistics of the Internet Software Consortium (www.isc.org/) indicate a growth from a few hundred thousand hosts in 1992 to 5 million in 1995, 36 million in 1998 and over 100 million in 2000.

2 Heinrich Klotz (ed.), *Kunst der Gegenwart: Museum für Neue Kunst*, exhibition catalogue (Karlsruhe: ZKM/Zentrum für Kunst und Medientechnologie, 1997; Munich: Prestel, 1997), p. 10.

3 Gerhard Johann Lischka, 'Media Art', in Gottfried Hattinger et al. (eds), *Ars Electronica: Festival für Kunst, Technologie und Gesellschaft, Linz 1986* (Linz: Linzer Veranstaltungsgesellschaft, 1986), pp. 16–17, here p. 17.

4 For a discussion of some of the interactive strategies of the 1980s, see Ann-Sargent Wooster, 'Reach Out and Touch Someone: the Romance of Interactivity', in Doug Hall and Sally Jo Fifer (eds), *Illuminating Video* (New York: Aperture, 1990), pp. 275–303; and David Rokeby, 'Transforming Mirrors: Subjectivity and Control in Interactive Media', in Simon Penny, *Critical Issues in Electronic Media* (Albany, NY: State University of New York Press, 1995), pp. 133–58.

5 David Z. Saltz, 'The Art of Interaction': Interactivity, Performativity and Computers', *Journal of Aesthetics and Art Criticism* 56:2 (Spring 1977), p. 120.

6 Roy Ascott, 'The Art of Intelligent Systems', Hannes Leopoldseder (ed.), *Der Prix ars electronica 1991* (Linz: Veritas, 1991), pp. 25–34, here p. 25.

7 For a discussion of the complex relationship between museums and a techno-art which no longer obeys the traditional aesthetic categories see Peter Weibel, 'Transformation der Techno-Ästhetik', in Florian Rötzer (ed.), *Digitaler Schein: Ästhetik der elektronischen Medien* (Frankfurt-am-Main: Suhrkamp, 1991), pp. 205–46.

8 See, for example, Mark Reaney, 'The Theatre of Virtual Reality' and 'Virtual Scenography', in *Theatre Design and Technology* 29:2 (Spring 1993); 32:1 (Winter 1996); Stephen A. Schrum (ed.), *Theatre in Cyberspace: Issues of Teaching, Acting, and Directing* (New York: Lang, 1999); David Z. Saltz, 'Live Media: Interactive Technology and Theatre', *Theatre Topics* 11:2 (September 2001), pp. 107–30.

9 See Claudio Pinhanez, 'Computer Theatre' (MIT Media Laboratory Perceptual Computing Science, 1996, and Claudio Pinhanez and Aaron Bobick, 'Using Computer Vision to Control a Reactive Computer Graphics Character in a Theater Play', in H. I. Christensen (ed.), *Computer Vision Systems* (Berlin: Springer, 1999). The state of research described above is poised to change dramatically in the first decade of the twenty-first century. While writing this chapter, focused on developments in the 1990s, I received information of new centres concerned with the study of cybernetic performances at MIT; Arizona State University; Ohio State University; University of Madison, Wisconsin; University of Texas, Austin; Simon Fraser University; Banff New Media Institute; ZKM Karlsruhe; and IRCAM Paris, to name but a few.

10   Eduardo Kac, 'On the Notion of Art in Visual Dialogue', in Karen O'Rourke (ed.), *Art-réseaux* (Paris: Centre d'Études et de Recherches en Arts Plastiques, 1992), pp. 20–1, here p. 21.

11   Simon Penny, 'Realities of the Virtual', in Hans Peter Schwarz and Jeffry Shaw (eds), *Media Art Perspectives: The Digital Challenge – Museums and Art Sciences Respond* (Ostfildern: Cantz, 1996), pp. 127–34, here pp. 130 and 132.

12   Charles Baudelaire, 'Salon de 1859', ch. 2: 'Le Public moderne et la photographie', in *Œuvres complètes* (Paris: Gallimard, 1961), p. 1034.

13   See the report by Stephen Jones, 'Towards a Philosophy of Virtual Reality: Issues Implicit in "Consciousness Reframed"', *Leonardo* 33 (2000), pp. 152–32.

14   'Jaron Lanier Interview', in Lynn Hershman-Leeson (ed.), *Clicking In: Hot Links to a Digital Culture* (Seattle, WA: Bay Press, 1996), pp. 43–53, here p. 45.

15   Tim Jordan, *Cyberpower: The Culture and Politics of Cyberspace and the Internet* (London: Routledge, 1999), p. 62.

16   See Steven Levy, *Hackers: Heroes of the Computer Revolution*, (Garden City, NY: Anchor Press, Doubleday, 1984), pp. 9–10. As Levy rightly emphasized, altering the mammoth programmes and functions of an IBM 704 or TX-0 'gave you not only an understanding of the system but an addictive control as well, along with the illusion that total control was just a few features away' (p. 61). This, of course, became a key motive for video game enthusiasts in the 1980s and 1990s.

17   See Leslie Haddon, 'Electronic and Computer Games', *Screen* 29:2 (Spring 1988), and Stephen D. Bristow, 'The History of Video Games', *IEEE Transactions on Consumer Electronics* (February 1977), pp. 58–68.

18   Figures are taken from Eugene Provenzo, *Video Kids: Making Sense of Nintendo* (Cambridge, MA: Harvard University Press, 1991), p. 10; and *Electronic Data Market Book* (Arlington, VA: Electronic Industries Alliance, 1998), p. 31.

19   Provenzo, *Video Kids*, pp. 11–13.

20   See Gillian Skirrow, 'Hellivision: an Analysis of Video Games', in M. Alvarado and J. O. Thompson (eds), *The Media Reader* (London: British Film Institute, 1990), p. 323.

21   Skirrow, 'Hellivision', p. 326.

22   Figures are taken from Provenzo, *Video Kids*, pp. 31–2.

23   Gary W. Selnow, 'Playing Videogames: the Electronic Friend', *Journal of Communication* 34:2 (Spring 1984), p. 153.

24   See Dave Grossman, *On Killing: The Psychological Cost of Learning to Kill in War and Society* (Boston, MA: Little, Brown, 1995).

25   Grossman, *On Killing*, pp. 304 and 310.

26   Margaret Morse, *Virtualities: Television, Media Art, and Cyberspace* (Bloomington, IN: Indiana University Press, 1998) p. 182.

27 I am much obliged to Ieuan A. Nicholas at the Virtual Reality Centre in the School of Engineering of Cardiff University for giving me a practical introduction to some of these applications.

28 Simon Penny, 'Virtual Reality as the Completion of the Enlightenment Project', in Gretchen Bender and Timothy Druckrey (eds), *Culture on the Brink: Ideologies of Technologies* (Seattle, WA: Bay Press, 1993), pp. 231–48, here p. 243.

29 N. Katherine Hayles, 'Embodied Virtualities: or How to Put Bodies Back into the Picture', in Mary Anne Moser and Douglas MacLeod (eds), *Immersed in Technology* (Cambridge, MA: MIT Press, 1996), pp. 1–28, here p. 1. See also her extensive discussion of embodied virtuality in N. Katherine Hayles, *How We Became Posthuman: Virtual Bodies in Cybernetics, Literature, and Informatics* (Chicago, IL: University of Chicago Press, 1996).

30 Jeffrey Shaw, 'Reise in virtuelle Welten', *Kunstforum International* 117 (1992), pp. 286–303, here p. 298.

31 Judith Halberstam and Ira Livingston (eds), *Posthuman Bodies* (Bloomington, IN: Indiana University Press, 1996), p. 3. See also the definitions of posthumanism in Tiziana Terranova, 'Post-Human Unbounded', in G. Robertson et al. (eds), *Future Natural: Nature, Science, Culture* (London: Routledge, 1996), and reprinted in David Bell and Barbara Kennedy (eds), *The Cyberculture Reader* (London: Routledge, 2000). Some artistic applications of the concept can be found in the exhibition catalogues *Post Human* (Lausanne: FAE Musée d'Art Contemporain, 1992) and *Le Corps mutant* (Paris: Galerie Enrico Navarra, 2000). See also Dietmar Kamper, 'Mimesis und Simulation: Von den Körpern zu den Maschinen', *Kunstforum International* 114 (July–August 1991), pp. 86–94; *Die Zukunft des Körpers I*, special issue of *Kunstforum International* 132 (November 1995–January 1996); Hayles, *How We Became Posthuman*; Ollivier Dyens, *Metal and Flesh: The Evolution of Man. Technology Takes Over* (Cambridge, MA: MIT Press, 2001).

32 See the documentation in James D. Paffrath and Stelarc (eds), *Obsolete Body/Suspensions/Stelarc* (Davis, CA: JP Publications, 1984).

33 See Cindy Carr, 'Before and After Science', *Village Voice*, 31 July 1984, pp. 77–8.

34 Interview with Stelarc in Paffrath and Stelarc, *Obsolete Body/Suspensions*, p. 16. The harness suspensions he referred to were carried out between 1970 and 1976.

35 See Fakir Musafar's homepage at www.bodyplay.com/, various articles on the subject in the journals *Body Play* and *Modern Primitives Quarterly*, and the many reports on spiritual journeys achieved by means of suspensions published under www.bmeworld.com/flesh/suspensions/private.

36 Stelarc, quoted in Paul McCarthy, 'The Body Obsolete', *High Performance* 24 (1983), p. 18.

37 Stelarc, statement dated 4 December 1977, in *Flash Art* 80–1 (February–April 1978), p. 54.

38 Stelarc, 'Electronic Voodoo', p. 112.

39 Stelarc, 'Telematic Tremors, Telematic Pleasures', p. 197.

40 Stelarc, 'Electronic Voodoo: Interview with Nicholas Zurbrugg', reprinted in Ashley Crawford and Ray Edgar (eds), *Transit Lounge: Wake-up Calls and Travelers' Tales from the Future* (North Ryde, NSW: Craftsman House, 1997), pp. 110–13, p. 111.

41 Mark Dery, *Escape Velocity: Cyberculture at the End of the Century* (London: Hodder & Stoughton, 1996), p. 159

42 Stelarc, 'The Involuntary, the Alien and the Automated: Choreographing Bodies, Robots & Phantoms', paper presented at www.stelarcova.com.au (accessed 2 May 2001).

43 The following outlines of Stelarc's performances paraphrase and summarize his own descriptions, which can be found on his website, www.stelarc.va.com.au. I would also like to express my gratitude to Nicholas Zurbrugg for providing me with several printed and videotaped interviews conducted in the 1980s and 1990s.

44 Dery, *Escape Velocity*, p. 155.

45 Stelarc, 'Parasite Visions: Alternate, Intimate and Involuntary Experiences', in Gerfried Stocker and Christine Schöpf (eds), *Ars Electronica 97 – Flesh Factor: Informationsmaschine Mensch* (Vienna: Springer, 1997), p. 152 (p. 412 in 2nd edn).

46 Stelarc, 'The Involuntary, the Alien and the Automated'.

47 A Ping is a test signal used to assess the density of Internet activity by measuring the echo times of the signal on a scale from 0 to 2,000 milliseconds.

48 Stelarc, 'Triggering an Evolutionary Dialectic', Paffrath and Stelarc, *Obsolete Body/Suspensions*, p. 52.

49 It was dated May 1910, but first published in F. T. Marinetti's *Guerra sola igiene del mondo* (1915). See F. T. Marinetti, *Teoria e invenzione futurista*, ed. L. de Maria (Milan: Mondadori, 1968), pp. 255–8, and F. T. Marinetti, *Selected Writings*, ed. R. W. Flint (London: Secker and Warburg, 1972), pp. 90–3.

50 See Günter Berghaus, 'From Futurism to Neo-Futurism: Continuities and Discontinuities in Twentieth-Century Avant-garde Performance', in Dietrich Scheunemann (ed.), *Avant-Garde/Neo-Avant-Garde* (Amsterdam: Rodopi, 2004), pp. 195–224.

Notes to Chapter 8: Epilogue

1 Interview with James Harding, in J. Harding, *The Contours of the Theatrical Avant-garde* (Ann Arbor, MI: University of Michigan Press, 2000), p. 207.

2 This was the title of a manifesto by the Futurist painter and stage designer Enrico Prampolini: *Bombardiamo le accademie* (1913), in which he expressed his opposition to the strongholds of traditionalism, entrenched conservatism and enemies of true art.

3 Hal Foster, *The Return of the Real: The Avant Garde at the End of the Century* (Cambridge, MA and London: MIT Press and October Books, 1996), p. 3.

4 Paul Mann, *The Theory Death of the Avant-Garde* (Bloomington, IN: Indiana University Press, 1991), p. 143.

5 Mann, *The Theory Death of the Avant-Garde*, p. 144.

6 Peter Bürger, *Theory of the Avant-garde*; I quote from a key passage in the American translation of 1984: 'Since now the protest of the historical avant-garde against art as institution is accepted as *art*, the gesture of protest of the neo-avant-garde becomes inauthentic. . . . The avant-garde intends the abolition of autonomous art by which it means that art is to be integrated into the praxis of life. This has not occurred, and presumably cannot occur, in bourgeois society unless it be as a false sublation of autonomous art' (Minneapolis, MN: University of Minnesota Press, 1984), pp. 53–4. This harsh judgement was already rebuked by Jochen Schulte-Sasse in his foreword to the American edition of the book, as well as by Benjamin Buchloh in his review in *Art in America* 72:10 (November 1984), pp. 10–21.

7 Foster, *The Return of the Real*, p. 14.

8 Just as Peter Bürger's *Der französische Surrealismus: Studien zum Problem der avantgardistischen Literatur* was a preliminary study for *Die Theorie der Avantgarde*, the latter paved the way for *Die Institutionen der Kunst*, written together with his wife Christa Bürger.

9 Ben Highmore, 'Avant-gardism and the Dialectic of Everyday Life', in Dietrich Scheunemann (ed.), *European Avant-garde: New Perspectives'* (Amsterdam: Rodopi, 2000), pp. 249–64, here p. 249.

Bibliography

Concepts of Modernism and of the Avant-garde
Historical Avant-garde Performance
Postwar Art and Culture, General
Postmodernism
Postwar Performance, General
Happening and Fluxus
Bodyart, Neoshamanism and Ritual Performance
Viennese Actionism
Video Art, Performance and Installation
Videodance and Cyberdance
Performance in Cyberspace

This selective bibliography is arranged in sections that correspond to chapters or sub-chapters of this volume. It contains works quoted in the notes as well as titles that may be useful for further readings. Exhibition catalogues related to individual artists have been entered under the artist's name. Catalogues on general topics are entered under the name of the editor or chief curator. A more extensive bibliography on the concept of the avant-garde and on various movements of the historical avant-garde can be found in the bibliography of my study *Theatre, Performance and the Historical Avant-garde* (Basingstoke: Palgrave Macmillan, 2005).

Concepts of Modernism and of the Avant-garde

Berman, Marshall, *All That is Solid Melts into Air: The Experience of Modernity* (New York: Schuster and Schuster, 1982).

Bradbury, Malcolm, and James McFarlane (eds), *Modernism, 1890–1930* (Harmondsworth: Penguin, 1976; 2nd rev. edn 1983).

Bürger, Peter, *Theory of the Avant-garde* (Minneapolis, MN: University of Minnesota Press, 1984).

Calinescu, Matei, *Five Faces of Modernity: Modernism, Avant-Garde, Decadence, Kitsch, Postmodernism* (Durham, NC: Duke University Press, 1987).

Eysteinsson, Astradur, *The Concept of Modernism* (Ithaca, NY, and London: Cornell University Press 1990).

Kirshner, Judith Russi, 'The Possibility of an Avant-Garde', *Formations* (Madison, WI) 2:2 (Fall 1985), 81–103.

Kuspit, Donald, *The Cult of the Avant-garde Artist* (Cambridge: Cambridge University Press, 1993).

Mann, Paul, *The Theory Death of the Avant-Garde* (Bloomington, IN: Indiana University Press, 1991).

Murphy, Richard, *Theorizing the Avant-garde: Modernism, Expressionism, and the Problem of Postmodernity* (Cambridge: Cambridge University Press, 1999).

Poggioli, Renato, *The Theory of the Avant-garde* (Cambridge, MA: Harvard University Press, 1968).

Scheunemann, Dietrich (ed.), *European Avant-garde: New Perspectives. Avantgarde – Avantgardekritik – Avantgardeforschung* (Amsterdam: Rodopi, 2000).

——, *Avant-Garde/Neo-Avant-Garde* (Amsterdam: Rodopi, 2004).

Weisgerber, Jean (ed.), *Les Avant-gardes littéraires au XXe siècle*, 2 vols (Budapest: Akadémiai Kiadó, 1984).

Historical Avant-garde Performance

Bablet, Denis, *The Revolution of the Stage: Design in the XXth Century* (Paris: Amiel, 1977).

Beaumont, Keith, *Alfred Jarry: A Critical and Biographical Study* (Leicester: Leicester Press, 1984).

Béhar, Henri, *Le Théâtre Dada et surréaliste* (Paris: Gallimard, 1979).

Berghaus, Günter, *Italian Futurist Theatre, 1909–1944* (Oxford: Clarendon Press, 1998).

——, *Theatre, Performance and the Historical Avant-garde* (Basingstoke: Palgrave Macmillan, 2005).

Berghaus, Günter (ed.), *International Futurism in Arts and Literature* (Berlin: DeGruyter, 2000).

Brescia, Anna Maria, *The Aesthetic Theories of Futurism*, PhD dissertation (New York: Columbia University, 1971; Ann Arbor, MI: University of Michigan, 1990).

Bronner, Stephen Eric, and Douglas Kellner, *Passion and Rebellion: The Expressionist Heritage* (London: Croom Helm, 1983).

Calandra, Denis, 'Georg Kaiser's "From Mourn to Midnight": the Nature of Expressionist Performance', *Theatre Quarterly* 6:21 (Spring 1976), 45–54.

Carlson, Marvin, *Performance: A Critical Introduction* (London: Routledge, 1996).

Durozoi, Gérard, *History of the Surrealist Movement* (Chicago, IL: University of Chicago Press, 2002).

Erickson, John D., *Dada: Performance, Poetry, and Art* (Boston: Twayne, 1984).

Foster, Stephen C., *'Event' Arts and Art Events* (Ann Arbor, MI: University of Michigan, 1988).

Goldberg, RoseLee, *Performance: Live Art 1909 to the Present*, 2nd rev. edn (London: Thames and Hudson, 1988).

Graver, David, *The Aesthetics of Disturbance: Anti-Art in Avant-garde Drama* (Ann Arbor, MI: University of Michigan Press, 1995).

Harding, James M. (ed.), *Contours of the Theatrical Avant-garde: Performance and Textuality* (Ann Arbor, MI: University of Michigan Press, 2000).

Kirby, Michael, *Futurist Performance*, 2nd edn (New York: PAJ Books, 1986).

Kuhns, David F., *German Expressionist Theatre: The Actor and the Stage* (Cambridge: Cambridge University Press, 1997).

Lippard, Lucy R. (ed.), *Dadas on Art* (Englewood Cliffs, NJ: Prentice-Hall, 1971).

Lista, Giovanni, *La Scène futuriste* (Paris: C.N.R.S., 1989).

Martin, Marianne W., *Futurist Art and Theory, 1909–1915*, 2nd edn (New York, Hacker, 1978).

Matthews, John H., *Theatre in Dada and Surrealism* (Syracuse, NY: Syracuse University Press, 1974)

Melzer, Annabelle, *Dada and Surrealist Performance* (New York: PAJ Books; and Baltimore, MD: Johns Hopkins Paperbacks, 1994).

Motherwell, Robert, *The Dada Painters and Poets*, 3rd edn (Cambridge, MA: Harvard University Press, 1989).

Nadeau, Maurice, *The History of Surrealism* (London: Cape, 1968).

Patterson, Michael, *The Revolution in German Theatre, 1900–1933* (London: Routledge & Kegan Paul, 1981).

Richter, Hans, *Dada, Art and Anti-art* (London: Thames and Hudson, 1965).

Rischbieter, Henning, and Wolfgang Storch (eds.), *Art and the Stage in the 20th Century: Painters and Sculptors Work for the Stage* (Greenwich, CT: New York Graphic Society, 1969).

Samuel, Richard, and Hinton Thomas, *Expressionism in German Life, Literature and the Theatre, 1910–1924*, 2nd edn (Philadelphia, PA: Saifer, 1971).

Schvey, Henry Ivan, *Oskar Kokoschka: The Painter as Playwright* (Detroit, MI: Wayne State University Press, 1982).

Shattuck, Roger, *The Banquet Years: The Origins of the Avant-Garde in France, 1885 to World War I*, 2nd rev. edn (New York: Vintage Books, 1968).

Taylor, Christina, *Futurism: Politics, Painting and Performance* (Ann Arbor, MI: Univrsity of Michigan Press, 1979).

Tisdall, Caroline, and Angelo Bozzolla, *Futurism*, 2nd edn (London: Thames and Hudson, 1985).

Postwar Art and Culture: General

Ackerman, James S., 'The Demise of the Avant-garde: Notes on the Sociology of Recent American Art', *Comparative Studies in Society and History* 11 (1969), 371–84.

Archer, Michael, *Art since 1960* (London: Thames and Hudson, 1997).

Ashton, Dore, *American Art since 1945* (New York: Oxford University Press, 1982).

Bolton, Richard, 'Enlightened Self-Interest: the Avant-garde in the 80s', *Afterimage* 16:7 (February 1989), 12–18.

Buchloh, Benjamin H.D., *Neo-Avant-garde and Culture Industry, 1955–75* (Cambridge, MA: MIT Press, 2000).

Butler, Christopher, *After the Wake: An Essay on the Contemporary Avant-Garde* (Oxford: Oxford University Press, 1980).

Calinescu, Matei, 'Avant-garde, Neo-Avant-garde, Post Modernism: the Culture of Crisis', *CLIO* 4:3 (June 1975), 317–40).

Crow, Thomas E., *The Rise of the Sixties: American and European Art in the Era of Dissent, 1955–69*, (London: Weidenfeld & Nicolson, 1996).

Fineberg, Jonathan, *Art since 1940: Strategies of Being*, 2nd edn (New York: Abrams, 2000).

Foster, Hal, *The Return of the Real: The Avant Garde at the End of the Century*, (Cambridge, MA and London: MIT Press and October Books, 1996).

Guilbaut, Serge, 'The New Adventures of the Avant-garde in America: Greenberg, Pollock, or From Trotskyism to the New Liberalism of the "Vital Center" ', *October* 15 (Winter 1980), 66–78.

Hapgood, Susan (ed.), *Neo-Dada: Redefining Art, 1958–1962* (New York: American Federation of Arts, and Universe Publishing, 1994).

Harris, Mary Emma, *The Arts at Black Mountain College* (Cambridge, MA: MIT Press, 1987).

Hobbs, Stuart D., *The End of the American Avant Garde* (New York: New York University Press, 1997).

Hoffman, Katherine, *Explorations: The Visual Arts since 1945* (New York: HarperCollins, 1991).

Hughes, Robert, 'The Decline and Fall of the Avant-Garde', in Gregory Battcock (ed.), *Idea Art: A Critical Anthology* (New York: Dutton, 1973).

Jencks, Charles, 'Postmodern and Late Modern: the Essential Definitions', *Chicago Review* 35:4 (1987), 31–58.

Klotz, Heinrich, *Kunst im 20. Jahrhundert: Moderne, Postmoderne, Zweite Moderne* (Munich: Beck, 1994).

Klotz, Heinrich (ed.), *Die Zweite Moderne: Eine Diagnose der Kunst der Gegenwart* (Munich: Beck, 1996).

Kuspit, Donald, *The New Subjectivism: Art in the 1980s* (Ann Arbor, MI: University of Michigan Research Press, 1988).

——, 'The Good Enough Artist: Beyond the Mainstream Avant-garde Artist', in Donald Kuspit, *Signs of Psyche in Modern and Postmodern Art* (Cambridge: Cambridge University Press, 1993), pp. 292–9.

Lucie-Smith, Edward, *Late-Modern: The Visual Arts since 1945* (New York: Oxford University Press, 1969).

Müller, Grégoire, *The New Avant-garde: Issues for the Art of the Seventies* (New York: Praeger, 1972).

Noszlopy, George T., 'The Embourgeoisement of Avant-garde Art', *Diogenes* 67 (Fall 1969), 83–109.

Phillips, Lisa (ed.), *Beat Culture and the New America, 1950–1965*, exhibition catalogue (New York: Whitney Museum of American Art, 1995–6).

Rorimer, Anne, *New Art in the 60s and 70s: Redefining Reality* (London: Thames & Hudson, 2001).

Saunders, Frances Stonor, *Who Paid the Piper? The CIA and the Cultural Cold War* (London: Granta Books, 1999).

Schrenk, Klaus (ed.), *Upheavals, Manifestos, Manifestations: Conceptions in the Arts at the Beginning of the Sixties: Berlin, Düsseldorf, Munich/Aufbrüche, Manifeste, Manifestationen: Positionen in der bildenden Kunst zu Beginn der 60er Jahre in Berlin, Düsseldorf und München* (Cologne: DuMont, 1984).

Szabolcsi, Miklós, 'Avant-garde, Neo-avant-garde, Modernism: Questions and Suggestions', *New Literary History* 3 (1971), 49–70.

Taylor, Brandon, *Avantgarde and After: Rethinking Art Now* (New York: Abrams, 1995).

Thomas, Karin, *Kunst in Deutschland seit 1945* (Cologne: DuMont, 2002).

Vergine, Lea, *Art on the Cutting Edge: A Guide to Contemporary Movements* (Milan: Skira, 2001).

Wallis, Brian (ed.), *Art After Modernism: Rethinking Representation* (New York: New Museum of Contemporary Art; Boston: Godine, 1984).

Weintraub, Linda, Arthur Coleman Danto, and Thomas McEvilley (eds), *Art on the Edge and Over: Searching for Art's Meaning in Contemporary Society, 1970s–1990s* (Litchfield, CT: Art Insights, 1996).

Wheeler, Daniel, *Art Since Mid-century* (London: Thames & Hudson, 1991).

Wood, Paul et al. (eds), *Modernism in Dispute: Art since the Forties* (New Haven, CT: Yale University Press, 1993).

Postmodernism

Appignanesi, Lisa (ed.), *Postmodernism: ICA Documents* (London: Free Association Books, 1989).

Ashley, David, *History without a Subject: The Postmodern Condition* (Boulder, CO: Westview Press, 1997).

Bertens, Hans, *The Idea of the Postmodern: A History* (London: Routledge, 1995).

Best, Steven, and Douglas Kellner, *Postmodern Theory: Critical Interrogations* (London: Macmillan, 1991).

Connor, Steven, *Postmodernist Culture: An Introduction to Theories of the Contemporary* (Oxford: Blackwell, 1997).

Dunn, Robert G., *Identity Crises: A Social Critique of Postmodernity* (Minneapolis, MN: University of Minnesota Press, 1998).

The Forest of Signs: Art in the Crisis of Representation, exhibition catalogue (Los Angeles: The Museum of Contemporary Art, 1989).

Foster, Hal (ed), *The Anti-Aesthetic: Essays on Postmodern Culture* (Port Townsend, WA: Bay Press, 1983).

Gaggi, Silvio, *Modern/Postmodern: A Study in Twentieth-Century Arts and Ideas* (Philadelphia, PA: University of Pennsylvania Press, 1989).

Hutcheon, Linda, *The Politics of Postmodernism* (London: Routledge, 1989).

——, *The Poetics of Postmodernism: History, Theory, Fiction* (London: Routledge, 1988).

Huyssen, Andreas, *After the Divide: Modernism, Mass Culture, Postmodernism* (Basingstoke: Macmillan, 1988).

Jameson, Fredric, *Cultural Turn: Selected Writings on the Postmodern, 1983–1998* (London: Verso, 1998).

Jencks, Charles, *What is Postmodernism?* (London: Academy Editions, 1986; 4th edn, 1996).

Jencks, Charles (ed.), *The Post-modern Reader* (London: Academy Editions, 1992).

Kohler, Michael, 'Postmodernism: Ein begriffsgeschichtlicher Überblick', *Amerikastudien* 22 (1977), 8–18.

Murphy, Richard, *Theorizing the Avant-garde: Modernism, Expressionism, and the Problem of Postmodernity* (Cambridge: Cambridge University Press, 1999).

Nicholson, Linda J. (ed.), *Feminism/Postmodernism* (London: Routledge, 1990).

Russell, Charles, 'Postmodernism and the Neo-avant-garde', in C. Russell, *Poets, Prophets, and Revolutionaries: The Literary Avant-Garde from Rimbaud through Postmodernism* (New York and Oxford: Oxford University Press, 1985).

Sandler, Irving, *Art of the Postmodern Era: From the Late 1960s to the Early 1990s* (New York: IconEditions, 1996).

Scott, Lash, and Jonathan Friedman (eds), *Modernity and Identity* (Oxford: Blackwell, 1992).

Silverman, Hugh J. (ed.), *Postmodernism: Philosophy and the Arts* (London: Routledge, 1990).

Smart, Barry, *Postmodernity* (London, Routledge, 1993).

Waugh, Patricia (ed.), *Postmodernity: A Reader* (London: Arnold, 1992).

Postwar Performance: General

Almhofer, Edith, *Performance Art: Die Kunst zu leben* (Vienna: Böhlau 1986).

Aronson, Arnold, *American Avant-garde Theatre: A History* (London: Routledge, 2000).

Aue, Walter (ed.), *PCA: Projecte, Concepte & Actionen* (Cologne: DuMont Schauberg, 1971).

Auslander, Philip, *From Acting to Performance: Essays in Modernism and Postmodernism* (London: Routledge, 1997).

Banes, Sally, *Subversive Expectations: Performance Art and Paratheatre in New York, 1976–85* (Ann Arbor, MI: University of Michigan Press, 1998).

Banes, Sally, and Noël Carroll, 'Performance Art/Art Performance', in Dennis Kennedy (ed.), *The Oxford Encyclopedia of Theatre and Performance* (Oxford: Oxford University Press, 2003), 1019–23.

Battcock, Gregory, and Robert Nickas (eds), *The Art of Performance: A Critical Anthology* (New York: Dutton, 1984).

Benamou, Michel, and Charles Caramello (eds), *Performance in Postmodern Culture* (Milwaukee, WI: Center for Twentieth-Century Studies, University of Wisconsin-Milwaukee, 1977).

Broadhurst, Susan, *Liminal Acts: A Critical Overview of Contemporary Performance and Theory* (London: Cassell, 1999).

Bronson, A. A., and Peggy Gale (eds), *Performance by Artists* (Toronto: Art Metropole, 1979).

Carr, Cindy, *On Edge: Performance at the End of the Twentieth Century* (Hanover, NH: Wesleyan University Press, 1993).

Childs, Nicky, and Jeni Walwin (eds), *A Split Second of Paradise: Live Art, Installation and Performance* (London: Rivers Oram Press, 1998).

Diederichs, Joachim, 'Zum Begriff Performance', *documenta 6*, vol. 1 (Kassel: Dierichs, 1977), 281–3.

Dolan, Jill, *Presence and Desire: Essays on Gender, Sexuality, Performance* (Ann Arbor, MI: University of Michigan Press, 1993).

Dreher, Thomas, *Performance Art nach 1945: Aktionstheater und Intermedia* (Munich: Fink, 2001).

Dupuy, Jean (ed.), *Collective Consciousness: Art Performances in the Seventies* (New York: Performing Arts Journal Publications, 1980).

Elwes, Catherine, 'Floating Femininity: a Look at Performance Art by Women', in Sarah Kent and Jacqueline Morreau (eds), *Women's Images of Men* (London: Writers and Readers Publishing Cooperative Society, 1985), pp. 164–93.

Felshin, Nina (ed.), *But is It Art? The Spirit of Art as Activism* (Seattle, WA: Bay Press, 1995).

Féral, Josette, 'What is Left of Performance Art? Autopsy of a Function, Birth of a Genre', *Discourse* 14:2 (Spring 1992), 142–62.

Fuchs, Elinor, *The Death of Character: Perspectives on Theater after Modernism* (Bloomington, IN: Indiana University Press, 1996).

Fusco, Coco (ed.), *Corpus Delecti: Performance Art of the Americas* (London: Routledge, 2000).

Ghinéa, Virgile, *Dada et Néo-Dada: Happening, Fluxus, Body-art, Land-art, Mail-art, Art conceptuel, poèmes, actions* (Luxembourg: Renaissance, 1978).

Glusberg, Jorge (ed.), *The Art of Performance*, exhibition catalogue (Venice: Palazzo Grassi, 1979).

Gribling, Frank, and Kirsti Jaervinen, *Beyond Performance* (Amsterdam: Arti Amicitiae, 1989).

Grüterich, Marlies, 'Performance–Musik–Demonstration', *Kunstforum International* 13 (February–April 1975), 130–66.

Harris, Geraldine, *Staging Femininities: Performance and Performativity* (Manchester: Manchester University Press, 1999).

Hart, Lynda, and Peggy Phelan (eds), *Acting Out: Feminist Performances* (Ann Arbor, MI: University of Michigan Press, 1993).

Haskell, Barbara, *Blam! The Explosion of Pop, Minimalism, and Performance, 1958–1964*, exhibition catalogue (New York: Whitney Museum of American Art, in association with W. W. Norton, 1984).

Hedden, Mark, 'Notes on Theater at Black Mountain College (1948–1952)', *Form* (Girton, Cambridge) 9 (April 1969), 18–20.

Howell John (ed.), *Breakthroughs: Avant-garde Artists in Europe and America, 1950–1990*, exhibition catalogue (Ohio: Wexner Centre for the Arts, 1990).

Inga-Pin, Luciano (ed.), *Performances: Happenings, Actions, Events, Activities, Installations* (Padua: Mastrogiacomo, 1978).

Innes, Christopher, *Avant Garde Theatre, 1892–1992* (London: Routledge, 1993).

Kaye, Nick (ed.), *Art into Theatre: Performance Interviews and Documents* (Amsterdam: Harwood, 1996).

Kostelanetz, Richard (ed.), *Scenarios: Scripts to Perform* (New York: Assembling Press, 1980).

——, *On Innovative Performance(s): Three Decades of Recollections on Alternative Theater* (Jefferson, NC: McFarland, 1994).

Loeffler, Carl E., and Darlene Tong (eds), *Performance Anthology: Source Book for a Decade of California Performance Art* (San Francisco, CA: Contemporary Arts Press, 1980; 2nd rev. edn, San Francisco, CA: Last Gasp Press and Contemporary Arts Press, 1989).

MacAdams, Dona Ann, *Caught in the Act: A Look at Multimedia Performance* (New York: Aperture, 1996).

Martins, Kirsten, and Peter P. J. Sohn (eds), *Performance: Eine andere Dimension/Performance: Another Dimension*, exhibition catalogue (Berlin: Künstlerhaus Bethanien, and Berlin: Frölich and Kaufmann, 1983).

Mehta, Xerxes, 'Some Versions of Performance Art', *Theatre Journal* 36 (1984), 164–98.

Mifflin, Margot, 'Performance Art: What is It and Where is It Going?' *ArtNews* 91:4 (April 1992), 84–9.

Montano, Linda (ed.), *Performance Artists Talking in the Eighties: Sex, Food, Money/Fame, Ritual/Death* (Berkeley, CA: University of California Press, 2000).

Performance, special issue of *Art-Rite* 10 (Fall 1975).

Performance, ed. Georg W. Schwarzbauer, special issue of *Kunstforum International* 24 (1977).

La Performance, exhibition catalogue (Bologna: Galleria Comunale d'Arte Moderna, 1977).

Performance Art, special issue of *Studio International* 192 (July 1976).

Performance Art into the 90s (London: Academy Editions, 1994).

Performance Art: (Some) Theory and (Selected) Practice at the End of this Century, ed. Martha Wilson, special issue of *Art Journal*, 56:4 (Winter 1997).

Performance Issue(s): Happening, Body, Spectacle, Virtual Reality, ed. Valie Export and Herbert Blau, special issue of *Discourse: Journal for Theoretical Studies in Media and Culture* 14:2 (Spring 1992).

La performance oggi: Settimana internazionale della performance, Bologna, 1–6 giugno 1977, exhibition catalogue (Bologna: Galleria Comunale d'Arte Moderna, 1977; Pollenza: La Nuova Foglio, 1978).

Performance und Performance Art, ed. Gerhard Johann Lischka, special issue of *Kunstforum International* 96 (August–October 1988).

Performance: Zwischen Kunst und Theater, special issue of *Kunstforum International* 58 (February 1983).

Pontbriant, Chanel (ed.), *Performance: Text(e)s & Documents* (Montreal: Parachute, 1981).

Roth, Moira (ed.), *The Amazing Decade: Women and Performance Art in America, 1970–1980* (Los Angeles/CA: Astro Artz, 1983).

Sangster, Gary (ed.), *Outside the Frame: Performance and the Object. A Survey History of Performance Art in the USA since 1950*, exhibition catalogue (Cleveland, OH: Cleveland Center for Contemporary Art, 1994).

Sayre, Henry M., *The Object of Performance: The American Avant-garde since 1970* (Chicago: Chicago University Press, 1989).

Schilling, Jürgen, *Aktionskunst: Identität von Kunst und Leben? Eine Dokumentation* (Lucerne: Bucher, 1978).

Schimmel, Paul (ed.), *Out of Action: Between Performance and the Object, 1949–1979* (London: Thames & Hudson, 1998).

Shank, Theodore, *Beyond the Boundaries: American Alternative Theatre*, 2nd rev. edn (Ann Arbor, MI: University of Michigan Press, 2002).

Stiles, Christine, and Peter Selz (eds), *Theories and Documents of Contemporary Art: A Sourcebook* (Berkeley, CA: University of California Press, 1996).

Styan, John L., *Modern Drama in Theory and Practice*, 3 vols (Cambridge: Cambridge University Press, 1981).

Walsh, Richard, *Radical Theatre in the Sixties and Seventies* (Keele: British Association for American Studies, 1993).

Weinberg, Mark S., *Challenging the Hierarchy: Collective Theatre in the United States* (New York: Greenwood Press, 1992).

Zimmer, Elizabeth, 'Has Performance Art Lost its Edge?', *Ms* 5:5 (March/April 1995), 78–83.

Zurbrugg Nicholas (ed.), *The Multimedia Text* (London: Academy Editions, 1995).

Happening and Fluxus

Allsop, Ric, Ken Friedman and Owen Smith (eds), *On Fluxus*, special issue of *Performance Research* 7:3 (September 2002).

Armstrong, Elizabeth, and Joan Rothfuss (eds), *In the Spirit of Fluxus*, exhibition catalogue (Minneapolis, MN: Walker Art Center, 1993).

Auslander, Philip, 'Fluxus Art-Amusement: The Music of the Future?', in James M. Harding (ed.), *Contours of the Theatrical Avant-garde: Performance and Textuality* (Ann Arbor, MI: University of Michigan Press, 2000), pp. 110–29.

Becker, Jürgen, and Wolf Vostell (eds), *Happenings, Fluxus, Pop Art, Nouveau Réalisme: Eine Dokumentation* (Reinbek: Rowohlt, 1965).

Behrens, Ditta, 'Pop, Happening und Fluxus: Künstlerinnen in den 60ern', in Baerbel Becker (ed.), *Unbekannte Wesen: Frauen in den 60er Jahren.* (Berlin: Elefantenpress, 1987), pp. 91–8.

Berger, Maurice, 'Forms of Violence: Neo-Dada Performance', in Susan Hapgood (ed.), *Neo-Dada: Redefining Art, 1958–1962* (New York: American Federation of Arts & Universe Publishing, 1994), pp. 67–84.

Berghaus, Günter, 'Happenings in Europe: Trends, Events and Leading Figures', in Mariellen Sandford (ed.), *Happenings and Other Acts* (New York: Routledge, 1995), pp. 310–88.

——, 'Tomas Schmit: a Fluxus Farewell to Perfection', *The Drama Review* 38:1, T141 (Spring 1994), 79–97.

Bertozzi, Barbara, and Klaus Wolbert (eds), *Gutai: Japanische Avantgarde/Japanese Avant-garde, 1945–1965*, exhibition catalogue (Darmstadt: Mathildenhöhe, 1991).

Beuckers, Klaus Gereon (ed.), *Zero-Studien: Aufsätze zur Düsseldorfer Gruppe Zero und ihrem Umkreis* (Münster: LIT Verlag für wissenschaftliche Literatur, 1997).

Block, René, and Anne Marie Freybourg (eds), *Wiesbaden Fluxus 1962–1982: Eine kleine Geschichte von Fluxus in drei Teilen*, exhibition catalogue (Wiesbaden: Museum Wiesbaden, 1983).

Bonito Oliva, Achille (ed.), *Ubi Fluxus ibi modus, 1990–1962*, exhibition catalogue (Venice: Ex Granai della Repubblica alle Zitelle, 1990; Milan: Mazzotta, 1990).

Bonnefoy, Françoise, Sarah Clément and Isabelle Sauvage (eds), *Gutai*, exhibition catalogue (Paris: Galerie Nationale du Jeu de Paume, 1999).

Brecht, George, *Jenseits von Ereignissen: Texte zu einer Heterospective von George Brecht*, exhibition catalogue (Berne: Kunsthalle, 1978).

Calder, John (ed.), *New Writers IV: Plays and Happenings* (London: Calder and Boyars, 1967).

Celant, Germano, *Piero Manzoni* (Milan: Charta, 1998).

Damsch-Wiehager, Renate (ed.), *ZERO Italien: Azimut/Azimuth 1959/69 in Milan. Und heute*, exhibition catalogue (Esslingen: Galerie der Stadt Esslingen, 1995–6; Ostfildern: Hatje, 1996).

——, *Zero und Paris 1960. Und heute*, exhibition catalogue (Esslingen: Galerie der Stadt Esslingen, 1997; Ostfildern: Hatje, 1997).

——, *Zero aus Deutschland 1957 bis 1966. Und heute*, exhibition catalogue (Esslingen: Galerie der Stadt Esslingen, 1999–2000; Hatje Cantz 1999).

Daniels, Dieter (ed.), *Fluxus: Ein Nachruf zu Lebzeiten*, special issue of *Kunstforum* 115 (September–October 1991).

Décollage, ed. Wolf Vostell, nos. 1 (1962) to 7 (1969).

Dietrich, Hans-Joachim, *Happenings (& actions): US pop art, nouveau réalisme, etc.* (Düsseldorf: Kalendar, 1965).

Document Gutai 1954–1972, exhibition catalogue (Ashiya: Ashiya Shiritsu Bijutsu Hakubutsukan, 1993).

Dreyfus, Charles (ed.), *Happenings and Fluxus* (Paris: Galerie 1900–2000, 1989).

Fetterman, William, *John Cage's Theatre Pieces: Notations and Performances* (Amsterdam: Harwood, 1996).

Filliou, Robert, *A Filliou Sampler* (New York: Something Else Press, 1967).

——, *Robert Filliou – Commemor*, exhibition catalogue (Aachen: Neue Galerie im Alten Kurhaus, 1970).

——, *Teaching and Learning as Performing Arts* (Cologne: Koenig, 1970).

——, *Robert Filliou*, exhibition catalogue (Munich: Galerie Buchholz, 1973).

——, *The Eternal Network Presents: Robert Filliou*, exhibition catalogue (Hanover: Sprengel Museum, 1984).

——, *Robert Filliou 1926–1987: Zum Gedächtnis,* exhibition catalogue (Düsseldorf: Städtische Kunsthalle, 1988).

——, *Robert Fillliou* [sic], exhibition catalogue (Paris: Centre Georges Pompidou, 1991).

——, *Robert Filliou: From Political to Poetical Economy*, exhibition catalogue (Vancouver: Morris and Helen Belkin Art Gallery, University of British Columbia, 1995).

Flux Attitudes, exhibition catalogue ed. Cornelia Lauf and Susan Hapgood (Buffalo, NY: Hallwalls Contemporary Arts Center, 1991).

Fluxus, special issue of *Flash Art* 84–5 (October–November 1978).

Fluxus, special issue of *Lightworks* 11–12 (Fall 1979).

Fluxus: A Conceptual History, ed. Estera Milan, special issue of *Visible Language* 26:1–2 (Winter/Spring 1992).

Fluxus: Aspekte eines Phänomens, exhibition catalogue (Wuppertal: Von der Heydt Museum, 1981–2).

Fluxus in Wiesbaden 1992, exhibition catalogue ed. René Block (Wiesbaden: Bellevue Saal et al., 1992).

Fluxus Research, ed. Jean Sellem, (Lund: Lund Art Press, 1991).

Fluxus subjektiv, exhibition catalogue ed. by Ursula Krinzinger (Vienna: Galerie Krinzinger, 1990).

Fluxus, 25 Years, exhibition catalogue (Williamstown, MA: Williams College Museum of Art, 1987–8).

Fluxus Virus 1962–1992, exhibition catalogue (Cologne: Galerie Schüppenhauer, 1992).

Fluxus. V TRE. ccV TRE, ed. George Brecht and Fluxus Editorial Council, nos. 1 (Jan. 1964) to 11 (1976) (reprinted Milan: Flash Art, King Kong International, n.d.).

Francblin, Catherine, *Les Nouveaux Réalistes* (Paris: Éditions du Regard, 1997).

Frank, Peter, 'Fluxus in New York', *Lightworks* 11/12 (Fall 1979), 29–36.

Friedman, Ken, *Events* (New York: Jaap Rietman, 1985).

——, *(Parts of) the Fluxus Saga. Part Two* (Oslo: Fluxforlaget, 1987).

——, *Fluxus 1992* (Budapest: Artpool, 1992).

Friedman, Ken (ed.), *The Fluxus Reader* (London: Academy Editions, 1998).

Hansen, Al [Alfred Earl], *A Primer of Happenings & Time/Space Art* (New York: Something Else Press, 1965).

——, *Performance/Live Art Notes* (Cologne: Hundertmark, 1981).

Hapgood, Susan, *Neo-Dada: Redefining Art, 1958–62*, exhibition catalogue (Scottsdale, AZ: Center for Art, 1994).

Hendricks, Jon (ed.), *Fluxus Codex* (Detroit, MI: Gilbert and Lila Silverman Fluxus Collection, in Association with H. N. Abrams, New York, 1988).

——, *Fluxus etc.: The Gilbert and Lila Silverman Collection*, exhibition catalogue (Bloomfield Hills, MI: Cranbrook Academy of Art, 1981).

——, *Fluxus, etc. Addenda 1: The Gilbert and Lila Silverman Collection* (New York: Ink &, 1983).

——, *Fluxus, etc. Addenda II: The Gilbert and Lila Silverman Collection* exhibition catalogue (Pasadena, CA: Baxter Art Gallery, California Institute of Technology, 1983).

Henri, Adrian, *Environments and Happenings* (London: Thames and Hudson, 1974).

Higgins, Dick, *One Hundred Plays* (New York: Higgins, 1961).

——, *Jefferson's Birthday* (New York: Something Else Press, 1964).

——, *Towards the 1970's* (Somerville, MA: Abyss Publications, 1969).

——, *A Dialectic of Centuries: Notes Towards a Theory of the New Arts* (New York: Printed Editions, 1978).

——, *Selected Early Works 1955–64* (Berlin: Ars Viva, 1982).

——, *The Poetics and Theory of the Intermedia* (Carbondale, IL: Southern Illinois University Press, 1984).

——, *Modernism since Postmodernism: Essays on Intermedia* (San Diego, CA: San Diego State University, 1997).

Higgins, Dick (ed.), *Manifestos* (New York: Something Else Press, 1966).

Hors limit: L'art et la vie, 1952–1994 exhibition catalogue (Paris: Centre Georges Pompidou, 1994–5).

Japon des avant gardes 1910–1970, exhibition catalogue (Paris: Centre Georges Pompidou, 1986).

Kahn, Annette, *Yves Klein: Le maître du bleu* (Paris: Stock, 2000).

Kaprow, Allan, *How to Make a Happening* (Vermont, NY: Something Else Press, 1965).

——, *Assemblage, Environments & Happenings* (New York: Abrams, 1966).

——, *Some Recent Happenings* (New York: Something Else Press, 1966).

——, 'Five Happenings', in John Calder (ed.), *New Writers IV: Plays and Happenings* (London: Calder and Boyars, 1967), pp. 81–106.

——, *Untitled Essay and Other Works* (New York: Something Else Press, 1967).

——, ' "Happenings" in the New York Scene', *Art News* 60:3 (May 1961), 36–9, 58–62.

——, *Days Off: A Calendar of Happenings* (New York: Museum of Modern Art, 1970).

——, 'Interview with Allan Kaprow', *Journal of Contemporary Art* 4:2 (Fall/Winter 1991), 56–69.

Kellein, Thomas, *'Fröhliche Wissenschaft'. Das Archiv Sohm*, exhibition catalogue (Stuttgart: Staatsgalerie, 1987).

——, *Fluxus*, (London: Thames & Hudson, 1995).

Kirby, Michael, *Happenings: An Illustrated Anthology* (New York: Dutton, 1965; London: Sidgwick & Jackson, 1967).

[Klein, Yves], *Yves Klein, 1928–1962: Selected Writings*, exhibition catalogue (London: Tate Gallery, 1974).

——, *Yves Klein*, exhibition catalogue, ed. Dieter Hönisch (Berlin: Nationalgalerie, 1976).

——, *Yves Klein 1928–1962: A Retrospective*, exhibition catalogue (Houston, TX: Rice University 1982; New York: The Arts Publisher, 1982).

——, *Yves Klein*, exhibition catalogue (Paris: Centre Georges Pompidou, 1983).

——, *Yves Klein: La Vie, la vie elle-même qui est l'art absolu*, exhibition catalogue (Nice: Musée d'Art Moderne et d'Art Contemporaine, 2000); English edn, *Yves Klein: Long Live the Immaterial*, exhibition catalogue ed. Gilbert Perlein and Bruno Corà (New York: Delano Greenidge Editions, 2000).

Knapstein, Gabriele, *George Brecht: Events. Über die Event-Partituren von George Brecht aus den Jahren 1959–1963* (Berlin: Wiens Verlag, 1999).

Knapstein, Gabriele, and Carola Bodenmüller, *Eine lange Geschichte mit vielen Knoten: Fluxus in Deutschland 1962–1994*, 2 vols, exhibition catalogue (Stuttgart: Institut für Auslandsbeziehungen, 1995).

Kostelanetz, Richard, *The Theatre of Mixed Means: An Introduction to Happenings, Kinetic Environments and Other Mixed-Means Performances* (New York: Dial Press, 1968; London: Pitman, 1970).

Kotz, Mary Lynn, *Rauschenberg: Art and Life* (New York: Abrams, 1990).

Kuhn, Anette, *Zero: Eine Avantgarde der sechziger Jahre* (Frankfurt-am-Main: Propyläen, 1991).

Kultermann, Udo, *Leben und Kunst: Zur Funktion der Intermedia* (Tübingen: Wasmuth, 1970); English edn, *Art and Life* (New York: Praeger, 1971).

——, *Art-Events and Happenings* (London: Mathews Miller Dunbar, 1971).

Lauf, Cornelia, and Susan Hapgood (eds), *FluxAttitudes*, exhibition catalogue (Buffalo, NY; Hallwalls Contemporary Arts Center, 1991; Gent: Imschoot, 1991).

Lebel, Jean-Jacques, *Le Happening* (Paris: Denoël, 1966).

——, *Happenings, interventions, et actions diverses (1962–1982)* (Vanves: Loques, 1982).

——, *Jean Jacques Lebel: Retour d'exil. Peintures, dessins, collages, 1954–1988*, exhibition catalogue (Paris: Galerie 1900–2000, 1988).

——, *Jean-Jacques Lebel: Des années cinquante aux années quatre-vingt-dix* (Milan: Mazzotta, 1991).

——, *Poésie directe: Des happenings à Polyphonix. Entretiens avec Arnaud Labelle-Rojoux et quelques documents* (Paris: Opus International, 1994).

——, *Jean Jacques Lebel: Bilder, Skulpturen, Installationen*, exhibition catalogue (Vienna: Museum moderner Kunst, 1998).

Leve, Manfred, *Aktionen, Vernissagen, Personen: Die rheinische Kunstszene der 50er und 60er Jahre. Eine Fotodokumentation* (Cologne: Rheinland-Verlag, 1982).

Loewen, Norma, *Experiments in Art and Technology: A Descriptive History of the Organization*, PhD dissertation, New York University, 1975.

[Manzoni, Piero], *Piero Manzoni: Catalogo generale*, ed. Germano Celant (Milan: Prearo, 1975).

——, *Piero Manzoni*, exhibition catalogue, ed. Germano Celant (Paris: Musée d'Art Moderne de la Ville de Paris, 1991).

——, *Piero Manzoni*, exhibition catalogue, ed. by Germano Celant (London: Serpentine Gallery, 1998; Milan: Charta, 1998).

Martel, Richard (ed.), *Art Action, 1958–1998* (Québec: Éditions Intervention, 2001).

McShine, Kynaston (ed.), *1961 BerlinArt 1987*, exhibition catalogue (New York: Museum of Modern Art; Munich: Prestel, 1987).

Milman, Estera (ed.), *Fluxus and Friends*, exhibition catalogue (Iowa City: University of Iowa Museum of Art, 1988).

Moore, Barbara, *Fluxus I: A History of the Edition* (New York: ReFlux Editions, 1984).

——, 'Charlotte Moorman: Eroticello Variations', *Ear Magazine: The Music News* 12:3 (May 1987), 16–19.

Moore, Barbara (ed.), *The World of Charlotte Moorman: Archive Catalogue* (New York: Bound and Unbound, 2000).

Munroe, Alexandra, *Japanese Art after 1945: Scream Against the Sky* (New York: Abrams, 1994).

O'Dell, Kathy, 'Fluxus feminus', *The Drama Review* 41:1 (T153) (Spring 1997), 43–60.

Oldenburg, Claes, *Injun & Other Histories (1960)* (New York: Something Else Press, 1966).

——, *Store Days: Documents from The Store (1961) and Ray Gun Theater (1962)* (New York: Something Else Press, 1967).

——, *Raw Notes: Documents and Scripts of The Performances Stars, Moveyhouse, Massage, The Typewriter, with Annotations by the Author* (Halifax, NS: Press of the Nova Scotia College of Art and Design, 1973).

——, *Claes Oldenburg: An Anthology* (New York: Guggenheim Museum, 1995).

Osaki, Shinichiro, Augusta Monferini and Marcella Cossu (eds), *Giappone all'a-vanguardia: Il gruppo Gutai negli anni cinquanta*, exhibition catalogue (Rome: Galleria Nazionale d'Arte Moderna, 1990–1; Milan: Electa, 1990).

Patterson, Ben, *'The Black & White File': A Primary Collection of Scores and Instructions for His Music, Events, Operas, Performances and Other Projects, 1958–1998* (Wiesbaden-Erbenheim: Patterson, 1999).

Phillpot, Clive (ed.), *Fluxus: Selections from the Gilbert and Lila Silverman Collection* (New York: Museum of Modern Art, 1988).

Piene, Otto, 'The Development of the Group Zero', *Times Literary Supplement*, 3 September 1964, 812–13.

[Rauschenberg, Robert], *Robert Rauschenberg*, exhibition catalogue (Washington DC: National Collection of Fine Arts, 1976).

——, *Rauschenberg Performance, 1954–1984*, exhibition catalogue, ed. Nina Sundell (Cleveland, OH: Cleveland Center for Contemporary Art, 1983).

Restany, Pierre, *Les Nouveaux Réalistes* (Paris, Éditions Planète, 1968); 2nd rev. edn, *Le Nouveau Réalisme* (Paris: Union Générale d'Éditions, 1978).

——, *Nouveau Réalism 1960/70*, exhibition catalogue (Paris: Galerie Mathias Fels, 1970).

——, 'The New Realism', *Art since Mid-century, vol. 2: Figurative Art* (Greenwich, CT: New York Graphic Society, 1971), pp. 242–71.

——, *Yves Klein* (Paris: Chêne, 1982; English edn, New York: Abrams, 1982).

——, *1960: Les Nouveaux Réalistes*, exhibition catalogue (Paris: Musée d'Art Moderne de la Ville de Paris, 1986).

——, *Nouveaux Réalistes Anni '60: La memoria viva di Milano*, exhibition catalogue (Milan: Fonte d'Abisso Arte, 1997).

Roberts, James, 'Painting as Performance', *Art in America* 80:5 (May 1992), 113–18, 155.

Ruhe, Harry, *Fluxus: The Most Radical and Experimental Art Movement of the Sixties*, exhibition catalogue (Amsterdam, 'A', Amstel 262, 1976).

Ruzicka, Joseph, 'Jim Dine and Performance', in John Elderfield (ed.), *American Art of the 1960s*, exhibition catalogue (New York: Museum of Modern Art, 1991), pp. 97–121; also in *Studies in Modern Performance* 1 (1991), 96–121.

Saint-Phalle, Niki de, *Niki de Saint-Phalle*, exhibition catalogue (Paris: Musée National d'Art Moderne, 1980).

——, *Niki de Saint-Phalle: Tirs … et autres révoltes, 1961–1964*, exhibition catalogue (Paris: Galerie de France, 1990).

——, *Niki de Saint Phalle*, exhibition catalogue ed. Pontus Hulten (Bonn: Kunst- und Ausstellungshalle der Bundesrepublik Deutschland, 1992; Stuttgart: Hatje, 1992).

Sandford, Mariellen R. (ed.) *Happenings and Other Acts* (London: Routledge, 1995).

Schröder, Johannes Lothar, *Identität, Überschreitung, Verwandlung: Happenings, Aktionen und Performances von bildenden Künstlern* (Münster: LIT, 1990).

Sell, Mike, 'The Avant-garde of Absorption: Happenings, Fluxus, and the Performance Economies of the American Sixties', *Rethinking Marxism* 10:2 (1998), 1–26.

——, 'Bad Memory: Text, Commodity, Happenings', James M. Harding (ed.), *Contours of the Theatrical Avant-garde: Performance and Textuality* (Ann Arbor, MI: University of Michigan Press, 2000), 157–175.

Smith, Owen F., *Fluxus: The History of an Attitude* (San Diego, CA: San Diego State University Press, 1998).

Sohm, Hans (ed.), *Happening und Fluxus*, exhibition catalogue (Cologne: Kölnischer Kunstverein, 1970–1).

Spector, Nancy, 'Rauschenberg and Performance, 1963–67: A "Poetry of Infinite Possibilities" ', in Walter Hopps and Susan Davidson (eds), *Robert Rauschenberg: A Retrospective*, exhibition catalogue (New York: Guggenheim Museum, 1999), pp. 226–45.

Stachelhaus, Heiner, *Zero: Heinz Mack, Otto Piene, Günther Uecker* (Düsseldorf: Econ, 1993).

Tono, Yoshiaki, 'Artists in the Early Sixties', in Shuji Takashina, Yoshiaki Tono and Yusuke Nakahara (eds), *Art in Japan Today* (Tokyo: Kinokuniya Book Store, 1974), pp. 16–21.

Truck, Fred, *George Maciunas: Fluxus and the Face of Time* (Des Moines, IA: Electric Bank, 1984).

Van der Marck, Jan, 'Piero Manzoni: An Exemplary Life', *Art in America* 61:3 (May–June 1973), 74–81.

Vautier, Ben, *Ben*, special issue of *Flash Art*, no. 23 (April 1971).

——, *Art = Ben* (Amsterdam: Stedelijk Museum, 1973).

——, *Ben doute tout*, special issue of *Art Thèmes* 78 (Winter 1994).

——, *Textes théoriques: Tracts 1960–74* (Milan: Politi, 1975).

——, *Théorie, 1965–1979* (Berlin: DAAD Galerie, 1979).

——, *Ben, pour ou contre: Une rétrospective*, exhibition catalogue (Marseille: MAC, Galeries Contemporaines des Musées de Marseille, 1995).

——, *Ma Vie, mes conneries, 1935–1997* (Nice: Z'éditions, 1997).

——, *Je cherche la vérité*, exhibition catalogue (Nice: Musée d'Art Moderne et d'Art Contemporaine, 2001; Paris: Flammarion, 2001).

Vierundzwanzig Stunden: Einzige vollständige Dokumentation eines Happenings (Itzehoe: Hansen and Hansen, 1965).

Vostell, Wolf, *Dé-coll/age Happenings* (New York: Something Else Press, 1966).

——, *Miss Vietnam, and Texts of Other Happenings* (San Francisco, CA: Nova Broadcast Press, 1968).

——, *Aktionen: Happenings und Demonstrationen seit 1965* (Reinbek: Rowohlt, 1970).

——, *Happening und Leben* (Neuwied: Luchterhand, 1970).

——, *Vostell: Environnements, Happenings, 1958–1974*, exhibition catalogue (Paris: ARC 2, Musée d'Art Moderne de la Ville de Paris, 1974–5).

——, *Vostell: Retrospektive, 1958–1974*, exhibition catalogue (Berlin: Nationalgalerie, 1975).

——, *Vostell und Berlin: Leben und Werk 1971–1981*, exhibition catalogue (Berlin: DAAD Galerie, 1982).

——, *Vostell*, exhibition catalogue (Bonn: Rheinisches Landesmuseum 1992).

——, *Vostell: Leben = Kunst = Leben*, exhibition catalogue (Gera: Kunstgalerie Lyra, 1993–4; Leipzig: Seemann, 1993).

Williams, Emmett, *My Life in Flux, and Vice Versa* (London: Thames & Hudson, 1992).

Williams, Emmett, and Ann Noël (eds), *Mr Fluxus: A Collective Portrait of George Maciunas, 1931–1978* (London: Thames & Hudson, 1997).

Young, La Monte, and Jackson MacLow (eds), *An Anthology* (New York: George Maciunas and Jackson MacLow [1963]); 2nd edn, *An Anthology of Chance Operations* (S.l.: Friedrich, 1970).

Zero: Bildvorstellungen einer europäischen Avantgarde, 1958–1964, exhibition catalogue (Zurich: Kunsthaus Zürich, 1979).

Zero: Eine europäische Avant-garde, exhibition catalogue (Essen: Galerie Neher, 1992).

Zero: Vision und Bewegung, exhibition catalogue (Munich: Städtische Galerie im Lenbachhaus, 1988).

Body Art, Neo-Shamanism and Ritual Performance

[Abramović, Marina], *Marina Abramović,* exhibition catalogue, ed. Friedrich Meschede (Berlin: Neue Nationalgalerie, 1993; Stuttgart: Cantz, 1993).

——, *Marina Abramović: Biography. In Collaboration with Charles Atlas* (Ostfildern: Cantz, 1994).

——, *Marina Abramović: Objects, Performance, Video, Sound,* exhibition catalogue, ed. by Chrissie Iles (Oxford: Museum of Modern Art, 1995).

——, *Cleaning the House,* ed. Johan Pijnappel (London: Academy Editions, 1995).

——, *Marina Abramović: Double Edge,* exhibition catalogue, ed. Beatrix Ruf and Markus Landert (Warth: Kunstmuseum des Kantons Thurgau, Kartause Ittingen, 1995–6; Sulgen: Niggli, 1996).

——, *Body: Marina Abramović,* exhibition catalogue, ed. Anthony Bond (Sydney, NSW: Art Gallery of New South Wales, 1997; Melbourne: Bookman Schwartz, 1997).

——, *Marina Abramović: Artist Body, Performances 1969–1998* (Milan: Charta, 1998).

——, *Marina Abramović: The Bridge/El puente: Marina Abramović exposición retrospectiva,* exhibition catalogue, ed. Pablo J. Rico (Valencia: Sala La Gallera, 1998).

Abramović, Marina, and Ulay [i.e. Uwe Laysiepen], *Relation/Works: 3 Performances,* exhibition catalogue (Innsbruck: Krinzinger, 1978).

——, *Ulay/Marina Abramović: Relation Work and Detour* (Amsterdam: Idea Books, 1980).

——, *Modus vivendi: Ulay & Marina Abramović Works 1980–1985,* exhibition catalogue, ed. Jan Debbaut (Eindhoven: Stedelijk Van Abbemuseum, 1985).

——, *The Lovers: The Great Wall Walk,* exhibition catalogue, ed. Marina Abramović, Ulay, and Dorine Mignot (Amsterdam: Stedelijk Museum, 1989).

——, *Marina Abramović: Sur la voie,* exhibition catalogue, ed. Paul-Hervé Parsy (Paris: Galeries Contemporaines du Musée National d'Art Moderne, and Centre Georges Pompidou, 1990).

——, *Ulay/Abramović: Performances, 1976–1988*, exhibition catalogue (Eindhoven: Stedelijk Van Abbemuseum, 1997).

Acconci, Vito, 'Performances', *Interfunktionen* (Cologne) 5 (November 1970), 138–42; 6 (September 1971), 21–6; 8 (January 1972), 14–26; 10 (1973), 39–53.

——, *Vito Acconci*, special issue of *Avalanche* 6 (Fall 1972).

——, *Vito Acconci*, exhibition catalogue, ed. Martin Kunz (Lucerne: Kunstmuseum, 1978).

——, *Vito Acconci: Interview by Robin White at Crown Point Press, Oakland, California, 1979*, special issue of *View* 2:5–6 (October–November 1979).

——, *Vito Acconci: A Retrospective, 1969 to 1980*, exhibition catalogue, ed. Judith Russi Kirshner (Chicago: Museum of Contemporary Art, 1980).

——, 'Biography of Work 1969–1981', *documenta 7*, vol. 1 (Kassel: Dierichs, 1982), 174–5.

——, *Vito Acconci*, special issue of *Profile* (Chicago) 4:3–4 (Summer 1984).

——, *Vito Acconci*, exhibition catalogue, ed. Amnon Barzel (Prato: Museo d'Arte Contemporanea Luigi Pecci, 1992; Florence: Giunti, 1991).

Acconci, Vito (ed.), *Street Works*, supplement to *0 to 9*, issue no. 6 (July 1969).

Adriani, Götz, Winfried Konnertz and Karin Thomas, *Joseph Beuys* (Cologne: DuMont, 1973; 3rd rev. edn, 1994) English edn, *Joseph Beuys: Life and Works* (Woodbury, NY: Barron's, 1979).

Allsop, Ric, and Scott deLahunta (eds), *The Connected Body? An Interdisciplinary Approach to the Body and Performance* (Amsterdam: Amsterdam School of Arts, 1996).

L'art au corps: Le corps exposé de Man Ray à nos jours, exhibition catalogue (Marseille: Musée de Marseille, 1996; 2nd edn, 1999; Marseille: MAC, Galeries Contemporaines des Musées de Marseille, 1996).

Art corporel, exhibition catalogue (Nevers: Maison de la Culture, 1981).

Berghaus, Günter (ed.), *On Ritual*, special issue of *Performance Research* 3:3 (Winter 1998.)

[Beuys, Joseph], *Joseph Beuys: Aktioner, Aktionen*, exhibition catalogue (Stockholm: Moderna Museet, 1971).

——, *Joseph Beuys*, exhibition catalogue, ed. Caroline Tisdall (New York: Guggenheim Museum 1979; London: Thames & Hudson, 1979).

——, *Joseph Beuys: In Memoriam Joseph Beuys. Obituaries, Essays, Speeches* (Bonn: Inter Nationes, 1986),

——, *Joseph Beuys: Social Sculpture, Invisible Sculpture, Alternative Society, Free International University, Conversation with Eddy Devolder* (Gerpinnes: Tandem, 1988).

——, *Joseph Beuys: Beyond the Border to Eurasia*, exhibition catalogue (Tokyo: Watarium, 1991).

——, *Manresa: Eine Fluxus-Demonstration als geistliche Übung nach Ignatius von Loyola*, ed. Friedhelm Mennekes (Frankfurt-am-Main: Insel, 1992).

——, *Energy Plan for the Western Man: Joseph Beuys in America. Writings by and*

Interviews with the Artist Compiled by Carin Kuoni (New York: Four Walls Eight Windows, 1993).

——, *Joseph Beuys: The Revolution Is Us*, exhibition catalogue, ed. Nesbitt Judith (Liverpool: Tate Gallery, Liverpool, 1993–94).

——, *Joseph Beuys: Arena. Where Would I Have Got If I Had Been Intelligent!*, ed. Lynne Cooke and Karen Kelly (New York: Dia Center for the Arts, 1994).

Billeter, Erika (ed.), *Mythos und Ritual in der Kunst der siebziger Jahre*, exhibition catalogue (Zurich: Kunsthaus, 1981).

Blau, Herbert, 'The Surpassing Body', *The Drama Review* 35:2 (T130) (Summer 1991), 74–98.

Bleeker, Maaike (ed.), *Bodycheck: Relocating the Body in Contemporary Performance Art* (Amsterdam: Rodopi, 2002).

Bodavinac, Zdenka (ed.), *Body and the East: From the 1960s to the Present*, exhibition catalogue (Ljubljana: Moderna galerija, 1998).

Body Art, special issue of *Data* (Milan) 12:4 (Summer 1974).

The Body in Performance, ed. Patrick Capbell, special issue of *Contemporary Theatre Review* 10:3 (2000).

Burkard, Lene et al. (eds), *Body as Membrane*, exhibition catalogue (Odense: Kunsthallen Brandts Klædefabrik, 1996).

Bussmann, Georg, and Thomas Kempas (eds), *Körpersprache*, exhibition catalogue (Berlin: Haus am Waldsee, 1975–6).

Butler, Judith, 'Performative Art and Gender Constitution: an Essay in Phenomenology and Feminist Theory', *Theatre Journal* 40 (1988), 519–31.

Capucci, Pier Luigi (ed.), *Il corpo tecnologico* (Bologna: Baskerville, 1994).

Chassey, Eric de (ed.), *[Corps] social*, exhibition catalogue (Paris: École Nationale Supérieure des Beaux-Arts, 1999).

Le Corps 1 and 2, special issues of *Chroniques de l'Art vivant* (Paris), nos. 40 (June 1973) and 41 (July 1973).

De Domizio Durini, Lucrezia, *The Felt Hat: Joseph Beuys, A Life Told* (Rome: Edizioni Carte Segrete, 1991; 2nd edn, Milan: Charta, 1997).

De Groen, Geoffrey, 'Barriers Beyond the Body: Stelarc', in G. de Groen (ed.), *Some Other Dream: The Artist, the Artworld and the Expatriate* (Sydney: Hale and Iremonger, 1984), pp. 79–117.

Diacono, Mario, *Vito Acconci: Dal testo-azione al corpo come testo* (New York: Out of London Press, A. H. Minters, 1975).

'Dix Questions sur l'art corporel et l'art sociologique: Un débat entre Hervé Fischer, Michel Jouniac, Gina Pane et Jean Paul Thenot', *Artitudes international* 2:6–8 (December 1973–March 1974), 4–16.

Dolan, Jill, *Presence and Desire: Essays on Gender, Sexuality, Performance* (Ann Arbor, MI: University of Michigan Press, 1993).

Durland, Steven, 'From Warriors and Saints to Lovers: Marina Abramović and Ulay', *High Performance* 9:2 (no. 34) (1986), 50–4.

Eiblmayr, Silvia, 'The Reflective Edge: a Female Concept of Self-Representation', *Performance Magazine* 55 (1988), 11–16.

——, *Die Frau als Bild: Der weibliche Körper in der Kunst des 20. Jahrhunderts* (Berlin: Reimer, 1993).

Engelbach, Barbara, *Zwischen Body Art und Videokunst: Körper und Video in der Aktionskunst um 1970* (Munich: Schreiber, 2001).

Featherstone, Mike (ed.), *Body Modification*, special issue of *Body & Society* 5:2–3 (September 1999; 2nd edn, London: Sage, 2000).

Fischer, Lili, 'Künstler/Schamanen', *Kunstforum International* 25 (1978), 54–109.

Forte, Jeanie Kay, 'Women's Performance Art: Feminism and Postmodernism', *Theatre Journal* 40 (1988), 217–35.

——, *Women in Performance Art: Feminism and Postmodernism* (Ann Arbor, MI: UMI Research Press, 1990).

Frueh, Joanna, 'The Body Through Women's Eyes', in Norma Broude and Mary D. Garrard (eds), *The Power of Feminist Art: The American Movement of the 1970s. History and Impact* (New York: Abrams, 1994).

Fuchs, Elinor, 'Staging the Obscene Body', *The Drama Review* 33:1 (T121) (Spring 1989), 33–58.

Gatens, Moira, 'Towards a Feminist Philosophy of the Body', in Barbara Caine et al. (eds), *Crossing Boundaries: Feminisms and the Critique of Knowledges* (Sydney: Allen and Unwin, 1988), pp. 59–70.

Gieseke, Frank, and Markert Albert, *Flieger, Filz und Vaterland: Eine erweiterte Beuys Biografie* (Berlin: Elefanten Press, 1996).

Haberl, Horst Gerhard (ed.), *Kunst als Lebensritual/Art as Living Ritual*, exhibition catalogue (Graz: 'Steirischer Herbst', 1974; Graz: Pool, 1974, special issue of *Pfirsich* 12–14 [1974]).

Hall, Donald, Thomas Laqueur and Helaine Posner (eds), *Corporeal Politics*, exhibition catalogue (Cambridge, MA: MIT, Press, 1992).

Irlandes, Alain, Alain Julien-Laferrière and Sophie Guillot de Suduiraut (eds), *Corps*, exhibition catalogue (Tours: Musée des Beaux-Arts, 1980).

Jappe, Elisabeth, 'Das Recht, fliegen zu können: Performance – Ritual und Haltung', *documenta 8*, vol. 1 (Kassel: Weber & Weidemeyer, 1989), 115–22.

——, *Performance, Ritual, Prozeß: Handbuch der Aktionskunst in Europa* (Munich: Prestel, 1993).

Jones, Amelia, *Body Art/Performing the Subject* (Minneapolis, MN: University of Minnesota Press, 1998).

Jones, Amelia, and Andrew Stephenson (eds), *Performing the Body/Performing the Text* (London: Routledge, 1999).

Jones, Ann Rosalind, 'Writing the Body: Towards an Understanding of *l'écriture féminine*', in Judith Newton and Deborah Rosenfelt (eds), *Feminist Criticism and Social Change: Sex, Class, and Race in Literature and Culture* (New York: Methuen, 1985), pp. 86–101.

Juro, Andrea, and V. Vale (eds), *Angry Women*, special issue of *RE/Search* no. 13 (San Francisco, CA: RE/Search Publications, 1991; reprinted New York: Juno Books, 1999).

Kaiser, W. M. H., *Vito Acconci: Poetry, Activities, Sculpture, Performances, Installations, Video* (Amsterdam: n.p., 1977).

Kern, Kersten Ann, *Staging Selves: Performing Women's Personal Narratives* (Ann Arbor, MI: University of Michigan Press, 1996).

Kubitza, Anette, *Fluxus, Flirt, Feminismus? Carolee Schneemanns Körperkunst und die Avantgarde* (Berlin: Reimer, 2002).

Künkler, Karoline, 'Die Künstlerin als "Schmerzensfrau"': Selbstverletzungsaktionen von Gina Pane', in Kathrin Hoffmann-Curtius and Silke Wenk (eds), *Mythen von Autorschaft und Weiblichkeit im 20. Jahrhundert* (Marburg: Jonas, 1997), pp. 196–205.

Licht, Ira (ed.), *Bodyworks*, exhibition catalogue (Chicago, IL: Museum of Contemporary Art, 1975).

Lippard, Lucy, 'The Pains and Pleasures of Rebirth: European and American Women's Body Art', *Art in America* 64:3 (May–June 1976), 73–81.

Malsch, Friedrich, 'Kämpfer und Liebende: 12 Jahre Marina Abramovic/Ulay', *Kunstforum International* 106 (March–April 1990), 228–45.

McEvilley, Thomas, 'Art in the Dark', *Artforum* 21:10 (June 1983), 62–71.

——, 'Marina Abramovic/Ulay', *Artforum* 22:1 (September 1983), 52–5.

Melchiorre, Virgilio, and Annamaria Cascetta (eds), *Il corpo in scena: La rappresentazione del corpo nella filosofia e nelle arti* (Milan: Vita e Pensiero, 1983).

Mit Haut und Haar: Körperkunst der 70er Jahre. Marina Abramović, Valie Export, Natalia LL, Friederike Petzold, exhibition catalogue (Aarau: Forum Schlossplatz, 1995).

Mladejovsky, Jan, 'Art and Sacrifice', *Flash Art* 80/81 (February–April 1978), 33–5.

Moffitt, John Francis, *Occultism in Avant-garde Art: The Case of Joseph Beuys* (Ann Arbor, MI: University of Michigan Press, 1988).

Müller, Martin, *Wie man dem toten Hasen die Bilder erklärt: Schamanismus und Erkenntnis im Werk von Joseph Beuys* (Alfter: Verlag und Datenbank für Geisteswissenschaften, 1994).

Nemser, Cindy, 'Subject–Object Body Art', *Arts Magazine* (New York) 46:1 (September–November 1971), 38–42.

Novakov, Anna (ed.), *Veiled Histories: The Body, Place, and Public Art* (New York: San Francisco Art Institute and Critical Press, 1997).

——, *Carnal Pleasures: Desire, Public Space and Contemporary Art* (San Francisco, CA: Clamor Editions, 1998).

O'Dell, Kathy, *Contract with the Skin: Masochism, Performance Art and the 1970s* (Minneapolis, MN: University of Minnesota Press, 1998).

[Pane, Gina], 'Dossier Gina Pane', *Artitudes international* 4:15–17 (October–December 1974), 33–52.

——, *Gina Pane: Partitions, opere multimedia, 1984–85*, exhibition catalogue, ed. Lea Vergine (Milan: Padiglione d'Arte Contemporanea, 1985; Milan: Mazzotta, 1985).

——, *Gina Pane: La légende dorée*, exhibition catalogue (Villeneuve-d'Ascq: Musée d'Art Moderne, 1986).

——, *Gina Pane*, exhibition catalogue (Troyes: Cadran Solaire, 1990–1).

——, *Gina Pane: Opere 1968–1990*, exhibition catalogue (Reggio Emilia: Chiostri di San Domenico, 1998–9; Milan: Charta, 1998).

——, *Gina Pane*, exhibition catalogue, ed. Servane Zanotti (Le Mans: École Supérieure des Beaux-Arts, 2000).

Pluchart, François, 'Risk as a Practice of Thought', *Flash Art* 80/81 (February–April 1978), 39–40.

——, *L'Art corporel* (Paris: Limage 2, 1983).

Pluchart, François (ed.), *L'Art corporel*, exhibition catalogue (Paris: Galerie Rodolphe Stadler, 1975).

Richard, Alain-Martin, and Clive Robertson (eds), *Performance au/in Canada, 1970–1990* (Québec: Éditions Interventions, 1991).

Roelens, Nathalie, and Wanda Strauven (eds), *Homo orthopedicus: Le corps et ses prothèses à l'époque (post)moderniste* (Paris: L'Harmattan, 2001).

Rubin, Arnold (ed.), *Marks of Civilization: Artistic Transformations of the Human Body* (Los Angeles, CA: Museum of Cultural History, 1988).

Savoca, Giuseppe, *Arte estrema: Dal teatro di performance degli anni Settanta alla body art estrema degli anni Novanta* (Rome: Castelvecchi, 1999).

Schneede, Marina, *Mit Haut und Haaren: Der Körper in der zeitgenössischen Kunst* (Cologne: DuMont, 2002).

Schneede, Uwe M., *Joseph Beuys, die Aktionen: Kommentiertes Werkverzeichnis mit fotografischen Dokumentationen* (Ostfildern: Hatje, 1994).

Schneemann, Carolee, *More than Meat Joy: Complete Performance Works and Selected Writings*, ed. Bruce McPherson (New Paltz, NY: Documentext, 1979; reprint, Kingston, NY: Documentext/McPherson, 1997).

——, *Carolee Schneemann: Up to and Including Her Limits*, exhibition catalogue (New York: New Museum of Contemporary Art, 1996).

——, *Imaging Her Erotics: Carolee Schneemann. Essays, Interviews, Projects* (Cambridge, MA: MIT Press, 2001).

Schneider, Rebecca, *The Explicit Body in Performance* (London: Routledge, 1997).

Senelick, Laurence (ed.), *Gender in Performance: The Presentation of Difference in the Performing Arts* (Hanover, NH: University Press of New England, 1992).

Sharp, Willoughby, 'Body Works: a Pre-critical, Non-definitive Survey of Very Recent Works Using the Human Body', *Avalanche* 1 (Fall 1970), 14–17.

Smith, Barbara T., 'Art and Ceremony: Performance, Ritual and Concern for the Earth', *High Performance* 10:4 (no. 40) (1987), 54–9.

Smith, Sidonie, *Subjectivity, Identity, and the Body: Women's Autobiographical Practices in the Twentieth Century* (Bloomington, IN: Indiana University Press, 1993).

Spector, Nancy, 'Performing the Body in the 1970s', in Jennifer Blessing (ed.), *Rrose is a rrose is a rrose: Gender Performance in Photography*, exhibition catalogue (New York: Guggenheim Museum, 1997).

Stachelhaus, Heiner, *Joseph Beuys* (Düsseldorf: Claassen, 1987; English edn, New York: Abbeville Press, 1991).

Stelarc [Stelios Arcadiou], *Obsolete Body/Suspensions/Stelarc*, ed. James D. Paffrath and Stelarc (Davis, CA: JP Publications, 1984).

[For other works, see section below on 'Performances in Cyberspace'.]

Thistlewood, David (ed.), *Joseph Beuys: Diverging Critiques* (Liverpool: Tate Gallery, 1995; Liverpool University Press, 1995).

Tisdall, Caroline, *Joseph Beuys: Coyote* (Munich: Schirmer–Mosel, 1976; 2nd edn, 1980).

——, *Joseph Beuys: We Go This Way* (London: Violette Editions, 1998).

Tronche, Anne, *Gina Pane: Actions* (Paris: Fall, 1997).

Tucker, Michael, *Dreaming with Open Eyes: The Shamanic Spirit in Twentieth-century Art and Culture* (London: Aquarian, and San Francisco: Harper, 1992).

Vanpeene, Michel (ed.), *Michel Journiac: L'enjeu de la représentation. Le corps. Actes des colloques 1987 & 1996* (Paris: Centre d'Études et de Recherches en Arts Plastiques, 1998).

Vergine, Lea, 'Bodylanguage', *Art & Artist* 9:6 (no. 102) (September 1974), 22–7.

——, *Il corpo come linguaggio: La body art e storie simili* (Milan: Prearo, 1974); English edn, *Body Art and Performance: The Body as Language* (Milan: Skira, 2000).

Warr, Tracey, and Amelia Jones (eds), *The Artist's Body* (London: Phaidon, 2000).

Wegener, Claudia, 'Manresa: Autobiography as Method', *Performance Research* 7:3 (September 2002), 30–46; 8:2 (June 2003), 117–34.

Viennese Actionism

Ausstellung Brus–Muehl–Nitsch: Vom Informel zum Aktionismus (Zurndorf: Archiv des Wiener Aktionismus, Friedrichshof, 1984).

Braun, Kerstin, *Der Wiener Aktionismus: Positionen und Prinzipien* (Vienna: Böhlau, 1999).

Drühl, Sven, 'Düstere Legenden: Vom Mythos des Suizids und der Autoamputation in der Aktionskunst', *Kunstforum International* 153 (January–March 2001), 74–8).

Engert, Rüdiger, 'Der Wiener Aktionismus', *Protokolle: Zeitschrift für Literatur und Kunst* 1 (1970), 152–69.

Friedl, Peter, 'Der zerrissene Dionysos: Annäherungen an Hermann Nitsch', *Vom anderen Theater* (Vienna: Wiener Festwochen, 1982), pp. 38–51.

Green, Malcolm (ed.), *Brus, Muehl, Nitsch, Schwarzkogler: Writings of the Vienna Actionists* (London: Atlas Press, 1999).

Günter Brus and Hermann Nitsch at White Box, exhibition catalogue (New York: White Box, 1999).

Hofmann, Werner, 'Die Wiener Aktionisten', *Luther und die Folgen für die Kunst*, exhibition catalogue (Hamburg: Kunsthalle, 1983), pp. 641–55.

Kirchner, Helmut, 'Orgies Mysteries Theater', *Formations* (Madison, WI) 2:2 (Spring 1985), 73–85.

Klockner, Hubert, *Wiener Aktionismus/Viennese Actionism, Wien/Vienna 1960–1971*, 2 vols (Klagenfurt: Ritter, 1989).

——, 'Gesture and the Object: Liberation as Aktion. A European Component of Performative Art', in Paul Schimmel (ed.), *Out of Actions: Between Performance and the Object* (London: Thames & Hudson, 1998), 159–95.

Levy, William, *Unser Freund Otto Mühl: Eine Studie zum Kulturschock* (Löhrbach: Der grüne Zweig, 1998).

Loers, Veit, 'Vom Mythos zur Synästhese: Bemerkungen zum Aktionismus von Hermann Nitsch', *Protokolle: Zeitschrift für Literatur und Kunst* 1/1990, 111–18.

Mühl, Otto, *Ausgewählte Arbeiten 1963–1986* (Vienna: Klocker, 1986).

——, *Mama und Papa: Materialaktion 63–69* (Frankfurt-am-Main: Kohlkunstverlag, [1969]).

——, *Otto Mühl 7*, exhibition catalogue, ed. Peter Noever and Bettina M. Busse (Vienna: Museum für angewandte Kunst, 1998; Ostfildern: Cantz, 1998).

——, *Otto Mühl: Aspekte einer Totalrevolution. Leben. Kunst. Werk*, ed. Eva Badura-Triska and Hubert Klocker (Vienna: Museum moderner Kunst Stiftung Ludwig, and Cologne: Koenig, 2004).

——, *Otto Mühl: Leben, Kunst, Werk, Aktion, Utopie, Malerei 1960–2004*, exhibition catalogue, ed. Peter Noever (Vienna: Museum für angewandte Kunst, 2004; Cologne: Koenig, 2004).

Nitsch, Hermann, 'Wien: Das O.M. Theater. Interview mit Hermann Nitsch', *Kunst: Magazin für moderne Malerei, Grafik, Plastik* 5:4–5 (April–June 1965), 82–4, 92.

——, *Orgien Mysterien Theater/Orgies Mysteries Theatre* (Darmstadt, März, 1969).

——, *Photodokumentation Aktionen 1960–1975*, exhibition catalogue (Innsbruck: Galerie Krinzinger, 1975).

——, *das orgien mysterien theater 2: theoretische schriften, partiturentwurf des 6tagespiels* (Naples, Reggio Emilia and Munich: Chiessi and Morra, 1976; 2nd edn, Bonn, Ottersheim, and Vienna: Octopus Okeanos Presse, 1990).

——, *1., 2., 3. und 5. abreaktionsspiel: urfassungen, polizeiberichte, gerichtsakten* (Naples: Morra, 1976).

——, *König Oedipus: eine spielbare Theorie des Dramas* (Naples: Morra, 1976; reprint, Berlin: Jochen Knoblauch und Edition Kalter Schweiss, 1986).

——, *Frühe Aktionen* (Naples: Morra, 1976).

——, *Das Orgien Mysterien Theater: Die Partituren aller aufgeführten Aktionen*, vol. 1: *1960–1979 (1.–32. Aktion)* (Naples: Morra, 1979); vol. 2: *1960–1979 (33.–65. Aktion)* (Vienna: Freibord; and Naples: Morra, 1986); vol. 4: *27.–30. Juli 1984 (80. Aktion)* (Vienna: Freibord, 1984); vols. 6–8: *Das 6tage Spiel 1998* (Vienna: Freibord, 1998).

——, *Behauptungen und Beschreibungen zum Projekt des Orgien Mysterien Theaters (Ordensregeln)*, ed. Arnulf Meifert (Altona-Hohengebraching: Das Hohe Gebrechen, 1981).

——, *Projekt Prinzendorf: Das Orgien Mysterien Theater von Hermann Nitsch. Entwürfe, Partituren, Bedingungen der Realisation*, ed. Otto Breicha, exhibition catalogue (Graz: Steirischer Herbst, Kulturhaus Graz, 1981; Vienna: Jugend und Volk, 1981).

——, 'Ich will ein Theater der Sinne', *Protokolle. Zeitschrift für Literatur und Kunst* 1/1990, 119–26.

——, *Die wortdichtung des orgien mysterien theaters (1957–1962)* (Prinzendorf: Das O.M. Theater, 1982); vol. 2: *Das orgien mysterien theater: die wortdichtung II* (Vienna: Freibord, 1996).

——, *Das orgien mysterien theater: partitur des 1. tages und der 1. nacht des 6tage spieles* (Prinzendorf: Verlag das O. M. theater, 1983).

——, *O.M. Theater Lesebuch*, ed. Gerhard Jaschke (Vienna: Freibord, 1983).

——, *Das Orgien Mysterien Theater, 1960-1983*, exhibition catalogue (Eindhoven: Stedelijk Van Abbemuseum, 1983).

——, *Hermann Nitsch: Das früheste Werk*, ed. Otmar Rychlik (Vienna: Sonderzahl, 1986).

——, *Die Architektur des Orgien Mysterien Theaters. The Architecture of the O.M. Theatre*, 2 vols (Munich: Jahn, 1987–1993).

——, *Hermann Nitsch 1960–1987*, exhibition catalogue (Naples: Museo Diego Aragona Pignatelli Cortes, 1987; Naples: Morra, 1987).

——, *Das rote Tuch: Der Mensch das Unappetitlichste Vieh. Hermann Nitsch, Das Orgien Mysterien Theater, Im Spiegel der Presse 1960–1988* (Vienna: Freibord, 1988).

——, *Das Orgien Mysterien Theater: Manifeste, Aufsätze, Vorträge* (Salzburg: Residenzverlag, 1990).

——, *Hermann Nitsch: Aktionsmalerei 1960–1963/1989–1990*, exhibition catalogue (Düsseldorf: Galerie Heike Curtze, 1990).

——, *Hermann Nitsch*, exhibition catalogue (Sevilla: EXPO 92, Pabellón de las Artes, 1992; Vienna: Bundesministerium für Unterricht und Kunst, 1992).

——, *Hermann Nitsch: Eine biographische Skizze*, exhibition catalogue (Krems-Stein: Kunsthalle Krems, 1994).

——, *Zur Theorie des Orgien Mysterien Theaters: Zweiter Versuch* (Salzburg: Residenz Verlag, 1995).

——, *Reizwort Nitsch. vol. 1: Der Blutprofessor eine Art Gedärme-Wüterich; vol. 2: Reizwort-Register zu 'Der Blutprofessor eine Art Gedärme-Wüterich'*, ed. Gerhard Jaschke (Vienna: Freibord, 1993; 2nd edn, Vienna: Sonderzahl, 1995).

——, *Hermann Nitsch Das Orgien Mysterien Theater* (Vienna: Museum moderner Kunst, Stiftung Ludwig, 1996).

——, *Hermann Nitsch: Das 6-tage-Spiel in Prinzendorf 1998. Relikte und Aktionsmalerei, Fotos und Video* (Vienna: Museum moderner Kunst, Stiftung Ludwig, 1999).

——, *Hermann Nitsch: Leben und Arbeit, aufgezeichnet von Danielle Spera* (Vienna: Brandstätter, 1999).

Noever, Peter (ed.), *Aktionsmalerei – Aktionismus, Wien 1960–1965*, exhibition catalogue (Vienna: Österreichisches Museum für angewandte Kunst, 1989).

Roussel, Danièle, *Der Wiener Aktionismus und die Österreicher: Gespräche* (Klagenfurt: Ritter, 1995).

Stärk, Ekkehard, *Hermann Nitschs 'Orgien Mysterien Theater' und die 'Hysterie der Griechen': Quellen und Traditionen im Wiener Antikebild seit 1900* (Munich: Fink, 1987).

Tsiakma, Katia, 'Hermann Nitsch: a Modern Ritual', *Studio International* 192:982 (July–August 1976), 13–15.

Ursprung, Philip, ' "Catholic Tastes": Hurting and Healing the Body in Viennese Actionism in the 1960s', in Amelia Jones and Andrew Stephenson (eds), *Performing the Body/Performing the Text* (London: Routledge, 1999), 138–52.

Von der Aktionsmalerei zum Aktionismus: Wien 1960–1965/From Action Painting to Actionism: Vienna 1960–1965. Günter Brus; Adolf Frohner; Otto Mühl; Hermann Nitsch; Alfons Schilling; Rudolf Schwarzkogler, exhibition catalogue (Kassel: Museum Fridericanum; Winterthur: Kunstmuseum; Edinburgh: Scottish National Gallery of Modern Art; Klagenfurt: Ritter, 1988).

Weibel, Peter, and Valie Export (eds), *Wien: Bildkompendium Wiener Aktionismus und Film* (Frankfurt-am-Main: Kohlkunstverlag, 1970).

Wiener Aktionismus prospektiv, special issue of *Protokolle: Zeitschrift für Literatur und Kunst* 2/1981 (Vienna: Jugend und Volk, 1981).

Video Art, Performance and Installation

About Time: Video, Performance and Installation by 21 Woman Artists, exhibition catalogue (London: Institute of Contemporary Arts, 1980).

[Acconci, Vito *See section on 'Body Art'*.]

Anderson, Laurie, *Words in Reverse* (Buffalo, NY: Hallwalls, 1979).

——, *Laurie Anderson: Interview by Robin White at Crown Point Press, Oakland, California, 1979*, special issue of *View* 2:8 (January 1980).

——, *Laurie Anderson: Works from 1969 to 1983*, exhibition catalogue, ed. Janet Kardon (Philadelphia, PA: Institute of Contemporary Art, University of Pennsylvania, 1983).

——, *United States* (New York: Harper and Row, 1984).

——, *Empty Places: A Performance* (New York: Harper Perennial, 1991).

——, *Stories from the Nerve Bible: A Retrospective, 1972–1992* (New York: Harper Perennial, 1994).

——, 'Laurie Anderson', *Parkett* 49 (1997), 126–67.

——, *The Record of the Time: Sound in the Work of Laurie Anderson*, exhibition catalogue, ed. Thierry Raspail (Lyon: Musée d'Art Contemporain, 2002).

Art vidéo – vidéo art, exhibition catalogue, ed. Dominique Bonnet Saint Georges (Lyon: Le Nouveau Musée, 1980).

Art vidéo: Retrospectives et perspectives, exhibition catalogue (Charleroi: Palais des Beaux-Arts, 1983).

L'arte elettronica: Metamorfosi e metafore, exhibition catalogue (Ferrara: Palazzo dei Diamanti, 2001).

Balkema, Annette W., and Henk Slager (eds), *Screen-Based Art* (Amsterdam: Rodopi, 2000).

Battcock, Gregory (ed.), *New Artists Video* (New York: Dutton, 1978).

Baumann, Hans D. et al. (eds), *Kunst und Medien: Materialien zur documenta 6* (Kassel: Stadtzeitung und Verlag, 1977).

Bellour, Raymond (ed.), *Eye for I: Video Self-Portraits*, exhibition catalogue (Muncie, IN: Ball State University Art Gallery, 1990; New York: Independent Curators Inc., 1989).

Birringer, Johannes, 'Video Art/Performance: a Border Theory', *Performing Arts Journal* 13:3 (September 1991), 54–84.

——, *Media and Performance: Along the Border* (Baltimore, MD: Johns Hopkins University Press, 1998).

Brüninghaus-Knubel, Cornelia, and Bettina Ruhrberg (eds), *Frischluft: Installation–Interaktion: Videokunst der 80er Jahre*, exhibition catalogue (Duisburg: Wilhelm Lehmbruck Museum, 1993).

Bunnage, Julia (ed), *Acting Out: The Body in Video, Then and Now*, exhibition catalogue (London: Royal College of Art, 1994).

Caldwell, John Thornton (ed.), *Electronic Media and Technoculture* (New Brunswick, NJ: Rutgers University Press, 2000).

Childs, Nicky, and Jeni Walwin (eds), *A Split Second of Paradise: Live Art, Installations and Performance* (London: Rivers Oram, 1998).

Chin, Daryl, 'Contemplating the Navel: the Use and Abuse of Video Art', *Performing Arts Journal* 4:1–2 (1979), 62–9.

Cirifino, Fabio et al. (eds), *Studio Azzurro: Ambienti sensibili. Esperienze tra interattivita e narrazione* (Milan: Electa, 1999).

Contemporary Video, special issue of *Performing Arts Journal* 18:3 (September 1996).

Cronn-Mills, Kristin Jean, *Performance and Problematization in Rhetorical Culture: The Example of Laurie Anderson*, PhD dissertation, Iowa State University, 1997.

Cubitt, Sean, *Timeshift: On Video Culture* (London: Routledge, 1991).

——, *Videography: Video Media as Art and Culture* (Basingstoke: Macmillan, 1993).

——, 'Laurie Anderson: Myth, Management, and Platitude', in John Roberts (ed.), *Art Has No History* (London: Verso, 1994), pp. 278–95.

——, *Digital Aesthetics* (London: Sage, 1998).

Davis, Douglas, and Allison Simmons (eds), *The New Television: A Public/Private Art* (Cambridge, MA: MIT Press, 1978).

Davis, Douglas, 'Video Obscura', *Artforum* 10:8 (April 1972), 64–71.

De Gaetano, Domenico (ed.), *Mutazioni elettroniche: Le immagine di Studio Azzurro* (Turin: Lindau, 1995).

Decker, Edith, *Paik Video* (Cologne: DuMont, 1988; English edn, New York: Barrytown, 1997).

Dossier Art Video, special issue of *Opus International* 54 (January 1975).

Duguet, Ann-Marie, *Vidéo: La mémoire au poing* (Paris: Hachette, 1981).

Ein anderes Klima: Künstlerinnen gebrauchen neue Medien, exhibition catalogue (Düsseldorf: Städtische Kunsthalle, 1986).

Electronic Undercurrents, vol. 1: *Art and Video in Europe*, ed. Lars Movin and Torben Christensen; vol. 2: *American Film and Video: Whitney Biennial*, ed. Vibeke Petersen and Marianne Torp Øckenholt; vol. 3: *Nam June Paik – Video Sculptures*, ed. Vibeke Petersen, exhibition catalogue (Copenhagen: Statens Museum for Kunst, 1996).

Engelbach, Barbara, *Zwischen Body Art und Videokunst: Körper und Video in der Aktionskunst um 1970* (Munich: Schreiber, 2001).

Export, Valie, *Works from 1968–1975: A Comprehension*, exhibition catalogue (Paris: Biennale de Paris, 1975).

——, *Valie Export: Dokumentations-Ausstellung des österreichischen Beitrages zur Biennale Venedig 1980*, exhibition catalogue (Vienna: Galerie in der Staastsoper, 1980).

——, 'Feministischer Aktionismus: Apekte', in Gislind Nabakowski et al. (eds), *Frauen in der Kunst*, vol. 1 (Frankfurt-am-Main: Suhrkamp, 1980), pp. 139–76.

——, *Das Reale und sein Double: Der Körper* (Berne: Benteli, 1987).

——, 'The Real and its Double: the Body', *Discourse: Journal for Theoretical Studies in Media and Culture* 11:1 (Fall–Winter 1988–9), 3–27.

——, 'Aspects of Feminist Actionism', *New German Critique* 47 (Spring–Summer 1989), 69–92.

——, *Valie Export*, exhibition catalogue, ed. Peter Assmann (Linz: Oberösterreichische Landesgalerie, 1992).

——, 'Persona, Proto-Performance, Politics: a Preface', *Discourse: Journal for Theoretical Studies in Media and Culture* 14:2 (Spring 1992), 26–35.

——, *White Cube, Black Box: Skulpturensammlung, Video, Installation, Film, Werkschau Valie Export und Gordon Matta-Clark. Vorträge. Reader zur Vortragsreihe/Ausstellung*, exhibition catalogue, ed. Sabine Breitwieser (Vienna: EA-Generali Foundation, 1996).

——, *Split:Reality Valie Export*, exhibition catalogue, ed. Monika Faber (Vienna: Museum moderner Kunst, Stiftung Ludwig Wien, 1997; 2nd rev. edn, Vienna: Springer, 1997).

——, *Werkschau III: Valie Export, Arbeiten von 1971–1998* (Vienna: Triton, 1998).

——, *Valie Export: Ob/De+Con(Struction)* (Philadelphia, PA: Goldie Paley Gallery at Moore College of Art and Design, 2001).

Fargier, Jean Paul, *Nam June Paik* (Paris: Art Press, 1989).

Frieling, Rudolf, and Dieter Daniels, *Medien Kunst Aktion: Die 60er und 70er Jahre in Deutschland/Media Art Action: The 1960s and 1970s in Germany* (Vienna: Springer, 2000).

338   Bibliography

Frohne, Ursula (ed.), *Video Cult/ures: Multimediale Installationen der 90er Jahre*, exhibition catalogue (Karlsruhe: Museum für Neue Kunst, ZKM/Zentrum für Kunst und Medientechnologie, 1999; Cologne: DuMont, 1999).

Gale, Peggy (ed.), *Video by Artists*, exhibition catalogue (Toronto: Art Metropole, 1976).

Gänsheimer, Susanne (ed.), *Video Art 1976–1990: The German Contribution*, exhibition catalogue (Munich: Goethe Institute, 1991).

German Video and Performance, exhibition catalogue (Toronto: A Space, 1980).

Gill, Johanna, *Video: State of the Art* (New York: Rockefeller Foundation, 1976).

——, *Artist's Video: The First Ten Years*, PhD dissertation (Providence, RI: Brown University, 1976).

Goldberg, RoseLee, *Laurie Anderson* (New York: Abrams, 2000).

Gordon, Mel, 'Laurie Anderson: Performance Artist', *The Drama Review* 24:2 (T86) (June 1980), 51–64.

——, 'Laurie Anderson's United States, Part II', *The Drama Review* 24:4 (T88) (December 1980), 112–15.

Gruber, Bettina, and Maria Vedder (eds), *Kunst und Video: Internationale Entwicklung und Künstler* (Cologne: DuMont, 1983).

Hall, Doug, and Sally Jo Fifer (eds), *Illuminating Video: An Essential Guide to Video Art* (New York: Aperture, 1990).

Hanhardt, John G. (ed.), *Video Culture: A Critical Investigation* (New York: Smith, 1986).

Hanley, JoAnn (ed.), *The First Generation: Women and Video, 1970–75*, exhibition catalogue (Montreal: Musée d'Art Contemporain de Montréal, 1993; New York: Independent Curators Inc., 1993).

Herzogenrath, Wulf, 'Fernsehen und Video: das Doppelgesicht eines neuen künstlerischen Mediums', *documenta 6*, vol. 2 (Kassel: Dierichs, 1977), 289–93.

——, *Nam June Paik: Fluxus, Video* (Munich: Schreiber, 1983).

——, *Mehr als Malerei: Vom Bauhaus zur Video-Skulptur* (Regensburg: Lindinger & Schmid, 1994).

Herzogenrath, Wulf (ed.), *Videokunst in Deutschland 1963–1982. Videobänder, Videoinstallationen, Video-Objekte, Videoperformances, Fotografien* (Stuttgart: Hatje, 1982).

Herzogenrath, Wulf, and Edith Decker (eds), *Video Skuptur: Retrospektiv und Aktuell 1963–1989* (Cologne: DuMont, 1989).

Herzogenrath, Wulf, Thomas W. Gaethgens, et al. (eds), *TV Kultur: Das Fernsehen in der Kunst seit 1879* (Dresden: Verlag der Kunst, 1997).

Het Lumineuze beeld/The Luminous Image, exhibition catalogue (Amsterdam: Stedelijk Museum, 1984; Maarssen: Schwartz, 1984).

Howell, John, *Laurie Anderson* (New York: Thunder's Mouth Press, 1992).

Huffman, Kathy Rae, and Dorine Mignot (eds), *The Arts for Television*, exhibition catalogue (Los Angeles, CA: Museum of Contemporary Art; Amsterdam: Stedelijk Museum, 1987).

International Video Art Symposium 1979 (Kingston, Ont.: Agnes Etherington Art Centre, 1979).

Jonas, Joan, 'Seven Years', *The Drama Review* 19:1 (T65) (March 1975), 13–17.

——, *Joan Jonas: Interview by Robin White at Crown Point Press, Oakland, California, 1979*, special issue of *View* 2:1 (April 1978).

——, *Joan Jonas: Scripts and Descriptions, 1968–1982*, exhibition catalogue, ed. Douglas Crimp (Berkeley, CA: University Art Museum, 1983).

——, *Joan Jonas: Works, 1968–1994*, exhibition catalogue, ed. Dorine Mignot (Amsterdam: Stedelijk Museum, 1994).

——, 'Interview with Joan Simon', *Art in America* 83:7 (July 1995), 73–9, 100–1.

——, *Joan Jonas: Performances, Film, Installations 1968–2000*, exhibition catalogue, ed. Johann-Karl Schmidt (Stuttgart: Galerie der Stadt Stuttgart, 2000–1; Stuttgart: Hatje Cantz, 2000).

Junker, Howard, 'Joan Jonas: the Mirror Staged', *Art in America* 69:2 (February 1981), 87–95.

Kapke, Barry, 'Body as Sign: Performance and Film Works of Valie Export', *High Performance*, 12:1 (no. 45) (Spring 1989), 34–7.

Krauss, Rosalind, 'Video: the Aesthetics of Narcissm', *October* 1 (Spring 1976), 51–64.

Krewani, Angela (ed.), *Artefacts, Artefictions: Crossovers between Contemporary Literatures, Media, Arts and Architectures* (Heidelberg: Winter, 2000).

Kurtz, Bruce, 'Video is Being Invented', *Arts Magazine* 47:3 (December 1972–January 1973), 37–44.

Lampalzer, Gerda, *Videokunst: Historischer Überblick und theoretische Zugänge* (Vienna: Promedia, 1992).

Landy, Leigh, and Antje von Graevenitz, ' "I Make Technology Ridiculous": the Unusual Dialectics of Nam June Paik', *Avant Garde* 7 (1992), 79–108.

Linard, Monique, and Irène Prax, *Images vidéo, images de soi, ou Narcisse au travail* (Paris: Dunod, 1984).

Linker, Kate, *Vito Acconci* (New York: Rizzoli, 1994).

——, 'Revisiting Narcissm in Video: the Voice of Vito Acconci', in Christopher Phillips (ed.), *Voices, Voces, Voix*, exhibition catalogue (Rotterdam: Witte de With Centre for Contemporary Art, 1998), pp. 137–49.

London, Barbara, 'Independent Video: The First Fifteen Years', *Artforum* 9:11 (1980), 38–41.

——, 'Electronic Explorations', *Art in America* 80:5 (May 1992), 120–8, 157.

London, Barbara (ed.), *Video Spaces: Eight Installations* (New York: Museum of Modern Art, 1995).

Lovejoy, Marjory, *Postmodern Currents: Art and Artists in the Age of Electronic Media* (Ann Arbor, MI: University of Michigan, 1989; 2nd edn, Englewood Cliffs, NJ: Prentice-Hall, 1992).

Margolies, John S., 'TV: the Next Medium', *Art in America* 57:5 (1969), 48–55.

Marsh, Ken, *Independent Video* (San Francisco, CA: Straight Arrow Books, 1974).

Mayer, Marc (ed.), *Being & Time: The Emergence of Video Projection*, exhibition catalogue (Buffalo, NY: Albright-Knox Art Gallery, 1996).

Maza, Monique, *Les Installations vidéo, 'œuvres d'art'* (Paris: L'Harmattan, 1998).

McKenzie, Jon, 'Laurie Anderson for Dummies', *The Drama Review* 41:2 (T154) (Summer 1997), 30–50.

Mediascape, exhibition catalogue (New York: Guggenheim Museum, 1996; New York: Abrams, 1997).

Mellencamp, Patricia, *Indiscretion: Avantgarde Film, Video, and Feminism* (Bloomington, IN: Indiana University Press, 1990).

Melville, Stephen, 'Between Art and Criticism: Mapping the Frame in *United States*', *Theatre Journal* 37 (1985), 31–43.

Mueller, Roswitha, *Valie Export: Fragments of the Imagination* (Bloomington, IN, 1994).

Munz, Thomas (ed.), *Real[work]: Film/Video, bildende Kunst, Internet, Performance* (Werkleitz, Tornitz: 4th Werkleitz-Biennale, 5–9 July 2000).

Nesweda, Peter, 'In Her Own Image: Valie Export, Artist and Feminist', *Arts Magazine* (New York) 65:9 (May 1991), 70–2.

Paik, Nam June, *Videa 'n' Videology 1959–1973*, exhibition catalogue, ed. Judson Rosebud (Syracuse, NY: Everson Museum of Art, 1974).

——, *Nam June Paik: Werke 1946–1976. Musik–Fluxus–Video*, exhibition catalogue, ed. Wulf Hertzogenrath (Cologne: Kölnischer Kunstverein, 1976–7).

——, *Nam June Paik*, exhibition catalogue, ed. John Hanham (New York: Whitney Museum of American Art, 1982; New York: W. W. Norton, 1982).

——, *Du cheval à Christo et autres écrits*, ed. Edith Decker and Irmeline Lebeer (Brussels: Lebeer Hossmann, 1993).

——, *Nam June Paik: Video Works 1963–88*, exhibition catalogue (London: Hayward Gallery, 1988).

——, *Niederschriften eines Kulturnomaden: Aphorismen, Briefe, Texte*, ed. Edith Decker (Cologne: DuMont, 1992).

——, *Nam June Paik: Eine DATA Bank,* exhibition catalogue, ed. Klaus Bußmann and Florian Matzner (Venice: La Biennale di Venezia. Padiglione Tedesco, 1993; Ostfildern: Cantz, 1993).

——, *Nam June Paik: Video Time – Video Space*, exhibition catalogue, ed. Toni Stooss and Thomas Kellein (Zurich: Kunsthaus; and Basel: Kunsthalle, 1991; English edn, New York: Abrams, 1993).

——, *Nam June Paik: Lo sciamano del video*, exhibition catalogue (Milan: Palazzo Reale, 1994; and Mazzotta, 1994).

——, 'Nam June Paik 1932–', in Lawrence J. Trudeau (ed.), *Modern Arts Criticism*, vol. 4 (Detroit, MI: Gale, 1994), pp. 198–228.

——, *Nam June Paik – Video Sculptures: Electronic Undercurrents*, exhibition catalogue, ed. Vibeke Petersen (Copenhagen: Statens Museum for Kunst, 1996).

——, *Nam June Paik: Fluxus/Video*, exhibition catalogue, ed. Wulf Herzogenrath (Bremen: Kunsthalle, 1999–2000).

——, *The Worlds of Nam June Paik,* exhibition catalogue, ed. John Hanham (New York: Guggenheim Museum, 2000).

——, *Nam June Paik: Fluxus und Videoskulptur,* exhibition catalogue, ed. Christoph Brockhaus and Gottlieb Leinz (Duisburg: Wilhelm Lehmbruck Museum, 2002).

Perrone, Jeff, 'The Ins and Outs of Video', *Artforum* 14:10 (June 1976), 53–7.

Pincus-Witten, Robert, 'Vito Acconci and the Conceptual Performance', *Artforum* 19:8 (April 1972), 47–9.

Prammer, Anita, *Valie Export: Eine multimediale Künstlerin* (Vienna: Wiener Frauenverlag, 1988).

Preikschat, Wolfgang, *Video: Die Poesie der neuen Medien* (Weinheim: Beltz, 1987).

Price, Jonathan, *Video-Visions: A Medium Discovers Itself* (New York: New American Library, 1977).

Prinz, Jessica, ' "Always Two Things Switching": Laurie Anderson's Alterity', in Marjorie Perloff (ed.), *Postmodern Genres* (Norman, OK: University of Oklahoma Press, 1988), pp. 150–74.

Rapaport, Herman, 'Can You Say Hello? Laurie Anderson's "United States"', *Theatre Journal* 38 (1986), 339–54; reprinted in *Art Criticism* 6:3 (1990), 43–62.

Reel Work: Artists' Film and Video of the 1970s, exhibition catalogue (North Miami, FL: Museum of Contemporary Art, 1996).

Rees, A. L., *A History of Experimental Film and Video: From the Canonical Avant-garde to Contemporary British Practice* (London: British Film Institute, 1999).

Rosler, Martha, 'Video: Shedding the Utopian Moment', *Block* 11 (Winter 1985–6), 27–39.

Rush, Michael, *New Media in Late 20th-Century Art* (London: Thames & Hudson, 1999).

——, *Video Art* (London: Thames & Hudson, 2003).

Ryan, Paul, 'A Genealogy of Video', *Leonardo* 21 (1988), 39–44.

Schneider, Ira, and Beryl Korot (eds), *Video Art: An Anthology* (New York: Harcourt Brace Jovanovich, 1976).

Schwarz, Hans Peter (ed.), *Media–Art–History: Media Museum* (Karlsruhe: ZKM Center for Art and Media, 1997; Munich: Prestel, 1997).

Schwarz, Hans Peter, and Jeffrey Shaw (eds), *Media Art Perspectives: The Digital Challenge – Museums and Art Sciences Respond* (Ostfildern: Cantz, 1996).

The Second Link: Viewpoints on Video in the Eighties, exhibition catalogue (Banff, Alberta: Walter Phillips Gallery and the Banff Centre School of Fine Arts, 1983).

Sturken, Marita, 'Feminist Video: Reiterating the Difference', *Afterimage*, April 1985, 9–11.

——, 'Revising Romance: New Feminist Video', *Art Journal* 45 (Fall 1985), 273–7.

Tamblyn, Christine, 'Video Art: an Historical Sketch', *High Performance* 10:1 (no. 37) (1987), 33–7.

Techno-Seduction: An Exhibition of Multimedia Installation Work by Forty Artists, exhibition catalogue (New York: Cooper Union for the Advancement of Science and Art, School of Art, 1997).

Tomkins, Calvin, 'Profiles: Video Visionary – Nam June Paik', *The New Yorker* 51:11 (5 May 1975), 44–79; reprinted in C. Tomkins, *The Scene: Reports on Post-modern Art* (New York: Viking Press, 1976, 195–226).

Torcelli, Nicoletta, *VideoKunstZeit: Von Acconci bis Viola* (Weimar: Verlag und Datenbank für Geisteswissenschaften, 1996).

Town, Elke (ed.), *Video by Artists 2*, exhibition catalogue (Toronto: Art Metropole, 1986).

Unnützer, Petra, 'Frauen, Kunst und Technik: von den Videopionierinnen zu den Medienkünstlern der 90er Jahre', *Bewegungskräfte: Künstlerinnen heute*, exhibition catalogue (Karlsruhe: Badischer Kunstverein, 1995), pp. 27–32.

Valentini, Valentina, *Teatro in immagine*, vol. 1: *Eventi performativi e nuovi media*, vol. 2: *Audivisivi per il teatro* (Rome: Bulzoni, 1987).

Valentini, Valentina (ed.), *La camera astratta: Tre spettacoli tra teatro e video. Studio Azzurro, Giorgio Barberio Corsetti* (Milan: Ubulibri, 1988).

——, *Studio Azzurro: Percorsi tra video, cinema e teatro* (Milan: Electa, 1995).

Video, special issue of *Lightworks: A Journal of Images, Ideas and Information* 1:5 (June 1976).

Video, special issue of *Performance* 52 (February/March 1988).

Vidéo, ed. Raymond Bellour and Anne-Marie Duguet, special issue of *Communications* 48 (1988).

Video: A Retrospective, 1974–1984, ed. Kathy Rae Huffman, exhibition catalogue (Long Beach, CA: Long Beach Museum of Art, 1984).

Vision & Television, exhibition catalogue (Waltham, MA: Rose Art Museum, Brandeis University, 1970).

Video Art, special issue of *Studio International* 191:981 (May/June 1976).

Video Art, exhibition catalogue (Philadelphia, PA: Institute of Contemporary Art, University of Pennsylvania, 1975).

Video Art: Expanded Forms, exhibition catalogue (New York: Whitney Museum of American Art, 1988).

Video Art/Video Alternatives, special issue of *High Performance* 10:1 (no. 37) (1987).

Vidéo Sculpture, exhibition catalogue (Marseille: Centre d'Art Contemporain, 1985; and ARCA, 1985).

The Video Show: Festival of Independent Video (London: Serpentine Gallery, and Arts Council of Great Britain, 1975).

Video: The Reflexive Medium, ed. Sara Hornbacher, special issue of *Art Journal* 45:3 (Fall 1985).

Videoscape: An Exhibition of Video Art, exhibition catalogue (Toronto: Art Gallery of Ontario, 1974–5).

Video – Zwanzig Jahre später, ed. Gislind Nabakowski, special issue of *Kunstforum International* 77/78 (January–February 1985).

Vidéo-vidéo, special issue of *Revue d'esthétique*, n.s. 10 (1986).

Walker, John A., *Art in the Age of Mass Media* (London: Pluto Press, 1983; 2nd edn, Boulder, CO: Westview Press, 1994; 3rd edn, London: Pluto Press, 2001).

Youngblood, Gene, *Expanded Cinema* (New York: Dutton, 1970).

Zell, Andrea, *Valie Export: Inszenierung von Schmerz. Selbstverletzung in den frühen Aktionen* (Berlin: Reimer, 2000).

Zippay, Lori (ed.), *Electronic Arts Intermix: Artists' Video. An International Guide* (New York: Cross River Press, 1991).

Videodance and Cyberdance

Allsop, Ric, and Scott deLahunta (eds), *The Connected Body? An Interdisciplinary Approach to the Body and Performance* (Amsterdam: Amsterdam School of Arts, 1996).

Becker, Nancy F., 'Filming Cunningham Dance: a Conversation with Charles Atlas (Part 1)', *Dance Theatre Journal* 1:1 (Spring 1983), 22–5.

Birringer, Johannes, 'The Intelligent Stage', *Performance Research* 6:2 (Summer 2001), 116–22.

Brightman, Peggy, 'Computer Dancemakers', *Leonardo* 23 (1990), 393–6.

Bush, Jeffrey, and Peter Z. Grossman, 'Videodance', *Dance Scope* 9:2 (Spring/Summer 1975), 11–17.

Celant, Germano (ed.), *Merce Cunningham*, exhibition catalogue (Barcelona: Fundació Antoni Tàpies, 1999; Milan: Charta, 1999).

Cine-Dance, special issue of *Dance Perspectives* 30 (Summer 1967).

Corin, Florence (ed.), *Danse et nouvelles technologies*, special issue of *Nouvelles de danse* 40–1 (Autumn–Winter 1999).

Cunningham, Merce, *Changes: Notes on Choreography*, ed. Frances Starr (New York: Something Else Press, 1968).

——, *The Dancer and the Dance: Merce Cunningham in Conversation with Jacqueline Lesschaeve* (London: Boyars, 1985).

Dance: A Future with Computer, special issue of *Dance Theatre Journal* 1:3 (August 1983).

Dance and Technology, special issue of *Interface*, Spring/Summer 1996.

Dance and Technology, ed. Richard Povall, special issue of *Dance Research Journal* 30:1 (Spring 1998).

Dance and Video, special issue of *Dance Theatre Journal* 1:4 (Autumn 1983).

Dancers on a Plane: Cage–Cunningham–Johns, exhibition catalogue (London: Anthony d'Offay Gallery, 1989; Liverpool: Tate Gallery, 1990; London: Thames & Hudson, 1990).

Dodds, Sherril, *Dance on Screen: Genres and Media from Hollywood to Experimental Art* (Basingstoke: Palgrave, 2001).

Fargier, Jean-Paul, 'Vidéo et danse: Danser maintenant', *Le Journal de Cahiers du Cinéma* 48 [*Cahiers du Cinéma* 367] (January 1985), XV–XVI.

Fetterman, William, 'Merce Cuningham and John Cage: Choreographic Cross-Currents', *Choreography and Dance* 4:3 (1997), 59–78.

Grossman, Peter Z., 'Talking with Merce Cunningham about Video', *Dance Scope* 13:2–3 (Winter–Spring 1979), 56–8.

Hodges, Mark, 'Computers and Dance', *Technology Review* 98:1 (January 1995), 20–1.

Jordan, Stephanie, and David Allen (eds), *Parallel Lines: Media Representations of Dance* (London: Libbey, 1993).

Klosty, James (ed.), *Merce Cunningham* (New York: Saturday Review Press, 1975; 2nd edn, New York: Limelight, 1986).

Kostelanetz, Richard (ed.), *Merce Cuningham: Dancing in Space and Time* (Pennington, NJ: A Cappella, 1992).

Kower, Yvonne, 'Being There: Dance Film / Video History – A Perspective', Hilary Trotter (ed.), *Is Technology the Future for Dance? The Green Mill Dance Project Papers 1995*, Canberra: Australian Dance Council, 1996, 84–94.

Kozel, Susan, 'Spacemaking: Experiences of a Virtual Body', *Dance Theatre Journal* 11:3 (Autumn 1994), 12–13, 31, 46–7.

Lockyer, Bob, 'Dance and Video: Random Thoughts', *Dance Theatre Journal* 1:4 (Autumn 1983), 13–16.

Lorber, Richard, 'Towards an Aesthetics of Videodance', *Arts in Society* 13:2 (Summer/Fall 1976), 242–53.

——, 'Experiments in Videodance', *Dance Scope* 12:1 (Fall–Winter 1977–7), 7–16.

Maletic, Vera, 'Videodance, Technology, Attitude Shift', *Dance Research Journal* 19:2 (Winter 1987–8), 3–7.

Mozafarian, Darius Masoud, *A Creative Synthesis of Dance and Video-Electronics: An Exploratory Investigation*, PhD dissertation (University of California at Los Angeles, 1974).

Neal, Nelson D, 'Early Television Dance', *Dance Scope* 13:2–3 (1979), 51–5.

Noll, A. Michael, 'Choreography and Computers', *Dance Magazine* 41:1 (January 1967), 43–5.

Politis, George, 'Computers and Dance: a Bibliography', *Leonardo* 23 (1990), 87–90.

Ramsey, Susie, 'Bring deinen Körper mit: Die Tanzszene und die neuen Technologien', *Kunstforum International* 133 (February–April 1996), 139–42.

Rosenberg, Douglas, 'Video Space: a Site for Choreography', *Leonardo* 33 (2000), 275–80.

Rosiny, Claudia, *Videotanz: Panorama einer intermedialen Kunstform* (Zurich: Chronos, 1999).

Ross, David A., 'Dance and the Video-Television Dialogue: a Problem of Location', *Art and Dance: Images of the Modern Dialogue, 1890–1980*, exhibition catalogue (Boston: Institute of Contemporary Art, 1982–3), pp. 97–106.

Rubidge, Sarah, 'Defining Digital Dance', *Dance Theatre Journal* 14:4 (Winter 1998), 41–5.

Schiphorst, Thecla, '*LifeForms*: Design Tools for Choreography', in A. William Smith (ed.), *Dance and Technology I: Moving Toward the Future* (Westerville, OH: Fullhouse, 1992), pp. 46–52.

——, 'Body Noise: Subtexts of Computers and Dance', *Computer Graphics* 31:1 (February 1997), 14–15.

——, 'Merce Cunningham: Making Dance with the Computer', *Choreography and Dance* 4:3 (1997), 79–98.

Smith, A. William (ed.), *Dance and Technology I: Moving Toward the Future. Proceedings of the First Annual Conference, 28 February to 1 March 1992, University of Wisconsin-Madison* (Westerville, OH: Fullhouse, 1992).

——, *Dance and Technology III: Transcending Boundaries. Proceedings of the Third Annual Conference, 18–21 May 1995, York University (North York), Toronto/Ont* (Columbus, OH: Fullhouse, 1995).

Tanz und Technologie, special issue of *Ballett International – Tanz aktuell* (August 1997).

Taub, Eric, 'Electronic Pulses Create Commitments: Videodance', *Dance Magazine* 54:8 (August 1980), 48–50.

Tee, Ernie, 'The Irreality of Dance', in Kathy Rae Huffman and Dorine Mignot (eds), *The Arts for Television*, exhibition catalogue (Los Angeles, CA: Museum of Contemporary Art; Amsterdam: Stedelijk Museum, 1987), pp. 54–65.

Vaccarino, Elisa, *La musa dello schermo freddo: Videodanza, computer e robot* (Genoa: Costa & Nolan, 1996).

Vaughan, David, *Merce Cunningham: 50 Years* (New York: Aperture, 1997).

'Videodance', *Ballett international – Tanz aktuell*, June 1999, 28–43.

Wechsler, Robert, 'Computers and Dance: Back to the Future', *Dance Research Journal* 30:1 (Spring 1998), 4–9.

Performance in Cyberspace

Ascott, Roy (ed.), *Art, Technology, Consciousness: Mind @ Large* (Oxford and Portland, OR: Intellect, 2000).

Ascott, Roy, and Carl Eugene Loeffler (eds), *Connectivity: Art and Interactive Telecommunication*, special issue of *Leonardo* 24:2 (1991).

Auslander, Philip, 'Cyberspace as a Performance Art Venue', *Performance Research* 6:2 (Summer 2001), 123–7.

Baumgärtel, Tilman, *[Net.art]: Materialien zur Netzkunst* (Nuremberg: Verlag für Moderne Kunst, 1999).

——, *[Net.art 2.0)]: Neue Materialien zur Netzkunst* (Nuremberg: Verlag für Moderne Kunst, 2001).

Bell, David, and Barbara M. Kennedy (eds), *The Cyberculture Reader* (London: Routledge, 2000).

Bender, Gretchen, and Timothy Druckrey (eds), *Culture on the Brink: Ideologies of Technologies* (Seattle, WA: Bay Press, 1993).

Benedikt, Michael (ed.), *Cyberspace: First Steps* (Boston, MA: MIT Press, 1992).

Braun, Claude M. J., and Josette Giroux, 'Arcade Video Games: Proxemic, Cognitive and Content Analyses', *Journal of Leisure Research* 21:2 (1989), 92–105.

Büscher, Barbara, 'Theater und elektronische Medien: Intermediale Praktiken in den siebziger und achziger Jahren', in Erika Fischer-Lichte, Wolfgang Greisenegger and Hans-Thies Lehmann (eds), *Arbeitsfelder der Theaterwissenschaft* (Tübingen: Narr, 1994), pp. 193–210.

Campbell-Kelly, Martin, and William Aspray, *Computer: A History of the Information Machine* (New York: Basic Books, 1996).

Case, Sue-Ellen, *The Domain-Matrix: Performing Lesbian at the End of Print Culture* (Bloomington, IN: Indiana University Press, 1996).

Cassell, Justine, and Henry Jenkins (eds), *From Barbie to Mortal Kombat: Gender and Computer Games* (Cambridge, MA: MIT Press, 1998).

Causey, Matthew, 'Postorganic Performance: The Appearance of Theater in Virtual Spaces', in Marie Laure Ryan (ed.), *Cyberspace Textuality: Computer Technology and Literary Theory* (Bloomington, IN: Indiana University Press, 1999), pp. 182–201.

Chateau, Dominique, and Bernard Darras (eds), *Arts et multimédia: L'œuvre d'art et sa reproduction à l'ère des média interactifs* (Paris: Publications de la Sorbonne, 1999).

Cirincione, Janine, and Brian d'Amato (eds), *Through the Looking Glass: Artists' First Encounters with Virtual Reality* (Jupiter, FL: Softworlds, 1992).

Computer and Art, special issue of *Art Journal* 49:3 (Fall 1990).

Cornwell, Regina, 'Interactive Art: Touching the "Body in the Mind" ', *Discourse: Theoretical Studies in Media and Culture* 14:2 (Spring 1992), 203–21.

Le Corps mutant, exhibition catalogue (Paris: Galerie Enrico Navarra, 2000).

Cyberart, special issues of *Art Journal*, 59:3 (Fall 2000), and 59:4 (Winter 2000).

Darley, Andrew, *Visual Digital Culture: Surface Play and Spectacle in New Media Genres* (London: Routledge, 2000).

Decker, Edith, and Peter Weibel (eds), *Vom Verschwinden der Ferne: Telekommunikation und Kunst*, exhibition catalogue (Frankfurt am Main: Deutsches Postmuseum, 1990–1; Cologne: DuMont, 1990).

Deitch, Jeffrey (ed.), *Post Human*, exhibition catalogue (Pully, Lausanne: FAE Musée d'Art Contemporain, 1992; Feldkirchen: Oktagon, 1992; English edn, Amsterdam: Idea Books, 1992; New York: Distributed Art Publishers, 1992).

Dery, Mark, *Escape Velocity: Cyberculture at the End of the Century* (London: Hodder & Stoughton, 1996).

Dery, Mark (ed.), *Flame Wars: The Discourse of Cyberculture* (Durham, NC: Duke University Press, 1993).

Dewdney, Christopher, *Last Flesh: Life in the Transhuman Era* (Toronto: HarperCollins, 1998).

Digital Reflections: The Dialogue of Art and Technology, ed. Johanna Drucker, special issue of *Art Journal* 56:3 (Fall 1997).

Dinkla, Söke, 'From Participation to Interaction: Towards the Origins of Interactive Art', in Lynn Hershman-Leeson (ed.), *Clicking In: Hot Links to a Digital Culture* (Seattle, WA: Bay Press, 1996), pp. 279–90, 357–8.

——, *Pioniere interaktiver Kunst von 1970 bis heute: Myron Krueger, Jeffrey*

Shaw, David Rokeby, Lynn Hershman, Grahame Weinbren, Ken Feingold (Ostfildern: Cantz, 1997).

Dinkla, Söke, and Cornelia Brüninghaus-Knubel (eds), *InterAct!: Schlüsselwerke interaktiver Kunst*, exhibition catalogue (Duisburg: Wilhelm Lehmbruck Museum, 1997; Ostfildern: Cantz, 1997).

Dixon, Steeve, 'Digits, Discourse and Documentation: Performance Research and Hypermedia', *The Drama Review* 43:1 (T161) (Spring 1999), 152–75.

Dovey, Jon (ed.), *Fractal Dreams: New Media in Social Context* (London: Lawrence & Wishart, 1996).

Druckrey, Timothy (ed.), *Electronic Culture: Technology and Visual Representation* (New York: Aperture, 1996).

——, *Ars Electronica: Facing the Future. A Survey of Two Decades* (Cambridge, MA: MIT Press, 1999).

Electra, exhibition catalogue (Paris: Musée d'Art Moderne de la Ville de Paris, 1983–4).

L'Ère binaire: Nouvelles interactions, exhibition catalogue (Brussels: Musée Communal d'Ixelles, 1992; Gent: Ludion, 1992); rev. German edn, *Binaera: 14 Interaktionen. Kunst und Technologie*, exhibition catalogue, ed. Toni Stooss and Eleonora Louis (Vienna: Kunsthalle Wien, 1993; Gent: Ludion, 1992).

Featherstone, Mike, and Roger Burrows (eds), *Cyberspace/Cyberbodies/Cyberpunk: Cultures of Technological Embodiment* (London: Sage, 1995).

Forester, Tom, *The Microelectronics Revolution: The Complete Guide to the New Technology and Its Impact on Society* (Cambridge, MA: MIT Press, 1981).

Franke, Herbert W., *Computer Graphics – Computer Art* (Berlin: Springer, 1971; 2nd rev. edn 1985).

——, *Wege zur Computerkunst* (Vienna: Edition Die Donau Hinunter, 1995).

Franke, Herbert W. (ed.), *Impulse Computerkunst: Graphik, Plastik, Musik, Film*, exhibition catalogue (Munich: Kunstverein München, 1970).

Frieling, Rudolf (ed.), *Medien Kunst aktuell/Current Media Art: Videokunst, CD-ROM, und Internetprojekte aus Deutschland* (Munich: Goethe-Institut, 1997).

Frieling, Rudolf, and Dieter Daniels (eds), *Medium Kunst Aktion/Medium Kunst Interaktion. Die 60er und 70er Jahre in Deutschland; Die 80er und 90er Jahre in Deutschland*, 2 vols (Vienna: Springer, 1997–2000).

Gehse, Kerstin, *Medien-Theater: Medieneinsatz und Wahrnehmungsstrategien in theatralen Projekten der Gegenwart* (Würzburg: Deutscher Wissenschaftlicher Verlag, 2001).

Goodman, Cynthia, *Digital Visions: Computers and Art* (New York: Abrams, 1987).

Grant-Ryan, Pamela (ed.), *Electronic Art*, special supplement of *Leonardo* (Oxford: Pergamon, 1988).

Greene, Rachel, 'Web Work: a History of Internet Art', *Artforum* 38:9 (May 2000), 162–7, 190.

Haddon, Leslie, 'Electronic and Computer Games', *Screen* 29:2 (Spring 1988), 52–73.

Hakken, David, *Cyborgs @ Cyberspace: An Ethnographer Looks to the Future* (London: Routledge, 1999).

Halberstam, Judith, and Ira Livingstone (eds), *Posthuman Bodies* (Bloomington, IN: Indiana University Press, 1996).

Haraway, Donna Jeanne, *Simians, Cyborgs, and Women: The Reinvention of Nature* (London: Free Association, 1991).

Harris, Jessica, *The Effects of Computer Games on Young Children: A Review of the Research* (London: Home Office Research, Development and Statistics Directorate, 2001).

Hayles, N. Katherine, 'The Seductions of Cyberspace', in Verena Andermatt Conley (ed.), *Rethinking Technologies* (Minneapolis, MN: University of Minnesota Press, 1993), 173–90.

——, *How We Became Posthuman: Virtual Bodies in Cybernetics, Literature, and Informatics* (Chicago, IL: University of Chicago Press, 1999).

Hayward, Philip, and Tana Wollen (eds), *Future Visions: New Technologies of the Screen* (London: British Film Institute, 1993).

Helsel, Sandra K., and Judith P. Roth (eds), *Virtual Reality: Theory, Practice and Promise* (Westport, CT: Meckler, 1991).

Herman, Leonard, *Phoenix: The Fall and Rise of Home Videogames* (Union, NJ: Rolenta Press, 1994).

Hershman-Leeson, Lynn (ed.), *Clicking In: Hot Links to a Digital Culture* (Seattle, WA: Bay Press, 1996).

Holtzman, Steven, *Digital Mosaics: The Aesthetics of Cyberspace* (New York: Simon and Schuster, 1997).

Homo zappiens zappiens, exhibition catalogue (Rennes: Centre d'Histoire de l'Art Contemporain à la Galerie Art et Essai, 1998; Rennes: Presses Universitaires de Rennes, 1998).

Hünnekens, Annette, *Der bewegte Betrachter: Theorien der interaktiven Medienkunst* (Cologne: Wienand, 1997).

Jones, Stephen, 'Towards a Philosophy of Virtual Reality: Issues Implicit in "Consciousness Reframed"', *Leonardo* 33 (2000), 125–32.

Jones, Steven G. (ed.), *CyberSociety: Computer-mediated Communication and Community* (Thousand Oakes, CA: Sage, 1998).

Jordan, Tim, *Cyberpower: The Culture and Politics of Cyberspace and the Internet* (London: Routledge, 1999).

Kinder, Marsha, *Playing with Power in Movies, Television and Video Games: From Muppet Babies to Teenage Mutant Ninja Turtles* (Berkeley, CA: University of California Press, 1991).

Kisseleva, Olga, *Cyberart: Un essai sur l'art du dialogue* (Paris: L'Harmattan, 1998).

Klonaris, Maria, and Katerina Thomadaki (eds), *Technologies et imaginaires: Art cinéma, art vidéo, art ordinateur* (Paris: Dis Voir, 1990).

——, *Mutations de l'image: Art cinéma/vidéo/ordinateur* (Paris: Astarti, 1994).

——, *Pour une écologie des média: Art, cinéma, vidéo, ordinateur* (Paris: Astarti, 1998).

Klotz, Heinrich, 'Zur Ästhetik der elektronischen Kunst', in H. Klotz, *Eine neue Hochschule (für neue Künste)* (Stuttgart: Cantz, 1995), 59–67.

Klotz, Heinrich (ed.), *Contemporary Art* (Karlsruhe: ZKM Centre for Art and Media; Munich: Prestel, 1997).

Klüver, Billy [Johan Wilhelm] (ed.), *Some More Beginnings: An Exhibition of Submitted Works Involving Technical Materials and Processes Organized by Staff and Members of 'Experiments in Art and Technology'*, exhibition catalogue (New York: Brooklyn Museum and Museum of Modern Art, 1968).

Konrad, Helga (ed.), *On-line: Kunst im Netz. On-line Symposion, 4.–7. März 1993, Palais Attems, Graz* (Graz: Steirische Kulturinitiative, 1993).

Kroker, Arthur, and Marilouise Kroker (eds), *Digital Deliriums* (New York: St Martin's Press, 1997).

Krueger, Myron W., *Artificial Reality* (Reading, MA: Addison-Wesley, 1983).

——, *Artificial Reality II* (Reading/MA: Addison-Wesley, 1991).

Kurzweil, Ray, *The Age of Intelligent Machines* (Cambridge, MA: MIT Press, 1990).

——, *The Age of Spiritual Machines: When Computers Exceed Human Intelligence* (New York: Viking, 1999).

Laurel, Brenda, *Computers as Theater* (Reading, MA: Addison-Wesley, 1991).

Levinson, Paul, *Digital McLuhan: A Guide to the Information Millennium* (London: Routledge, 1999).

Lichty, Patrick, 'The Cybernetics of Performance and New Media Art', *Leonardo* 33 (2000), 351–4.

Lischka, Gerhard Johann, and Peter Weibel (eds), *Im Netz der Systeme: Für eine interaktive Kunst*, special issue of *Kunstforum International 103* (September–October 1989).

Loveless, Richard L. (ed.), *The Computer Revolution and the Arts* (Tampa, FL: University of South Florida Press, 1989).

Ludlow, Peter (ed.), *High Noon on the Electronic Frontier: Conceptual Issues in Cyberspace* (Cambridge, MA: MIT Press, 1996).

Lunenfeld, Peter, *Snap to Grid: A User's Guide to Digital Arts, Media, and Culture* (Cambridge, MA: MIT Press, 2000).

Lunenfeld, Peter (ed.), *The Digital Dialectic: New Essays on New Media* (Cambridge, MA: MIT Press, 1999).

The Media Arts in Transition, exhibition catalogue (Minneapolis, MN: Walker Art Center, 1983).

Morse, Margaret, *Virtualities: Television, Media Art, and Cyberculture* (Bloomington, IN: Indiana University Press, 1998).

Moser, Mary Anne, and Douglas MacLeod (eds), *Immersed in Technology: Art and Virtual Environments* (Cambridge, MA: MIT Press, 1996).

Mulder, Arjen, and Maaike Post, *Book for the Electronic Arts* (Amsterdam: De Balie, 2000).

Myers, David, 'Computer Game Genres', *Play & Culture* 3 (1990), 286–301.

netz.kunst Jahrbuch 98/99 (Nuremberg: Verlag für Moderne Kunst, 1999).

Netzkunst, special issue of *Kritische Berichte* 26:1 (1998) (Marburg: Jonas-Verlag, 1998).

Nichols, Bill, 'The Work of Culture in the Age of Cybernetic Systems', *Screen* 29:1 (Winter 1988), 22–46.

O'Rourke, Karen (ed.), *Art-réseaux* (Paris: Centre d'Études et de Recherches en Arts Plastiques, 1992).

Oslin, George P., *The Story of Telecommunications* (Macon, GA: Mercer University Press, 1992).

Penley, Constance, and Andrew Ross (eds), *Technoculture* (Minneapolis, MN: University of Minnesota Press, 1991).

Penny, Simon (ed.), *Critical Issues in the Electronic Media* (Albany, NY: State University of New York Press, 1995).

Perlin, Ken, and Athomas Goldberg, 'Improv: a System for Scripting Interactive Actors in Virtual Worlds', *Siggraph '96: Proceedings of the 23rd Annual Conference on Computer Graphics and Interactive Techniques* (New York: ACM Press, 1996), 205–16.

Perry, Tekla, Carol Truxal, and Paul Wallich, 'Video Games: The Electronic Big Bang', *Institute of Electrical and Electronics Engineers Spectrum* 19:12 (December 1982), 20–33.

Pinhanez, Claudio C. and Aaron F. Bobick, 'Using Computer Vision to Control a Reactive Computer Graphics Character in a Theater Play', in Henrik I. Christensen (ed.), *Computer Vision Systems: First International Conference, ICVS '99, Las Palmas, Gran Canaria, Spain, January 13–15, 1999. Proceedings* (Berlin: Springer, 1999), pp. 66–82.

Poole, Steven, *Trigger Happy: The Inner Life of Videogames* (London: Fourth Estate, 2000).

Popper, Frank, *Art: Action and Participation* (New York: New York University Press, 1975).

——, *Art of the Electronic Age* (New York: Abrams, 1993).

Price, John A., 'Social Science Research on Video Games', *Journal of Popular Culture* 18:4 (Spring 1985), 111–26.

Provenzo, Eugene F., *Video Kids: Making Sense of Nintendo* (Cambridge, MA: Harvard University Press, 1991).

Ranzenbacher, Heimo, Jutta Schmiederer, and Gerfried Stocker (eds), *Zero: The Art of Being Everywhere*, exhibition catalogue (Graz: Steirische Kulturinitiative, 1992–3).

Reaney, Mark, 'The Theatre of Virtual Reality: Designing Scenery in an Imaginary World', *Theatre Design and Technology* 29:2 (Spring 1993), 29–32.

——, 'Virtual Scenography: the Actor Audience Computer Interface', *Theatre Design and Technology* 32:1 (Winter 1996), 36–43.

Reichardt, Jasia, *The Computer in Art* (London: Studio Vista 1971).

Reichardt, Jasia (ed.), *Cybernetic Serendipity: The Computer and the Arts*, 2nd rev. edn (London: Studio International, 1968).

——, *Cybernetics, Art and Ideas* (London: Studio Vista, 1971).

Rheingold, Howard, *Virtual Reality* (New York: Summit Books, 1991; 2nd edn, New York: Touchstone, 1992).

Rindler, Robert (ed.), *Techno Seduction: An Exhibition of Multimedia Installation Work by Forty Artists*, exhibition catalogue (New York: The Cooper Union for the Advancement of Science and Art, School of Art, 1997).

Robins, Kevin, and Frank Webster, *Times of the Technoculture: From the Information Society to the Virtual Life* (London: Routledge, 1999).

Rogers-Lafferty, Sarah, *Body Mécanique: Artistic Explorations of Digital Realms* (Columbus, OH: Wexner Center for the Arts, 1998–9).

Rötzer, Florian, *Digitale Weltentwürfe: Streifzüge durch die Netzkultur* (Munich: Hanser, 1998).

Rötzer, Florian (ed.), *Ästhetik des Immateriellen: Zum Verhältnis von Kunst und Neuen Technologien*, 2 vols, special issues of *Kunstforum International* 97 (November–December 1988); and 98 (January–February 1989).

——, *Digitaler Schein: Ästhetik der elekronischen Medien* (Frankfurt-am-Main: Suhrkamp, 1991).

——, *Die Zukunft des Körpers*, special issues of *Kunstforum International* 132 (November 1995 to January 1996); 133 (February–March 1996).

Rötzer, Florian, and Peter Weibel (eds), *Strategien des Scheins: Kunst, Computer, Medien* (Munich: Boer, 1991).

——, *Cyberspace: Zum medialen Gesamtkunstwerk* (Munich: Boer, 1993).

Rutsky, R. L., *High Technē: Art and Technology from the Machine Aesthetics to the Posthuman* (Minneapolis, MN: University of Minnesota Press, 1999).

Ryan, Marie Laure (ed.), *Cyberspace Textuality: Computer Technology and Literary Theory* (Bloomington, IN: Indiana University Press, 1999).

Saltz, David Z., 'The Art of Interaction: Interactivity, Performativity, and Computers', *Journal of Aesthetics and Art Criticism* 56:2 (Spring 1997), 117–27.

——, 'Live Media: Interactive Technology and Theatre', *Theatre Topics* 11:2 (September 2001), 107–30.

——, 'The Collaborative Subject: Telerobotic Performance and Identity', *Performance Research* 6:3 (Winter 2001), 70–83.

Sarkis, Mona, *Blick, Stimme und (k)ein Körper: Der Einsatz elektronischer Medien im Theater und in interaktiven Installationen* (Stuttgart: M und P Verlag für Wissenschaft und Forschung, 1997).

Schrum, Stephen A. (ed.), *Theatre in Cyberspace: Issues of Teaching, Acting, and Directing* (New York: Lang, 1999).

Schwarz, Hans Peter (ed.), *Media–Art–History: Media Museum* (Karlsruhe: ZKM Center for Art and Media; Munich: Prestel, 1997).

Schwartz, Hans Peter, and Jeffrey Shaw (eds), *Media Art Perspective: The Digital Challenge – Museums and Art Sciences Respond* (Ostfildern: Cantz, 1996).

Selnow, Gary W., 'Playing Videogames: the Electronic Friend', *Journal of Communication* 34:2 (Spring 1984), 148–56.

Sherman, Barrie, and Phil Judkins, *Glimpses of Heaven, Visions of Hell: Virtual Reality and its Implications*, 2nd rev. edn (London: Coronet Books, 1993).

Shields, Rob (ed.), *Cultures of Internet: Virtual Spaces, Real Histories, Living Bodies* (London: Sage, 1996).

Skirrow, Gilian, 'Hellivision: an Analysis of Video Games', in Manuel Alvarado and John O. Thompson (eds), *The Media Reader* (London: British Film Institute, 1990), pp. 321–38.

Smith, Marc A. and Peter Kollock (eds), *Communities in Cyberspace* (London: Routledge, 1999).

Software: Information Technology. Its New Meaning for Art, exhibition catalogue (New York: Jewish Museum, 1970).

Sommerer, Christa, and Laurent Mignonneau (eds), *Art@science* (Vienna: Springer, 1998).

Springer, Claudia, *Electronic Eros: Bodies and Desire in the Postindustrial Age* (Austin, TX: Texas University Press, 1996).

Stelarc [Stelios Arcadiou], *Obsolete Body/Suspensions/Stelarc* (ed.) by James D. Paffrath and Stelarc (Davis, CA: JP Publications, 1984).

——, 'Beyond the Body', *New Music Articles* (Melbourne) 6 (1986–7), 27–30.

——, 'Prosthetics, Robotics and Remote Existence: Postevolutionary Strategies', *Leonardo* 24:5 (1991), 591–5.

——, 'Enhanced Gestures/Obsolete Desire', in Karl Gerbel and Peter Weibel (eds), *Ars Electronica 92: Die Welt von Innen/The World from Within – Endo & Nano* (Vienna: PVS Verleger, 1992, 233–9.

——, 'Electronic Voodoo: Interview with Nicholas Zurbrugg', *21.C* (Melbourne) 2 (1995), 44–9; reprinted in Ashley Crawford and Ray Edgar (eds), *Transit Lounge: Wake-up Calls and Travelers' Tales from the Future* (North Ryde NSW: Craftsman House, 1997), pp. 110–3

——, 'Stelarc, ou le mythe de Faust: Entretien entre Stelarc et Jacques Donguy', *L'art au corps: Le corps exposé de Man Ray à nos jours*, exhibition catalogue (Marseille: Musée de Marseille, 1996); pp. 211–20.

——, 'From Psycho to Cyber Strategies: Prosthetics, Robotics and Remote Existence', *Canadian Theatre Review* 86 (Spring 1996), 19–23.

——, 'An Interview with Stelarc by G. J. Hilton', *P-Form* 42 (Winter 1996/97), 6–8.

——, 'Parasite Visions: Alternate, Intimate and Involuntary Experiences', in Gerfried Stocker and Christine Schöpf (eds), *Ars Electronica 97 – Flesh Factor: Informationsmaschine Mensch* (Vienna: Springer, 1997), pp. 148–56; reprinted in Timothy Druckrey (ed.), *Ars Electronica: Facing the Future. A Survey of Two Decades* (Cambridge, MA: MIT Press, 1999, 411–15; and *Body & Society* 5:2–3 (September 1999), 117–28.

——, 'From Psycho-Body to Cyber-Systems: Images of Post-human Entities', in Joan Broadhurst Dixon and Eric Cassiday (eds), *Virtual Futures: Cyberotics, Technology and Post-human Pragmatism* (London: Routledge, 1998); revised in David Bell and Barbara M. Kennedy (eds), *The Cyberculture Reader* (London: Routledge, 2000), pp. 560–76.

——, 'Telematic Tremors, Telematic Pleasures: Stelarc's Internet Performances. Stelarc in Conversation with Nicholas Zurbrugg', in Anna Novakov (ed.), *Carnal Pleasures: Desire, Public Space, and Contemporary Art* (San Francisco, CA: Clamor Editions, 1998), pp. 167–203.

——, 'Interview Stelarc', in Arjen Mulder and Maaike Post, *Book for the Electronic Arts* (Amsterdam: De Balie, 2000), pp. 24–32.

——, 'In Dialogue with "Posthuman" Bodies: Inteview with Stelarc [by Ross Farnell]', *Body & Society* 5:2-3 (September 1999), 129–47.

Stone, Allucquére Rosanne, *The War of Desire and Technology at the Close of the Mechanical Age* (Cambridge: MIT Press, 1996).

textualités&nouvelles_technologies, ed. Eric Sadin, special issue of *[:éc/art s:]* 2 (2000–1).

Thalmann, Nadia Magnenat, and Daniel Thalmann (eds), *Artificial Life and Virtual Reality* (Chichester: Wiley, 1994).

Théâtre et technologie, special issue of *Théâtre/Public* 127 (January–February 1996).

Tofts, Darren, and Murray McKeich, *Memory Trade: Prehistory of Cyberculture* (North Ryde, NSW: Interface, 1998).

Turkle, Sherry, *The Second Self: Computers and the Human Spirit* (New York: Simon & Schuster, 1984).

——, *Life on the Screen: Identity in the Age of the Internet* (New York: Simon & Schuster, 1995).

Unruh, Delbert, 'Virtual Reality in the Theatre: New Questions about Time and Space', *Theatre Design and Technology* 32:1 (Winter 1996), 44–7.

Weibel, Peter, and Timothy Druckrey (eds), *Net Condition: Art and Global Media*, exhibition catalogue (Graz: Steirischer Herbst; Karlsruhe: ZKM/Zentrum für Kunst und Medientechnologie, 1998–2000; Cambridge, MA: MIT Press, 2001).

Wirths, Axel (ed.), *Der elektronische Raum: 15 Positionen zu Medienkunst* (Ostfildern: Cantz, 1998).

Wolmark, Jenny (ed.), *Cybersexualities: A Reader on Feminist Theory, Cyborgs and Cyberspace* (Edinburgh: Edinburgh University Press, 1999).

Wood, John (ed.), *The Virtual Embodied: Presence/Practice/Technology* (London: Routledge, 1998).

Zylinska, Joanna (ed.), *The Cyborg Eyperiments: The Extension of the Body in the Media Age* (London: Continuum, 2002).

Subject Index

354

Name Index